DESTINATION

COCKTAILS

SANTA
MONICA
PRESS

Published by:

Santa Monica Press LLC
P.O. Box 850
Solana Beach, CA 92075
1-800-784-9553
www.santamonicapress.com
books@santamonicapress.com

Printed in the United States

Santa Monica Press books are available at special quantity discounts when purchased in bulk by corporations, organizations, or groups. Please call our Special Sales department at 1-800-784-9553.

ISBN-13 978-1-59580-072-5

Library of Congress Cataloging-in-Publication Data

Teitelbaum, James, 1967-
 Destination cocktails : the traveler's guide to superior libations / by James Teitelbaum.
   p. cm.
 ISBN 978-1-59580-072-5
1. Cocktails—Guidebooks. 2. Bars (Drinking establishments)—Guidebooks. I. Title.
TX951.T435 2012
641.87'4—dc23
                              2012010798

Cover design by Michael Kellner
Interior design and production by Future Studio

DESTINATION
COCKTAILS

THE TRAVELER'S GUIDE TO SUPERIOR LIBATIONS

James Teitelbaum

CONTENTS

INTERNATIONAL | 270

DESTINATION: NIGHTCAP | 399

Original craft cocktail recipes to enjoy at home.

"Fortunately, there is gin, the sole glimmer of light in this darkness. Do you feel the golden, copper-colored light it kindles in you? I like walking through the city of an evening in the warmth of gin."

—ALBERT CAMUS

CRAFT COCKTAILS
WHAT ARE THEY, AND WHY NOW?

There are two types of bar in the world: the ones that care about making great cocktails, and the ones that don't.

One would think that the latter would be the minority. After all, people go to bars for drinks. What are the chances of a bar succeeding as a business if the drinks are not good?

The chances are excellent, actually. In our fast-paced society, people are generally more concerned with saving money and with immediate satisfaction than they are with quality. Good drinks are expensive, and they take time to make. This isn't always desirable for a customer, and subsequently it isn't healthy for a bar owner's bottom line. Fast and cheap seems to be what people want, and that's what keeps the cash rolling in.

Let's compare this to the restaurant industry. Looking at the total number of restaurants that exist in any given city, and then looking at how many of them are fast food joints, the fast food joints are a clear majority. And yet, fast food isn't especially tasty, it's almost always really bad for your health, and it's almost never made fresh. It's usually processed in a foreboding factory somewhere, and then shipped off to a franchise that may be hundreds of miles away. There, it is reheated indifferently by someone making a little bit over minimum wage. The sad truth is that in the 21st century, the majority of people in industrialized nations are content to eat in an industrialized manner. Eating this way may taste bad, it may be the cause of obesity and other diseases resulting from poor nutrition, and it may have harmful effects on the environment, but it's fast and cheap, and that's what people seem to want.

These same principles apply to bars as well. For every really nice cocktail bar that serves the sort of delicious libations we'll be exploring in these pages, there are 10 bars that serve something mediocre, and 100 that can't muster much more than a shot of rail-quality liquor and a factory-brewed beer.

We can think of the latter as fast-food bars.

Whether this is acceptable or not is up to you. We're not going to be judgmental here. If you want to eat crappy food and drink crappy booze, that's your call, not ours. Have a good time. All the time. If you want to make a buck *selling* fast food or owning a high-volume bar, that's also up to you. Best of luck. But we are positive that there are people out there who demand better, people who require certain reasonable levels of quality in their food and drink. To accommodate these people, there are quality restaurants in every city in the civilized world. However, there is an interesting phenomenon at work here. When dining out, there are choices— you can get something fast and processed, or something fresh and yummy. When drinking, you'd think the same was true, but often it isn't. If you want a shot and a beer, go to your local dive bar. Easy. If you want a nice cocktail, go to a classy hotel bar, or a good restaurant, or swanky lounge . . . right?

Not so easy.

For reasons we'll speculate on in a moment, it is a lot harder to get a solid cocktail than it is to get a solid meal. There are many, many elegant restaurants, five-star hotels, and expensively designed ultra-lounges that look and feel as though they *should* serve delicious cocktails. Many of them certainly charge you as if they are giving you something special. But the bulk of them don't. Mediocrity abounds, even when gussied up with an ersatz layer of elegance. Fantastic restaurants that win accolades from food critics may still give you an indifferently prepared cocktail. Trendy clubs that draw in celebrities, or hotels designed by rock star architects still don't typically seem willing or able to create solid bar programs.

Why is this the case?

The answer requires a quick history lesson.

There have been many books written about the history of the cocktail, and there have been many studies made of the trends and habits of drinkers in modern society. We won't rehash this material in these pages (much).

But, as briefly as we can muster:

Toward the end of the 18th century, popular drink categories included flips, posses, punches, juleps, swizzles, toddies, bucks, mules, and slings. Each of these involved a specific technique of combining liquor with other ingredients to enhance the flavor of a base spirit (rum, whiskey, gin, brandy, etc.). For example, if your drink contained liquor and ginger beer it was called a buck (or a mule); if it had liquor, citrus, and soda water it was a fizz; and if it had liquor, egg, sugar, and spice it was a flip. And so on. The catch-all usage of "cocktail" to describe all of these drink categories hadn't evolved yet. The first recorded use of the word dates to 1803, when it described a specific style of drink, a cousin to the aforementioned toddies and juleps. Said to be a good hangover remedy, the "cock's tail" was something for the early morning. By 1806, the cocktail was formally defined as liquor with sugar, water, and bitters added. Punches, flips, and posses were still considered to be different types of drinks.

At that point, drinking liquor in public bars and saloons was not yet allowed in the United States; however, this was changed in 1832 by the Pioneer Inn and Tavern Law. During this era, the art of the bartender truly began to develop toward its first golden age. In 1862, pioneer mixologist Jerry Thomas wrote *Bar-Tenders Guide: A Complete Cyclopedia of Plain and Fancy Drinks*, which contained 600

recipes plus instructions for making certain ingredients. Among the punches, swizzles, and slings, there were 10 variants on the cocktail. At some point in the ensuing decades, "cocktail" became a blanket term for all mixed alcoholic drinks, including all of the varieties named above. It was in these years, the late 19th and early 20th centuries, that so many of the cocktails we take for granted today were invented by Thomas and his contemporaries (such as Harry Johnson and Ada Coleman).

It was also in these years that the etiquette and expectations of service and hospitality that we enjoy today were formalized. Thomas was a consummate host, and he was also a man who knew how to work the media. Before telephones, television, or Twitter, Thomas guaranteed his own celebrity by traveling to San Francisco, New York, New Orleans, and Chicago to quickly set up bars that lasted just long enough to solidify his fame in those towns before he moved on. Interestingly, those are probably the four best towns in the U.S. to drink in today. Ultimately, Thomas, Coleman, Johnson, and their peers left behind a legacy of fantastic creations that survive to this day.

This golden age of cocktailing should not be underestimated. Americans drank well for close to a century until, half a century after Thomas's book was published, World War I began. Just after that, the Volstead Act was passed into law, stating that "no person shall manufacture, sell, barter, transport, import, export, deliver, or furnish any intoxicating liquor . . ." Volumes have been written about the 14 years of Prohibition that followed, but the net result is that all of the creativity and hard work Thomas and his peers put into developing a dizzying array of classic drinks was essentially forgotten. Although Prohibition was repealed on December 5, 1933, the damage was done: Americans had become used to disguising the taste of their so-called bathtub gin with mountains of sugar in order to make it palatable, and most career bartenders had moved on to other trades or to other continents. Revelers in Europe and Cuba, among other places, drank quite well during the 1920s. But before cocktailing as a culinary art could recover in the United States, World War II began. Supplies of booze became scarce worldwide, and people could not be concerned with making flips and slings while Adolph Hitler was marching across Europe.

By the late 1940s, booze companies were beginning to rebound, and they wanted to get their products into the marketplace as quickly as possible. They pushed blended whiskies (which contained unaged whiskey combined with smaller amounts of the superior aged products) because they were faster to produce. They also heavily marketed a new spirit that was fast and cheap to make and had almost no flavor, making it easy to mix with almost anything. For many drinkers, it soon replaced gin as the base spirit in the newly trendy Martini.

By the 1950s, the American palate for cocktails had withered, unused since before the time of World War I. The world had moved on. Expectations had been lowered by the scarcity of quality cocktails over the decades. Once a person is used to mediocrity, they don't know to demand quality. Business owners aren't going to improve things if their customers seem content. A vicious circle develops. Why go the extra mile and absorb the extra expense, says the smart businessman, if our customers don't know or care when confronted with something superior?

Thus, appropriate styles of drinks for a new generation and a new business model were marketed. The highball—simply base spirit over ice, topped with a carbonated beverage—was just the sort of thing that the new jet-age ultraconsumerist America of the 1950s was ready to be sold. The versatile highball was considered modern, and it was fast and cheap to make. Gin and tonic. Whiskey and soda. Rum and cola. There are several points to make about the highball. First, its purpose wasn't to enhance and add dimension to the base spirit, as the best recipes of the golden age were, but rather to obscure the taste of mediocre spirits under sweet mixers, as people had been trained to do during Prohibition. Second, the liquor itself, now buried under factory-produced cola, was often of less than great quality. After all, why use the good stuff if the customer can't taste it? Thus, the appreciation of quality spirits for their own merit continued to diminish, and the American palate became even less sophisticated.

Aiding the devolution of the tipple was the increasing ubiquity of handy hoses that squirted out carbonated products, and could be simultaneously connected to several different canisters of carbonated mixer. All that was required from a bartender now was to pour a shot of gin while squirting tonic from the hose, or to pour a shot of whiskey while squirting cola from the hose. With truly skilled bartenders no longer *required*, bars discovered that they could cheaply hire good-looking and energetic college kids, any of whom could pour a hundred highballs an hour, raking in big profits for high-volume bars.

The old guard had truly passed; soon there were few bartenders who really had any idea of how to make proper, old-style cocktails at all, and even fewer who cared to learn. And the customers? Most of their *parents* hadn't even been born by the end of the golden age, so their taste buds just didn't know what they were missing.

It can be noted that the Polynesian Pop or "tiki" trend of the 1930s to 1960s did produce some lovely drinks. Sadly, by the end of the 1960s, the tropical drinks of the tiki trend were becoming just as hard to find in their original unadulterated forms as the traditional-style cocktails of Harry Johnson's era. Like the golden age classics of Johnson's time, the tiki drinks were considered too complicated, expensive, or time-consuming for most bars to want to deal with.

By the mid-1980s, the classic cocktail was all but dead in the United States. Fascinatingly, it was enjoying great popularity in Japan, and it still does today. The Japanese are masters at taking other people's inventions, stripping them down to their core, and figuring out ways to improve them. The cocktail, as a quintessentially

American art form, was being deconstructed and revered across the Pacific. Kazuo Uyeda, now 65 years old and still the owner of an intimate bar in Ginza, Tokyo, spent the 1980s innovating shaker techniques, developing theories on the usage of ice, and perfecting other minutiae that would eventually become influential around the globe.

Back in America, the return of the classic cocktail was inevitable, perhaps due to nostalgia, and perhaps due to people beginning to realize there was more to nightlife than highballs. A few bartenders remembered that there could be true craftsmanship and culinary excellence involved in their work. They knew cocktails had the potential to be every bit as pleasing to the palate as a fine meal was. They knew that a century ago people had enjoyed something special, and it was time to bring that level of quality into the modern age. Credit for launching what we'll call the *craft cocktail movement* is most often given to Dale DeGroff, who was working in New York's Rainbow Room at the time. Most of the people working in the craft cocktail sector today weren't around yet when DeGroff began working his magic, but the halcyon days at the Rainbow Room are spoken of with great reverence by those who were there.

DeGroff wasn't alone, however. Others, elsewhere, had similar convictions, and over the past 20 years, the great American cocktail has made a comeback that has truly begun to grow in exponential leaps since the mid-2000s.

And now, here we are. Back to an age where a proper cocktail can (theoretically) be imbibed in most major cities.

Sometimes.

There is still this nagging question of why many of the best upscale restaurants and hotel bars still serve crummy cocktails with their (potentially) great meals and (potentially) great service. People expect good food and good service, but many of these same people are absolutely content with lousy drinks (and that's exactly what they're getting). We don't have a definitive solution to this phenomenon, but we do have a solid and simple theory (*lex parsimoniae*).

Quality liquor was either illegal or hard to get for several decades of the 20th century. Good food, on the other hand, was neither illegal nor rare at any point (in the United States, at least). And, people need to eat. But they don't *need* to drink booze. So, for most people, there isn't as much urgency to explore the culinary possibilities of a handcrafted cocktail as there is motivation to eat well. Thus, between the lack of exigency and the lingering effects of the world wars and Prohibition, cocktail culture is still struggling to catch up to the culinary world, and it is several decades behind. Give the beleaguered and underappreciated tipple some time; it shall find its place in the culinary world soon enough!

Is it actually catching up though?

Really?

Yes.

Yes it is.

We're getting there. DeGroff and his kindred spirits got the ball rolling. This ball is getting bigger and it is gaining momentum, fast. But craft cocktails aren't quite mainstream yet; you still aren't guaranteed a great drink in any given nice restaurant or swanky lounge you may visit.

That's why this book exists.

Destination: Cocktails is a guide to the bars on the cutting edge of the craft cocktail movement. It profiles several hundred destinations that are doing things *properly*. It will introduce you to the people and the places that care enough to give you a quality experience for your money. This book will point you to the swanky lounges (and the dive bars), the five-star hotel bars (and the neighborhood

taverns), and the high-end restaurants (and the low-end restaurants) that are backing up their pretense of class (or distinct lack thereof) with one crucial thing: an amazing cocktail.

With luck, there won't be so much need for a book like this a decade from now; it would be fantastic to see great cocktails routinely served in *all* the places where you might expect them today (no, not in dive bars, which we also love, but at least in the better restaurants, hotels, and lounges). It would be fantastic to see the trend toward universal excellence continue and last, instead of just being seen as a post-millennial fad when the current decade is looked back upon. Many expensive eateries are improving their bar programs surely, steadily, visibly, and remarkably, but we're not yet at critical mass where a nice restaurant can be expected to also serve a nice cocktail. Quality cocktailing is still a *movement*, even at the very top of the dining spectrum. Thus, we think the craft cocktail phenomenon shares a deeper kinship to the Slow Food movement.

Slow Food was founded in 1986 by Carlo Petrini. With members in 132 countries, the movement is an antithesis to fast food's ideals and methods. It aims to preserve regional cuisines and to proliferate traditional farming of animals and plants while supporting small local businesses. It is a return to eating wholesome, healthy food, created locally by people tending to nature, as opposed to processed food made by people tending to factories. Many of the bars in this book also adhere to these principles, which, of course, were not part of a "movement" in the days of Jerry Thomas. It was simply the way things were done, all the time, by necessity, in both the food and liquor worlds. Whether bar owners and bartenders at craft cocktail bars today consider themselves ecologically-minded or not, they are adhering to principles of Slow Food by default, just as they follow in Thomas's footsteps by choice. In this book, we'll be paying special attention to the bars that do consciously and conscientiously adhere to what we'd like to think of as the "slow drinks" credo (with a nod to like-minded writer Wayne Curtis, whose blog is called *Slow Cocktails*).

All right, enough with the manifesto already.

You want to drink.

But first, a few rules . . .

DESTINATION: COCKTAILS

HOUSE RULES

Some of the bars profiled in this book have chosen to post rules on their front doors, menus, websites, or restrooms. A selection of these rules from various bars includes:

"No stupid drinks."

"Please don't bring anyone with you that you wouldn't take home for dinner with your mother."

"Gentlemen shall not approach unescorted ladies without an introduction."

"Exit the bar briskly and silently. People are trying to sleep across the street."

In the spirit of having some fun with the "house rules" seen in many bars, here are a few things to keep in mind while perusing this tome. This will give you a set of starting points for getting the most out of this book, and an idea of what sort of places are profiled in these pages.

1. Atmosphere
This book is about great drinks.

The only criteria for inclusion is that the bar consistently and reliably serves a superior cocktail. That said, atmosphere is important. Good service is *very* important. A lack of deafeningly loud music or multiple televisions is a good management choice, too.

But all of these are secondary in the context of *Destination: Cocktails*. In this book, you'll find both stinky dive bars and five-star hotel lounges. You will find bars that have been open since the 19th century, and others that have been open since 2012. You will find loud, rowdy places, and you will find oases of tranquility. You will even find a few Michelin-starred restaurants right alongside at least one bar in a building that used to sell Michelin tires.

All of these bars will make you a solid cocktail, crafted with care.

All that mattered when a bar was considered for inclusion in this book was **what was in the glass**. We like to think there is a bar for every personality type in *Destination: Cocktails*, provided that this person cares about what they're drinking.

2. Pretension and pomposity

We've already mentioned bars that post lists of house rules. In theory, it is a positive thing that many contemporary watering holes are encouraging people to behave like grown-ups. On the other hand, it's kind of sad that we live in a society where people can't figure out, on their own, that wearing flip-flops to a five-star hotel bar is a bad idea, that whistling isn't a good way to get a bartender's attention, and that yapping on your cell phone in a quiet lounge or restaurant is still tacky.

Yes, it is.

Go outside.

Unfortunately, those who think these behaviors are acceptable seem to be the same people who use the word "pretentious" to describe lounges that simply ask you to behave like a lady or a gentleman.

That said, we have to admit that just a few of the businesses in these pages might indeed be a little pompous. A very small percentage of them do seem to forget that at the end of the night, they're still just slinging hootch. There's nothing inherently classy about selling or buying something that is going to ruin your health and eventually make you start talking like an idiot. Expensive booze will transform you into just as much of a troll as the cheaper variety will. It just tastes better going down the hatch.

While we regret to say that a handful of the establishments

"freshly crafted cocktails" or "speakeasy menu." Many of these bars are still using canned juice and syrups full of evil high fructose corn syrup, and will routinely serve you rail-quality booze (none of these places made the cut for inclusion in *Destination: Cocktails*). Their unimaginative menus are still full of 1980s-style drinks with names that end with "-tini," but which now sport gratuitous persimmon or basil. Sleeve garters, a mustache, and a bottle of Peychaud's bitters do not a skilled bartender make.

The first time we experienced a bartender dipping a little straw into the drink he had just mixed, and then taking a little taste to make sure it was just right, we were impressed. When we saw a young lady do this six years later before serving a vile cocktail that wouldn't have made the cut at TGIFriday's, we realized that a craft cocktail backlash was imminent. Her tasting of the drink was all for show. The poor girl had no idea what she was tasting, and wouldn't have known if it was good or not if her job depended on it. It should have.

A mass awareness of the craft cocktail may be upon us. If the quality can be maintained, then wider acceptance and more options for the thirsty customer are a very good thing. Universal awesomeness and a comprehensive raising of the bar are positive developments for everyone involved. But if we may venture an opinion, all bartenders must master the classics before thinking that they can put aquavit, yuzu, Malört, St. Germain, rye, cardamom, and three kinds of bitters into the same glass and expect to make it work.

6. Your homework

This book is designed so as not to require the reader to have an expert foreknowledge of craft cocktails. We don't want to alienate the newbies among you, but we are going to assume you have a *small* amount of experience. There are a dozen or two drinks that are absolutely intrinsic to a baseline knowledge of mixology, and these drinks are referenced again and again throughout this text. If you're still confused as to what's in them, we recommend working your way through these classics during your next few nights out, before moving up to more exotic potions. This could be seen as the reciprocal of asking bartenders to avoid overreach: train your palate to love the classics and then take it from there. Once you get acquainted with them, you'll see why they've lasted, in many cases, for over a century.

Within the context of this book, this list of standards includes: the Aviation, the Bee's Knees, the Corpse Reviver #2, the Daiquiri, the French 75, the Gimlet, the Last Word, the Manhattan, the Margarita, the Martinez, the Martini, the Mint Julep, the Mojito, the Negroni, the Old-Fashioned, the Piña Colada, the Rob Roy, the Sazerac, and the Sidecar.

There are many other drinks that many people would rightly consider to be bona fide classics, but we will include the basic ingredients for all drinks, save for the ones listed above, as they come up in the text.

Please also keep in mind that as much as we're huge fans of these classics and others, we'll be featuring house original cocktails for the bars we visit as often as we can. After all, virtually any of the bars in this book can make you a flawless Manhattan or a perfect Negroni, but we want to turn you on to some of the creative work that the amazing bartenders featured in this book are doing. If some of them are over-reaching, we'll leave that up to you to decide for yourself.

We're also going to assume that the reader knows the difference between gin, rum, whiskey, tequila, absinthe, and brandy, and has at least a passing clue what calvados, applejack, cachaça, armagnac, and cognac are. ((Hint: these are all types of liquor, or in the context of a cocktail, they're referred to as a "base spirit.") We're also expecting a passing familiarity with certain extremely popular and common liqueur brands such as Cointreau, Grand Marnier, Chartreuse, Campari, Bénédictine, Pernod, and various crèmes (crème de cacao, crème de cassis, etc).

7. Making the cut

The joy of watching the craft cocktail movement spread is that there are now a whole lot of places making great drinks. This wasn't the case as recently as six years ago, when a solid Sidecar was elusive even in New York or San Francisco. Today, there are plenty of places who *get* it, and who are doing it right. This is fantastic for you, but tricky for us!

Destination: Cocktails is not even going to pretend to be

comprehensive. New and quite worthy bars are opening all the time, and they are destinations that cocktail lovers will doubtlessly enjoy. Other fantastic bars, sadly, are also closing, but this seems to be happening at a slower rate than the openings, fueling evidence of the impending mainstream desire for slow drinks. There are also plenty of fantastic bars already thriving in toddling towns that we just couldn't manage a visit to.

So, in these pages you'll find a curated selection of bars that have maintained a consistent buzz in the cocktail community. These are the places that come up in conversation again and again when talking to the international community of distillers, bartenders, cocktail enthusiasts, and bar owners. The ones that (in some cases) win awards, and (in other cases) *should* be winning awards.

There are more.

Omissions are regretted. If your favorite bar, or *your* bar, is not in this book, then it is either for lack of space, or because you're in a town that we just couldn't get to this time around . . . or maybe it's because your bar program sucks.

8. Last call

For most of the cities we visited, we've included a section called "Last Call!" at the end of those cities' listings. It is here that you can read a little bit about some additional places that might be worth a visit. Some are solid destinations, but we just didn't have space to give them full profiles. Some are brand-new and we weren't able to research them more thoroughly (read: we haven't had to be carried out of the place yet). Others are businesses that aren't *quite* up to the high standards exemplified in the main profiles, but which may still be worth a visit for various reasons. In many cases, we might mention what it was that made us decide that this bar wasn't quite A+ material. It is our hope that these instances will be read constructively. It's also our hope that readers will support these places so that they may thrive and, hopefully, continue to improve.

9. Obsolescence

Things change fast in the bar business. We have tried to make this book as up to date as possible, but bars do close, move, drop cocktails from their menus, and raise their prices. Their operating hours fluctuate. Their happy hour policies and schedules change. Their specials and promotions begin and end. Bartenders move on to other bars or other careers. Concepts change. Aliens blow up cities.

If you have any doubts, we've provided phone numbers for just about every bar in this book. Give 'em a call and make sure they'll be there when you plan to be. This is also why we haven't listed hours of operation or happy hour parameters—they're just too wildly subject to change. Call or visit their website. A few locations also require reservations; we have tried to note those.

10. Whiskey or whisky?

The Old Irish term for whiskey was *uisce beatha*, or "water of life." Our term for whiskey is "yes, please." Those of you who love whiskey (or whisky) already know about the difference in spelling: the lovely liquor made from mash of grain is called "whisky" in Scotland and Canada; it's called "whiskey" more or less everywhere else.

Since it is awkward and kind of lame to use "whisk(e)y" throughout this book, "whiskey" will be used as a blanket term, except when referring specifically to Scotch or Canadian whisky.

Since we're on the topic—the names of cocktails will be capitalized. This book is all about cocktails, of course. There'd be nothing to write about without The Last Word, so the drinks are given respect by using caps. This also helps them to stand out in the text. For liquors, brand names are capitalized (Ron Zacapa) but categories of liquor are not (rum). Liqueurs are capitalized when mentioned by brand name (Chartreuse) but not by style (herbal liqueur). Exceptions are when the type of liquor or liqueur appear specifically in the brand name. For example, "falernum" need not be capitalized in most cases, but "John D. Taylor's Velvet Falernum" will be. The tricky bits are in liquor types that are derived from a place. Champagne, curaçao, and bourbon have more or less lost their strong associations to the Champagne region of France, the Dutch island of Curaçao, and Bourbon County, Kentucky, and are no longer commonly capitalized. But what about hootch that comes from Cognac, Armagnac, or Calvados? In solidarity with champagne, curaçao, and bourbon, capitalization of cognac, armagnac, and calvados shall also be denied.

11. Beer, wine, food, and booze à la carte

Virtually every bar in this book also sells beer, wine, and liquor by the shot. A large number of these bars are within restaurants, or at least they sell some food. We'll be mentioning food in a brief way when applicable, so you may plan your drinking and dining combinations accordingly. In the interest of space and focus, we'll only mention beer, wine, and booze served neat from time to time, when there's special reason to. For the most part, consider it a given that in the majority of businesses listed in this book, the selections of potables adjunct to the cocktail menu are of an equivalent style as the cocktails themselves, are at as high a standard, and are appropriate to the atmosphere or mood of the business being profiled.

12. Bartender

We asked a few dozen bartenders and bar owners the same question: "Do you prefer the term bartender, bar chef, mixologist, shaker monkey, or something else? Why?" Their answers were surprising and often a lot of fun. You'll see their comments in little boxes throughout the book.

13. The bottom line

Sometimes your author needs his constant companion Gal Friday Night (note-taker, monkey wrangler, schedule keeper, mobile CFO, and royal cocktail co-tester) to remind him that this is just booze we're talking about here.

Firewater.

Likker.

Hootch.

It is *recreation*.

We definitely demand a certain level of quality from anything we are going to pour down our gullets—if you're reading this, perhaps you do, too—but let's not take this *too* seriously.

Let's have some fun.

The endlessly efficient Gal Friday Night is ready with our tickets, our itinerary, all of our cash (she doesn't trust writers with money) and a big-ass bottle of water to keep us hydrated.

She says: Let's go!

UNITED STATES

Beginning in New York, a world nexus for cocktail destinations, and ending on the other side of the continent in San Diego, we've planned a roughly east-to-west road trip across the U.S. for your tippling adventures. Your ultimate cocktail crawl begins here and now—don't forget to send us a postcard!

NEW YORK

New York is the cocktail capital of North America. There are also amazing things going on in Chicago and San Francisco. New Orleans has the claim to history, while Los Angeles, Portland, Seattle, and other towns are representing strongly as well. But they all pale next to New York. Listing every decent tipple to be found in this toddling town is an impossible task; the following is a selection of the very best.

1534

20 Prince Street
New York, NY
212.966.5073
www.jacquesnyc.com

A number of bars in this book post rules forbidding men to approach unescorted ladies, but there are just a few that make this approach *mandatory*. There is no mistaking rule #5 at 1534: "If a beautiful woman/man is by themselves, you must attempt conversation and attempt courtship." This rule may or may not be trumped, should the situation arise, by #6: "When an awesome power ballad is playing you must sing along." This rule seems to be taken to heart at 1534; the bar can get pretty noisy. Their stated mission is to serve the same quality of drinks that other slow drink bars do, but without what they perceive as a snooty atmosphere.

Launched in November 2010, 1534 was named by owner Jacques Oauri after the year when French colonist Jacques Cartier set out for the New World. The bar 1534 can be found below Jacques Downtown (the sister restaurant to Jacques Brasserie at 204–206 East 85th Street; 212.327.2272). Unsurprisingly, the fare is inspired by France and her colonies, including moules et frites ($19), trout with almond lemon sauce

($21), and warm goat cheese Napoleon ($10).

Be careful navigating the narrow staircase as you head downstairs to slurp up some cocktails. This bar is not large, with only four seats, standing room for maybe a dozen, and a few leather banquettes. The decor recalls a festive governor's home in a hot climate: sconces and chandeliers, coffered ceilings, a leafy pattern on the wallpaper, and rugs over a tiled floor. Head bartender Justin Noel (of consulting firm Contemporary Cocktails, who also put together the Breslin) is responsible for the menu. Looking like a passport, it maintains the French colonial theme, aiming to spotlight the ingredients and flavors of France's many diverse (ex)territories. Absinthe fountains have been repurposed as punch bowls; punch is also served tableside in vintage teapots with an array of DIY garnishes (service for 3, 6, or 10 at $35/$65/$130). Gal Friday Night was reminded of her years living in Tanzania by the Zanzibar punch (Appleton Reserve rum, tahini, coconut milk, coffee tincture, fresh nutmeg). French Indochina is evoked with the Haloong Bay punch (green tea-infused gin, yuzu juice, pineapple juice, lime juice, ginger-infused agave syrup). The Americas have inspired Ponche de Xochiquetzal punch, named in honor of the Aztec goddess of fertility (reposado tequila, coffee liqueur, Combier Liqueur d'Orange, Bénédictine, sherry, lemon juice).

All of these punches are hard to resist, and we haven't even breached the single-portion menu selections yet. Let's do it: Tahitian 75 (Bluecoat gin, dry champagne, lemon juice, hibiscus syrup, edible flower garnish), Colonial Holiday (Laird's applejack, East India

sherry, John D. Taylor's Velvet Falernum, lime juice, coffee grind garnish), and Saigon Folly (pepper-infused gin, lemongrass syrup, Crème Yvette, lemon juice, soda). All cocktails are $12.

À la tienne!

Angel's Share

8 Stuyvesant Street
New York, NY
212.777.5415

Choosing a booze-related name isn't uncommon for a bar. Some simply pick the name of a spirit or cocktail and run with it, like Absinthe (see page 206) or Rob Roy (page 176). You know exactly what you're in for at these places. Far fewer bars are named for the *complete absence* of a spirit. In distilling terminology, the "angel's share" is the quantity of product lost to evaporation while a spirit is aging. In New York terminology, Angel's Share is a pioneer on the craft cocktail scene, having been open for over a decade now.

Located behind Village Yokocho, a venerable yakitori joint (which itself is above St. Marks Bookstore), Angel's Share is accessed by a subtle door in the back of the eatery. It can hardly be thought of as a "speakeasy," though; their big picture windows allow fantastic views of the tourists, artists, and NYU students navigating the bustling East Village. There's no "bustling" inside Angel's Share, however. This heavenly little oasis in the big city absolutely refuses to seat parties larger than four people, and its servers will harp on you if you raise your voice. They'll give you hell for standing, too. Within a room decorated in damask curtains, deco-ish wood paneling, a mural of painted cherubs (with one lil' devil), and plush leather seats, the smartly-dressed bartenders serve a lovely menu of cocktails.

Many of the libations have an Asian flair, using shiso, ume, lychee, and passion fruit flavors. The barmen, some of whom were trained by the legendary master bartenders of Tokyo's Ginza district, seem reluctant to go off-menu; perhaps they're too occupied carving the ice by hand, which isn't an unworthy endeavor. All cocktails are in the $15 range. We were fascinated by the possibilities of the Stormy Weather (rye infused with Fuji apple and cinnamon,

lime juice, ginger wine, ground ginger, ginger ale), Mack the Knife (gin, whiskey, cinnamon, cayenne pepper, grapefruit juice, flamed thyme), Del Sasser (house-infused bacon bourbon, plum liquor, lime juice, pomegranate juice, balsamic honey, Argentine bitters), and Green Haze (gin, kiwi juice, grapefruit juice, yuzu juice, cucumber). Bar snacks include sashimi, dim sum, fried oysters, and Japanese sausage.

Brandy Library

25 N. Moore Street
New York, NY
212.226.5545
www.brandylibrary.com

There are two types of bar in the world: those that can sell you a snifter full of century-old brandy, and those that can't. Brandy Library is currently in the latter category, but if their supply of 1914 Pierre Ferrand cognac holds out just a little longer, they will joining the elite "century club" very soon.

Opened in 2004 by Flavien Desoblin, Brandy Library carries a reported 1,500 brands of brandy on its amber-lit shelves, accessed by waitstaff elegantly scampering up library ladders. You won't see much clear liquor on that wall; this is a place for bourbon, cognac, Scotch, and armagnac. The collection is curated by Brandy Library's on-site team of spirit sommeliers, who will help you choose a libation if the extensive menu becomes overwhelming. In order to make sure your selection is exactly what you want, Desoblin assures us that "we always show the bottle and give a taste for approval

before pouring." For the indecisive or adventurous, they offer spirits flights for $31–$88. Naturally, local products occupy those shelves as well, including whiskeys from Hudson Valley, Kings County, Breuklen, Delaware Phoenix, MacKenzie, and Warwick distilleries.

Cocktails (all $14) are served in vintage-inspired glassware. Although there are around 100 available, Desoblin says, "We make them in the most classic form possible, trying to stay away from the hip and trendy mixology abuse."

The syllogistic Gal Friday Night liked the looks of the Paradox (armagnac, orange liqueur, Amarula liqueur) and the Peaches and Cream (cognac, crème de pêche, port wine reduction, cream). The creamy Amarula is made from the fruit of the African Marula tree. My eyes were drawn to the Creold Fashioned (bourbon, Clément Créole Shrubb, orange juice, cherry, bitters). Yours should be, too. Desoblin pointed out that their number-one cocktail has always been the Sidecar. "Along with the Old-Fashioned," he said, "we are told by our customers that it's better than anywhere else." The Sidecar (brandy, Cointreau, lemon juice) is elegant in its simplicity, but it is also tricky to get *just right*. The solution here? Pierre Ferrand,

of course. No, not the 1914 stuff. Brandy Library has its own house VSOP Cognac made by Ferrand, and this is what you'll find in the Sidecar. Where appropriate, cocktails may be mixed with house-made chocolate liqueur, peanut butter liqueur, ginger beer, coffee liqueur, and orange simple syrup.

A short menu of decadent bites and entrees (house cognac-cured foie gras, Malai tikka, croque monsieur, smoked salmon, coq au vin, etc.) is served until late, and ranges from $8 to $19. You won't find buffalo wings at Brandy Library because—as the menu wryly states—they could never match the ones at Hooters. Gal Friday Night, a former Hooter's corporate executive, disagrees.

Located in TriBeCa, the dimly-lit Brandy Library is decorated in plush leather chairs and mahogany. Monday night patrons may enjoy the sounds of Joel Forrester on the piano. The room exudes maleness, and the upscale crowd of Wall Street types are all—as defined by door policy—over 25. Definitely the sort of customer who can afford the 1914 Pierre Ferrand at $230 per snifter.

B ars named after drinks that were named after 19th-century social clubs seem to be a popular New York phenomenon. We'll discuss the Pegu Club—the classic bar, the drink, and the modern bar—later, but first let's talk Clover.

Clover Club

210 Smith Street
New York, NY
718.855.7939
www.cloverclubny.com

First mentioned in print in 1911, the Clover Club cocktail was named for a Philadelphia journalist's society, hosted in the Bellevue-Stratford Hotel from 1882 until the 1920s. Recipes for the libation vary, but the constants over the past century have been gin, raspberry syrup, lemon, and egg white; variations utilize vermouth, grenadine, or lime. Crosby Gaige, who wrote several great cocktail guides in the 1940s, deemed this tipple worthy of his "Hall of Fame."

New York cocktail impresario Julie Reiner opened her Brooklyn reincarnation of Clover Club in 2008 with partner Susan Fedroff. Reiner, who is also a partner at the Flatiron Lounge (see page 42) and Lani Kai (page 43), arrived in New York in 1997. She created beverage programs for a few bars before opening Flatiron in 2003.

Clover Club moves slightly away from the moody paradigm so prevalent in nearby Manhattan by featuring tall windows, which let bright light in. This illuminates the 19th-century mahogany back bar, exposed brick, a fireplace surrounded by marble, intricate antique tiles on the floor, and oriental rugs. The spacious opulence of the front room is complimented with a smaller and more intimate back room.

The menu at Clover Club is both a primer to pre-Prohibition potables and a showcase for Reiner's talents. It includes sections for cobblers, smashes, punches, and other mixed drink categories dating from a time before "cocktail" became the boilerplate term that it is. Fairly detailed explanations of each group of drinks are thoughtfully provided for newbs still getting up to speed. We're here to help, kids.

Wanting to explore some of Reiner's own inventions, Gal Friday Night and I were drawn to two further sections: "Porch Drinks," which is a new category of libation invented at Clover Club ("a long format drink that you would want to enjoy on a hot evening"), and "Clover Club Greatest Hits." Most drinks are reasonably priced (for New York) at $12.

Thus spoke Friday: Bitter Tom (gin, Campari, Bénédictine, grapefruit juice, lemon juice, pomegranate molasses) and Nightvision (spice-infused aquavit, carrot juice, lemon juice, ginger syrup). Aquavit (also called aqua vitae or akvavit, and related to eau de vie, arrack, and schnapps) is a family of fruit-based brandies popular all over Europe and beyond. Two deceptively simple cocktails looked good as well: Brunswick Sour (white rum, lime juice, ruby port) and the classic Improved Whiskey Cocktail (rye, maraschino liqueur, absinthe, bitters). We are humbled, once again, to be reminded that the simplest of recipes can be magic when amalgamated and agitated by accomplished appendages.

Clover Club also has a light food menu (most dishes are $8–$16), which may include smoked bluefish rillette, steak over toast, mac and cheese, pulled pork minis, and charcuterie. They also have a brunch menu, with full cocktail service all day long. We like.

Since its launch on January 1, 2007, Death & Co has become a cornerstone of New York's cocktail scene. The head bartender of Dave Kaplan's lauded bar is currently Thomas Waugh (who took the reins from previous bar chiefs Brian Miller and Phil Ward), but veteran Joaquín Simó is the longest-standing man behind the stick at Death & Co. Prior to settling in for a night of cocktailing, Simó provided some insight on the original concept: "A small, intimate space in which beautifully crafted cocktails could be enjoyed in a civilized atmosphere. We are a dark, windowless space, so there's a sense of heightened isolation from the noise and bustle of the East Village, as well as the weather."

Death & Co isn't hard to find. There is nothing subtle about a huge wooden door flanked by two columns, standing out from everything else on the block. The bar does not accept reservations. Simó calls it "a completely democratic establishment which operates on a first-come, first-serve basis."

The menu launched with a mere seven drinks in 2007, but soon swelled dramatically, peaking at over 90 libations. Some of the added drinks were tiki-style, courtesy of Miller. "We were among the first cocktail bars to start treating tiki drinks seriously," says Simó. Death & Co also offers punch service—their "classicist response to the bottle service trend that was so popular in lounges and clubs."

Death & Co makes its own ginger, grenadine, demerara, cinnamon bark, vanilla, orgeat, raspberry, and acacia honey syrups all year round, and adds other flavors, such as passion fruit, cumin, hibiscus, curried ginger, and various tea infusions, according to season. Expect to see baking spices, apple, pear, and pumpkin during the cooler months and more fresh herbs, berries, and cucumber in the warmer months. The same ingredients are used in-house infusions (pineapple and sage tequila, spiced pecan bourbon, Fuji apple scotch) along with a wide variety of teas and herbal blends.

These ingredients are, to say the least, put to good use at Death & Co. "To get someone's eyes to light up the first time they realize they don't actually hate gin or tequila, [that] they hate crappy versions of those products mixed carelessly with even worse mixers, is a beautiful part of our job," says Simó. "Then we can start introducing them to aquavit or mezcal and really begin to open up new worlds of flavors and experiences to their palates."

All right, we are convinced. Let's have a look at that extensive booze book of theirs, which is filled with quotes from illuminated lushes like Ernest Hemingway, Hunter S. Thompson, and President Roosevelt. A musical theme seemed to develop as we picked out a selection of delectable libations (all $13): the Cure For Pain (Rittenhouse rye, George T. Stagg bourbon, Carpano Antica Formula vermouth, Otima 10-year tawny port, white crème de cacao, Campari, orange twist) may or may not be named for the song/album by Morphine, while Pressure Drop (Ransom Old Tom gin, Meletti amaro, Dolin dry vermouth, Clear Creek pear brandy, Angostura bitters) may or may not be named for the song by the Maytals (and the Clash . . . and the Specials . . .). Slap and Pickle (Krogstad aquavit, muddled cucumber, lime juice, grenadine, cucumber wedge) is probably *not* named after Squeeze's "Slap and Tickle" (we're really pushing it here). The possibilities within Golden Beautiful (Herradura reposado tequila, lime juice, passion fruit purée, vanilla syrup, Campari, club soda) are also especially intriguing. Someone write a song, quick, so we can drink this one.

For the hungry, Death & Co offers a dozen or so small plates, not limited to truffle macaroni ($10), goat cheese profiteroles ($12), and crab fritters ($14), courtesy of chef Luis Gonzalez.

Dram

177 S. 4th Street
New York, NY
718.486.3726
www.drambar.com

Some bar menus are house-driven, meaning that the bar manager or head mixologist created the menu, and the bar staff is expected to stick with it. Others are bartender-driven, meaning that the people making your drinks are trusted enough to follow their instincts (and customer guidance) to create something unique. Within the context of the bars featured in this book, bartender-driven bars aren't especially rare. The entire city of Seattle seems to adhere militantly to this philosophy, actually. Dram does, too.

Tom Chadwick opened Dram in the spring of 2010. The bar had been in the works since 2004, which might be some sort of record. Having seen enough fancy-pants craft cocktail bars open up during Dram's lengthy gestation period, Chadwick realized that Brooklyn really needed a bar that could do high-end cocktails in a neighborhood bar environment. What makes Dram special, however, are Chadwick's choices about which bartenders to keep on hand. In addition to a solid cast of reliable regulars, Dram rotates in guests from a litany of top-tier houses of liquid worship, not limited to: Death & Co, Flatiron Lounge, Prime Meats, Clover Club, and even Experimental Cocktail Club. Consult the calendar on their website to see who is working tonight.

Make no mistake, the house team is not to be underestimated. Frank Cisneros is also a sommelier and will just as likely make you a great cocktail as suggest a perfect wine. Or he'll slap a beer on the bar in front of you, if that's your fancy. Egalitarian Dram strives to be just as friendly to the shot-and-beer crowd as they are to the cocktail nerds.

Among the locals grooving to indie rock, the free-thinking Gal Friday Night went Behind God's Back (rum, cane syrup, pineapple juice, cinnamon, orgeat; $9), before moving on to a Pressgang Swizzle (Smith & Cross rum, Hayman's Old Tom gin, ginger syrup, grapefruit juice, lime juice, orgeat, bitters; $9). Meanwhile, I was intrigued by the East Coast take on aged cocktails, a trend that has been very popular on the West Coast and in London the past couple of years. Dram claims to have been the first place in

New York to serve them.

Another trend embraced by Dram before anyone else in New York has us on the fence: draft cocktails. Pre-batched cocktails can work—after all, that's what a punch is, and that's currently trendy, too. But we've all worked so hard to get heinous squirt guns and rubber hoses banished from bars. Barrel aging done properly adds cohesiveness and deeply layered flavors to a cocktail, but what does being squirted up a hose add to the drink, other than bartender efficiency? The jury is out on this one.

Across the street is Pies 'n' Thighs. Yes, it's fried stuff—like chicken and catfish—with pie (166 S. 4th Street; 347.529.6090; www.piesnthighs.com). Keeping that particular temptation at bay (for the moment), Dram offers a few enticing nibbles of its own, including American farmstand cheeses ($10/two, $18/four), charcuterie ($21), house-made salted caramels ($1 each), and forest mushroom fondue ($10).

Dutch Kills

27-24 Jackson Avenue
New York, NY
718.383.2724
www.dutchkillsbar.com

While all but the staunchest of so-called speakeasies will gladly provide any interested customer with their address, there aren't many whose entire website consists of nothing other than 11 separate sets of directions for finding them. Welcome to Dutch Kills in Long Island City. If you get lost, it is not their fault.

Long Island City is actually the westernmost section of Queens, just over the river from Manhattan. The area was once home to factories and bakeries, and now hosts the New York metro area's largest conglomeration of art galleries and artists' spaces. Within Long Island City is the smaller neighborhood of Dutch Kills, home to the bar in question.

Richard Boccato and Sasha Petraske (of Milk & Honey; Petraske also owns Little Branch) teamed with Ian Present to open

Dutch Kills in May 2009. Of the many bars that evoke the era of Jerry Thomas and the golden age of barcraft, Dutch Kills is among those that take the concept most to heart. Sawdust covers the floors, the menu is scribbled on chalkboards, bartenders rock ersatz period attire, and on selected nights, live ragtime and early jazz is performed on an upright piano. Low ceilings, dim lights, coffered mahogany walls, antique cash registers. Outside, you'll be looking for a small white neon sign that simply says "BAR." Jerry Thomas never saw a neon sign in his life, but we'll let that small detail pass.

Before we settle in for a drinkie, let's talk ice. Using the right ice in a cocktail is a crucial aspect of mixology which ought never to be underestimated. When ice is in a shaker or a glass, it will melt, altering the water content of a drink, and therefore altering taste and consistency. Ice management is how a bartender maintains control over the dilution and the temperature of a drink. The ice in a glass also contributes to the experience of drinking the beverage; the ice's size, shape, texture, and temperature all matter. Ice does exist at different temperatures. A colder and more dense cube will cool your drink more effectively while taking longer to melt. Win-win.

The Japanese understand this. During the 1980s, when the American cocktail was at it's nadir, the Japanese were developing influential ice programs and shaker techniques. Apparently, the Dutch get it, too; what we see at Dutch Kills is a killer ice

program. In fact, the bar's owners have launched Hundredweight Ice and Cocktail Services, which does ice manufacturing and consultation for other bars. You'll also hear the name Kold-Draft thrown about quite a lot. This company has been making ice machines since 1955 and is considered the best of the best for delivering ice that is colder, harder, and clearer than any other. Many of the businesses in this book use Kold-Draft machines whenever possible. The company's website also claims that their machines "have been carefully developed to be more energy- and water-efficient than standard ice machines." Cool.

Without ceremony or confusion, Gal Friday Night gave in to temptation with a New Order (bourbon, lemon juice, rhubarb bitters, crème de cacao), while I went for the smoky Don Lockwood (bourbon, Islay Scotch whisky, chocolate bitters, maple syrup, orange peel). Also intriguing were the Taj Majal (Laird's applejack, Beefeater gin, apricot liqueur, lime juice) and the Infante (tequila, lime juice, orgeat, nutmeg).

Dutch Kills serves no food, but they don't seem to mind if you order from local take-out joints, such as Sage General Store (24–20 Jackson Avenue; 718.361.0707).

Anyway, you're still wondering about the name. Who calls a neighborhood "Dutch Kills"? Easy there, pardner; *kills* means "creek" in the tongue of the Dutch, who settled the area in 1643. Dutch Creek. Kinda homey, actually.

Elsa

217 E. 3rd Street
New York, NY
917.882.7395
www.elsabar.com

It could be said that certain bars come across as being especially masculine, and others may present a more feminine environment. At the risk of getting into messy gender role stereotypes here, we just can't deny that a bar filled with heavy mahogany, plush maroon leather furniture, and taxidermy mammals is never going to be defined as "feminine." Conversely, there are definitely places that seem to have a vibe more alluring to estrogen, and I'm thinking that a certain New York bar named after 1920s fashion icon Elsa Schiaparelli might be one of them.

Maybe it's the rows of candles, the checkerboard floor, the orchids set into alcoves along spotless creamy walls, the booths of blond wood, or the copy of Schiaparelli's *Time* magazine cover on a back wall. Maybe it's because the place feels airy and clean, or the fact that the hyperosmic Gal Friday Night was impressed with the scent in the restroom. It could be the antique Singer sewing machine that doubles as a beer tap, or the neon sign outside depicting a fashionable girl with a Martini glass. Or, just maybe, it is a neat alcove inside the bar with women's clothing for sale.

This is where the chick thing ends, though. Elsa also has a full-service bespoke tailor at the front of the property. Gentlemen may have their suits custom-fitted by Jake Mueser during normal business hours, and may also do so two nights a week during bar hours. This is really handy for those who spill drinks on themselves. The well-coordinated Gal Friday Night never has that problem, so her perusal of the fashions on hand were purely recreational. I, on the other hand, had to buy myself an entire suit after absently letting a Jaszek (Laird's applejack, falernum, lime juice, Angostura bitters, orange bitters) dribble down my Nat Nast. Bitters stains.

Examining the cocktail menu housed within the cover of a vintage book (most drinks are right around $10), we gravitated toward the S. M. Jenkins Cocktail (gin, cucumber, lime juice, falernum, Pimm's, ginger ale). We were given pause by a trio of morbidly named drinks apparently inspired by the likes of Vladimir Nabikov and Neil Young: Suicide Song, Invitation to a Beheading, and Cortez Killer. Maybe they need to let Joy Division inspire a cocktail, too, if Dutch Kills (see page 36) doesn't beat them to it.

Elsa has a limited menu of snacks, gets a little louder than you'd expect, and has recently expanded its drink menu to two dozen-ish libations. Let us all toast Moctezuma II and Elsa Schiaparelli in our stylish new duds!

It is worthy of some note that Employees Only opened on December 5. What's so special about December 5? Ask any of the Employees Only owners (Jason Kosmas, Igor Hadzismajlovic, Henry LaFargue, Dushan Zaric, and Billy Gilroy) and

Employees Only

510 Hudson Street
New York, NY
212.242.3021
www.employeesonlynyc.com

they'll remind you that December 5 is the cocktail enthusiast's national holiday—Repeal Day. In fact, www.repealday.org says: "Unlike St. Patrick's Day or Cinco de Mayo, Repeal Day is a day that all Americans have a part in observing, because it's written in our constitution. No other holiday celebrates the laws that guarantee our rights, and Repeal Day has everything to do with our personal pleasures."

We'll drink to that. In fact, we'll drink to that at Employees Only, if possible. In their 2010 book *Speakeasy*, Kosmas and Zaric discuss the genesis of the bar: "Our ambitions were simple; we would open up a first class cocktail bar that would be entirely owner operated. . . . We wanted to transport people back to a time when drinking cocktails was part of a lifestyle, to romanticize it. A secluded destination was ideal for this concept to keep out the distractions of daily life. With the fear-ridden climate of the nation [in 2004], we sought to provide a carefree atmosphere where people could let go of their inhibitions and have fun."

In keeping with these refreshingly old-school values and their stated mission to evoke the American 1920s, the mahogany walls, marble floor, and pressed-tin ceiling tiles give Employees Only a decidedly art deco feel. In order to get in, however, you'll have to look for the red neon sign advertising a psychic. That's the place.

Cocktails (glad you asked) are $14/$15 and include a mix of classics with a few decidedly newfangled ideas. We were immediately drawn to the Lazy Lover (Leblon cachaça, jalapeño-infused green Chartreuse, Bénédictine, lime juice, agave nectar). That's yum at first sight. But wait, seriously. *Jalapeño-infused green Chartreuse*? How crazy are these people going to get with the housemade ingredients?

This crazy: honey vanilla orange syrup, pineapple syrup, mint syrup, ginger syrup, crema de mezcal, ginger beer, grenadine, lime cordial, wild strawberry cordial, hibiscus cordial, vermouth de Provence, chai-infused Italian vermouth, rooibos-infused bianco vermouth, lavender-infused Plymouth gin, peach-infused bourbon, English bishop, absinthe bitters, quinine bitters, quince bitters, five-spice bitters, sangrita, and ruby red grapefruit cordial. Some of these are available for retail purchase and, as Zaric unabashedly enthused, "Dude . . . they all rock in their own right!" Employees

Only lets some of the other local kids play, too. You'll find Finger Lakes Distilling Company's rye whiskey and raspberry, cherry, and cassis liqueurs behind the bar.

"We are very proud to have been a part of the resurgence of the cocktail culture," says Zaric, "and have been privileged to teach many, many young men and women who made the choice to be professional bartenders. For us, this is an opportunity to serve our teachers by passing on the lineage in the right way."

A full menu of food, courtesy of chef Julia Jaksic, contains selections like seared salmon ($24), elk loin ($37), and spaghetti ($16), alongside appetizers like bacon-wrapped lamb chops ($16).

Macao Trading Co. (311 Church Street #1; 212.431.8750; www.macaonyc.com) is the second restaurant from the owners of Employees Only. Designed to evoke a port warehouse, they serve Portuguese and Chinese cuisine (ah, together at last!), a combo that actually makes more sense when you consider the intensive contributions to maritime exploration made by the Portuguese in the 15th and 16th centuries. Jorge Álvares and his contemporaries began trading heavily in Macao after 1513, and now we may toast their impending 500th anniversary. Try the Mah-Johng (Chivas 12-year Scotch whisky, Navan vanilla liqueur, Carpano Antica Formula vermouth, Macao five-spice bitters; $15) or the Hong Kong Cocktail (Pueblo Viejo blanco tequila, Dow's fine ruby port, lemon juice, pandan leaf syrup; $14).

"A fully developed, grown-up bartender is much more than just a drink maker. The more [a bartender] is able to consistently make guests happier than they were when they came in, the more rewarding it gets. Drinks become phenomenal, empathy arises as understanding of human nature grows, and there is this professional manner of conduct. Guests react to this on a very deep level."
—DUSHAN ZARIC, Employees Only

to 2009's *Beach Bum Berry Remixed*) and Martin Cate's San Francisco Bay Area bars (Forbidden Island and Smuggler's Cove) had a lot to do with bringing people's attitudes around. But really, if there is one person in New York who has been rooting for tropical-style drinks all along, it's Julie Reiner.

Born in Hawaii, Reiner is known for her two other bars, Flat-iron Lounge and Clover Club. A careful look at the menus in these establishments reveal that there has always been a hint of exotica in her recipes, a slight preference for unusual fruits and spices collected from around the globe. Thus, at Lani Kai, Reiner is able to let loose and indulge those passions. And we all win.

Kai is Hawaiian for "sea," while *lani* can mean "chief," "heaven," or "sky." We're thinking "sky" in this case, because the big windows let in plenty of light, providing sunshine to more plants than we have seen in a bar since before Pat Nagel paintings were hip. Blond wood, a bit of woven matting, and a fireplace in the downstairs level keep Lani Kai feeling simultaneously cozy and tropical without ever crossing the line into the depths of actual tiki—there are no taxidermy pufferfish lamps or wooden deities with oversized phalluses to be found here.

A Shaheen-clad Gal Friday Night navigated us to Lani Kai, where islands in the Pacific (Oahu) and Atlantic (Manhattan) are connected through a continent of cocktails. The menu is divided into a half-dozen sections containing 40-ish drinks. The temptation to test drive classics like the Mai Tai might be trumped by the lust for new adventures; our eyes kept sliding back to the Leilani's Fizz (gin, lychee, lime juice, lemongrass syrup, and club soda), the Hamilton Park Swizzle (Laird's applejack infused with mango black tea, Palo Cortado sherry, pineapple syrup, lime juice, house falernum), the Manolin (aquavit, white rum, yellow Chartreuse, lime juice, grapefruit syrup, kafir lime), and the Black Pearl (bourbon, Cruzan Black Strap rum, demerara, aromatic bitters). All are $13. There are quite a few tea infusions on the menu, too, which suggests an Asian influence.

Lani Kai is open for Hawaiian-style brunch (lobster benedict, Kailua pork and grits, pressed Spam and cheese) and evening eats (crab wontons, escabeche tacos, various sliders), all of which are $7–$14.

In the spectrum of swanky to divey bar environments, Little Branch might be the bar that falls exactly in the middle, a veritable fulcrum with both ends of the continuum teetering in careful balance. It has a relaxed adult atmosphere, but graffiti covers the building's exterior. There are deco details in the design, but a little bit of basement dampness lingers in the air. Carefully curated jazz provides the soundtrack, but the furniture is arranged sort of randomly. The one thing that tips Little Branch into the realm of the sublime is ownership and cocktails from the capable hands of Sasha Petraske, also the co-owner of Milk & Honey (see pages 49 and 296).

Little Branch

20 7th Avenue South
New York, NY
212.929.4360

Petraske is a fella who can always be relied upon to deliver a solid tipple. Under low ceilings lit by candles, the scene is set for live jazz on selected evenings. Little Branch is all about getting the balance right. This isn't a jazz snob place where absolute silence is expected during the performances, but it *is* a place where people are expected to keep their voices down, even when there isn't live music.

The prepared Gal Friday Night arrived with a few classics in mind; she knew that the drink menu here is rather short and ought to be considered a source of inspiration more than a definitive index of possibilities. The bar stewards will gladly draw from their encyclopedic knowledge to make you something based on your taste and temper. In a mood for classics, we happily quaffed a Twentieth Century (gin, Lillet Blanc, crème de cacao, lemon juice), a Last Word (gin, green Chartreuse, Luxardo maraschino, lemon juice), and a Mint Julep variant (bourbon, simple syrup, mint) served properly in an ice-packed metal julep cup with a metal straw.

What's that playing on the sound system? "One mint julep was the cause of it all." Hmmm . . . let's have another.

Maison Premiere

298 Bedford Avenue
New York, NY
347.335.0446
www.maisonpremiere.com

Let's cut to the chase: absinthe and oysters. That's right, absinthe and oysters. We could probably end this profile of Maison Premiere right now; you've got all you really need to know. But let's go a little deeper.

Maison Premiere was opened in early 2011 in the Williamsburg area of Brooklyn. Josh Boissy (of Le Barricou) owns the joint with partner Krystof Zizka. Maxwell Britten (of Freemans and Jack the Horse) is the chief mixologist.

The cocktail list is absolutely skewed toward drinks from (or associated with) New Orleans. Among the 18 cocktails are two Hurricane variants, a Pimm's Cup, a Vieux Carré, a French 75, a Cocktail à la Louisiane, a Moviegoer (by Chris Hannah of Arnaud's French 75 bar), and no less than four juleps. Oddly, there is no Sazerac on the menu, but we have no doubts that they can whip one up for you. Drinks are $8–$14. There are also some solid wines for sale, many of which are organic and/or biodynamic.

The thirsty Gal Friday Night immediately wanted the Naked Cowboy, the Chatham, the Ninimoto, and the Wellfleet. When I raised a skeptical eyebrow at her ordering four drinks at once, she reminded me that those are varieties of oyster. Right. I knew that. Um, these things make you horny, right?

But honestly, you're going to come here for absinthe, which does indeed pair nicely with oysters. The absinthe might not cause a stirring in your loins, but it might make you see either green fairies or pink elephants. Boissy currently has 25 absinthes on the menu, and he claims to be on a mission to assemble the biggest collection in the United States. A worthy endeavor, sir.

Most absinthe orders will pass under the unmistakable marble obelisk on the bar, a faithful recreation of the absinthe fountain at the Old Absinthe

House in New Orleans. The green stone, the brass taps, and even the statue of Napoleon atop the tower all take one right back to Bourbon Street at 5:00 AM. Remember that? No, I don't either.

The Napoleon statue was created by the same sculptor who did the one in New Orleans. Boissy got it on Ebay (we couldn't make that up, and we didn't). Designers John and Kevin McCormick (Moto, Five Leaves, Smith & Mills) aimed to make the interior look like something seen in the French Quarter a century ago, and by and large they've succeeded. Of course, the decades of grime and velociraptor-sized "palmetto bugs" that you'll pretend to ignore at the Old Absinthe House aren't present here, so the convincing fake-old of Maison Premiere might actually be preferable to the authentic patina of the bar's Southern inspiration.

On the other side of the absinthe menu we discover . . . more cocktails! There are eight more tipples ($10–$12), that will make a believer out of you. We like the looks of the Turn of the Century (Kubler absinthe, Lillet Blanc vermouth, crème de cacao, lemon juice; $12), and the Lafitte's Swizzle (Pernod 68 absinthe, lime juice, house-made orgeat; $11).

Is that *la fée verte* that we see at the end of the bar, or is it the ghost of Hemingway? Never mind, let us try one more. Off-menu, for those celebrating: the Death in the Afternoon (absinthe, champagne). You don't need an occasion, champagne is its *own* occasion. Absinthe might be, too. Oysters definitely are.

◆

Mayahuel was unleashed by Philip Ward and Ravi DeRossi of Death & Co (see page 33) in mid-2009. The festive upstairs level of the bar is dark and decorated in red. The stained glass and church pews recall the set of a Jodorowsky film. Downstairs is where

Mayahuel

304 E. 6th Street
New York, NY
212.253.5888
www.mayahuelny.com

the real magic happens. There are, to put it mildly, a couple of mezcals, tequilas, and other related intoxicants here, and *si, si, si,* they make cocktails with them.

"*Para todo mal, mezcal, y para todo bien también,*" say the Oaxacans. The multilingual Gal Friday Night says: "Look it up." Her further sage advice: "Let's get a drink."

More than 40 cocktails divided into six categories, and not a rum, gin, or brandy in sight. Our eyes were immediately drawn to the Amor Morado (tequila blanco, sloe gin, crème de violette, absinthe, grapefruit juice, lemon juice; $13) and the Cinnsation (mezcal, mulled apple cider, lemon juice, cinnamon bark, Peychaud's bitters; $14). We also spied the Trato Hecho (pineapple-infused mezcal, green Chartreuse, Luxardo maraschino, lime juice; $14), which seems suspiciously like a Last Word with mezcal in place of gin. Gee, I wonder what *trato hecho* means? The repetitive Gal Friday Night says: "Look it up."

They also serve food at Mayahuel, by courtesy of chef Luis Gonzales. Small bites such as seared shrimp and chorizo with roasted red pepper, braised pork belly with papaya-mango mustard, popcorn sprinkled with lime, cotija cheese, and ancho chilis, or churros y chocolate will set you back $5–$21.

La ultima palabra: Mayahuel was the Aztec goddess of the maguey plant in pre-Columbian Mesoamerica. She is also associated with reproduction and sustenance. To me, that means eating, drinking, and screwing. We like this woman. In order to feed her children (called the *Centzon Totochtin*—the Four Hundred Rabbits) she had many breasts, which themselves symbolize drunkenness in the local mythology. I'm just going to leave that alone.

A BIT ON TEQUILA & MEZCAL

There are two kinds of hootch made from the agave plant: tequila and mezcal. Actually, that's not entirely true, and it reminds me of that quip from *The Blues Brothers*: "We play both kinds of music here—country and western." So it is with tequila and mezcal. Mezcal is the result of fermenting sap from the flower stalk of the agave plant. Tequila is actually one variety of mezcal, just as rye and bourbon are both types of American whiskey. Tequila, according to an agreement between Mexico and the European Union, must be made from the Weber blue agave plant, and must come from certain Mexican states. This agreement wasn't officially ratified until 2001, so who knows what you were drinking in college. Explains a lot, doesn't it? Other mezcal drinks, including the ones made from the agave variant maguey, come from all over central Mexico.

M ilk & Honey is one of the very few bars you'll read about in this book that are currently *not* open for business. New York's inaugural neo-speakeasy was among the first to feature a secret location, an unmarked door, and a list of

Milk & Honey

www.mlkhny.com
(entrance by referral and appointment only)

rules ("name-dropping and starfucking" were forbidden). Opening in January 2000, Milk & Honey was far ahead of the curve, and essentially became the template for dozens of bars that have opened around the world in the 21st century. As of this writing, the bar has closed, but they plan to reopen (further uptown from its former location at 134 Eldridge Street) in the very near future—hence this placeholder listing.

The classic location at 134 Eldridge Street has been renamed **Attaboy,** and is owned by Sam Ross and Michael McIlroy, a pair of Milk & Honey bartenders. M&H owner Sasha Petraske is their

same team culpable for Long Island City's Dutch Kills (see page 36), the bar briefly known as Painkiller opened in May 2010. (We have no doubts that Giuseppe Gonzalez and Richard Boccato's third bar will be called Killer Queen, Kill Bill, or the Killing Moon. Seriously guys, you're scaring us with all the killing. Is this a New York thing?) After 11 months of business, a certain rum company that had trademarked the name Painkiller in order to "own" a drink (which was invented before this brand of rum existed) sued the bar. Painkiller renamed themselves PKNY, and a few hundred bartenders promptly stopped using the rum product in question. It's nice to have friends.

There are a lot of rum bars out there, but there is only one that combines craft-attention to classic tiki drinks with a Polynesian-meets-1970s-NYC environment. The small, narrow, subterranean space that PKNY occupies is decked out in plenty of bamboo, red leather booths, and graffiti-style murals. PKNY combines downtown with tiki, and *aloha* with a healthy dose of urban living. It's a cocktail of wooden masks and paintings of nude *wahines*, infused in a what might have been a punk bar had it opened a few decades earlier. We are reminded of Milwaukee's **Foundation Bar** (2718 N. Bremen Street, Milwaukee, WI; 414.374.2587; www. foundationbar.com), which *did* start as a punk bar and went tiki later, except that PKNY just threw all of it into the blender at once. Another connection between metropolis and Micronesia is tattoos, and you'll find your share of them at PKNY. Exhibit A: bartender Natalie Jacob (who also works at Dutch Kills), whose many inventions include the African Queen (rum, calvados, lime juice, orgeat, cinnamon).

The huge menu contains many tiki classics, plus some original permutations—the Suffering Bastard (traditionally: gin, bourbon, lime juice, ginger ale/beer, Angostura bitters) now has a family, including brothers Inglorious Bastard and Dead Bastard (each contains slightly different base liquor ratios). Similarly, their Mai Tai (traditionally: two rums, lime juice, orgeat, orange curaçao, mint sprig) is augmented with deviations like the Kon-Tiki Mai Tai (rum, lime juice, honey, ginger syrup, Pernod, orange juice).

Head bartender Valentin Gonzalez may build further bridges between the city and the islands, as with Donn Beach's 151 Swizzle (151 demerara rum, lime juice, simple syrup, absinthe, grated nutmeg, cinnamon), which shares the menu with a Negroni Swizzle (Beefeater gin, sweet vermouth, Campari, soda, pinch of salt). Drinks are generally $12–$16, and contain as many house-made ingredients as possible.

Okole maluna!

There are two types of bar in the world: those that serve free hot dogs, and those that are speakeasy-format joints hidden within hot dog stands. Unlike PKNY, the chow at Crif Dogs is not free, but they do some pretty interesting things with encased meats (such as the Chang Dog: a bacon-wrapped, deep-fried Crif dog buried under kimchi from Momofuku). So, it may be worth fortifying yourself there before entering PDT.

Please Don't Tell

113 St. Marks Place
New York, NY
212.614.0386
www.pdtnyc.com

The East Village bar is accessed via a vintage phone booth in the back corner of Crif Dogs. You'll pick up the phone and dial; those with reservations will be let in, while non-reserved patrons may be allowed in, if there is room. Reservations may be made each day via phone starting at 3:00 PM.

Once inside the bar, the atmosphere completely changes. The small space seats no more than 45 people and is decorated in taxidermy animals mounted on bare brick walls. Some of the animals are just heads, and we are not going to speculate on what became horseshoe-shaped bars allow a trio of bartenders to work autonomously while keeping the invariably large and sometimes noisy crowds serviced. The orderly workspaces are conspicuously free of visible bottles, giving the bar area a streamlined appearance. Bowls of fruit and herbs are the only immediate cues as to what is happening here. Most of the work is done at the soapstone tables behind each bar, above which you'll spy an assortment of vintage barware.

The menuless Drink initially relied upon its bartenders to create custom beverages based on the whim of the customer. A top-10 list on a blackboard has since been added to aid the indecisive. Misty Kalkofen, founder of the Boston chapter of LUPEC (Ladies United for the Preservation of Endangered Cocktails) can often be found behind one of Drink's three bars. A regular face in national bartending competitions, Kalkofen has been noted for creating drinks such as the In Vida Veritas (Del Maguey mezcal vida, Zirbenz pine liqueur, Nux Alpina walnut liqueur, Bénédictine, xocolate molé bitters, orange oil) and the Guadalajara (El Tesoro Reposado tequila, Fernet-Branca amaro, agave syrup, xocolate molé bitters, grapefruit oil). Drink also serves a few canapés from a seasonally rotating menu, as well as popcorn delivered by your server.

Lynch also maintains a handful of other restaurants. Cocktailers and oenophiles might be most interested in the aforementioned **No. 9 Park** (9 Park Street, 6th floor; 617.742.9991; www.no9park. com), which is where Lynch and John Gertsen first teamed up. Although Gertsen is now based at Drink, the small bar in the front café area of No. 9 Park still serves a tasty array of libations. Anglophile Gal Friday Night liked the Park Street Cup (Pimm's, Peychaud's bitters, lemon juice, egg white, hefeweizen beer). Ask barman Brendan Mercure for a list of their whiskeys, absinthes, and house drinks. Move toward the Bullfinch-style building's two dining rooms for some of Lynch's spendy Alsace-inspired fare.

Reports have been surfacing that Kalkofen will also be involved in **Brick & Mortar** (569 Massachusetts Avenue) in the Central Square area of Cambridge, to be opened by Patrick Sullivan of the fondly-remembered B-Side Lounge. Central Square is also known for solid cocktail programs at **Green Street Grill** (280 Green Street, Cambridge, MA; 617.876.1655; www. greenstreetgrill.com), **Craigie on Main** (853 Main Street, Cambridge, MA; 617.497.5511; www.craigieonmain.com), and **Rendezvous** (502 Massachusetts Avenue, Cambridge, MA; 617.576.1900; www.rendezvouscentralsquare.com).

◆

The vast majority of bars near major-league ballparks are going to be filled with far too many televisions, mass-produced beverages that barely deserve to be called beer, and a rowdy crowd of sports fans. For those who don't

| **Eastern Standard** |
| Hotel Commonwealth |
| 528 Commonwealth Avenue |
| Boston, MA |
| 617.532.9100 |
| www.easternstandardboston.com |

care for this particular paradigm, visitors to Boston's Fenway Park area will be pleasantly surprised by Eastern Standard.

Eastern Standard's long marble bar seems perpetually busy, with multiple bartenders all working at once to get drinks out to the bar customers, as well as to the elegant bistro-style restaurant and the sidewalk patio. While sports fans may eschew Eastern Standard, the cavernous space does attract a diverse crowd ranging from Boston University students to mature corporate types. The bar and restaurant are located inside Kenmore Square's Hotel Commonwealth and are frequently cited as being among the very best on the East Coast. The credit for this could be distributed among their hardworking and award-winning team of bartenders, but we must give special props to the bar director, Jackson Cannon.

A co-founder of the Jack Rose Society, a group of Boston bartenders dedicated to exploring and preserving classic cocktails, Cannon can trace the roots of his interest in mixology to Hemingway's *The Sun Also Rises*, which he read as a young man. He has taken this exploration further than most, traveling to Italy to learn about vermouth production, and to France to seek out the Benedictine monks.

Cannon's cocktail menu is packed with a variety of classics and classic-inspired house creations, mostly in the $10–$12 range. Most of them are described a bit cryptically, with the ingredients

only hinted at. The wonderful Seelbach, for example, is "a happy accident, we are told. Maker's Mark with aromatic bitters." What they leave out is that the drink is topped with champagne, and that the aromatic bitters consists of a whopping seven dashes each of Angostura and Peychaud's. This drink also appears in Ted Haigh's crucial tome *Vintage Spirits and Forgotten Cocktails*. Another winking reference to this book appears on Eastern Standard's menu, just a bit below the Seelbach: the Pink Lady is "not a secret anymore" (Haigh mischievously listed the Pink Lady as the "Secret Cocktail").

After quaffing Eastern Standard's rendition of the classic Belle de Jour (Bénédictine, cognac, grenadine, lemon juice, champagne), the resourceful Gal Friday Night managed to dig up the ingredients for a few particularly tasty-looking house creations, such as the Periodista (Myers's dark rum, Marie Brizard Apry, orange liqueur, lime juice), and the 261 Cocktail (Sazerac rye, Bénédictine, orange juice, Angostura bitters).

Yes, please.

Reports have been surfacing that Cannon will be involved in **Hawthorne** (500A Commonwealth Avenue; 617.532.9150; www. thehawthornebar.com), located in the space once occupied by Foundation Lounge in the Kenmore Square area. Word has it that bartenders from Drink, Eastern Standard, Lineage, and New York's Flatiron Lounge will be on hand.

WASHINGTON, DC

The capital of the USA is home to a solid handful of fantastic cocktail bars and (unsurprisingly) a few upscale restaurants that have been elevating their cocktail programs in recent years. From the long list of candidates, we'd vote for the following.

A t 1021 7th Street NW, you'll find two very different craft cocktail bars under the same roof. The Passenger is a loud and festive neighborhood bar that just happens to make excellent cocktails. Columbia Room is a more elegant 10-seat oasis that offers a considerably quieter and more decorous drinking experience.

Columbia Room
&
The Passenger

1021 7th Street NW
Washington, DC
202.393.0336 (Columbia Room)
202.393.0220 (The Passenger)
www.passengerdc.com

The Passenger was opened five blocks from Chinatown in November 2009 by bartending brothers Derek and Tom Brown. With head bartender Alexandra Bookless at the helm, the menu-free Passenger prides itself on steering milquetoast highball hoisters into more interesting directions. Angie Salame of Derek Brown's consulting company, Laughing Cocktail, says: "I'm most proud of the fact that people who previously would have been ordering a safe drink feel comfortable enough in our bar that they tell us what they like and let us go crazy. It's very flattering that they trust us enough to guide their cocktail experience, which is for many of them, their first one."

Naturally, the Passenger supports local brands (such as rye whiskey, gin, and Mosby's Spirit from Catoctin Creek distillery). House syrups and infusions include cinnamon syrup, mango syrup, black pepper/orange/tea syrup, celery-infused Rhum Agricole, and black-pepper-infused gin. Salame says that after scoring some local mint from a farmers' market, the Passenger responded by featuring an entire cocktail list dedicated to drinks containing mint. Capital idea.

Seasonal comfort food comes from chef Joe Rumberger. Before heading over to the considerably less raucous Columbia Room, we tried a quick Cocktail à la Louisiane (rye whiskey, absinthe, Bénédictine), and toasted William Howard Taft.

Run as a separate business from the Passenger, Columbia Room was opened by Derek Brown in March 2010. Brown's bio states that his "love of bartending stems as much from books, maps, and molecules as from working behind the stick." Katie Nelson is the lead bartender in Brown's absence.

The bar seats 10 people in a quiet atmosphere decorated with big glass jars full of roots and spices: quassia, cardamom, dried lemon peel, coriander, sweetgrass, and lavender, for starters. "It's one of the highlights of the job that each week we go to the farmers' markets and check out what's fresh and in season," Salame says. "This little ritual gives us lots of inspiration for our upcoming food pairings and opening cocktails. We try to make the cocktails and food pairing as seasonally-directed as

possible." Columbia Room keeps a small garden on the roof where they grow herbs for cocktail garnishes. In 2011 they established a beehive to produce honey for the drinks.

Columbia Room also makes their own aquavit, featuring bright dried citrus peel notes and spices like cardamom and black pepper, in addition to the expected caraway and fennel flavors. Bluecoat gin from nearby Pennsylvania is featured as a local spirit as well. House-made syrups include simple syrup made with turbinado sugar, sirop de gomme, grenadine, and orgeat. Ice is hand-carved.

Entry to the Columbia Room requires reservations. The bar

offers most guests a prix fixe tasting menu ($64) consisting of an amuse-bouche, a pre-selected seasonal cocktail du jour, a small plate of food, and a bespoke cocktail designed for the customer on the spot. À la carte cocktails are available as well, and may be a better bargain at $17 each. Wait, $17 is a bargain? Welcome to *Destination: Cocktails* in DC, my friends.

Gal Friday Night, who speaks fluent Nahuatl, was intrigued by the Aztec's Mark (Bulleit rye, dark crème de cacao, lemon juice, bitters, Tabasco), but I like the idea of the full experience, putting myself into the capable hands of Brown or Nelson and seeing where the evening lands. We like to think that Grover Cleveland (leader of the "Bourbon Democrats") would have done the same.

⬥

There are bars that cultivate an atmosphere conducive to conversation, and there are those where you have to shout to be heard. If we told you that Eric Hilton of the DJ duo Thievery Corporation opened a bar (with partners Yama Jewanyi and Farid Ali), on which end of the amplitude spectrum would you place it? Adjust your expectations accordingly, because head bartender Jon Harris reports that the Gibson "is dedicated to cocktails and conversation. We provide a laid-back, relaxed environment. We require that all guests remain seated, so we never have a huge crowd. You never have to yell to talk to your friends."

> **The Gibson**
>
> 2009 14th Street NW
> Washington, DC
> 202.232.2156
> www.thegibsondc.com

The bi-level Gibson opened in November 2008 in DC's hip U Street corridor, with an initial focus on classics such as the Old-Fashioned and the Sazerac. Once drinkers in the nation's capital

became reacquainted with tippling the way people quaffed in Teddy Roosevelt's era, the Gibson began rolling out house creations and upping their level of complexity, particularly in their cozy lower-level "Black Bar." One example is the Uncle Simon (pipe tobacco infused chocolate ganache, Smith & Cross rum, Drambuie liqueur, kirschwasser, hot water, topped with coconut milk marshmallow fluff).

Upstairs, the brighter "White Bar" maintains the menu of classic drinks, organized by flavor profile (sweet, sour, bitter, dry). The White Bar tends to be more low-key and doesn't have as strict a reservation policy as the Black Bar does (use the Gibson's website to make a reservation for the Black Bar; the White Bar accepts walk-ins up to a capacity of 48 people). A seasonal patio is the most casual of the three areas, adds 40 more seats, and focuses on lighter summery drinks such as punches.

Fresh from a visit to the Smithsonian's cocktail library (er, don't go looking for it), Gal Friday Night went for Tom Bullock's 1917 creation, Bliz's Royal Rickey (Old Tom gin, dry vermouth, raspberry syrup, lime juice, ginger ale), while I was drawn to the Black Roses (Leblon cachaça, Dolin rouge vermouth, crème de violette, Angostura bitters, rose water). Drinks are $11–$16.

Naturally, the citrus is squeezed daily, and syrups such as simple, grenadine, orgeat, raspberry, honey, vanilla cream, mango, and pineapple are made in-house. The Gibson has also created an Ambrosia syrup (honey, vanilla, raspberry) and several bitters, including the Saffron bitters, (inspired by Spanish flavors), Angel's bitters (based on a perfume recipe found in a late 19th-century *New York*

Times article), and Opium Den bitters (created to mimic the smell of a 19th-century opium den in Hong Kong). The list is rounded out with coffee, cherry, peach, and Hellfire bitters (ancho, chipotle, and habanero peppers blended with spices, citrus, and quinine).

The Gibson is also working with more unusual ingredients, such as avocado. Harris explains: "On a lark we roasted avocado pits and found the aroma to be unbelievably rich. Similar to Cynar, but with the distinct nutty-fatty aroma of avocado pits. Paired with reposado tequila, sherry, and crème de cacao, it was quite the experience. An ode to Mexico!" Harris also commissioned local gelato purveyor Dolcezza to create custom flavors to use in "grown-up floats." The Angostura gelato was used to make a variant on the classic Champagne Cocktail. Harris expands on the concept: "[We used the] Beetroot-Green Peppercorn gelato to make a crazy-ass drink called the Slightly Odd Duck (gin, mango syrup, balsam fir needle tincture, bitter lemon soda). It was a nod to Heston Blumenthal, chef at the Fat Duck restaurant. Initially comes out like a dry Martini, crisp and clean, but when the bright pink gelato starts to melt you get a completely different experience."

Visitors poking their heads into the Gibson on selected nights may also be treated to the mixology skills of Derek Brown, cocktail columnist for the *Atlantic* online.

Some bars serve rather predictable fare, and others may indulge in more questionable content. I usually keep my poker face on when perusing menus, but if Gal Friday Night sees my eyebrow twitch in response to a listed ingredient, she'll invariably order that cocktail and make me drink

PS 7's

777 I Street NW
Washington, DC
202.742.8550
www.ps7restaurant.com

it. All of it. This once resulted in me drinking a liquefied centipede in Beijing, but that's a story for another book. Although the menu at PS 7's contains a few cocktails with questionable content, you may want to ask head bartender Gina Chersevani for the Questionable Content. This is her version of the Bartender's Choice, and it is usually a solid option at Chersevani's bar. Committed to fresh ingredients and to supporting local farmers' markets (as so many of the bars in this book are), PS 7's Questionable Content is almost guaranteed to contain something fresh and recently alive. (But not *quite* as recently alive as a centipede. Unless, of course, Ms. Chersevani wants to take that as a challenge.)

For the less adventurous, there is a menu of around 18 seasonal cocktails, including the g.H. Sazerac (Old Overholt rye, Kübler absinthe, shiraz syrup; $10) and the En Rogue (Philadelphia's Shine White whiskey, Cointreau, Bitterman's orange bitters; $11). We were also intrigued by the B&B(&b) (Makers Mark whiskey, beet syrup, bitters; $10). The beet syrup is made in-house of course, and uses one vanilla bean per bottle as the requisite (un)questionabl(y) awesome content. Local roots and veggies also make an appearance in the Rocky's Doctor (Plymouth gin, Domaine de Canton ginger liqueur, strawberry purée, rhubarb and ginger syrup, cinnamon, lemon juice).

PS 7's opened in 2006, right in the Penn Quarter area between Capitol Hill and the White House. The interior is bright and sleek, going for a more contemporary cosmopolitan vibe rather than the dark and cozy atmosphere so prevalent in lounges.

The bar is only one side of PS 7's, of course. Owner Peter Smith (note his initials and the street address and do the math if you're sober enough) is also the chef of the restaurant. In keeping with the local and sustainable vibe, Smith collects mash (the solids left over after fermentation of a spirit) from the nearby Blue Coat and Cacoctin Creek distilleries. From the mash, he makes both a powder and an oil, as sampled in his gin-cured lomo and his arugula salad dressed in gin-oil vinaigrette. Naturally, if you're in DC you're also going to want to try a half-smoke, the capital's local street delicacy. A combo of half pork and half beef is smoked and then doused in veal chili, aged cheddar cheese, chives, and dijon mustard ($12, lunch only). I'm sure Smith would prefer, however, for us to mention proper dinner fare such as rockfish stew ($28) from the Aqua menu, or the seared duck breast ($29) from the Terra menu.

Back to the bar ('cause that's how we roll after dinner). Gal Friday Night wanted a Pimpin' Pimms (Pimm's, Oxley gin, strawberries, tarragon, rhubarb), but I was still stuck on the Questionable

Content. I had to staple my brow into place so I didn't end up with the Sav U'R Cereal (cereal milk, Old Overholt rye, St. Elizabeth allspice dram). Are we talking about Frankenberry-infused milk here? In a cocktail? Did Benjamin Harrison drink these?

◄●►

Of the many bars that fly the Jolly Roger, we have pirate-themed bars, rum bars, and average random bars that seem to think having a pirate flag on the wall is a cool thing to do. We are not inclined to disagree with this decor

PX

Eamonn's A Dublin Chipper
728 King Street
Alexandria, VA
703.299.8384
www.eamonnsdublinchipper.com

option. But there is one other place that you might see the Jolly Roger: in the window of Eamonn's A Dublin Chipper, an Irish fish and chip shop gone classy.

Opened in a historic townhouse among the international eateries of Old Town, Cathal and Meshelle Armstrong's chippery flies the skull and crossbones on selected nights. On those nights, you'll want to walk down the alley next to the historic 18th-century building, look for the blue light next to a nondescript (and locked) door, and wait. Hint: use the number above for reservations, since a scant eight seats are held for walk-ins. Pending approval (gents should be in jackets), you'll be escorted up a flight of stairs to a room that seats about three dozen. Last redecorated in the era of William McKin-

ley (apparently), the space is still finished in the original dark wood, including built-ins and moldings, and has added a collection of vintage cocktail shakers, cut-glass chandeliers, and lots of candles. Sorry mateys, the Jolly Roger is not to be seen up here;

that's downstairs in the chippery.

Here, in the hidden PX, you'll most likely be served a drink by "liquid savant" Todd Thrasher. In addition to being the sommelier at Eve, the Armstrongs' other restaurant, Thrasher is the mastermind behind PX. Opened in 2006, PX stands for "Personne Extraordinaire" and is the French equivalent of the English term "VIP." It is the stated goal of Thrasher and the Armstrongs to treat all of their customers in a manner befitting the PX or VIP. Part of this includes making superior libations, of course.

The menu typically contains about 18 drinks (usually $11–$14), which are mostly Thrasher's creations. He also creates as many of the ingredients for these drinks as possible, including seven types of bitters (lemon, peach, mint, cherry, orange, kumquat, cranberry), orange soda, and tonic water. Naturally, juices are squeezed fresh daily, and even eggs are sourced locally, from Polyface Farm.

Keeping with the Irish theme established downstairs, we were drawn to the Irish Flip (Powers Irish whiskey, cream, sugar, nutmeg). Gal Friday Night is Irish by birth, and flipped over my drink, but got more excited about a southern variant, the Chicas Flip (Hendrick's gin, lemon juice, cream, rose water). Switching to something that promised to be lighter and crisper, the Sweet Basil looked good, too (London dry gin, Lillet Blanc, basil leaves, simple syrup).

LAST CALL!

More Destinations to Explore in the Washington, DC Area

Jason Stritch can often be found behind the stick at **Rasika Penn Quarter** (633 D Street NW; 202.637.1222; www.rasikarestaurant.com), an upscale and trendy Indian-American fusion restaurant. The South Asian cuisine is echoed in the cocktail list with ingredients like star-anise smoked sugar and scorched juniper. Try the Ginger Pom Pisco Sour (pisco, pomegranate juice, Domaine de Canton ginger liqueur, scarlet seeds). This may be the only Indian business in this book, but the idea of cocktails paired with this cuisine is an exciting proposition that ought to be explored further.

One of our primary lieutenants has spent some considerable time in DC, and recommends the following restaurants, which he has reputably reported to be destinations for worthy tipples:

- **Againn** (1099 New York Avenue NW; 202.639.9830; www.againndc.com)
- **Estadio** (1520 14th Street NW; 202.319.1404; www.estadio-dc.com)
- **The Majestic by Gwen** (1368 H Street NE; 202.388.1204; majestic-by-gwen.tripod.com)
- **Oyamel** (401 7th Street NW; 202.628.1005; www.oyamel.com)
- **Proof** (775 G Street NW; 202.737.7663; www.proofdc.com)
- **Room 11** (3234 11th Street NW; 202.332.3234; www.room11dc.com)

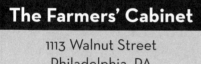

PHILADELPHIA

Perhaps thought of as a dark horse on the East Coast cocktail scene, Philly doesn't have quite the visibility of New York, DC, or Boston, but the City of Brotherly Love has a few very worthy destinations quietly earning accolades and pouring fantastic cocktails.

The Farmers' Cabinet

1113 Walnut Street
Philadelphia, PA
215.923.1113
www.thefarmerscabinet.com

There are two types of bar in the world: the ones for cocktails and the ones for beer. The Farmers' Cabinet opened in 2011 with one of each type on-site. The beer bar serves house-made brews by Terry Hawbaker, plus a fine selection of European beers (think: Belgium). The cocktail bar is overseen by Damon Dyer, formerly of Brooklyn's Clover Club. The whole operation—which also encompasses a rather spendy restaurant—is the work of Matt and Colleen Swartz with Matt Scheller (the trio also opened Fork & Barrel, Tap & Table, and the Bookstore).

The owners hand-built the space, which has a warm, woody, rustic 19th-century feel and is decorated with beer casks, taxidermy animal busts, exposed wooden beams, touches of Damask wallpaper, Mason jar lanterns, and communal dining tables. The walk-up window for cheese and house-made charcuterie is cool, as is the live Dixieland music (full bands on weekends and occasional piano on weeknights). Historians among you will note with some appreciation that the *Farmer's Cabinet* was the New England newspaper that contained the first-ever confirmed usage of the word "cocktail" in 1803. The farm-to-table dining philosophy at the Farmers' Cabinet makes the appellation all the more appropriate.

Phoebe Esmon—President of the United States Bartenders' Guild's Pennsylvania chapter—may be found behind the bar on most nights. Esmon is developing her own vermouth and has several house bitters (including a narcissus bitters and a ginger tincture) already in use. House-made syrups include strawberry-rhubarb ratafia and celery flavors. Every Tuesday, Esmon hits the local farmers' market and uses that day's haul to create two original cocktails, served that night as part of the bar's Fresh Market Tuesday. More dear to the heart of Gal Friday Night, however, was a menu of eight drinks inspired by the Tom Waits LP *Small Change*. Naturally, we were drawn toward Waitsisms like The Barstools Are On Fire (rye whiskey, barrel-aged apple-chestnut shrub, honey, clove, orange peel) and the Raconteurs and Roustabouts (cucumber gin, candied ginger, lime juice, white pepper, saffron, spiced beet soda).

Those suspecting that a bar so rooted in the 19th century might have forgotten its roots need look no further than the "Foundations" end of the menu, which keeps things simple with early purist choices such as Sour, Daisy, Crusta, and, yes, Cocktail. Listed as a specifically defined recipe, the Cocktail at the Farmers' Cabinet will get you what we now call an Old-Fashioned; that's where the name of that drink came from. The original 1800s Cocktail made the old-fashioned way, before all mixed drinks became known generically as "cocktails," became known as the Old-Fashioned. Someone did their homework, apparently.

The beer bar across the room is alluded to in the beer-less but beer-inspired Cockaigne (cognac, strawberries, apple cider vinegar, orange bitters, sugar, sparkling wine), which was designed to resemble a Belgian lambic. The Farmers' Cabinet also offers a bespoke Whiskey Sour, which compliments the requisite sugar and lemon juice with your choice of Irish whiskey, rye, Scotch, Japanese whiskey, bourbon, or un-aged White Dog whiskey. Their barrel-aged Martinez stows this classic proto-Martini away for 30 days in a used bourbon barrel before serving. All cocktails are $12.

Also worth a mention is one of Swartz and Scheller's other businesses, **The Bookstore Speakeasy** (336 Adams Street, Bethlehem, PA; 610.867.1100). With shelves of books along the walls of a small anteroom and menus hidden in the books laid out on the tables inside the hidden bar, the only further thing needed to keep literate cocktail nerds happy is a jazz trio swingin' along as we sip our $11 cocktails . . . at a vintage copper bar . . . by candlelight.

LAST CALL!

Another Destination to Explore in Philadelphia

Southwark Restaurant (701 S. 4th Street; 215.238.1888; www.southwarkrestaurant.com) was opened by Sheri and Kip Waide in 2004, with Sheri handling the kitchen duties and Kip manning the bar. Just off chaotic South Street in Philadelphia's Queen Village area, the mahogany bar is host to just as many diners as the dining room. Be warned, however, that it can get a bit loud at the bar. The restaurant's French-influenced cuisine is heavily dependent on local farmers and co-ops for produce. This simplicity is reflected in the menu, which simply lists the dishes as "duck," "trout," "pork," etc. ($23–$28). This same sensibility of simplicity pervades Kip's bar, which is focused on classics such as the Corpse Reviver #2, the Martinez, the Sidecar, and, of course, the requisite Philadelphian (Laird's apple brandy, port, orange juice, ginger ale). House creations are minimal at Southwark, but the bar does have a signature beverage: the Southwark Cocktail (Willet single-barrel rye, Meletti amaro, Rare Wine Co. Ben Franklin madeira). These drinks are bolstered by what Southwark claims are among the largest gin and rye collections in the country. Naturally, you'll see Philly's Bluecoat gin on that list.

CLEVELAND

Cleveland boasts one of the top three symphonies in the United States, a great theater district, world-class hospitals, a very solid art museum that's free every day, some nice 19th-century architecture, and an "emerald necklace" of parks surrounding the metro area, plus various sports teams and touristy things like the Rock and Roll Hall of Fame and Museum. So why is there really only *one* seriously kick-ass cocktail bar there? Hard to say, but the one they do have is in the same league as their orchestra and hospitals—world-class stuff, my friends.

We've been glad to see so many new slow drinks bars opening during the past three or four years. But then there are the ones that go back more than 15 years, predating even the best that New York, Chicago, and San Francisco have to offer. Where might you find one of these pioneers?

Try Cleveland.

Fascinated by the look of the cocktails he'd see in the Cleveland *Plain Dealer*'s annual cocktail supplement (ah, the 1960s . . .), young Paulius Nasvytis's earliest interest in cocktails was strictly based on

Velvet Tango Room

2095 Columbus Road
Cleveland, OH
216.241.8869
www.velvettangoroom.com

their visual appeal. In the 1970s, he watched the bartenders at work at his Lithuanian father's social club. "The bartenders were making great Manhattans," he says, "pouring drinks that were 20 years out of date. But by the 1970s [given the state of cocktail culture then], cocktails two decades behind the times were a *good* thing." During the next two decades, Nasvytis worked for a dizzying array

of respected Cleveland restaurants until it was time to open his own place. Citing the myriad difficulties that come with opening a restaurant, but wanting to provide his customers with an adult, upscale experience, the idea for the Velvet Tango Room was hatched.

Opened in 1996, the Velvet Tango Room is furnished in a warm 1930s vibe, with a tasteful collection of vintage glassware and an antique mahogany backbar. A small black-and-white television shows classic movies with the sound off. Up two steps from the bar area is a lounge featuring a piano, some davenports, and an old console radio with a cool monkey lamp atop it (the same one that Arnaud's in New Orleans has!). The piano is put to good use seven nights a week by a variety of local jazzers who may be joined by bass or sax. Beyond that is a mirrored door leading to a private event room (added in 1999) containing another bar, another piano, a fireplace, and more plush seating.

The Velvet Tango Room's signature drink is the French 75 (another Arnaud's parallel!). Back in 1996 when, as Paulius says, "everything was shot out of a hose," this drink led to the bar's early success. In 2006, the bar revamped and renewed its commitment to doing the classics properly.

"The East Coast does their thing," says Paulius, "riffing on the classics, taking an Old-Fashioned and tweaking it, customizing it. The West Coast does their thing with organic and natural and using yogurt or whatever. It's like jazz, sometimes it works when all of the players are playing well together, and sometimes, not so much. What we do at the Velvet Tango Room is to define what we say is the standard for a cocktail, and present the best possible take on that. We set a baseline."

Not everything is old-fashioned here, however. The Velvet Tango Room may be unique in its 21st-century methodology for pouring drinks. There is neither free-pour nor jigger seen behind the bar; they measure their drinks by the gram, by the drop, using a digital scale. Their scales are zeroed after placing a shaker full of ice on them, and each ingredient is added by *weight*. This gives their recipes a precise and uncanny repeatability which rivals that of any other bar in this book.

After a dozen visits to the Velvet Tango Room, we have yet to be disappointed. We've enjoyed Sazeracs there that clean the floor with any found in New Orleans and Manhattans that rival New York's best. We've also enjoyed our traditional classic VTR drink, the Widow's Kiss (calvados, green Chartreuse, Bénédictine, Angostura bitters) each time we've passed through Cleveland. As should you. Gal Friday Night's is one of the few house creations— the Rangpur Gimlet, which substitutes the disappointing modern-day version of Rose's lime juice with fresh lime and sugar, and uses Tanqueray Rangpur gin for a further bit of lime-y kick. (Rangpur limes are an orange-colored lime from India that are distilled into this gin, along with ginger and bay leaves, as opposed to being added later as an infusion.) We also like the Velvet Tango Room's Spicy Chica, a rum drink prepared with house-made ginger syrup and a dash of cinnamon on top.

The bar also offers a short menu of snacks and desserts, including a chocolate fondue. It is also kind of cool that there are little bottles of bitters and real pomegranate grenadine on each table, kinda like salt and pepper for your drinks.

All cocktails are priced at $15, which might fly in New York but seems spendy in Cleveland. Nasvytis points out that live music with no cover charge, free easy parking, and generously-sized pours bring things into alignment. Uncle!

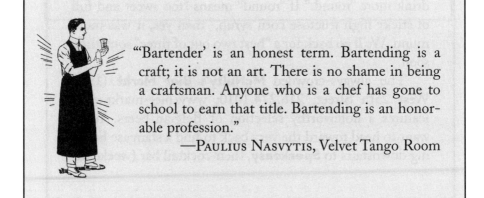

"'Bartender' is an honest term. Bartending is a craft; it is not an art. There is no shame in being a craftsman. Anyone who is a chef has gone to school to earn that title. Bartending is an honorable profession."
—PAULIUS NASVYTIS, Velvet Tango Room

for a bar, and it seems that Chicago's new Barrelhouse Flat has taken all three to heart.

Opened in late October 2011 and located at the edge of the DePaul University campus in Lincoln Park, the bar was created by Violet Hour alumnus Stephen Cole, with Greg Buttera of both Sable and the Aviary. Split over two levels of a space that was, until recently, a succession of college dive bars, the interior of the 1892 building was redesigned by Patry + Kline of Los Angeles. They've installed a jukebox full of early blues and ragtime, cattle-branded stools along the lengthy bar, and a live barrelhouse pianist. Two rows of booths opposite the bar provide plenty of seating, but the tile walls and collegiate crowd almost guarantee a bit of noise. If things get a bit raucous for your taste, check with the hostess in the back of the room for access to the more tranquil upper level. That bar has just six seats, but the three connected rooms feature dim lighting, a fireplace, comfy parlor seating in two of the rooms, and a custom-built pool table in the third.

The epic-length menu of classic libations contains all of the usual suspects, most of them untampered with. However, Cole and Buttera have dug deep and unearthed a few that even experienced cocktail nerds might find unfamiliar. We were drawn to the Holland Pride (Bols genever, sweet vermouth, absinthe, orange bitters), the Mamie Taylor (Scotch whisky, lime juice, simple syrup, ginger beer), and the Swiss Ess (cognac, maraschino liqueur, absinthe, simple syrup, egg white, soda). We followed this up by having bartender Maren whip up a custom beverage (although she is a student of mortuary science, we resisted asking her to make us a Corpse Reviver #2 or a Zombie; both are on the menu). Cocktails are generally $9.

Locally-sourced ingredients are used in the creation of the bar's house-made bitters, syrups, and sodas. A focus on punches is evident in potions like the Golden Fleece punch (gin, Drambuie liqueur, green tea, lemon juice, pineapple syrup) and the classic Fish House punch (Jamaican rum, cognac, peach brandy, lemon juice, sugar). Four punches are available at a time, and are listed on a blackboard downstairs. Upstairs, a cart is wheeled around, offering tableside punch service as you relax in a wingback chair.

French-inspired food includes Barrelhouse Flat's lauded pig face poutine ($13), sweetbread bites ($9), and a seasonal paté ($10), which contrast with the daily popcorn ($4) and cotton candy ($5).

Take the advice of Mary Johnson: "If you women want a good time, stop by this barrelhouse flat of mine."

Boka, it seems, is a bit of a popular name for bars. Seattle, New York, and Gatineau (Quebec) all have Bokas. London has a hotel by that name, and Serbia has a town called Boka. Let us also not forget the U.K.-based Boka Records. Of all these options, it is the Boka in Chicago that you may want to

Boka

1729 N. Halsted Street
Chicago, Il
312.337.6070
www.bokachicago.com

visit first, for it is here that you'll be treated to the inimitable talents of Ben Schiller, resident mixologist for the Boka Restaurant Group. After working as a sommelier around Chicago, Schiller was hired at In Fine Spirits—a bar equally well-loved for its wine list and its cocktails—before joining the Boka Group in 2009.

Although he prides himself on keeping things simple, Schiller always seems to be going the extra mile to make his drinks special. One example is the Smoking Jacket. Using a hand-held culinary smoker, Schiller smokes Evan Williams single-barrel bourbon with applewood, cherrywood, and hickory. House-made grenadine and lime juice round out the recipe. Schiller is also a fan of innovation and creativity, trying to come up with new concepts but without getting needlessly complex. Witness the Trade Secret (Small's gin, celery juice, lime juice, egg white, Chartreuse VEP mist; $12) or the Longship (North Shore aquavit, Bas armagnac, ginger, Angostura bitters; $12). We like the use of the local aquavit from Chicago's

www.greeneyelounge.com). There's no drawing at the Drawing Room, apparently, so they have to do it at Green Eye. Gal Friday Night, exemplar of all factotum, thinks he's a slacker, but I'm not going to be the one to tell him that.

To be fair, the credit for the Drawing Room's international reputation must be shared with "Master Bartenders" Cristiana DeLucca and Sergio Serna. We'd be remiss if we didn't mention their inventions, such as the Dance, Dance (Milagro reposado tequila, allspice dram, Cynar bitter aperitif, lime juice) and the For Medicinal Use Only (Pierre Ferrand Ambre cognac, Bénédictine, Fernet-Branca amaro, maple syrup, Lahproaig Scotch whisky rinse), respectively.

Classics are treated with respect at the Drawing Room, and we were happy to see standards like the Jack Rose on the menu, although there seems to be an uncontrollable urge to tinker; witness the "Drawing Room" Manhattan and the "Improved" Blood & Sand. Each seasonal menu ends with a few cocktails from friends, on loan from bars you'll read about elsewhere in this book. All cocktails are $13.

Naturally, attention is carefully paid to the bar's ice program, while selected syrups, sodas, and other ingredients are made in-house. We always like to see the use of local spirits, such as the North Shore aquavit mentioned above (North Shore also conjures an array of quite lovely gins and absinthes).

The sleek room is decorated with zebrawood walls, white curtains, and low seats, which are good for training tall guys to be contortionists. There's room for about 60 at the Drawing Room, but the bar itself seats a scant half-dozen. Those wishing to watch Joly and company work their magic, however, may be treated to tableside mixology from a custom-designed roving drink cart. This little bit of whiz-bang might be eclipsed by something far more subtle and more infinitely practical: a magnetic panel at the end of the bar, keeping all manner of knives, peelers, and bottle openers within easy reach. It's almost some sort of weird kinetic action art piece.

Though primarily a lounge, the Drawing Room offers small plates of food courtesy of Nick Lecass, who accompanies Joly to the farmers' markets each week to seek out synergies. We were intrigued by the lemongrass mussels ($13), root vegetable tart ($12), and monkfish cassoulet ($28). We also vaguely recall a fine little plate of tiny quails and something wonderful that had to do with fried avocado, all devoured during some hazy distant past adventure. Gal Friday Night must not have been around that night, or there would be copious evidence in the form of detailed notes and high-definition 3D movies.

An Andersonville wine shop dubbed **In Fine Spirits** was founded by Jill and Shane Kissack in 2004. Johnnie Grozenski and Paul Hasenwinkel joined the partnership in 2007 to develop the adjacent bar, which opened in

Premise

Chicago, IL
773.334.9463
www.premisechicago.com

April of 2008, and closed in March 2012. The shop sells a concise but solid variety of wines, and just a few bottles of the hard stuff, including local brands such as Koval and North Shore.

Next door, the original bar served up a selection of wines predominantly from the New World and some lovely artisanal cheeses, flatbreads, and charcuterie, plus the best cocktails north of Diversey Parkway (did you know that Diversey was named for Michael Diversey, a 19th-century beer brewer?).

In spring of 2012, the bar was redeveloped as a restaurant called Premise. The upper floor (which was formerly a private party room) is now an intimate cocktail lounge. Both are "too new to review," but we visited the upstairs lounge and were suitably impressed. Meanwhile, head bartenders Cody Modeer and Anne Carlson have moved on to open their own place, **Ward Eight** (629 Howard Street, Evanston, IL).

We're sure that Modeer and Carlson will continue the impressive efforts that made In Fine Spirits the only real destination cocktail bar on Chicago's far north side. For example, Modeer has reverse-engineered two liqueurs rare in the U.S.—Swedish punsch and Amer Picon—so as to be able to serve classic cocktails such as the Have a Heart and the Brooklyn, among others.

Amer is the French equivalent of amaro, that category of bitter spirits that the Italians love so much (Averna, Fernet, Ramazotti, Cynar, etc.). Amer Picon is a bittersweet French aperitif with orange notes. Though inexpensive in Europe, it hasn't been imported into the US of A for decades. Amer Picon is available in two varieties in Europe, the standard digestif and a lighter version meant to be mixed with beer. Modeer blends an orange tincture and an herbal bitters (both made in-house) with cane sugar to approximate Amer Picon (Jamie Boudreau of Canon in Seattle makes Amer Boudreau from orange tincture mixed with Ramazotti). In any case, it's a necessary ingredient in the Brooklyn (rye, maraschino liqueur, dry vermouth, and your favorite ersatz Amer Picon). Have a Heart dates from 1934. Modeer recreates the required but rarely imported Swedish punsch with a combination of Batavia Arrack, sugar, citrus, tea, and rum. Add this to Broker's London dry gin, lime juice, and grenadine (or try amarena cherry syrup). Batavia Arrack is a liquor distilled in Indonesia from sugar cane, making it a relative of rum and cachaça.

Carlson put the In Fine Spirits' private barrel of Elmer T. Lee bourbon to good use with the Elmer Tea (Elmer T. Lee bourbon, tea, lemon juice, peach bitters, lemon wheel). It was also during Carlson's reign that we had a few of the best Deshlers in the realm of foggy memory (Benchmark bourbon, Lillet Rouge, Prunier Liqueur d'Orange, Peychaud's bitters). Maybe it's the substitution of Cointreau for the Prunier (possibly), or of Dubonnet for Lillet (possibly not), or maybe it's just because Anne rocks (probably).

Although the Andersonville area is infrequently visited by tourists, the strip of Clark Street just north of Foster Avenue is a thriving nightlife area for locals. Don't miss Chicago's premier brew destination, **The Hopleaf Bar** (5148 N. Clark Street; 773.334.9851; www.hopleaf.com), or any of the dozen-plus good-to-great restaurants along this stretch of road.

Nuevo Latino restaurant Nacional 27 was a rare Chicago outpost for a *real* cocktail, prior to the yummy booze explosion resulting from the 2007 openings of the Vio-

Nacional 27

325 W. Huron Street
Chicago, IL
312.664.2727
www.n27chicago.com

let Hour and the Drawing Room. The restaurant's not-so-secret weapon was advanced sommelier Adam Seger. Seger had previously run the restaurants at the Seelbach Hilton (see page 120) in Louisville, where he resurrected the amazing and long-lost Seelbach Cocktail. After moving to Chicago, he became the cocktail advisor for the Lettuce Entertain You restaurant group, and creator of Hum liqueur. Seger's cocktails stand as classic early examples of the "raiding the kitchen" school of recipe invention, and they still define that style of mixology. *New City* magazine called him "the Charlie Trotter of Cocktails," an appellation that is not undeserved.

Seger has left N27 to focus on Hum, but his legacy still informs the restaurant's bar program. House-made ingredients include Licor 27 (a take on Licor 43), falernum, a recreation of the vanished rum-based Pimm's No. 4, sweet vermouth, and all sorts of bitters. The "Luxe" El Corazon is the restaurant's signature cocktail, a Margarita variation with Corzo anejo tequila, passion fruit juice, pomegranate juice, a float of Del Maguey single village mezcal, and a variable seasonal fruit (blood orange, peaches, sour cherries, raspberries, etc.). Seger's legacy also includes the LookBetterNaked Margarita (Partida Reposado tequila, Sambazon organic acai juice, agave nectar, rosemary, egg white, lime juice). Rum and pisco are used frequently here; classics at Nacional 27 are unsurpringly biased towards twists on the Latin litany. Drinks based on Caipirinhas, Mojitos, Pisco Sours, and Margaritas are $9–$14.

When Nacional 27 opened in 1998, Randy Zweiban's kitchen was focused on street-food-turned-haute-cuisine from 27 different Latin nations. Zweiban has also moved on, opening **Province** (161 N. Jefferson Street; 312.669.9900; www. provincerestaurant.com), but the current menu stays fresh with dishes like smoked chicken empanadas, pumpkin and goat cheese

croquetas, prime chimi-churri-crusted sirloin, slow-roasted Gunthorp Farms pork "cubano," and a selection of ceviche variations ($6–$21).

Later in the evening, the restaurant becomes more clubby as live percussionists join the DJs and an affluent, trendy crowd comes out to dance. In these hours, the cocktails aren't always shaken with quite the same skill as the hips of the customers. Go early for a relaxed dinner and drinks, go late for the salsa and merengue.

Salud!

Sable

Hotel Palomar
505 North State Street
Chicago, IL
312.755.9704
www.sablechicago.com

We've seen some elaborate cocktail menus in our day, but check out the one at Sable—it is divided into nine enigmatically-named chapters, finally ending with an epilogue (which quotes Frank Sinatra, no less).

River North's "gastro-lounge" is attached to the new Kimpton Hotel Palomar, which opened in April 2010. Running about half the length of the block, the 40-foot bar is one of the longest in Chicago. Glass tables and display cases, quartz lightboxes, and laser-cut backlights feel ultra-contemporary. Look for the 16-seat patio should you visit during the annual three-week period when Chicago's weather might make al fresco imbibing a desirable proposition. Speaking of the weather, and the planet that said weather envelops, Sable conforms to Kimpton's EarthCare program, recycling whenever possible and using biodegradable materials.

The overlord of cocktails for the Kimpton hotel group is Jacques

Bezuidenhout, a London expat based in San Francisco. However, when visiting Sable, you're much more likely to meet Mike Ryan, the head bartender. Ryan began as a chef, working at molecular gastronomy restaurant Moto from 2005 to 2008. After discovering a love for bartending at sister restaurant Otom, he was lured over to the Violet Hour, where he honed his mixology skills under head bartender Mike Rubel.

Upon arriving at Sable, Ryan created the Marionette (El Tesoro Platinum tequila, Luxardo maraschino liqueur, Peychaud's bitters, crème de menthe, lime juice), in homage to the Violet Hour's Marion. Other Ryan creations include the Speaking in Tongues (mezcal, Luxardo amaro, lemon juice, simple syrup, Angostura bitters, Peychaud's bitters, muddled strawberry) and the Fedora Cocktail (Buffalo Trace bourbon, grenadine, simple syrup, lemon juice, pinch of salt, fresh thyme), a nod to the vintage-styled wardrobes sported by so many craft bartenders. All cocktails are $13.

The lengthy cocktail menu is by no means all-Ryan, however. In addition to a solid list of standards, fully half of the several dozen originals on hand are attributable to the rest of the bar staff, such as bartender Fred Sarkis. Naturally, the bar makes its own syrups, infusions, tinctures, and bitters, and hatches perfect ice from its Kold-Draft machine. Sable also offers one of the largest brown spirits collections in Chicago. Their 20-page list (a separate document from the cocktail menu) lists 120 single malt Scotches, 19 blended Scotches, 82 American whiskeys, and further whiskeys from Ireland, Japan, and even India. For those looking to work their way through this beast, Sable offers Whiskey Wednesdays, with a different distillery, region, or style featured each week. Tequilas, rums, gins, and genevers round out the list.

Still thirsty? Try a wine selected by master sommelier Emily Wines (yes, Wines is her surname), perhaps paired with some chow from chef Heather Terhune, a 10-year veteran of the nearby Atwood Café. The modern American menu (divided into hors d'oeuvres, fish, farm and garden, and meat), encourages social dining and is designed so that any item can be an entree or an appetizer.

"So," sings Francis Albert at the very end, "make it one for my baby, and one more for the road."

Sepia

123 N. Jefferson Street
Chicago, IL
312.441.1920
www.sepiachicago.com

With so many bars housed in 20th- or 21st-century buildings, it's always really cool to see the ones housed in edifices built during the age of Jerry Thomas himself. There's just something special about drinking a Sazerac in a 19th-century building. Authentic patina can't be bought, it has to be earned. There are a few bars in this book that were indeed constructed in the age of sepia-tinted photographs, and one in particular was named to specifically evoke this era.

Sepia is a stylish West Loop restaurant housed in a former 1890s print shop. A collection of old Chicago memorabilia, exposed brick, antique cameras, leather tabletops, and lots of wood preserve the warm 19th-century atmosphere, although Mylar chandeliers are one of the few modern touches. Owner Emmanuel Nony designed the art nouveau-inspired floor himself. French by birth, Nony opened Sepia in 2007 after stints in Florida and the well-regarded NoMi in the Park Hyatt Chicago.

In February 2009 Josh Pearson took over the bar program from Peter Vestinos, having newly arrived in Chicago from Australia by way of Vancouver. By the end of that year, Sepia was on track for a Michelin star. Sepia's well-regarded cocktail list is complimented

by an exhaustive wine selection.

As Pearson and I had both recently spent time in Gal Friday Night's homeland of Canada, he insisted that we try a Toronto, a simple but effective classic-era drink (Rittenhouse rye, Fernet-Branca amaro, and a dribble of simple syrup—"just enough to take the edge off of the Fernet"). All drinks are $10–$12. All the infusions are made in-house and the juices squeezed fresh.

Next, we tried Dale DeGroff's Sazerac variant, the Sazerac Royale (Sazerac rye, cognac, Herbsaint wash, sugar, Peychaud's bitters, champagne) and the crisp and well-balanced Monk's Daiquiri (Cockspur rum, yellow Chartreuse, grapefruit juice, lime juice, simple syrup). We also noted that Sepia's French 75 replaces the champagne with demi-sec sparkling rosé. Clearly, based on this trio of variants, Pearson is a fan of using classics as starting points for subtle variations. This is taken even further in the Cognac et Framboise, a Sidecar with raspberry-apple foam, and the Spring Old-Fashioned, in which 1792 Bourbon is infused with fresh rosehip. Pearson also recommended an untitled combo of Old Raj gin, green Chartreuse, and lemon juice in equal parts; sort of a Last Word without the cherry flavor, or a Las Wor, if we may. We'd had quite enough by that point (believe it or not), but Gal Friday Night insisted that we go back (twist my arm, babe) when bartender Bill was working. How can I deny a request like that from a lady?

We were especially impressed by Bill's own Pear in the Pipe (Sombra mezcal, house walnut syrup, lemon juice, green Chartreuse, Angostura bitters, orange flower water, Bordelet Poire sparkling cider). This one was inspired by the pear/walnut salad on the restaurant's menu, combined with Bill's first taste of mezcal.

Speaking of the restaurant, that's the bailiwick of Nony's fellow NoMi alumnus Andrew Zimmerman. Sepia's kitchen is another of the many adherents to the welcome "natural, organic, sustainable, local" credo. We liked the looks of the tandoori-marinated sturgeon ($28), root vegetable pot pie ($26), and cider-braised pork shank ($29) after starting with the chicken-fried quail ($14) and charcuterie ($15).

The Violet Hour

1520 N. Damen Avenue
Chicago, IL
773.252.1500
www.theviolethour.com

Of the many bars in the world, only a handful can boast of being the bar that virtually defines a certain city's cocktail identity. Whether or not the Violet Hour serves the *best* drinks in Chicago is open for debate—it is certainly a strong contender—but it is probably the first place the average cosmopolitan cocktailian thinks of when contemplating the idea of properly administered fortification in the City of Big Shoulders.

The Violet Hour opened with little fanfare in the summer of 2007, hidden behind a graffiti-covered wall that has since become a streetside gallery. A new mural by a local artist can be seen every few months. A lone yellow bulb above the door indicates where the bar is and when it is open. The bar is a collaboration between Terry Alexander, Jason Cott, Peter Garfield, Donny Media, and chief mixologist Toby Maloney. Maloney and Alexander (who is also responsible for beloved Chicago spots such as Mia Francesca, Soul Kitchen, and Danny's Tavern) first hatched the idea for the Violet Hour after working together in several other establishments.

With its elegant 19th-century French salon interior (high-backed chairs, periwinkle walls, crown molding, and huge tapestry curtains dividing the room), the Violet Hour is aimed at grown-ups and conversation. "It is not a 'woo hoo!' type of bar," Maloney says. "Ladylike squeals of delight are encouraged. 'Chug, chug, chug, high-five!' are out of place. Every bar does not need to be all things to all people. When [a bar tries] to become this obsequious jack of all trades, you are hospitable to none. I wish that people put in as much thought to the bars that they go to as to the restaurants."

Speaking of restaurants, the Violet Hour features a small menu of light food (a dozen selections at $8–$12), but we know what you're here for: cocktails.

The menu adheres to what Maloney calls "a philosophy of minimalism—we look to the classics and use them as a template to create cocktails that have a whiff of the familiar but with an updated twist." The three dozen-ish inventions on the menu at any given moment are rotated seasonally. Although most of the drink names won't be immediately familiar to cocktail newbies, Maloney is careful not to alienate potential converts to the cocktail cause. "You shouldn't have to have read a manual before you walk into a bar," he says. "It's no fun to be faced with a plethora of choices that you don't understand." Thus, the bar staff are patient, discussing better options and upgrades with people who may need to be gently helped away from their comfort zones.

We've made a dent in the menu, but dammit, it keeps changing, so we have to keep going back. All drinks are $12. Some longtime

favorites include the Poor Liza (pear brandy, green Chartreuse, simple syrup, lemon juice, Peychaud's bitters, flaming orange peel zest), the El Diablo (Sauza Hornitos tequila, lemon juice, soda water, ginger syrup, float of crème de cassis), the Zarzamora (Wild Turkey 101 whiskey, muddled blackberries, Fernet-Branca amaro, orange bitters, float of cola), and the near-legendary Juliet and Romeo (Plymouth gin, mint, cucumber, rose water, Angostura bitters, lime juice, simple syrup). Maloney's current favorite is a Bramble variant called the Ramble On (Death's Door gin, lemon juice, simple syrup, Campari, Briottet crème de cassis).

Naturally, all syrups, all juice, about 20 bitters, and a couple of macerations are done in-house. "We get all our spices and even our demerara from Terra Spice, a local company, and it makes all the difference," Maloney says. "Our hibiscus simple syrup is able to capture Hawaii in a bottle."

The Violet Hour, like the Teardrop in Portland or New York's Pegu Club, seems to be a spawning ground for creative mixologists; alumni include Brad Bolt of Chicago's Bar DeVille, Mike Ryan of Chicago's Sable, Kirk Estopinal of New Orleans' Cure, Stephen Cole of Chicago's Barrelhouse Flat, and Ira Koppelwitz of Milwaukee's Bittercube, among many others. All of these men deserve the accolades that they're awarded elsewhere in this book, and the current roster of barkeeps at the Violet Hour are probably destined for the same sort of success. "I am most proud of the staff," says Maloney. "It is the staff that keeps studying, comes in off-hours to help out others, and day after day is professional, enthusiastic, and loves the minutiae."

Viva la minutiae!

Directly across the street from the Violet Hour (and owned by some of the same partners) is the Tex-Mex-themed **Big Star** (1531 N. Damen Avenue; 773.235.4039; www.bigstarchicago.com). This festive bar is always packed full of revelers looking for elevated, Mexican-inspired food (both inside the restaurant and at a takeout window) by Paul Kahan. The food is paired with well-crafted but no-nonsense cocktails focused on bourbon, rye, and tequila by Michael Rubel of the Violet Hour. Try the Taco de Huitlacoche ($3) or the Tostada de Calabacitas ($4) paired with a Bakersfield Buck (Old Heaven Hill whiskey, lime juice, Gosling's ginger beer; $7), or a Stockyard Pony (Elmer T. Lee bourbon, Aperol aperitif, lemon juice, demerara sugar, Angostura bitters; $7). Note the turntables behind the bar, with bartenders spinning vinyl between drink orders. Dig it.

There are bars where customers go to drink, and there are bars where bartenders go to drink. Weegee's is the latter. But don't be misled: the Aviary, this is not.

Weegee's Lounge

3659 W. Armitage Avenue
Chicago, IL
773.384.0707
www.weegeeslounge.com

Opened in mid-2006 by former photography student Alex Huebner, Weegee's is named after the famous 1940s Los Angeles crime scene photographer Arthur "Weegee" Fellig. Like the scene in so many of Fellig's photos, the bar is in a somewhat gritty neighborhood. It is also an archetypical Chicago neighborhood bar in every sense—the restored tin ceiling, the classic Brunswick back bar, and the soundtrack of classic jazz records all pair with the photo booth, the Weegee photos on the walls, and a giant antique photo enlarger to enhance the photography theme without being over the top. Even the (free) shuffleboard game is cool.

Aside from the friendly and relaxed atmosphere, the draw here is the booze, and lots of it. Working without any kitchen facilities at all, Weegee's does one thing very well: booze in a glass. You're not going to get drinks heavy on fresh-squeezed juice at Weegee's, and house-made syrups are also at a minimum. There's just nowhere to make this stuff. So instead of using canned or artificial ingredients, what you'll get is a menu of cocktails that don't *need* this stuff. We've all paged through a cocktail menu and seen that one drink tucked in there that is made of liquor, liquor, and liquor, with maybe a liqueur in there for good measure. Take all of those drinks, compile 'em into one document, and you have Weegee's menu. This is the real deal. With no nonsense.

Most of Weegee's drinks are in the $8–$11 range. Their Sazerac is solid, and the Jack Rabbit (Laird's applejack, locally produced maple syrup, a hint of orange juice, and a peel of lemon) is reliable. Martinis are perfect, naturally, but we should have known better than to ask for an off-menu Sidecar; there's going to be a problem with the lemon juice. We also like the Sit and Spin, which bravely combines Michigan's New Holland Hopquila and Chicago-based Hum liqueur. This bears further discussion, actually, since Huebner is a huge proponent of using local and handcrafted spirits. You won't find a house-made, barrel-aged tarragon-honey-yuzu liqueur at Weegee's, but you will find whiskeys, gins, and rums by small-batch distilleries from all over the Midwest and beyond.

Hence the population of bartenders blowing off steam at the shuffleboard table during their nights off, while a Mexican guy shoots Polaroids of you for $5. No attitude, no doorman, no food, just booze in a glass with a room full of friendly locals.

The Whistler

2421 N. Milwaukee Avenue
Chicago, IL
773.227.3530
www.whistlerchicago.com

There are two types of bar in the world: those with an art gallery on the premises, and those without. Actually, there are a fair number of bars in the "with art gallery" category, so let's say that there are those that offer craft bartending classes, and those that don't. But, actually . . . at least one solid bar in each major city is doing classes these days, so let's say that there are those affiliated with a record label, and those that are not so tuneful. In the case of the Whistler, let's just say that there is only one bar we know of that will gladly handle all of the above, and then there are those who think that simply rocking a dartboard is pure magic. There is no dartboard at the Whistler.

The Whistler was opened in the autumn of 2008 by Robert Brenner and Billy Helmkamp (of Chicago's Whistler Records), along with partner and former lead bartender Paul McGee. The lauded McGee departed from the Whistler in February 2012, leaving longtime co-bartender Eric Henry behind the stick.

The Whistler is a rather small space, but with large ambitions. In keeping with the young and arty Logan Square neighborhood, it aims to provide a space for live music, DJs, poetry, and film screenings while maintaining an art gallery in its storefront windows. Look for new art on display every two months. The sparse space, not-especially-decorated in exposed brick, holds about 75 people and gets crowded and loud when you'd expect it to. A seasonal patio holds another 50.

All of this is augmented by the Whistler's carefully mixed and reasonably priced cocktails (most are $8). Their mandate is to be a neighborhood bar that just happens to have excellent cocktails. The proof is in the customers: the average crowd at the Whistler seems to consist equally of people on both ends of the cocktail–PBR spectrum. Let's skip the PBR end, since it's always cocktail hour for Gal Friday Night and she calls the shots. Oh, are we doing shots? Hang on. *Kanpai!* Okay, we're back.

The bar's seasonal menu usually contains a concise eight drinks, combining a few carefully selected classics with a few house creations. The Whistler is partial to minimalism, and in the spirit of the classics, they prefer to keep their own inventions limited to three or four quality ingredients. Witness the Big Bend No. 2 (Azul reposado tequila, Cherry Heering, lime juice, Cynar amaro, chipotle tincture) or the Viking Funeral (North Shore aquavit, Luxardo Amaro Abano, lemon juice, egg white). Pre-Prohibition classics are given an update now and again, such as adding a little bit of extra apple whiskey to the Orchard Old-Fashioned (Old Overholt rye, Leopold Bros. apple whiskey, demerara syrup, Angostura bitters). Modern classics may also be altered ever so slightly, as in adding a bit of extra ginger liqueur to Audrey Saunders' Gin-Gin Mule (Broker's gin, ginger liqueur, lime juice, ginger beer, Angostura bitters, mint).

The bar makes some of their syrups and tinctures in-house but also likes to support small businesses, buying product from B. G. Reynolds (of Portland) and Small Hand Foods (of San Francisco). In the summer, they get herbs from an after-school garden project maintained by inner-city teens.

The Whistler also holds cocktail classes on Sunday afternoons, but we're almost more intrigued by the idea that there's never a cover for Patsy Cline tribute bands, Bollywood films, the Orange Alert reading series, shows by Brenner's band Black Apple, and movieoke once a month (like karaoke, but the people onstage are acting out movie scenes). We're there for all of it.

Paul McGee's new project will be a tiki bar in the basement of a new country bar (both currently unnamed) at 435 N. Clark Street. That one should be open sometime in 2012, and will be owned by Ed Warm and Tom DiSanto with R. J. and Jerrod Melman, who own several trendy downtown clubs and restaurants. McGee promises craft-level attention to an array of classic and modern tropical drinks in what will become the only tiki bar currently operating within the Chicago city limits.

LAST CALL!

More Destinations to Explore in Chicago

The Aviary (955 W. Fulton Market; www.theaviary.com) is rock star chef Grant Achatz's take on a molecular mixology bar. Achatz is also the man behind Alinea, currently the only restaurant in Chicago with three Michelin stars. The sleek upstairs space at the Aviary features bartenders shaking it up in birdcages, but there's a bit less of the performance art happening in **The Office,** an invitation-only private bar downstairs. Tasting menus are $165, while single cocktails will set you back $16–$18 on average and top out at $28 for a Black Truffle Negroni. Although beverages prepared with the aid of a rotary evaporator or liquid nitrogen do manage to set a new bar for presentation, you'll visit the Aviary once for the thoroughly impressive whiz-bang, and then visit the Whistler (see page 102) for a perfectly respectable $8 Manhattan.

   The Bedford (1612 West Division Street; 773.235.8800; www.bedfordchicago.com) opened in April 2011. The bar is housed in the spacious and well-lit basement level of a landmark bank building. A giant vault door is the centerpiece of a large room that also has safety deposit boxes embedded in the walls above plush booths. Equal parts bar and restaurant, the Bedford is full of trendy Wicker Parkers enjoying drinks such as the Jackknife Judy (Templeton rye, Cynar aperitif, orange bitters, Muscat dessert wine, Rishi vanilla black tea reduction;

$11). Mixologist/manager Pete Gugni says the Bedford is "not a cocktail bar, but a bar that does cocktails."

At venerable multi-award-winning restaurant **Blackbird** (619 W. Randolph Street; 312.715.0708; www. blackbirdrestaurant. com), Lynn House (an alumnus of the Drawing Room and graham elliot restaurant) arranges seasonal cocktail menus by theme. She's been known to source ingredients from the most local place possible: her backyard. Witness the London Calling, a Pimm's Cup variant made with apple butter from her own apple trees (gin, Pimm's, cucumber soda, ginger syrup, apple butter). That same "farm" supplies the mint for the Plum Smash, a drink showcasing cognac, House's preferred spirit (cognac, muddled plums, lime, mint, mint blossoms). We've also enjoyed her Starry Night (Ron Zacapa rum, Jans Dutch liqueur, hot coffee, Angostura-infused whipped cream, vanilla sugar) and her Oz (Pierre Ferrand Ambre cognac, plum wine, Gruet Blanc de Noir champagne, lemon juice, apple cider vinegar gastrique), which was named after the legendary Chicago jazz club. Blackbird cocktails are in the $12 range.

The **Gilt Bar** (230 W. Kinzie Street; 312.464.9544; www.giltbarchicago.com) is a restaurant with a solid bar, sporting a menu of decadent food (ham and cheese fondue, mushroom and truffle pasta, pork belly, truffle fries) and lengthy lists of wine, beers, and spirits. Cocktail seekers will want to find their way to the intimate **Curio Bar,** Gilt's "secret" basement cocktail lounge, where you may sample Curio-exclusive libations such as the Oaxacan Old-Fashioned (mezcal, sugar, bitters), and the Trade Winds (Myers's rum, Matusalem rum, apricot liqueur, coconut cream). Sounds good, but what's up with using Myers's in a $12 cocktail? They're redeemed by a staff of knowledgeable bartenders

who will gladly whip up an omakase cocktail or pour from a solid menu of standards. Curio Bar opens at 7:00 PM. On selected nights, the sound of DJs or live jazz fills the small, cozy, candlelit space.

Very close to Gilt is **Hubbard Inn** (110 W. Hubbard Street; 312.222.1331; www.hubbardinn.com). We're not sure who was more pompous and uninviting during our visit, the door staff or the other customers, but let's stick to the drinks here. Our first round was served by a friendly and talented guy from Cleveland. Our second was presented by an aloof amateur from (apparently) Applebee's. We like the spirits selection and the drinks list (with highlights written on a huge chalkboard above the bar), so we're going to sneak back in to give them a second chance . . . when "Cleveland Rocks" is working.

Longman and Eagle (2657 N. Kedzie Avenue; 773.276.7110; www.longmanandeagle.com) is in the hip Logan Square neighborhood. Opening for coffee at 8:00 AM, the restaurant remains open through dinner. Overnight, Longman and Eagle offers six inn-style rooms ($75–$200 per night). Sleep, refresh, and repeat. Decor includes art by a different Chicago artist in each room, plus furniture by Mode Carpentry, which designed Longman and Eagle's bar and worked on the Violet Hour and

the Whistler. The whiskey-centric cocktail list contains classics such as the Full House (Laird's applejack bonded, Bénédictine, yellow Chartreuse, aromatic bitters). Nerdery alert: this is actually the Full House #2 and is essentially the same as a Widow's Kiss, but slightly rebalanced—the Full House #1 is rum, Swedish Punsch, and dry vermouth. Chef Jared Wentworth is focused on local and sustainable regional dishes. The continually malleable menu may contain delectables such as Slagel Family Farm's half duck ($24) or pot-au-feu of Swan Creek Farms' beef short rib ($29), plus a variety of small plates and sandwiches.

To date, **Maria's Packaged Goods & Community Bar** (960 W. 31st Street; 773.890.0588; www.community-bar. com) in the Bridgeport neighborhood is the only South Side bar to embrace slow drinking. Owned until recently

by Maria Marszewski (known as "the Peggy Guggenheim of Bridgeport"), the bar has been run by her two sons since 2010. A classic Chicago-style bar is hidden behind a nondescript door within a liquor store that is decorated with dozens of ventriloquist's dummies. You'll know Maria's by the antique back bar, pressed tin ceiling, and yes, chandeliers made from bomber bottles. Most of the decor is reclaimed/recycled/reused. Maria's also supports and helps to foster the rapidly growing arts community in up-and-coming Bridgeport. Themed DJ nights range from punk to funk, and from exotica to Latina discoteca. The bartenders at the small and always-packed space offer renamed twists on classics (all $8–$9), such as the Nordic 75, Maria's Manhattan, A Dark and Stormy Night, and the Side Bahr (Knob Creek bourbon, Grand Marnier, organic apple juice, lemon juice) by bartender Nick Bahr.

Maude's Liquor Bar (840 W. Randolph Street; 312.243.9712; www.maudesliquorbar.com) is owned by the same people as Curio Bar. They serve decadent Franco-Belgian-inspired food (pommes frites with aioli, mussels, cassoulet, foie gras pâté) in a bistro environment: old wood, mirrors, and white ceramic tile. And a cabinet of curiosities. We *love* that. The concise cocktail menu specializes in smashes: whiskey smash, Grand Marnier smash, Smoky Violet smash, and the massively intriguing Chartreuse smash.

Colleen Flaherty's **Tiny Lounge** (4352 N. Leavitt Street; 773.463.0396; www.tinylounge.com) can be found in the pleasant Lincoln Square area, which is also home to a small German community (with access to relevant food/beer). Intriguing original drinks such as the Lakshmi (Hendrick's gin, St. Germain elderflower liqueur, Berentzen pear brandy, cava; $10) vary wildly in quality based on who is making them. Tiny Lounge has a solid beer list and tasty small plates for the peckish.

MILWAUKEE

Milwaukee may be the city we have to blame for Miller Lite, but we have to cut them some slack, because they're also the only city on the globe with a professional sports team—at any level, and in any sport—named after booze (the Brewers). Milwaukee also has a versatile craft distillery (Great Lakes) and a handful of microbreweries that easily redeem them for Lite indiscretions. Plus, Death's Door Spirits distillery is just down the road in Madison. Cocktails? They've got those here, too!

Milwaukee is the sort of town where an elegant restaurant will shamelessly compliment your cocktail with bacon-and-cheese-dusted pork rinds,

Beta by Sabor

777 North Water Street
Milwaukee, WI
414.431.3106
www.saborbrazil.net

served with a Martini glass full of pure honey, *and make it work*.

Beta by Sabor is the cocktails-and-small-plates annex to Sabor, Milwaukee's upscale Brazilian steakhouse. Upon its opening in July 2011, Beta's chef, Mitch Ciohon, combined the South American menu of Sabor with some decidedly Milwaukeean touches to create a cosmopolitan yet comfortably midwestern hybrid. At the bar, we tried the aforementioned pork rinds ($4), as well as some perfectly seared scallops served with a fried banana and bacon purée ($9), and then an absolutely decadent dish of little fried chicken breasts stacked high on waffles with a whiskey apple syrup ($8.50).

As we worked our way through three cocktails, we enjoyed the small and bright space, which looks out onto trendy Water Street. All of our drinks were house creations, although the menu does contain a few classics as well. Bar manager Bill Dumas describes the menu as "twists on old classics, updated." When we asked for

the Scudetto (pineapple-infused Plymouth gin, Campari, egg white; $9), bartender Marc's eyes lit up. "That's the good one!" he enthused. One would hope they all are . . . but the Scudetto was definitely a good place to start. I would have used a little more Campari in the sweet drink, but then again I drink that stuff for breakfast. Speaking of breakfast (I guess the waffles got us into that mood), we moved on to a more whiskey-forward invention, the Kentucky Breakfast Old-Fashioned (bacon-infused Knob Creek bourbon, maple syrup, Luxardo maraschino; $9). The garnish: a tall and crispy slab of perfectly straight bacon sticking up out of the rocks glass.

Dumas told us that the menu changes seasonally, as Marc pointed out the array of Bittercube and Great Lakes Distillery products behind the bar. Great Lakes' Rehorst gin is used for all of Beta's infusions.

◆━▶━

Bryant's Cocktail Lounge

1579 S. 9th Street
Milwaukee, WI
414.383.2620
www.bryantscocktaillounge.com

A surprisingly large number of the bars in Milwaukee look more or less like your hip uncle's bachelor pad, circa 1968. We can't discuss **At Random** (2501 S. Delaware Avenue, 414.481.8030) at any length in this book—even though it was opened by an ex-Bryant's bartender—since the drinks just aren't especially amazing. It is, however, definitely worth a stop for a heavy dose of post-Rat Pack splendiferousness.

Bryant's, on the other hand, does deliver fantastic libations, in an atmosphere of untouched temporal flashback from the years when leatherette sofas, fake plants wrapped in Christmas lights, and swingin' swag lamps were all the rage. Their tipples are all more than worthy of imbibing within a room that can only be described as swanky.

The story of Bryant's narrow escape from oblivion is worth noting. In 1938, Bryant Sharp opened his bar on the corner of 9th and Lapham, in what looks more or less like a typical neighborhood house. Three years later, he stopped selling beer and switched to an all-cocktails format. Loyal customer Pat Malmberg bought the lounge after Sharp's death, and maintained its reputation for great cocktails and groovy vibes even as it recovered from a 1971 fire. The bar closed after Malberg's passing in 2007. At the time, Bryant's had been the oldest continually-operating cocktail bar in Milwaukee. Nine months later (in July of 2008) it was rescued by new owner John Dye, now the second consecutive loyal customer to save Bryant's by buying the place.

The veteran bartenders at the menuless Bryant's version 1.0 were said to have 500 recipes committed to memory, and they encouraged customers to order by flavor. The new Bryant's 2.0 has recruited new bartenders (the old-timers had all retired or moved to other jobs during the 2007 hiatus). However, the vibe inside is more or less unchanged, right down to the aquarium, velvet wallpaper, plush booths, and original McIntosh hi-fi playing swingin' classics.

Visitors to the modern remix of Bryant's will find the new staff to be fully up to the task of keeping their predecessor's legacy alive. We've tried the "bartender's choice" a few times ($7–$10). On one

chilly night, we asked for something with "Chartreuse and a warm brown base liquor." We were promptly handed a rocks glass full of rye and Chartreuse, neat, with a lemon peel. We'd been hoping for something a bit more challenging, perhaps less of a strictly literal interpretation of our request, but hey, this was exactly what we asked for, and it was good.

Playing it a bit safer, we went for some Bryant's house classics, such as the Kismet (Southern Comfort whiskey, lemon, secret house-made syrups). This led us down an exciting and dangerous road toward some of Malmberg's seasonal punches, which also contain secret proprietary ingredients. In fact, Bryant's has been doing house-made syrups for decades, perhaps out of necessity, or perhaps out of creative inspiration. In either case, it's fantastic to see them surviving and carrying on through their eighth decade in business.

The Hamilton

823 E. Hamilton Street
Milwaukee, WI
414.223.1020
www.thehamiltonmke.com

There are two midwestern bars that will greet you with big blue curtains as you walk in. One is Chicago's the Violet Hour, whose periwinkle draperies are nearly as iconic as their drinks (see page 98). The other is the Hamilton, whose royal blue curtains are not their only visual parallels to the Violet Hour: a gilt-framed mirror and big marble lamps on the bar recall the Chicago bar's elegance as well. Let us not mistake the Hamilton for lil' Violet Hour, however; the mere 90 miles that separate Chicago and Milwaukee is more than enough distance to allow the bars their own identities.

The Hamilton was opened in February 2011 by Kimberly Floyd. "[I was inspired by] the original salons of the 1700s, where artists, writers, intellectuals, men, and women first got together to socialize," Floyd says. "The inspiration merged with the idea of a hotel lobby, because the Hamilton sounded like a hotel, plus I liked the idea of travelers passing through."

The Hamilton's concise cocktail list (10 drinks, all $9), curated by co-lead bartenders Nic Behrends and Caleb Anderson, is divided into three sections: Prologue, Dialogue, and Epilogue. We began with the Marionette, which is notable for containing no less than three locally-made products: Roaring Dan's rum from Great Lakes Distillery, Bittercube Jamaican #1 bitters, and house-made ginger syrup. Lime juice and demerara syrup complete this tropical-style

drink, which is strained into a rocks glass. Gal Friday Night's off-menu French 75 was presented in a Martini glass. We also tried a Windsor Forest (Citadelle gin, lime juice, green Chartreuse, rosemary tincture) and the nearly identical-looking Zeppelin (house-blended Koval white whiskey, lemon juice, Luxardo maraschino, crème de violette). The house-blended Koval white whiskey is interesting. The Hamilton has taken *all five* of the white whiskey varieties from Chicago's Koval distillery and created a custom blend for in-house use.

"We have a great passion for all aspects of alcohol-making," says Floyd, "from the people who put all the ingredients together, to the grapes, grains, herbs, locations, distillation, aging, and finally, the flavor." Indeed, in addition to growing rosemary and basil on their back deck, the Hamilton likes to infuse genever gin with tea from local distributor Rishi. They also use Rishi tea in their green tea honey syrup.

Creative ingredients at the Hamilton don't seem to be confined to the glass. "We took these ingredients—creativity, technique, and passion—and transformed an old garage into a gorgeous lounge," Floyd says. "We used those same ingredients to inspire our cocktails. The result is a fun and interesting staff with fantastic patrons."

The Hamilton also has a list of over 50 wines and champagnes, a private party room, a small outdoor patio, and a private parking lot (free).

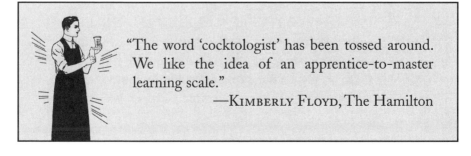

"The word 'cocktologist' has been tossed around. We like the idea of an apprentice-to-master learning scale."
—KIMBERLY FLOYD, The Hamilton

LAST CALL!
More Destinations to Explore in Milwaukee

Just around the corner from Great Lakes Distillery (visible from their parking lot, in fact) is the motorcycle-friendly Iron Horse Hotel (500 W. Florida Street; 414.374.4766; www.theironhorsehotel.com). Located in a century-old warehouse, the hotel has been accumulating high accolades. Their bar is called **Branded,** and its chief mixologist, Clint Sterwald, has generated a bit of hype as well. Drinks weigh in at $10–$15 and include several made with Great Lakes Distillery products.

BYO Studio Lounge (2246 S. Kinnickinnic Avenue; 414.489.7474; www.byostudio.com) was opened as an art gallery in 2009, and owner Ken Yandell added a full bar in 2010. We like the idea of an art gallery/cocktail lounge hybrid. Art so often feels like an afterthought in restaurants and lounges, and the only booze you're usually going to get in an art gallery is Stumble Home, er, Sutter Home merlot. The cocktail menu at BYO (where, it might be noted, you *can't* "bring your own") leans heavily toward the South American end of the spectrum with Caipirinhas, Mojitos, and Margaritas dominating the list. "I like visiting that part of the world," Yandell explains simply.

Distil (722 N. Milwaukee Street; 414.220.9411; www. distilmilwaukee.com) is a rockin' bar in a festive area filled with nightlife. Dark wood, low light, and sports on several televisions give it a masculine feeling, as does the impressive and lengthy leather-bound spirits and cocktails menu. Their Absinthe Sour is a solid drink, well-balanced and velvety on the tongue as properly diluted absinthe tends to be, but Gal Friday Night's drink wasn't strained properly and had a lot of icebergs in it. She *hates* that! The Manhattan we tried was better than most. All were in coupe glasses for $12.

ST. LOUIS

The Gateway to the West may be famous for Eero Saarinen's modernist arch, but there's at least one cocktail bar that makes Mound City worth a visit, too.

There are two types of bar in the world: those owned by anesthesiologists, and those that should be. Seriously, it is awesome and appropriate, when considering all the branches of medical practice, that an anesthesiologist owns this bar. (A hepatologist would be even more apropos, but that's not quite so fun. Maybe a herpetologist would be better still. Those guys are good at keeping the lounge lizards lubricated.)

Dr. Gurpreet Padda (also owner of Chuy Arzola's and Café Ventana) opened Sanctuaria in the Grove, a shopping and nightlife district within St. Louis. The large black-

Sanctuaria

4198 Manchester Avenue
Saint Louis, MO
314.535.9700
www.sanctuariastl.com

and-red sign outside is lettered in the sort of spiky gothic font that might lead one to believe that they were about to enter a speed metal club. Inside, you'll find a whimsical Latin theme where Mexican Day of the Dead figurines are juxtaposed with a big metal tree behind the bar. The ceiling is papered with Mexican movie posters, Che Guevara iconography, and Spanish liquor ads. The room is also decorated with artifacts from 17th- and 18th-century churches and a giant mirror from Peru.

Formerly of Chicago's In Fine Spirits, bar manager and mixologist Matt Seiter has been on board since the Sanctuaria opened in early 2010. Seiter's menu takes full advantage of the bar's private

barrel of Elijah Craig 12-year bourbon, plus a list of perennial favorites and a list of drinks submitted by members of Sanctuaria's
cocktail club. For a $20 club membership fee, the brave customer
will be given a menu of 150 drinks. When all of the $8 libations
have been sampled, the corpse/customer will thereafter get every
third drink for free, for the life of the bar. This club is a fun idea,
and the fact that members have submitted drinks that have made
it onto the bar's menu is really cool. That's a nice effort at engag-
ing customers and keeping them involved, eroding the barriers between mixologist and barfly.

Sanctuaria is also experimenting with cocktails on tap, a concept that we have expressed doubts about elsewhere in this book.
Their take on the idea involves batching 4.5 gallons of a drink,
adding ice, and then allowing it to thaw, simulating the natural
way that ice would impart water to a shaken cocktail. The ice is
removed when the right water ratio is achieved. Refrigeration is
then kept at at 38 degrees until the beverage is tapped. One drink
served this way is the Uncommon Ground (Scotch whisky, cognac,
cinnamon syrup, malbec wine, passion fruit juice, baked apple bitters), which also gets just a little bit of carbonation from the carbon
dioxide gun as it is served.

Of the house cocktails, we were drawn to the Prince of Jalis-
co (reposado tequila, crème de cacao, orange juice, lemon juice,

cracked espresso beans), the Turmoil (rye whiskey, Bénédictine, lemon juice, crème de cacao, lemon balm leaves), and the Autumn Blush (North Shore No. 11 gin, lime juice, crème de violette, sprig of lavender, grape juice spiced with thyme, sage, and cinnamon). It's always great to see products in use from Chicago's North Shore Distillery. This is just the beginning of Sanctuaria's mission to use craft, local, and indie products; you won't see many huge mass-market booze brands behind their bar. Seiter makes many of the syrups himself and sources fresh herbs from the bar's garden.

In the kitchen, chef Chris Lee creates generously-portioned "wild tapas," including goat cheese fritters, smoked shrimp salad, vaca frita with chimichurri, quinoa with piquillos, and a weekly locavore special made from whatever he can rustle up at the market.

LAST CALL!
More Destinations to Explore in St. Louis

At **Taste** (4584 Laclede Avenue; 314.361.1200; www.tastebarstl.com), you may meet Ted Kilgore (a founding member of the local USBG chapter, who is recognized by many as an elder statesman of the St. Louis cocktail scene) as you dine from a dinner menu by owner and head chef Adam Altnether. **Danno's American Pub** (7895 Watson Road; 314.395.3000) is primarily a beer joint featuring local bands, but Chris Muether has been expanding the cocktail end of the bar program since 2009. **DeMun Oyster Bar** (740 Demun Avenue, Clayton, MO; 314.725.0322; www.demunoysterbar.com) features solid cocktails by T. J. Vytlacil and Chad George. In September 2011, Vytlacil and Adam Frager (formerly of Pi) launched **Blood and Sand** (1500 St. Charles Street; 314.241.7263; www.bloodandsandstl.com), a private cocktail club with a monthly membership fee, and food by Chris Bork. That's one to watch.

LOUISVILLE

All right, sluggers, do you need a reason to visit Derby City? Here are a few very good ones.

Proof on Main

21c Museum Hotel
702 W. Main Street
Louisville, KY
502.217.6360
www.proofonmain.com

One would think there'd be more great cocktail bars located in Kentucky, the home-state of bourbon, America's spirit. Alas, we're guessing that most visitors might prefer to drink Bourbon County's eponymous beverage neat. One Mint Julep might change a few minds. In Louisville, the best bar in town also has the added attraction of being attached to a swell contemporary art gallery and a swanky contemporary hotel, all located on what was once known as Whiskey Row.

The 21c Museum Hotel and Art Gallery was conceived by art collectors Laura Lee Brown and Steve Wilson, who opened the space in 2006. Brown and Wilson stitched four 18th-century tobacco and bourbon warehouses together, leaving brickwork, leaded glass transoms, and arches intact. This vintage/modern hybrid structure was designed to house their extensive art collection, plus the hotel and Proof on Main. Since it is part of the hotel's public areas, the art museum never closes. The 9,000 square feet of gallery space features solo and group exhibitions and site-specific commissioned installations, all dating from the 21st century.

At the bar, head bartender Jenni Pittman likes making classics such as the Mint Julep, the French 75, the Gimlet, and the lesser-known Gold Rush (Woodford Reserve bourbon, lemon juice, honey syrup) when she isn't designing new drinks. Sticking with the local bourbon theme, Gal Friday Night and I were drawn to the Bourbon Cider (bourbon, apple cider, sugar, lemon juice, cloves, ginger, cinnamon), and a riff on the classic Presbyterian called the Naughty Presbyterian (Old Forester bourbon, Grand Marnier, ginger beer). Proof on Main also hosts an annual Repeal Day party (December 5). Naturally, they also sell a comprehensive selection of Kentucky bourbons and ryes.

In the restaurant, Chef Michael Paley adds an Italian flavor to his Southern-style cooking in dishes like pan-roasted Berkshire pork ($28), Hudson Valley duck ($29), and chickpea and country ham fritter ($9).

LAST CALL!
More Destinations to Explore in the Louisville Area

Proof on Main's Whiskey Row location is an inspired choice. This global nexus for bourbon is a great place to launch your road trip of bourbon distillery tours. Louisville tourists can grab **Urban Bourbon Trail** maps, leading them to restaurants and bars that spotlight nearby Bourbon County's most famous export. Ironically, Bourbon County itself is dry, but a recent addendum to the law allows historic sites to serve alcohol. Thus, the nine active distilleries in Kentucky can now legally offer tastings and samples of their products; eight of them currently do so. Coalescing into the Bourbon Trail campaign just after the millennium, these eight businesses offer tours akin to those offered in various wine regions around the world. Visitors may want to

time their visit to coincide with the annual Kentucky Bourbon Festival held every September in Bardstown.

Equus Restaurant's **Equus & Jack's Lounge** (122 Sears Avenue; 502.897.9721; www. equusrestaurant.com) has been open since 1985, and bartender Joy Perrine has been there the whole time. They feature 150 bourbons at the bar and a short menu of seasonal cocktails that all seem to feature Woodford Reserve bourbon, including their signature pour, the Bourbonball (Woodford Reserve bourbon, Tuaca liqueur, crème de cacao). Originally produced in Italy, the brandy-based Tuaca is now made in Louisville, and has a dominant vanilla flavor with orange notes.

Kevin Grangier of the Village Anchor gave his restaurant's bar the appropriate appellation **Sea Hag** (11507 Park Road, Anchorage, KY; 502.708.1850; www. villageanchor.com). They've got an extensive bourbon selection listed by proof, and cocktails by Adam Underwood and Jared Schubert under bar master Jim Murphy. Cuisine includes shrimp and grits ($25), grilled salmon ($25), and fried chicken ($16).

One last stop for Lousiville visitors should be the historic **Seelbach Hilton Hotel** (500 S. 4th Street; 502.585.3200; www.seelbachhilton.com). Built in 1905, the Seelbach is often considered the finest hotel in Kentucky. F. Scott Fitzgerald featured the Seelbach in *The Great Gatsby* as the location of the wedding scene. The Seelbach is also the home of the classic Seelbach Cocktail, which was created in 1917. Forgotten for decades, the recipe was rediscovered by Adam Seger (creator of the Chicago-based Hum liqueur) and later disseminated via Ted Haigh's mandatory

tome *Vintage Spirits and Forgotten Cocktails.* You'll be mixing bourbon, Cointreau, champagne, and *seven dashes each* of Angostura and Peychaud's bitters into that puppy. It works. Oh my, how it works.

NASHVILLE

Music City USA is home to a whole lot of bars, and most of 'em are great places to hear live music while drinking canned beer. That's not a bad thing, but sometimes you need a solid cocktail. Have no fear; we have reconnoitered two houses of mixology that are shaking things up with the best of them.

The bars in Nashville all seem to make you want to feel at home. Or at least "at house." We'll discuss chateau Patterson below, but first, let us visit East Nashville's Holland House. Created

Holland House Bar & Refuge

935 W. Eastland Avenue
Nashville, TN
615.262.4190
www.hollandhousebarandrefuge.com

by Holland-born Cees Brinkman with noted Nashville bartender Terrell Raley, East Nashville's Holland House opened in March 2010. The restaurant and bar offers upscale dining and drinking in a spacious and inviting room decorated with two maple bars, 20-foot barrel-vaulted ceilings, and no less than 16 chandeliers. They also rescued some of their interior wood from a local barn, which is just the beginning of their commitment to keeping things local.

Lead bartender Jeremiah Blake says that the use of Tennessee ingredients is a "Nashville pride thing," and that they source local products whenever possible, right down to their suspenders-and-bow-tie uniforms, which are tailored in town. The bar serves the new Collier and McKeel whiskey, as well as old standby Prichard's whisky, and Blake's personal favorite, George Dickel whiskey. Blake is also in charge of cocktail development and the creation of house-made bitters, cordials, and syrups. "I don't think anybody is making as much product as we are," he says. "With our syrups, it takes two days of prep time to get ready for one week of service."

Looking over the menu, we were enticed by many of the 20-ish cocktails labeled "Contemporary" (mostly $10), especially the Daisy If You Do (bourbon, Bénédictine, CioCiaro amaro, lemon juice, grapefruit juice, agave syrup, Angostura bitters, Fee Brothers Whiskey Barrel-Aged bitters). This drink is just one of roughly 100 libations that the bar staff has created in the two years they've been open. Blake attributes this creativity to Raley, calling him "a bad-ass" before elaborating: "[Raley] was doing [craft cocktails] in Nashville before anyone, but he didn't get the recognition because it wasn't a national craze yet. He's really generous with his time and has taught me *so* much."

Holland House's "Historical" cocktails are also seasonally selected; a summer visit will be heavy on the Mojito, the Pimm's Cup, the Pisco Sour, and the Mint Julep. We like that the American South and South America are well-represented in these warm weather menu choices. We also like the idea of a Weekender Punch ($5), which is available on Friday and Saturday from 9:00 PM "till the bowl is empty," and a daily featured drink which is offered for half price. Their ginger ice cubes are a nice touch as well.

Holland House also offers a solid food menu, which changes seasonally and is—of course—locally-sourced when possible. Some regionally-inspired selections include brunch dishes like pulled pork polenta ($8) and crab oscar ($12), and dinner selections such as pan-seared, wild-caught Kentucky catfish ($22) and honey-roasted spring hen ($21).

---◆---

The Patterson House

1711 Division Street
Nashville, TN
615.636.7724
www.thepattersonnashville.com

As stated above, there are multiple bars named after houses in Nashville, but if we're discussing sheer historic awesomeness, we have to give the edge to the Patterson House. The historic ex-residence is named for former Tennessee governor Malcolm R. Patterson, who attempted to block Prohibition on the state or national levels, arguing that legislating what people imbibe was something to be decided on a local level. His veto was overruled.

The Patterson House opened in April 2009, near distinguished universities Belmont and Vandy, by distinguished brothers Benjamin and Max Goldberg. The bar was inspired by a 2008 visit to Chicago's the Violet Hour. Benjamin Goldberg was so impressed with the Chicago bar that he hired Violet Hour mastermind Tobey Maloney and his consulting partner Jason Cott to get the Patterson House up and running.

Maloney and Cott brought a few Violet Hour classics to Patterson House, such as the legenday Juliet and Romeo (gin, rose water, cucumber, mint). Don't be fooled into thinking Patterson is a Violet Hour clone, however; the menu has diverged into its own realm. Gal Friday Night was seduced by the El Diablo (reposado tequila, lemon juice, ginger syrup, crème de cassis, club soda, garnish of candied ginger), whereas your humble narrator went for the Bacon Old-Fashioned (bacon-infused Four Roses from the bar's private barrel, demerara syrup, Peychaud's bitters). The ice ball in the Old-Fashioned is carved to order, and is from a mold made in Japan. Keeping with the bourbon theme—we're so close to Kentucky, after all—we were also intrigued by the Duck Hunter (Pritchard's Sweet Lucy bourbon, lemon juice, egg yolk, St. Elizabeth allspice dram, Regan's orange bitters). We also liked the idea of a local rum making a strong showing in the land of whiskey, as used in the Kelso Daiquiri (Prichard's Tennessee Crystal rum, lime juice, simple syrup). Most drinks are $12.

The dark, romantic atmosphere at the Patterson House is the work of Landy Gardner, who surrounded the 30-seat, 68-foot bar with dim Edison bulb lighting, shelves full of old books, and chandeliers bouncing their luminescence off of silvery wallpaper. The book motif is continued with the presentation of your bill tucked inside a tome of its own. Also in keeping with the Violet Hour's ethos, heavy curtains in the foyer keep you from the good stuff until the host confirms that there are seats available. At the Patterson House, there is no standing room and "no starfucking" (Maloney will cop to stealing that particular decree from another of his alma maters, New York's Milk & Honey). While you're waiting, drool over the barrel of whiskey in the foyer, custom-blended by the

Four Roses' master distillers in Lawrenceburg. This house batch has been awarded its own cocktail, the Patterson House Brooklyn (Four Roses whiskey, Amer Picon aperitif, Luxardo maraschino liqueur, blood orange bitters).

The bar also offers a small menu of food. The Elvis is decidedly a local favorite: peanut butter, banana, honey, and Benton bacon smashed into a panini. The shrimp corndogs with curried ketchup and the black-eyed pea hummus seem contemporary but also decidedly Southern.

In late 2011, the Goldberg brothers opened **The Catbird Seat** in the space above the Patterson House (615.248.8458). This small and exclusive restaurant is already being called the best in Nashville by some critics. Two dozen diners sit at a bar-like table around three sides of an open kitchen, and personally interact with the chef as dinner is prepared. The multi-course prix fixe menu changes weekly. Chefs Josh Habiger and Erik Anderson met at Alinea in Chicago, strengthening the connection between Chicago and 1711 Division Street in Nashville. Want more? The Catbird Seat has hired Jane Lopes of the Violet Hour as their beverage director. She's focusing on "unique, interesting, small-production finds," which could be wine, beer, cocktails, or some combination thereof.

ATLANTA

The deepest bits of the South don't seem to have embraced the cocktail renaissance quite yet, but when it happens (and it will), it seems likely that Atlanta will be where it starts. The sole bar listed here will hopefully provide the impetus for more adventurous mixology across the Bible Belt. One thing is for sure—they'll all be serving Presbyterians!

Visiting a bar called Prohibition might give the savvy customer pause. After all, the cocktails that most bars served during the 13 most hated years in the history of America were expensive, and by all accounts they were borderline undrinkable. We are pretty sure that

Prohibition

56 E. Andrews Drive NW
Atlanta, GA
404.869.1132
www.prohibitionatl.com

owner/bartender Steve De Haan's intent was to keep the so-called speakeasy concept in place, while offering libations more palatable to pre- or post-Prohibition tastes than those of Prohibition proper. This does seem to be the case, as Prohibition's menu of "prescriptions" offers such classics as the Clover Club, the Aviation, and the Dark and Stormy, along with more contemporary favorites like the Bramble and the Gin Gin Mule. All are $12.

The bar opened in September of 2009 in the slick new shopping area of Andrews Square. The incongruous red phone booth among the trendy fashion shops is the secret entrance to Prohibition, which is below the Stout Irish Pub. The windowless Prohibition may appeal to cigar smokers as much as cocktail enthusiasts, with nearly two dozen stogies in the humidor. The basement space does get smoky, so this is absolutely a destination for cigar-loving cocktailians only. Food may be ordered in from Cellar 56 next door.

MIAMI

Trendy Miami is a perfect spot to establish a craft cocktail outpost. A number of highly-regarded locations are popping up, but our tantalizingly brief visit left us unable to explore them in depth. Yet. Thus, we're headed straight to the "Last Call!" section here to spotlight a few places that have shown up on our cocktail-radar.

LAST CALL!
Destinations to Explore in Miami

The Bar at Sra. Martinez (4000 NE Second Avenue; 305.573.5474; www.sramartinez.com) is housed in a historic 1920s post office. This is chef Michelle Bernstein's spendy Design District spot for tapas. Up a discreet staircase to the second floor, you'll find a bar that seats less than 20. You'll also find house-made bitters and mixers combined with hand-squeezed juices and fresh herbs. Of course, the art, music, and late-night action Miami is known for

can be found here as well, but perhaps in a slightly more refined environment than you'll get in South Beach. A South American bent to the cocktails seems to balance the Spanish cuisine, so the festive Gal Friday Night gravitated toward the Flor de Espana (Oloroso sherry, Johnnie Walker Black, egg white, lemon juice, allspice miel), while her *compadre el escribidor* went for a taste of the Bar's bacon bourbon served neat, and then went Between the Cheets (Salignac cognac, Cointreau, house-made crème de chai, lemon juice). All cocktails are $9.

At **Michael's Genuine Food & Drink** (130 NE 40th Street; 305.573.5550; www.michaelsgenuine.com) in the Design District, Michael Schwartz (of Nemo and Afterglo) serves up fresh, locally-sourced, and seasonal food

made in a wood-fired oven. The casual bistro with culinary fare seats 90, with 14 seats at the bar. Mixologist Ryan Goodspeed makes hyphenated syrups like rosemary-cherry, ginger-lemongrass, and blueberry-tarragon. He says that the rosemary-cherry is also made into a soda, which features in their Manhattan variant. "We have a forager," he says, "that brings back some amazing fruits and vegetables from the Homestead area. If I can't use something in a cocktail, then I will try to use it as a garnish. If it's in season, I try to use it!" Goodspeed's personal picks for further Miami cocktails are the Cuban/Latin-inspired drinks at **Florida Room** in the Delano Hotel (1685 Collins Avenue, Miami Beach; 305.674.6152; www.delano-hotel.com) and **Sustain** (3252 NE 1st Avenue, #107; 305.424.9079; www.sustainmiami.com).

FORT LAUDERDALE

When driving south along the Space Coast of Florida to explore Miami, there is one place we'll definitely be stopping at along the way: Mai-Kai.

Mai-Kai

3599 North US 1
Fort Lauderdale, FL
305.947.9052
www.maikai.com

During the past few years, we have finally seen craft cocktail bars begin to embrace the tropical drink genre. It is great to see big city cocktail bars carrying this torch, but let's face it—the best place to get a classic tiki drink is in a classic tiki bar . . . when they do it right. Such as at Mai-Kai.

The Mai-Kai story begins in the early 1950s. Chicago brothers Robert and Jack Thornton had learned the craft of bartending from Donn Beach and others. By 1956, they'd begun construction of Mai-Kai with a mixology assist from Beach's former right-hand man, Mariano Licudine. In the 1960s, additions were made to the supper club by the renowned team of architect George Nakashima and designer Florian Gabriel, expanding Mai-Kai to 489 seats in seven rooms (named Samoa, Lanai, Tahiti, Tonga, Hawaii, New Guinea, and Moorea), and then another 150 in the vintage 1970s Molokai Bar.

At the Molokai Bar, there is not a bottle in sight, nor a bartender to be found. Cocktail waitresses (in bikini tops, matching mini-mini-mini sarongs, and big smiles), take your drink orders and deliver them to the team of master mixologists secretly concealed in a hidden laboratory. After a short wait, the potions are delivered to you. It fascinates us that Chicago über-chef Grant Aschatz has borrowed a similar concept, more than half a century later, for his 2011 bar the Aviary. He was lauded for (among many other things) the novelty of opening a bar with neither bottle nor shaker monkey in sight. Noted.

The rum collection at the Mai-Kai is the stuff of legend. They have been accumulating the noble spirit for 56 years now, and there are rums served here that you will never see anywhere else. In fact, you won't even see them at Mai-Kai, because they're in the liquor kitchen. This, my poor deprived (or depraved) rummy friends, is where the term "suffering bastard" is best used, because that rum collection is quite something, but you'll probably never get anywhere near it.

Catch the floor show and some dinner while you're there (make a reservation for a timed seating), then have a walk around the huge restaurant and back gardens to see the single spot on earth that best defines "tiki."

NEW ORLEANS

Few cities can boast that they are the birthplace of a greater number of important pre-Prohibition cocktails than New Orleans. Drinks that hail from the Crescent City include the crucial Ramos Gin Fizz (by Henry Ramos, 1880s), the delicious Brandy Crusta (Joseph Santini, 1850s), and the mighty Sazerac (Antoine Amadie Peychaud, prior to 1850; possibly the first modern cocktail). Post-Prohibition saw things pick up again with the untouchable Vieux Carré (Walter Bergeron, 1930s). Additionally, the Pimm's Cup, the French 75, and the Mint Julep were invented elsewhere, but still have strong associations with this town. This is also the place where Peychaud first created his bitters in 1830. A trio of newer bars are keeping New Orleans' reputation for innovation alive, while a healthy list of historic destinations will entertain visitors for as long as their livers can handle it. This is a town with a rich culture and a richly cultured array of people behind the bars. In the next few pages, you'll meet mixologists who speak fluent Latin, teach yoga, and recite poetry as they shake juleps.

Arnaud's French 75 Bar

813 Rue Bienville
New Orleans, LA
504.523.5433
www.arnaudsrestaurant.com

The French 75 Bar is just a small part of the Arnaud's complex, which consists of multiple dining rooms serving elegant elevations of traditional Creole cooking, plus a few banquet rooms, several bars, and yes, the Germaine Cazenave Wells Mardi Gras Museum. Wells was the daughter of Count Arnaud, who founded the original restaurant in 1918. She was the queen of 22 Mardi Gras balls between 1937 and 1968. Her collection of costumes is pretty spectacular, and somehow the crumbling 1950s mannequins that the costumes so stylishly adorn are endearing in their own right. Of course.

The French 75 Bar was added to the ever-expanding Arnaud's in 1979 as the Grill Bar; the name was changed to the French 75 Bar in 2003. The 19th-century antique back bar is often manned by Chris Hannah, a passionate student of the classics and creator of his own concoctions as well. Hannah is committed to using fresh ingredients paired with house-made drams, liqueurs, and syrups. This is especially evident in the Winter Waltz (rye, cognac, Averna amaro, allspice dram, and a garnish of a whole star anise). We're also fans of his Rebennack (rye, Averna amaro, Clement Creole Shrubb, Peychaud's bitters).

Of course, you'll want to try Hannah's French 75 (gin or cognac, lemon juice, sugar, champagne). There is some debate as to whether the gin version or the cognac version came first. Harry Craddock published the gin version in his indispensable *Savoy Cocktail Book* (1930), but it seems likely that the cognac version predates that. After all, it was invented in Paris at Harry's Bar and named after a bit of heavy artillery first used in World War I. The French were certainly more likely to mix with cognac than with gin during that era.

The comfortable seats in the French 75 Bar are arranged in small festive groups, commonly occupied by tourists enjoying drinks and cigars. Vintage-style lamps are in the form of monkeys dressed as bellboys. Of course. Visitors wishing to avoid the smoke may want to explore Arnaud's vintage 1918 Richelieu Bar. The structure dates back to the 18th century, and is allegedly haunted. Of course.

◆

There are two kinds of bartenders in the world: the friendly ones and the truculent ones. And then there are the bartenders that turn surliness into an art form. Those, should the customer be in just the right frame of mind, might come full circle

Bar Tonique

820 N. Rampart Street
New Orleans, LA
504.324.6045
www.bartonique.com

and become endearing in their cantankerousness as they thrust a cocktail across the bar at you. Visiting Bar Tonique on a slow and relaxed Sunday night, the Ramos Gin Fizz that eventually landed in my sweaty hands was so transcendent that we tipped the brusque bartender more than his abrupt attitude might normally warrant. The same moody mixologist prepared a Mai Tai for Gal Friday Night, and we have to confess that Trader Vic, had he been alive to taste it, would doubtlessly have approved.

Hidden away in an easy-to-miss spot across the street from the art deco entrance to Louis Armstrong Park, Bar Tonique is a cozy and casual neighborhood bar. Opened in August 2008 by the owners of the Delachaise, the interior is decorated in exposed brick, a few leather banquettes, candles, and a large blackboard listing a few dozen drinks of particular note. These libations are almost exclusively classics, which are the focus of Bar Tonique's cocktail program. Their commitment to making classics properly is demonstrated by what's in the glass, but is also hinted at on their menu, which lists the creation date for each drink listed. This veritable history lesson begins with the Mint Julep (1803; $8) and lands in relatively modern times with the Vieux Carré (1938; $7), which was invented a few blocks away at the Monteleone Hotel's Carousel Bar (see page 139). Along the way, there are 20 other classics, most dating from the 19th century. Your Widow's Kiss, Pimm's Cup, or Whiskey Smash are all in the $7/$8 range.

A shorter list of featured cocktails includes contemporary selections from Bar Tonique's staff, each credited to the mixologist who invented it. Gal Friday Night liked the looks of the Bitter Harvest by Steven Wilshire (Bernheim's wheat whiskey, Averna amaro, St. Elizabeth allspice dram, bitters; $9). Tonic water, ginger beer, and other ingredients are all made in-house, and are complimented with an extensive selection of bitters and tinctures.

The bar's very reasonable prices for classics made with craft and care are reason enough to stop in at Bar Tonique, but the fact that they stay open quite late (or until quite early, rather) makes it an attractive late-night (early morning) destination for New Orleans bartenders looking to unwind after a shift.

Some bars are destinations because of their cocktails, while others are destinations because of the bartender *and* the cocktails. Bar UnCommon is in the latter category, of course.

Bar UnCommon

Renaissance Pere Marquette Hotel
817 Common Street
New Orleans, LA
504.525.1111
www.baruncommon.com

The Renaissance Pere Marquette Hotel was built in 1925. Bar UnCommon opened in 2008, after renovations to the hotel were made in the wake of Hurricane Katrina. The ultra contemporary and brightly-lit lounge is not precisely where one might expect to find the best Juleps in the South, but this is a case of the man, not the room, making all the difference.

Fourth generation New Orleans bartender Chris McMillian spent some time in the Richelieu Bar within Arnaud's, as well as the Library Lounge in the Ritz-Carlton New Orleans, before settling in at Bar UnCommon. You'll find the friendly McMillian reliably shaking up a wide variety of libations, including his two specialties: Ramos Gin Fizz and Mint Julep.

The Ramos Gin Fizz is one of the drinks that defines New Orleans. Most bars in the Big Easy will make you one, but most will fail to do so *properly*. McMillian will not fail to do so properly. The Ramos Brothers Saloon was just a block away from the Pere Marquette, and was open from the 1880s until the dawn of Prohibition in 1919. Henry Ramos was one of the most famous bartenders of the era. His signature drink was made with London dry gin, lime juice, lemon juice, simple syrup, orange flower water, vanilla extract, heavy cream, egg white, and club soda. After getting everything balanced properly, you'll need to shake this puppy for two whole minutes to get the proper consistency.

While he's shaking up your liquid masterpiece, McMillian may start reciting verse. We've never bothered to ask him why. Doesn't matter. It works. A true ambassador for his hometown's cocktail history, McMillian is also a co-founder of the Museum of American Cocktail (see page 137).

Cure

4905 Freret Street
New Orleans, LA
504.302.2357
www.curenola.com

You don't see many bars whose decor features a six-foot-tall diagram showing the dissection of a cockroach, as if pulled straight from a 1920s college entomology lecture. This unusual design decision *might* function as a sort of tongue-in-cheek acknowledgment of the most ubiquitous of Louisiana's local fauna. Otherwise, it's just weird. Fortunately, Cure's location in New Orleans places them firmly on the non-creepy end of the very small spectrum of bars using insects as a legitimate decor scheme. Or, *pictures of* insects, anyway; let us be clear that we've never seen a *real* bug in the immaculate Cure.

What we have seen in this former firehouse, built in 1905, are plenty of challenging cocktails. Example: the Gunshop Fizz, which contains two full ounces of Peychaud's bitters. This unlikely drink could once be found in *Rogue Cocktails*, which co-author Kirk Estopinal calls "a cocktail guide for the bartender who wants to introduce their customers to a libation that is challenging, complex, and, most importantly, a new experience." Estopinal and co-Creator Maks Pazuniak (of the Counting Room in Brooklyn) have since replaced the book with a new edition/sequel, *Beta Cocktails*. If nothing else, Cure and *Rogue/Beta Cocktails* can be used as a fascinating microcosm for the migration of the modern tipple. The Art of Choke, for example, was invented by Kyle Davidson while

Estopinal was working with him at the Violet Hour in Chicago. Estopinal brought the drink to New Orleans and published it in *Rogue Cocktails*, and it is now served all over the world. This drink has become something of a modern classic with its bold combination of Cynar aperitif, Flor de Caña white rum, green Chartreuse, demerara syrup, lime juice, and Angostura bitters. The pun in the drink's name comes from one of the 13 herbs and plants used to distill Cynar: artichokes.

Although the Cure team makes the usual (and unusual) array of house ingredients (bitters, vermouth, syrups, tonic water, liqueurs, shrubs, cocktail cherries), Estopinal's house kümmel is an especially unique and exciting thing to see in an American bar. Kümmel is a liqueur made with caraway seed, cumin, and fennel, and is popular in the Netherlands, Germany, and Russia.

We enjoyed Nick Deitrich's Scotch & Salt (Dewar's Blended Scotch whisky, Cocchi Americano aperitif wine, Cocchi Vermouth di Torino, grapefruit juice, smoked salt tincture, orange peel; $9) and Mike Yusko's the Drink of Laughter & Forgetting (Cynar amaro, green Chartreuse, lime juice, demerara, Angostura bitters; $9). Not sure if that one is named for Milan Kundera or David Sylvian, but the inclusion of bartender Rhiannon Enlil's Bees for Pele twists the classic Bee's Knees into a tiki direction, while obtusely referencing Sylvian once again (La Favorite rhum agricole blanc, yellow Chartreuse, lemon juice, honey, house spice bitters, Angostura bitters; $11). You may have noted by now that all drinks are credited to the bartenders who created them. Cure isn't the only bar that does this, but it is always fantastic to see credit given where due to creative people who work hard.

Owner Neil Bodenheimer placed Cure in New Orleans' Freret neighborhood, far, far away from the French Quarter or most of the other tourist destinations. "[Cure was] inspired by the historical period when cocktails grew out of medicine and home remedies," Estopinal says. "Our idea at Cure is to reintroduce our guests to another time where the experience of having a cocktail and a bite to eat was both healthful and enjoyable." Coming from the home of Peychaud's bitters—originally sold as one of the aforementioned home remedies—there couldn't be a better town in which to espouse this philosophy.

Light but tasty treats at Cure include a list of $4 bar snacks, including goat cheese dates with pancetta, bourbon-roasted almonds and pecans, and white chocolate blackberries. Cure also serves slightly more substantial fare, such as a cured meat and cheese plate ($22), spicy Jamaican meat pie ($9), and peach and speck tartines ($10).

Bellocq, a new bar opened by Bodenheimer, Estopinal, and Matthew Kohnke, is located within the new Hotel Modern (936 St. Charles Avenue; 800.684.9525; www.thehotelmodern.com/bellocq). Named for New Orleans photographer E. J. Bellocq, the bar compliments a restaurant called Tamarind by Dominique, curated by chef Dominique Macquet.

Iris

Bienville House Hotel
321 N. Peters Street
New Orleans, LA
504.299.3944
www.irisneworleans.com

Many bars featured in this book use fresh ingredients, perhaps sourced locally and sustainably. But then there are the bars that seem to have an entire freaking garden growing behind the bar, along with preparatory tools such as a gigantic cutting board and a huge wooden sledgehammer. And really, huge wooden sledgehammers are what separate a great cocktail bar from a merely good one. But back to this garden of theirs. It is possible that no other bar in this book has more spermatophytes in use than Iris does. That's really saying something.

Chef Ian Schnoebelen and his partner Laurie Casebonne opened Iris in 2006, less than a year after Hurricane Katrina subsided. The original location was an old shack in Carrollton, a neighborhood in uptown New Orleans. In 2008, the restaurant moved to the Bienville House Hotel along the outskirts of the French Quarter. Iris serves an undeniably American cuisine, but one which is influenced by France (where Schnobelen was trained) and Asia. The menu changes daily based on what's available locally, but typical dishes include their take on gulf shrimp, given an Asian twist with coconut broth, baby bok choy, pickled shimeji mushrooms, basil coulis, and fried ginger ($26).

Sharon Floyd was in charge of the cocktail program until March 2012 (we look forward to meeting her successor), and made full use of the jungle behind her bar. Seasonal fruits and herbs are used to great effect at Iris, both for taste and for smell, which is a focus for Floyd. Ingredients like pine needles, lemongrass, and pandan leaf bring fresh, clean scents to her libations.

The Asian influence that Schnoebelen brings to the food at Iris is carried over to the bar. Iris maintains a selection of sakes, which are sometimes used in their cocktails. The Western Disguise (Oronoco rum, Well of Wisdom sake, Campari, sweet basil, reduction of soy sauce and pineapple) uses the soy to bring a little salinity to the drink, tying together the sweet and bitter aspects of the pineapple and Campari. The extensive vegetation in Iris's vision is also demonstrated in the Stems and Stalks (lemongrass-infused mezcal, St. Germain elderflower liqueur, Herbsaint pastis, celery juice, rosewater, citrus syrup) and the Todo Bien (Sombra mezcal, yellow Chartreuse, pineapple juice, coriander, sage). All cocktails are $11.

Oh, and the sledgehammer? Combine that with the handy Lewis bag—a canvas sack used for crushing ice—and you might have had a chance to see Floyd working off the sort of stress that yoga (her daytime job) just can't handle. We're sure the new mixo is going to be a prizefighter or something.

Museum of the American Cocktail

Riverwalk Marketplace
1 Poydras Street, Suite 169
New Orleans, LA
504.569.0405
www.museumoftheamericancocktail.org

The Museum of the American Cocktail in New Orleans is a single-room museum located within the Southern Food and Beverage Museum in the Riverwalk Marketplace mall. The exhibits

are devoted to tracing the history of the cocktail from the very first punches through the golden age of Jerry Thomas and then straight into the present day. About three dozen display cases contain a dizzying array of artifacts and plenty of informative text that will keep the average visitor occupied for an hour or two, and then there is the rest of the Food and Beverage museum to explore.

You'll find it all at the end of the food court (natch), near the Julia Street entrance to the Riverwalk Mall; this is the entrance furthest away from the French Quarter. Admission is $10.

FIRST CALL!

Historic Destinations to Explore in New Orleans

More so than any other city covered in this book, New Orleans contains a group of timeless bars whose historical legacy make them can't-miss destinations for the traveling cocktail enthusiast. Although we've grouped them here in a special "First Call!" section, be warned that they all serve cocktails that vary wildly in quality. Adjust epicurean expectations accordingly, but revel in the exhaustive history of 19th-century American boozing, as evidenced in the classic bars of New Orleans.

There are bar experiences where the room is spinning after you've had too many drinks, and then there are ones where parts of the room are spinning before you've even had breakfast. Welcome to the **Carousel Bar** (Hotel Monteleone, 214 Royal Street; 504.523.3341; www.hotelmonteleone.com). Antonio Monteleone, a cobbler from Sicily, built

the hotel in 1886, and the Carousel Bar was added in 1949. The bar itself is stationary, but the ring of seats surrounding the circular libation station rotates once every 20 minutes or so. The chair backs are all hand-painted with motifs of circus animals, which are complimented by the tent-like canopy above the spinning apparatus. This bar is the birthplace of the Vieux Carré (rye, cognac, dry vermouth, Bénédictine, Peychaud's bitters, Angostura bitters), which was first poured in this hotel by Walter Bergeron in 1938. *Vieux carré* is French for "old square," and is the Creole name for the French Quarter. The Monteleone has been host to musicians such as Louis Prima and Liberace, and has been a favorite flop house for authors including Hemingway, Faulkner, Capote, Tennessee Williams, and many others.

Napoleon House (500 Chartres Street; 504.522.4152; www.napoleonhouse.com) is named for Napoleon Bonaparte, of course. All the best bars are named for dictators. Nicholas Girod (mayor of New Orleans from 1812 to 1815) once lived in the building, and offered Napoleon the option of crashing there during the French ruler's 1821 exile. Napoleon didn't show up, time passed, and now it's a bar. Owned by the Impastato family since 1914, Napoleon House is known for Sazeracs and Pimm's Cups. It is said that the senior Impastato pushed the Pimm's Cup on people because he didn't like seeing customers get too wasted, and we all know how hard it is to get hammered on the gentle Pimm's.

The **Old Absinthe House** (240 Bourbon Street; 504.523.3181; www.oldabsinthehouse.com) typifies the palpable sense of history in New Orleans. The building was erected by Spanish importers Francisco Juncadella and Pedro Font in 1806. Over the next few decades, it evolved into an epicurie, a boot shop, and then a coffee house. Jacinto Aleix, a nephew of Juncadella's widow, started serving absinthe frappés in the 1840s, until Cayetano Ferrer bought the place in 1874 and renamed it the Absinthe Room. During the 1920s, the current owners violated Prohibition so many times that they were forced to sell off everything in the bar, including the iconic absinthe fountain topped with a brass statue of Napoleon Bonaparte. This was miraculously restored to the premises in 2005. Mark Twain, Oscar Wilde, William Thackeray, and Walt Whitman drank here, and Aleister Crowley is said to have written *The Green Goddess* here. Nowadays, you'll find wasted tourists spilling out onto the sidewalk from a dusty and rowdy bar filled with football memorabilia.

The **Sazerac Bar** (Roosevelt Hotel, 123 Baronne Street; 504.648.1200; www.therooseveltneworleans.com) was opened in 1923 and still retains its art deco vibe, historic Paul Ninas murals, and African walnut bar. The elegant hotel was restored after Hurricane Katrina and reopened with much fanfare in 2009. The Sazerac was not invented in this bar, but they will definitely serve you one.

Tujague's (823 Decatur Street; 504.525.8676; www. tujaguesrestaurant.com) is the second-oldest restaurant in New Orleans (the oldest is Antoine's). They opened in 1856, across the street from the French Market. In the bar half of the business, you'll have to stand at their antique cypress bar, as there are no stools (but there are four small tables along the opposite wall). Diners in the restaurant half may sit more comfortably as they sip Sazeracs and Absinthe Frappés.

LAST CALL!

More Destinations to Explore in New Orleans

Here are a few more contemporary slow drinks destinations that you might want to visit in New Orleans—yes, in addition to all of the historic places listed above.

There are two types of bar in New Orleans: those on Bourbon Street, and those that people over the age of 22 may want to visit. Oddly enough, **Bourbon House** (144 Bourbon Street; 504.522.0111; www.bourbonhouse.com)

is both. The house drink here might be the Bourbon Milk Punch (bourbon or brandy, milk, simple syrup, vanilla extract, nutmeg), which is what you'll want to sip while munching on crystal alligator (croc meat with spicy barbecue sauce and blue cheese dressing). Legend has it that the process of aging whiskey in charred barrels was discovered by accident when white whiskey was floated downriver from Kentucky to New Orleans. The charred barrels helped prevent contamination, but the five-month journey resulted in a transformed product by the time the hootch arrived in the Big Easy. Suffice to say, people liked it. Bourbon House pays homage to this history by offering around 90 American whiskeys. They also host events sponsored by the New Orleans Bourbon Society.

Brennan's (417 Royal Street; 504.525.9711; www.brennansneworleans.com) is part of a dynasty of restaurants founded by Owen Brennan. The Creole restaurant was opened in 1946 and more than a dozen others followed (including Bourbon House which is currently owned by another branch of the Brennan family). Try the Absinthe Suissesse (absinthe, cream, orgeat, egg white, orange flower water) or the Ojen Frappé (ojen, Peychaud's bitters, seltzer water). Ojen, which went out of production a few years ago, was a Spanish anise-flavored liqueur that was consumed for good luck on Fat Tuesday. The last 6,000 bottles were made available exclusively in the New Orleans area until selling out in 2009; a few places, such as Brennan's and Lüke, are still serving it. Enjoy it while you can!

Cochon (930 Tchoupitoulas Street; 504.588.2123; www.cochonrestaurant.com) is one of those restaurants that seems custom-made for special occasions. Their fully decadent food menu is festooned with items like fried rabbit livers with pepper jelly toast ($9), goat feta and pears ($12), oyster and bacon sandwiches ($15), and Louisiana cochon with turnips, cabbage, and cracklins ($23). Yeah, for once we were distracted from the solid cocktail menu. For a minute. Their attached butcher shop, **Butcher** (930 Tchoupitoulas Street; 504.588.7675), sells fantastic house-cured meats, small plates (duck pastrami sliders; $6), charcuterie, sandwiches, and a few selected cocktails. The same company also owns **Herbsaint** (701 Saint Charles Avenue; 504.524.4114; www.herbsaint.com), another worthy destination for solid upscale dining and cocktails.

Green Goddess (307 Exchange Place; 504.301.3347; www.greengoddessnola.com) is located in a tiny (or let us say *cozy*) space just around the corner from the Monteleone Hotel. They serve an eclectic array of food from all over the globe and some solidly-prepared cocktails, such as the Gentle Giant (green Chartreuse, G'Vine gin, lime juice, lotus tea, float of Clear Creek Douglas Fir eau de vie; $15) and the Col. Ferrari, a Manhattan variant (Buffalo Trace bourbon, Bonal aperitif, Fernet-Branca amaro; $9). Their wine list is rather impressive, too.

Loa (221 Camp Street; 504.553.9550; www.ihhotel. com) is located inside the International House Hotel, and is the current home of bartender Alan Walter. Moving on from his previous gig sharing the bar with Sharon Floyd at Iris, Walter has brought the herbacious textures of Iris with him to Loa. Try the Rites of Spring with tarragon, mint, and Lakeview pine-needle-infused Velvet Falernum. Walter speaks fluent Latin and writes plays when not making his own infusions. If he wrote plays *about* making his own infusions, we'd see those, too.

Lüke (333 St. Charles Avenue; 504.378.2840; www. lukeneworleans.com) is chef John Besh's brasserie and homage to old New Orleans French-German restaurants. Lüke combines cuisines from France, Germany, and New Orleans in a space that feels much older (in a good way) than its 2007 vintage.

AUSTIN

One might think that edgy Austin would be wiping the floor with more conservative Houston—or any other place south of the Mason-Dixon line—in the cocktail world. Alas, pickings seem to be slim in the City of the Violet Crown. Here are just a few very good reasons to visit the town that has launched a local campaign to "keep Austin weird."

Bar Congress

200 Congress Avenue
Austin, TX
512.827.2760
www.congressaustin.com

There are two types of bar in the world: those that are within stumbling distance of your home, and those that are in the same building as your $7 million luxury condo. The Austonian condo tower boasts 56 floors, 188 residences, a ton of original art on the premises, and three conjoined places to eat and drink. Congress Restaurant, Bar Congress, and Second Bar + Kitchen all opened at the very end of 2010. All three share one large space. Chef David Bull calls the prix fixe menu at Second Bar + Kitchen "Natural American" cuisine. Seasonal and local small plates ($8–$14), large plates ($16–$24), and pizzas ($12–$16) compliment the slightly more elegant fare at Congress, where a three-course menu is $75 and a seven-course tasting menu will set you back $115. That's about 1/61,000th the cost of a 56th-floor penthouse mortgage.

Right between the two eateries is Bar Congress, where Jason Stevens (of the Tigress, East Side Show Room, and Austin-based bitters company Bad Dog Bar Craft) has recently taken over for founding bar manager Adam Bryan, also formerly of East Side Showroom. Bar Congress is a narrow space, with its scant 22 seats separated from the two restaurant dining rooms by curtains.

Although sommelier June Rodil (once awarded the title of Texas's Best Sommelier) curates a solid selection of European wines, you'll also want to visit bartender Brian Dressel. He might mix you one of the bar's twists on classics, such as the Congress GT (Cascade-hopped gin, house quinine, grapefruit bitters, seltzer; $8) or the Corpse Reviver #33 (Bols genever, Acqua de Cedro grappa, lemon juice, celery bitters; $14). Gal Friday Night was honestly more drawn to creations like the Preferred Lies (Earl Grey-infused bourbon, apple drinking vinegar, Domaine de Canton foam; $13) and the Montegomatica (J. Wray & Nephew overproof rum, Fernet-Branca amaro, John D. Taylor's Velvet Falernum, lime juice, float of Cruzan blackstrap rum; $13). We also liked the Walker Manhattan (Michter's US 1 Straight Rye, Vya red vermouth, Angostura bitters, Regan's orange bitters; $12). Austin's own Treaty Oak rum is used in the Velpar (Treaty Oak rum, lemon juice, St. Germain elderflower liqueur, absinthe). The Treaty Oak, by the way, is the last surviving tree from a grove of 14 that were sacred to the Comanche and Tonkawa peoples. Velpar is a hardwood herbicide that was used to vandalize the tree in 1989 and nearly killed it.

◆▶

As far as we know, all of the bars that serve cocktails named after Finnish modernist architects are located—as unlikely as this may seem—in Austin, Texas. Austin isn't a world hotbed for modernism, but it is a place that prides itself

East Side Show Room

1100 East 6th Street
Austin, TX
512.467.4280
www.eastsideshowroom.com

on being weird. Thus: the Mondays With Aalto (Krogstad aquavit, lemon juice, crème de cacao, Triplum orange liqueur, crème de violette), named in honor of the great Alvar Aalto.

We like Aalto's Finlandia Hall (1962–71) and his Museum

of Modern Art in Aalborg, Denmark (1958–72) enough that his touch is sorely missed when viewing the building that now houses East Side Show Room. The plain, square, white-brick box (a former grocery store), built in the early 20th century, is only slightly younger than Aalto himself (born in 1898).

Inside, the mother-daughter team of owners have kept the brick exposed and added subdued lighting, metal sculptures by co-owner Mickie Spencer, huge old wooden kegs, and candlelit café tables with coins embedded in them. The cozy, casual café atmosphere is a place where, on any given night, you might catch poetry or literature readings, contemporary dance, live music (with jazz and European folk influences), silent movies projected on the walls, theater, or puppet shows. (And really, the puppet shows are the reason we go to most bars.) Interestingly, almost all of the art, furniture, and decor in East Side Showroom is for sale, giving us a clue as to what inspired the café's name.

Since opening in 2009, the bar has been the stomping ground for current and former Bar Congress honchos Jason Stevens and Adam Bryan, as well as for Contigo's current bar manager, Houston Eaves. Clearly it's a nexus for Austin's cocktail community. Current executive barkeep Chauncy James oversees the creation of syrups, tinctures, infusions, and the preserving of pickles, cherries, and fruits. Herbs are picked fresh each day, probably not long after the juice is squeezed. A concise menu of 15-ish cocktails is heavily weighted toward unmolested standards (French 75, Margarita, Pimm's Cup), but a few house creations looked tempting, including the Devil in Texas (Ocho reposado tequila, lemon juice, ginger, crème de cassis; $11) and the Blush (aquavit, grapefruit juice, St. Germain elder-flower liqueur, Cocchi Americano aperitif wine, "bubbles"; $10).

Executive chef Sonya Cote's Texas chow (think bison carpaccio) comes from one of the 30 local farms that the restaurant supports. In fact, you can't help but see the list on every table, outlining where every ingredient is sourced from. Most of it is pretty close by (in Texas terms, "close by" is plus or minus 300 miles, so in this case it's all *very* close by).

LAST CALL!
More Destinations to Explore in Austin

The Belmont (305 W. 6th Street; 512.457.0300; www. thebelmontaustin.com) is a convincingly-decorated throwback to mid-century America. Designed to evoke a classic-era restaurant and bar, the Belmont is all about dark wood and green leather booths. They also have an outdoor patio where contemporary live music can be enjoyed. Dinner fare is mainly from local farms, and includes choices in keeping with the decor: tilapia, beef medallions, and meatloaf. The cocktail menu is divided between Martinis, Cocktails, and Mojitos n' Muddles, with their Old-Fashioned considered a muddle, and their Sidecar considered a Martini. "During the winter months," says chief mixo Larry Miller II, "the menu will adjust by adding on some rich dessert Martinis in exchange for the fresh fruit Martinis."

Created as an homage to the Contigo Ranch in South Texas, **Contigo** (2027 Anchor Lane; 512.614.2260; www. contigotexas.com) is a neighborhood eatery in the Mueller development in central East Austin. All of the restaurant's rustic wood furniture was hand-built by Brian Chilton. Cocktails are hand-built by mixologist Houston Eaves with the aid of local bees, as in the classic Bee's Knees (gin, Contigo Ranch honey, lemon juice; $7). Eaves is also crafting house-made bitters, syrups, and liqueurs. Being in Texas, beer taps are made from antlers.

Fino (2905 San Gabriel Street; 512.474.2905; www. finoaustin.com) opened in July 2005, serving modern Mediterranean cuisine in a bright second-floor space. Original chief mixologist Bill Norris has left, with Josh Loving now behind the stick. We liked the ideas behind the Pim Pim Pot-Still (Pimm's, Smith & Cross pot-still rum, St. Elizabeth allspice dram, allspice syrup, Chinese five-spice bitters; $10) and Ghost of the Pine (Rittenhouse rye, Nux Alpina walnut liqueur, Zirbenz Stone Pine liqueur, Del Maguey Chichicapa mezcal, Lapsang Souchong tea, orange bitters; $12).

Haddingtons (601 W. 6th Street; 512.992.0204; www. haddingtonsrestaurant.com) is named after the ship that owner Michael Polombo's great-grandfather captained. Chef Chris Turgeon serves classic American fare such as hanger steak ($25), buttermilk chicken ($18), and salmon and corn fritters ($12). Bill Norris, formerly of Fino, is slinging drinks such as a duck fat rye Sazerac, working alongside head bartender Brandon Burkart and DC transplant Tiffany Short, who is known for her vegetable infusions. Classics are $9, while house creations are $10. We were drawn to the Flippin' Wisenheimer (Old Tom gin, wheat beer, orange liqueur, allspice, acid phosphate, farm egg).

Péché (208 W. 4th Street; 512.494.4011; www. pecheaustin.com) serves French comfort food sourced locally, as envisioned by chef Jason Dodge and mixologist/ owner Rob Pate, paired with plenty of absinthe. The extremely long bar is dotted with absinthe fountains; library ladders behind the bar are required to reach booze stacked up on shelves that reach toward the ceiling. At marble tables or on comfy sofas, you may sample libations from a long list of classics and classic variants, such as the Final Say ($10), a variant on the Last Word that substitutes rye for the traditional gin. Also behind the stick are Madelyn Kay and Russel Davis, who is responsible for the Devil's Cocktail (gin, Paula's Texas Lemon, St. Germain elderflower liqueur, lime juice, honey jalapeño syrup, Angostura bitters).

HOUSTON

Space City has its fair share of bars and barbecues, but we want to direct you to one of those must-visit places that cocktail nerds just won't stop talking about: Anvil Bar and Refuge.

S ome bars are named subtly or cryptically, whereas others just seem to be begging for us to start making puns. In the case of Anvil, the thing that is the most (ahem) *striking* about the place is how the locals enjoy (um) *pounding* cocktails without getting too (errr) *hammered*,

Anvil Bar & Refuge

1424 Westheimer Road
Houston, TX
713.523.1622
www.anvilhouston.com

although the good-looking among you might get (this is pushing it) *hit on*.

All right, with that nonsense out of the way, the name Anvil actually comes from the owner Bobby Heugel's perspective on drink-making. He prefers to keep things simple, working with the same old-fashioned attention to craftsmanship that you'd find in the shop of a 19th-century carpenter, cooper, glazier, or, yes, blacksmith. There are no arm garters or ironic mustaches at Anvil; the 19th-century fashions of New York bartenders just don't fit in with a Texas mindset. You will find ample nods to the past in the decor, however, which was collected by Heugel and co-owners Kevin Floyd and Steve Flippo in the months prior to the bar's March 2009 launch. Shelving from a piano store that Heugel and Floyd worked in as teens is just the beginning. Vintage glassware comes from thrift shops in the Montrose area. Purse hooks under a weathered steel bar are made from rail ties. Even the building itself echoes a workshop vibe, since it was built in the 1950s as a tire store.

In addition to a chalkboard listing a half-dozen daily cocktail recommendations, Anvil's menu contains around 15 originals, and another 15 featured classics. Of course, the drinks on this menu are made with house-made bitters, sodas, infusions, ginger beer, and liqueurs, all built from ingredients sourced locally when possible. Some of their bitters and syrups are available for sale. For the serious historians among you (that's all of you, right?), Anvil offers a list of 100 cocktails that everyone should try at least once. Their own explanation sums it up: "We at Anvil would be remiss in our duties if we did not mention that there are certain libations we feel you should try at least once in you life . . . for better or worse." A two-sided card lets you check them off, from Absinthe drip to Zombie.

As for the originals, Anvil's most popular might be Huegel's the Brave (Del Maguey Chichicapa mezcal, Hacienda de Chihuahua Sotol Plata mezcal, Averna amaro, orange curaçao, Angostura bitters, flamed orange zest; $12). Chris Frankel devised the Leyden Jar (genever, Pimms No. 1, Pineau des Charentes aperitif, cane vinegar, raisin; $8), while Ornella Ashcroft is responsible for the Smoke & Mirrors (rye, Fernet-Branca amaro, crème de cacao, lemon juice, black peppercorn, egg white; $10). Simplifying things a bit is Matt Tanner's Bitter Julep (gin, Campari, sugar, mint; $9).

Anvil's modest food selections are courtesy of chef Dax McAnear. His menu includes flatbreads, sandwiches, charcuterie, and cheese from Houston Dairymaids. More Anvilisms: plan for some extra time to find parking when visiting Anvil, and be prepared for the fact that the 85-capacity room feels crowded and quite loud at 60. Management usually caps admission around there, so be prepared for a wait on the weekends.

Anvil began holding cocktail classes in mid-2010. They also offer a short list of hard-to-find beers, including one that is casked. Tuesday is tiki night.

Huegel and chef Chris Shepherd (of Catalan) also opened **Underbelly** (1100 Westheimer Road; 713.528.9800; www.underbellyhouston.com) in late 2011. Verily defining Texas eating, the restaurant has its own butcher shop on premises, so that pigs, grass-fed cows, goats, and fish are as fresh as possible. Cocktail news forthcoming . . .

T here are two
types of bar
in the world: those
with a giant bea-
ver painted on the
side of the build-
ing, and those with
a giant platypus

Beaver's

2310 Decatur Street
Houston, TX
713.864.2328
www.beavershouston.com

painted on the side of the building. If a bar doesn't have either of
these, it probably isn't worth visiting.

Monica Pope's restaurant opened in late 2007, within a rather
storied example of beaver-badged real estate. The previous bar on
the site—also called Beaver's—replaced a business called Doodie's
(we couldn't make this up) in what was once an icehouse during
pre-refrigeration times. In your great-granpappy's heyday, an icehouse was the only place where one could obtain ice in Texas, and
in due course icehouses became community gathering places. Bar
manager Eric Cody tells us that Beaver's aims to maintain that casual neighborhood vibe while serving top-tier cocktails and—of
course—live-fire, slow-cooked barbecue.

Cody is not shy about discussing Beaver's place in more recent
history. "Beaver's was one of the bars that sparked the cocktail revolution in Houston," he says. "As the first mixology and classic cocktail bar in the city, Beaver's has been the starting point for many
of Houston's well-known mixologists, such as Bobby Heugel and
Kevin Floyd of Anvil Bar and Refuge, and other great mixologists
like Claire Sprouse."

Cody is clearly enamored with Houston and its environs. "Beaver's is all about local, all the way from the food and drinks to the
building and design," he enthuses. "We support local products every
chance we can." A glance behind the bar might reveal Texas spirits
such as Treaty Oak rum and gin, Paula's Texas Lemon and Paula's
Texas Orange liqueurs, Railean rum, Balcones Baby Blue whisky,
Balcones True Blue whisky, Balcones Rumble liqueur, and others
(Balcones chooses to spell "whisky" the Scotch/Canadian way).

These products are put to very good use in some of the house
cocktails, including the Dip Slip Fizz by Sprouse, a variation of
the Ramos Gin Fizz (Balcones Rumble, lemon juice, lime juice,

lavender-infused honey, cream, egg white, and lavender-black-tea tincture), and the No Name Punch by Eric Cody (Treaty Oak rum, Domaine de Canton ginger liqueur, Mathilde peach brandy, St. Germain elderflower liqueur, and lemon juice). Balcones Rumble is a unique liquor distilled from Texas wildflower honey, Mission figs, and turbinado sugar. It isn't rum, but it may be closer to rum than it is to any other liquor. Given the barbecue specialties on the food menu, it should come as no surprise that the bar also smokes rye whiskey for their Smoky Julep (smoked rye, powdered sugar, mint). They also do a Bloody Mary variation with powdered bacon fat, sugar, and salt mix on the rim of the glass, garnished with a strip of candied bacon.

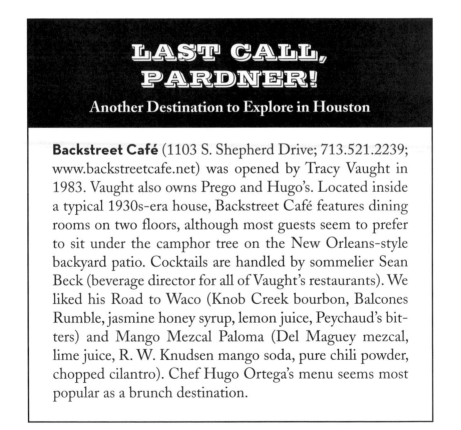

LAST CALL, PARDNER!

Another Destination to Explore in Houston

Backstreet Café (1103 S. Shepherd Drive; 713.521.2239; www.backstreetcafe.net) was opened by Tracy Vaught in 1983. Vaught also owns Prego and Hugo's. Located inside a typical 1930s-era house, Backstreet Café features dining rooms on two floors, although most guests seem to prefer to sit under the camphor tree on the New Orleans-style backyard patio. Cocktails are handled by sommelier Sean Beck (beverage director for all of Vaught's restaurants). We liked his Road to Waco (Knob Creek bourbon, Balcones Rumble, jasmine honey syrup, lemon juice, Peychaud's bitters) and Mango Mezcal Paloma (Del Maguey mezcal, lime juice, R. W. Knudsen mango soda, pure chili powder, chopped cilantro). Chef Hugo Ortega's menu seems most popular as a brunch destination.

DENVER

The Mile-High City has a very nice cocktail scene developing. It is certainly the very best in the Mountain time zone. Need somewhere to stop over when driving between Chicago and the West Coast? Make it the Queen City of the Plains.

Sometimes a bar is just a bar, and if the drinks are solid, that's all that matters (within these pages, at least). Some bars are decorated quite well, but that doesn't necessarily mean there's a *concept* in place. As for the concept bars/restaurants, we can talk tiki plenty (and already have), but we can also consider the wide spectrum separating Planet Hollywood from Hollywood's the Edison (see page 257), and everything in-between. The only real question is whether the concept works or not.

Beatrice & Woodsley

38 S. Broadway Street
Denver, CO
303.777.3505
www.beatriceandwoodsley.com

At Denver's whimsical Beatrice and Woodsley (opened in May 2008), the concept works. The atmosphere is supposedly based on a 19th-century folk tale (of which we could find no record outside of the restaurant's press). Beatrice, the porcelain and proper daughter of a French winemaker, is in love with burly rural cooper Woodsley. He builds her a rustic cabin, and a century later, you're dining in its remains as the woods creep in to reclaim it. Fair enough. Aspen trunks "grow" from floor to ceiling, chainsaws decorate the backbar, old wooden planks cover the walls, and wispy, diaphanous curtains separate the booths. Yellow gels cover the windows and filter the bright mountain sunlight, so that you're dining in a permanent golden dawn. An interesting, if confusing, pulley system operates the bathroom sinks, which are outside of the restrooms, barley hidden behind a trellis. Fellow diners may watch you wash up (and you're *so busted* if you don't). In short, Beatrice and Woodsley works

as a more feminine take on the endless macho-rustic decor schemes seen all over this part of the country.

Well, actually, it works only if the food and drink do. (Hint: they do.)

Owners Kevin Delk and John Skogstad (of Mario's Double Daughter's Salotto and Two-Fisted Mario's Pizza) decided on small plates equally inspired by the 19th and 21st centuries for their cuisine. Executive chef Pete List offers hearty options like whole roasted Colorado striped bass ($35), herb'd, garlic'd, and roasted leg o' lamb ($26), and country ground duck ($18). The crawfish beignets ($9) and crispy veal sweetbreads ($12) looked quite nice, too.

At the bar, Gal Friday Night (who has a masters degree in folklore) started with their daily restorative ($8), which ended up being a little bowl of chowder, before ordering the Garter in Eden (Hendricks gin, dandelion root simple syrup, lemon juice, muddled apple and cucumber; $11). Served on the rocks, it is light, crisp, and lemony, with cuke finish. In the Beet n' Path (Montanya Oro rum, white-tea-and-brown-sugar simple syrup, beet juice, lemon, splash soda; $9), the beet is present but not overbearing, but we could have used a touch more of that yummy locally-made Montanya rum. The Europa 51 (Right gin, Cynar bitter aperitif, apple juice, citrus pepper tincture, orange peel; $11) is intense, just how we like it. The Cupacabra (tequila, St. Germain elderflower liqueur, lemon juice, orange juice, Fresno chili-honey syrup) is no longer on the menu, but you might be able to ask for the honey-ish yet peppery libation.

The booze collection among the chainsaws behind the bar is well-curated; any bar that invests in Chartreuse VEP is all right in our book (*this* book, in fact), and the local Montanya rum and Leopold Bros. gin work too.

If you're in the mood for something completely different, try

Sputnik, virtually across the street (3 S. Broadway; 720.570.4503; www.sputnikdenver.com). Cool twentysomething rockers, vaguely 1950s decor, good beer, satisfying bar food, and a photo booth. It probably doesn't belong in this book, but you might like this one after you've got the midnight hour and three fancy-pants cocktail bars behind you.

When called for, most bars will blend their own rums (such as when preparing one of the many tiki drinks that re-

Colt & Gray

1553 Platte Street #120
Denver, CO
303.477.1447
www.coltandgray.com

quire two or three different rums). But Colt & Gray have gone a step further. They have developed their own carefully balanced house blend, and they've done so with admirable components: Pyrat, Matusalem 12-year, and Cruzan Black Strap. They call the blend simply "XO," and we were lucky enough to try it in the AlcaRon (XO rum, Cynar bitter aperitif, house grapefruit bitters; $9).

Colt & Gray opened in August of 2009. Nelson Perkins and Allie Perkins are the owners, and Nelson is the executive chef. The chief mixologist is Kevin Burke. While looking over the dinner menu (a few selections: foie gras terrine, sautéed sweetbreads, seared King salmon, steak tartare, roasted free-range "Buddhist" chicken breast, and several programs of cheese and charcuterie), we had a chat with Burke. "The restaurant is, at it's core, an American restaurant drawing extensively from Western European cuisine," he said. "We focus on having close relationships with our farmers and producers. This translates to the bar program as well, where we have been chosen to showcase several highly-allocated wines, beers, and spirits. We try to provide a service to the neighborhood, and strive to be a place where anyone can come in, have a cocktail and unwind with a little snack, or come in for a multi-course tasting menu paired with selections from our cellar." Indeed, upon entering the restaurant, Gal Friday

Night remarked that it felt upscale in there, with a well-dressed clientele of young professionals and an impossibly cute hostess. But the fact that they let *me* in gives legitimacy to Burke's "anyone can come in . . ." line. Whew. I need another drink.

Parker, the co-bar manager, gave us a menu neatly divided between Original Cocktails and Vintage Cocktails. We went for the Hapsburg, which seemed like it might do the trick (Bols genever, Krogstad aquavit, Ramazotti amaro, Rothman & Winter apricot brandy; $11). It did. We also liked the look of house creation the B3 (bourbon, Bénédictine, Bonal Gentiane-Quina aperitif wine), and the Whimpering Barback (hibiscus-infused gin, lime juice, orgeat, house ginger beer).

We liked seeing the Caprock gin (from Hotchkiss, Colorado's Peak Spirits) behind the bar. "We always try to feature at least one locally-made spirit in the cocktail menu at all times," Burke remarked. To wit: the Colorado Dachshund (Leopold Bros. American small batch whiskey, Avery Joe's pilsner, ginger, grapefruit juice). Of course, Colt & Grey make their own falernum, orgeat, and pimento dram, among more complex ingredients. "We try to make as much in-house as we can," Burke said. "We are very lucky to have access to the kitchen's Cryovac and immersion circulators, this permits us to effectively 'vacuum distill' ingredients for test batches and recipe creation. Currently we are infusing gin with local pluots [plum–apricot hybrids] to make our take on a sloe gin."

* * *

Root Down

1600 W. 33rd Street
Denver, CO
303.993.4200
www.rootdowndenver.com

The Beastie Boys recorded "Root Down" in 1995, largely basing the track on the eponymous 1972 ditty by legendary jazz organist Jimmy Smith. I did a gig with him once (ask me in person). So, how many degrees of separation does that give me from Root Down? Only one. We went there.

Jimmy Smith named his tune after a bit of jazz slang that directs players to get back to the root of a song after a jam. This back-to-basics approach lends itself to the restaurant/bar's philosophy too. "When the whole cocktail craze hit, you basically had to go to New York, Chicago, or San Francisco to get a good cocktail," says head mixologist Mike Henderson. "With that came some serious attitude, and rightfully so, but it took some of the fun out of going to a bar. Luckily now some of those attitudes are going away and it's getting back to being all about service and the guest. Don't get me wrong, I think going to a speakeasy style bar like [Please Don't Tell] in New York is one of the most 'fun' cocktail experiences on the planet. But for the everyday drinker I think they just want to relax, have a good time, and know that the people on the other side of the bar are looking out to make sure they have a great experience."

Gal Friday Night and I were pleased to peruse a "field to fork" menu containing "globally influenced seasonal cuisine," such as organic risotto ($13), Maple Leaf Farms hoisin duck confit slider ($13), and Rocky Mountain bistro beef tender ($27).

In a restaurant that prides itself on things like being 100 percent wind-powered, being built and finished with 70 percent reclaimed and recycled materials, and who list shout-outs to 20 local suppliers on their menu, the bar program must follow suit. According to Henderson, seasonality comes into play more so than any other single component. "When we're getting ready to launch a new menu, the first thing I do is go and talk to the chefs," he says. "I want to find out not only what's going to be in season but more importantly what they are going to be using on the menu so that the drinks can ultimately compliment the food."

A straight line can be drawn from this philosophy to the wide array of Colorado products behind the bar, including hootch from Leopold Bros., Stranahan's, Peak Spirits, Boca Loca cachaça, and Peach Street Distillers. "These guys all make great products and we definitely like to support the home team," says Henderson. This attitude is supported by cocktails including the Cardamom Gin Fizz (Cap Rock organic gin, Domaine de Canton ginger liqueur, lime juice, cardamom simple syrup, cream, soda), the Blackberry Smash (Leopold Bros. blackberry whiskey, Grand Marnier, lemon juice, mint), and the Blood Orange Caipirinha (Boca Loca cachaça, sugar, lime juice, blood orange juice). All are $9/$10. We also tried the sweet and nutty Fig Thyme Out (fig-thyme-infused bourbon, Nocello walnut liqueur, cranberry juice, lemon juice; $10).

Now we're thinking of that other Jimmy Smith track. No, not "Back at the Chicken Shack," or "Picknickin'," or "Pork Chop," or even "One Mint Julep" . . . no, bust out the vinyl, kids, we'll let you figure it out for yourselves.

"I think what I'm always trying to be is a 'beverage professional.' I think it's something more bartenders should consider. Look, if you are behind the bar, you can't just know about cocktails. You have to know about beer, wine, tea, coffee, water, and even soda now. It's not enough in our industry anymore to just be a cocktail dork, you have to go beyond that."

—MIKE HENDERSON, Root Down

Occidental

3301 Tejon Street
Denver, CO
303.284.0053
www.thesqueakybean.net

There is a bar at 3301 Tejon Street. You'll want to visit it. But pay attention, this gets tricky (drawing your own Venn diagram may help).

Johnny Ballen and Josh Olsen opened a bar called Squeaky Bean at 3301 Tejon Street, featuring chow by chef Max MacKissock, but it soon closed. Before it closed, bartender Sean Kenyon left Steuben's to work at Squeaky

Bean. After Squeaky Bean closed, Kenyon opened a bar called Williams & Graham (see page 161). Meanwhile, some of the owners of Squeaky Bean shrank the kitchen and reopened in the same space, with a new name: Occidental. Then, some of the owners of Squeaky Bean found a new space across town and reopened a new Squeaky Bean 2.0, calling it Squeaky Bean (again).

We visited 3301 Tejon Street when it was Squeaky Bean 1.0, and were thrilled with the Squeaky Spritz (prosecco, Aperol aperitif, sparkling water, castel vetrano olive; $8) and the Proximus Marg (Proximus silver tequila, Rothman orchard pear brandy, agave nectar, lime juice; $8). "It tastes like a really good margarita," said the succinct Gal Friday Night. "Lime-y and light." That's about all we can ask for. Except for another drink. The Drinkable Molly Brown (Stranahan's Colorado whiskey, Rothman apricot liqueur, Kopke 10-year tawny port, pure cinnamon extract; $10) is another drink, and we asked for it, and we drank it. And we liked it.

Now you have twice the options. Occidental at 3301 Tejon Street is even more cocktail-focused than Squeaky Bean 1.0 was, and that's a very good thing. Not that it was bad before, mind you. But there's less of a food menu there now. The new **Squeaky Bean** will be located in the historic Saddlery Building (500 Wynkoop Street), built in 1900. Ballen says that the new location's larger kitchen will expand upon the previous version's chow, while carrying over the great cocktails, toy pigs, and Farrah Fawcett shrine.

◄─◄►►─►

There are a lot of businesses in this book that do good things for their communities. Supporting local brands and farmers is something we've been less than subtle about pointing out, but of course communities can be

Steuben's Food Service

523 E. 17th Avenue
Denver, CO
303.830.1001
www.steubens.com

supported in many other ways. According to their website, Steuben's has been helping the Denver area by making charitable donations to

no less than 50 orga-
nizations each year.
That's your booze
money at work,
people. We like the
idea that some of
the income from the
last few drinks we
quaffed at Steuben's
went toward schools,
arts organizations, hospitals, and environmental preservation groups.
It is kind of poetic that by trashing our livers, we are helping some
little kid manage leukemia.

Barkeep! Another round! We've got kids to save!

Josh Wolkon and his wife Jen launched Vesta Dipping Grill
in 1996, and followed that success with Steuben's Food Service
in the Uptown area of Denver. Next, Brandon and Emily Bieder-
man helped them get Steuben's Food Truck rolling, and in 2012,
with the help of Jeff Bustos, they will open a new space adjacent to
Steuben's (17th and Pennsylvania) that will include another dining
room, another bar, and a ping pong parlor.

Wolkon named Steuben's after the Boston restaurant that his
great-uncles Max and Joe opened in 1945. Subsequently, the graph-
ic design (and to a degree, the interior design) of Steuben's screams
1945. Vintage cocktail shakers above the bar underline the hints of
mid-century modern flavor found in the decor. The exposed brick
and ductwork, however, feel more contemporary and industrial.

Bar manager Randy Layman replaced longstanding Steuben's
icon Sean Kenyon in September of 2010, moving over from his
post at Vesta. Mixologists Mark Grounds, Courtney Wilson, and
Randy's twin brother, Ryan, complete the current team.

Mark was on duty when we darkened Steuben's door. To the
sound of Elvis Costello, the Clash, and New Order's "Ceremony,"
we perused a solid beer list (loaded with Colorado selections), an
array of wines, ports, and punches, a long booze list, and a Scorpion
Bowl for $16. As for cocktails, we spied 16 classics on the menu
and 10 house creations.

First down the hatch was the Uptown Cocktail (rye, Carpano

Antica Formula vermouth, Campari, roasted apples, cinnamon-infused simple syrup), which is a close relative of the classic Boulevardier (bourbon, Campari, sweet vermouth). Is it a Negroni with bourbon or a Manhattan with Campari? You be the judge; add cinnamon and apples and it's something new altogether.

Next up were the Eleventh Hour (Leopold gin, Rothman & Winter Orchard Apricot liqueur, lemon-ginger simple syrup, lemon juice, St. Elizabeth allspice dram), the 100 Years Cocktail (Leopold Bros. rye, Peach Street peach brandy, Ramazzotti amaro, orange bitters), and Steuben's Rock & Rye (Wild Turkey 101 rye infused with orange zest and lemon zest, clove, cassia bark, horehound, rock candy). Horehound, by the by, is an herb used as a natural cough suppressant, and is used here as nod to the era when bitters had medicinal uses, and were sweetened to make them more palatable. This is where the first cocktails came from, over 200 years ago.

Steuben's is also known for American comfort food: lobster roll, fried chicken, mac and cheese. No one said *Latin* America was excluded, so we went for the Cubano—a big slice of ham, pulled pork, cheese, and pickles. Delicious and sloppy as hell.

At this time we'd like to turn your attention to Don Hermann and Sons kosher dill pickles. These are the best pickles ever. They're made in Garrettsville, Ohio, a rural community about 40 miles southeast of Cleveland. We have never seen them anywhere except for in a couple of east side Jewish delis near Cleveland. Anyway, they have them at Steuben's, which might be a phenomenon even more worthy of admiration than the Wolkon family's charitable contributions.

Maybe.

—◀●▶—

Which bars are our very, very, very favorites? The ones that sell books *and* booze! Located in a building that was originally a drugstore and a soda fountain, Williams & Graham Booksellers opened on

November 15, 2011. They sell books about cocktail history, modern recipe books, reprints of 19th-century recipe books, books by famous boozers (from Hemingway to Bukowski), and hopefully at least one cocktail travel guide (cough). The shop also sells bar utensils. The hostesses, erm . . . shop girls in the bookstore may not admit that there's something special behind one of the bookshelves, but those in the know just might be admitted to the speakeasy (gasp! Scandalous!) if there's room in the 62-person capacity space.

Owners Todd Colehour (of Kona Grill) and Sean Kenyon (of more or less all the other Denver bars listed above) aren't precious or pompous about their theme; they want the bar to be seen as a neighborhood bar, in spite of the subterfuge required for entry. Their team is complimented by Josh Smith (of TAG), Jason Patz, and bar manager Courtney Wilson (Steuben's). Low lighting is provided by candles, with the sounds of jazz filling a room of deep wood and original tin ceilings. Velvet curtains frame brown leather booths separated from the bar by a waist-high bookshelf.

The menu—which the slightly nerdy and always awesome Gal Friday Night called "slightly nerdy/awesome"—features essays from modern spirits writers such as Danny Valdez, Paul Pacult, Dave Wondrich, and Steve Olsen. Among this wholesome literature are a selection of drinks that are kept simple and elegant, crafted in pre-Prohibition style. The word "molecular" is rarely uttered within these walls.

Williams & Graham also offers a small menu of four appetizers, four entrees, and four desserts by David Bumgardner of Highland Tavern, served until late.

Z Cuisine Parisian Bistrot & À Côté Bar à Absinthe

2239 W. 30th Avenue
Denver, CO
303.477.1111
www.zcuisineonline.com

No matter how good a restaurant may be, sometimes you need to go next door. Z Cuisine was opened in 2004 by chef Patrick Dupays, who was intent on serving the sort of rural French cooking

he grew up on. The popularity of the 35-seat restaurant led him to open À Côté (literally: "next door") in 2007. Initially created as a place for customers to have a glass of wine while waiting for a table, À Côté has developed its own identity. Located on a quiet street corner in a hilly residential neighborhood a fair distance from downtown Denver, the area is appropriate to the French countryside motif that Z Cuisine and À Côté aim to evoke. Art nouveau details in zinc and copper are appropriate anomalies; the cozy and woody interior is really all about the mismatched furniture, the menu on a chalkboard, a found-glass chandelier, folksy art, and French movies projected on À Côté's wall.

Wanting something different from wine, yet still associated with France, Dupays decided to make À Côté an absinthe bar. About a dozen absinthes are available in the $7–$10 range. Kübler, La Fée, Le Tourment Vert, St. George, Marteau, Libertine, and the locally-made Leopold Bros. are usually found on the absinthe list. Of course, traditional absinthe drip service is available, but it did give us pause when our bartender tried to pull out the flamethrower, given how traditionally executed every other aspect of À Côté is. For those looking for something more cocktail-ish, mixologist Kristian Kelly is on hand to whip up libations such as the Mile High Manhattan (Stranahan's Colorado whiskey, Leopold Bros. apple whiskey, Peychaud's bitters, Lillet Rouge, house-brandied cherries; $10).

All of the food at Z Cuisine and À Côté comes from a local farm or provider, with Dupays buying from local and organic farmers twice a week and planning the menu around what's available. Small plates are a specialty at À Côté. The charcuterie board is excellent; when we visited, it was loaded up with two cheeses, three meats, house-made conserves, and various nuts and dried fruits. The patés and cassoulet are notable, too, and we also liked the tartine croque madame gratineé (ham, cheese, egg, organic greens).

À ta santé!

LAST CALL!

More Destinations to Explore in Denver

We're now at the point in this book where we must discuss bars that rock murals of Adolph Hitler on the walls, or at least used to. **The Cruise Room** (1600 17th Street; 303.825.1107; www.theoxfordhotel.com) in the historic Oxford Hotel opened on December 6, 1933, the day after Repeal Day. The neon-lit art deco bar hasn't changed at all, except for the addition of a jukebox (still loaded with 45s) and the mid-1940s destruction of a bas-relief depicting a toasting Hitler. This bit of art was one of a dozen bas-reliefs, the rest of which still decorate the bar, depicting leaders of many nations toasting in their native tongues (*Prosit! Hoot mon! Slanta mah! Na zdorovie! Skal!*). Remember that in 1934, Hitler was *Time* magazine's Man of the Year! A decade later, more modern perspectives brought this piece of art down forever. Although we were unimpressed with the house cocktail menu, the bartenders (in their dinner jackets and black bow ties) can mix up any of the classics. Paintings in the lobby (by H. Harmon) show the exploration of the West. Nearby, the Brown Palace Hotel (321 17th Street; 800.321.2599; www.brownpalace.com) has a 1930s nautical bar and restaurant called **Ship Tavern.**

   Elway's (2500 E. 1st Avenue, Unit 101; 303.399.5353; www.elways.com) is the Cherry Creek neighborhood's local spendy dining option. It is also the place to find bar manager Ky Belk, often regarded as the founding father of the modern Denver cocktail scene. His signature drink is an unnamed combo of gin, muddled strawberries, ground black pepper, lemon juice, and agave nectar. Food at the restaurant is from chef Tyler Wiard. They've also got locations downtown and in the resort town of Vail.

It seems as though Mile High City has got medicinal marijuana dispensaries on every other block. It's really fascinating to see legal pot dealers taking over old gas stations and florist shops. Thus, it almost seems routine to make

assumptions about the plants growing in a hydroponic garden behind the bar at **Green Russell** (1422 Larimer Street; 303.893.6505; www greenrussell.com). But don't get too excited; although the bar is Denver's entry into the speakeasy paradigm, the plants growing here are kumquat, Thai basil, Meyer lemon, and even a bay tree.

Named for William Greenberry Russell, the first man to discover gold in the Rockies, the bar was opened in November 2010 by Frank and Jacqueline Bonanno. Enter via Wednesday's Pie Shop, which does pie and cocktail pairings on Wednesdays (um, yes, cocktails and pie, *please*). Under the low ceiling and between the two ice stations (where 300-pound blocks are chipped to order), bartender Alexandra Parks can whip you up the Repeal (rye, Strega herbal liqueur, aquavit, Cynar bitter aperitif, vanilla cardamom bitters) or the Mile High Club Cocktail (genever,

Punt E Mes vermouth, yellow Chartreuse, orange juice) until you reach the Bitter End (Russell's 10-year rye, Domain de Canton ginger liqueur, lime juice, prosecco, Fernet-Branca amaro). All drinks are $12.

Right across the street is **TAG** (1441 Larimer Street; 303.996.9985; www.tag-restaurant.com), a swanky Larimer Square restaurant and raw bar by Troy Atherton Guard and Leigh Sullivan-Guard. Troy has cooked in Hawaii, Hong Kong, Tokyo, Singapore, and New York. His menu echoes his passport in dishes like flash-seared hiramasa in a yuzu sauce topped with jalapeño and Pop Rocks. (Pop Rocks!) Bar manager Mike Henderson works with well-regarded bartenders Jared Boller and James Lee, who has returned to Denver after a stint in Salida. (Salida!) Asian and local influences show up in the Where There's A Will (Yamazaki 12-year whiskey, lime juice, ginger beer), and the Hot For Teacher (Leopold Bros. apple whiskey, maple extract, fresh citrus). Drinks are $10.

The Thin Man (2015 E. 17th Avenue; 303.320.7814; www.thinmantavern.com) is full of plenty of religious effigies so you can feel the holy spirits, which are Chartreuse or Bénédictine as far as Gal Friday Night is concerned. We sipped both of these monk-made liqueurs neat, since this isn't a cocktail-focused bar per se. But when we think of *The Thin Man* we think of Nick and Nora Charles, the patron saints of cocktail-swilling couples, so we toasted them and moved on. Thin Man also offers a buck off of any of their single-malts "if your [*sic*] wearing a kilt."

Finally, if you make it over to Boulder, we've heard good things about **Bitter Bar** (835 Walnut Street, Boulder, CO; 303.442.3050; www.thebitterbar.com), where Mark Stoddard serves up things like his Grassy Knoll (gin, verjus, dry vermouth, sauvignon blanc, celery bitters). Did we count three products made from white grapes in that glass? Yup!

RENO

"I shot a man in Reno, just to watch him die." Well, actually, we did some shots in Reno, and the next day we wanted to die. The Biggest Little City in the World doesn't have as many marriage chapels as Las Vegas does, but it does have the Chapel Tavern.

L as Vegas bars are defined by velvet ropes, expensive sound and lighting systems, and trendy tourists, while Reno bars are defined by swinging doors, broken sound and lighting systems, and rough locals. Las Vegas is Katy Perry, and Reno is Tom Waits. We prefer Reno.

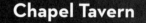

Chapel Tavern

1495 S. Virginia Street
Reno, NV
775.324.2244
www.chapeltavern.com

T. Duncan Mitchell opened the Chapel Tavern in June 2007. His goal was to serve craft cocktails in a "neighborhood bar" environment. "My favorite bars at the time were Bourbon & Branch, Alembic, Slanted Door, and the like [all in San Francsico]," he says. "I really admired what they were doing and wanted to bring some of that to Reno." However, given the local culture at the time, there was no way a pompous lounge would fly. "We try very hard to present these drinks in an unpretentious, non-judgmental environment," Mitchell says. "Reno has gotten up to speed very quickly over the last four years since we opened, and I am very proud and impressed at the cultural zeitgeist we are experiencing."

Indeed, the tiny, dimly-lit bar feels casual. Decorated with exposed brick walls, metal tables, antlers from various mammals, a pool table, and a television at either end of the bar, the place feels welcoming to the pub crowd. Here is a plan as worthy as it is stealthy: create a bar that feels familiar, and then slip in the craft cocktails.

Thus, Chapel Tavern offers a seasonally-based menu of 8 to 10 cocktails—"whatever looks good and is ripe at the time is what we are making." Mitchell is a fan of the classics, focusing on flips, smashes, juleps, slings, and bucks, but he enjoys taking them in new directions. "The drinks are full cocktail geekery with my own little private jokes built in," he says. "I really try to create things with the idea of keeping up with or maybe even impressing say, Erik Adkins or Thad Vogler, should they ever stop by. If I even come close to that goal, then I feel I am doing a great job."

The bar staff will also willingly make any of the classics and has around 80 whiskeys and over 100 beers on offer.

An impressive variety of syrups are made in-house: grenadine, honey syrup, ginger syrup, honey-ginger syrup, Earl Grey sherbet, blackberry shrub, palm sugar syrup, pineapple gomme, watermelon syrup, wine syrup, and a few others. They also pickle their own vegetables for use in their extremely popular Bloody Mary; the rotating blend may include cauliflower, carrots, green beans, okra, garlic, pearl onions, peppers, and others.

With all cocktails reasonably priced at $8, we found ourselves intrigued by the Dutchman vs. Baron (genever, marischino, Rosato vermouth, lemon juice), the Harlan Sun (unaged whiskey, Montenegro amaro, Carpano Antica Formula vermouth), and of course the Creole Buck (Barbancourt 5-Star Haitian rum, ginger honey syrup, yellow Chartreuse, lime juice). It's very cool to note that for each Creole Buck sold, Chapel Tavern will donate two bucks to Haitian disaster relief.

Mitchell is proud of the change he has helped bring to Reno's barflies. "I set out with the goal of bringing cocktail culture to Reno, and it has been and continues to be a profound success," he says. "Not that I can take all the credit. Others in town have done their fair share as well. People that used to drink nothing but Pabst and Jameson are now cocktail enthusiasts, whiskey experts, and hop-heads. Nothing makes me happier than turning someone on to their new favorite drink."

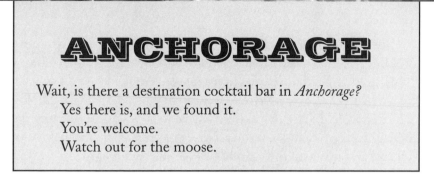

ANCHORAGE

Wait, is there a destination cocktail bar in *Anchorage?*
Yes there is, and we found it.
You're welcome.
Watch out for the moose.

You know you're in Alaska when the bartender whips out a photo album and shows you pictures of grizzly bears in the front yard of his home. To be honest, we didn't go to Alaska looking for cocktails. We went there looking for fresh salmon,

Corsair Restaurant

944 W. 5th Avenue
Anchorage, AK
907.278.4502

auroras borealis, and Tlingit totem poles. We found all of that and also ate reindeer sausage, saw some whales, and completely unexpectedly discovered the Corsair.

The restaurant looks rather uninviting from the outside, as it is located in the basement of a virtually windowless concrete box that passes for the annex of a Best Western Hotel. Inside, it is decorated with a nautical motif that feels like a Trader Vic's, but without any tikis. Dinner here is pricey, and the vintage 1970s room is showing its age.

But what do you know—their cocktail menu is pretty impressive. In addition to the detailed and proper Sazerac that we cheerfully imbibed, the booze selection includes Alaskan rarities such as Chartreuse VEP, Fernet-Branca, rums from Lemon Hart, Diplomatico, and R. L. Seale's, plus extensive lists of wine, port, brandy, cognac, armagnac, and calvados. This is impressive no matter where you are, and it is astounding and unique in Anchorage.

In the mood for a snack after watching Gal Friday Night land a few prize salmons, we got a small plate of smoked salmon lox, a bowl of French onion soup, a glass of Malbec, and that Sazerac. They were all very good, and set us back $37.50 plus a tip for Andy the bartender. Andy claims to be the longest-standing bartender in Anchorage, having been at the Corsair for about 33 years. He says that a certain Stan at **Club Paris** (417 W. 5th Avenue; 907.277.6332; www.clubparisrestaurant.com) is the second-longest-standing, but that Stan is "a little rough around the edges" (Club Paris is also a little rough around the edges, but you must check out their great neon sign). Andy does know his stuff, that's for sure, and would do just fine working in any classic bar in Manhattan. But when he pulled out that photo album full of wildlife and started showing us the various visitors to his home (uh, the grizzly bears were just for starters), there was no mistake; he is clearly a proud Alaskan.

SEATTLE & TACOMA

During an exhaustive research mission in 2011, we discovered that enthusiasm for quality cocktails in the Pacific Northwest is absolutely exploding. We'll start with a bar in nearby Tacoma before rolling north to Jet City.

Chris Keil opened 1022 South in March 2009. Located in the Hilltop neighborhood just a mile or two off of I-5, Keil envisioned 1022 South as a neighborhood bar with high-quality drinks. "At the end of the day, while we take our jobs very seriously, we are not curing cancer," he says. "Drinking should be about community and fun, which is what we're really about even if we're putting a bunch of crazy stuff in the shaker tins or making old-timey cocktails."

1022 South

1022 South J Street
Tacoma, WA
253.627.8588
www.1022south.com

We have to disagree with Keil's statement about curing cancer, however. If there is any cocktail bar in this book that has a prayer of truly curing what ails you, it may be 1022 South (also see Keefer Bar in Vancouver, page 275). The three cocktails we quaffed contained (collectively) goji berry, horny goat weed, lavender, tulsi, chamomile, jiaogulan, and ginseng. There was some booze in there somewhere, too, but seriously, we felt ready to climb Mount Rainier after drinking here. It's visible from the street outside the bar, so go for it. Keil explains that 1022 South created their beverages "with a conscientious observance of what has come before and with an acknowledgment that the distinction between bartenders and apothecaries was once only loosely made." Yeah, we are buying that. Seriously.

Our bevvies, by the by, were the Holy Word (Evan Williams whiskey, green Chartreuse, jiaogulan/tulsi syrup, lemon juice; $10), the dry and chai-forward Revolver (Barbancourt 8-year rum, masala chai, lemon juice, maca-ginseng-infused honey; $8), and the herbacious Reishi Cocktail (mezcal, horny goat weed, reishi syrup, Goji berry, Angostura bitters; $10), which will appeal to amari fans, though it doesn't contain any. We also liked the looks of the La Gitana (sherry, allspice dram, sotol, lavender-chamomile honey, hellfire bitters; $10), but they were out of sotol. Any of the words in this paragraph that don't otherwise appear in this book are herbs and spices that are probably good for you, especially if you're from China, or from Gal Friday Night's former homeland of India.

In addition to all of the exotic infusions, 1022 South makes a lot of their more common mixers in-house, including hibiscus-coriander syrup, reishi syrup, jiaogulan-tulsi syrup, cola, tonic, ginger beer, and a seasonal dandelion-burdock root beer. Herbs in the mint-cilantro-serrano syrup are organic, as is the basil in the basil syrup and most of the botanicals in the cola and tonic. We feel better already. Keeping the spirits local too, Keil says that the bar uses "a lot of spirits from Oregon," plus Voyager gin and their house absinthe, Pacifique, from Woodinville's Pacific Distillery. To wit, the bar's variant of the Corpse Reviver #2, the 1022 Corpse Reviver, is gin, lemon juice, honey, Cocchi Americano aperitif wine, Pacifique absinthe, and cayenne. Ten bucks well spent.

With only a dry cleaner next door and small working-class homes all around otherwise, this tiny space is indeed a neighborhood bar. About 10 seats and four tables fill a room piled up with random books, tall vertical shelves of booze stacked up 12 feet high, and a small patio out front.

Gal Friday Night was feeling peckish, so we indulged in the day's cheese selection ($5), a plate of stuffed red peppers ($5), and a croque monsieur ($8), but I was eyeballing the smoked salmon plate ($12). Next time . . .

Keil leaves us with this: "I tend to look at the bar in terms of growth. We can always be better, make drinks faster, be more innovative, and treat people better."

Wait, it gets *better*?

Angostura bitters is often used to finish cocktails, but how many businesses can you name that use Angostura bitters to finish *the bar?* It's true. When we visited Canon in autumn of 2011, just prior to their opening day, chief mixologist Jamie Boudreau (who co-owns the bar with

Canon: Whiskey & Bitters Emporium

928 12th Avenue
Seattle, WA
206.552.9755
www.canonseattle.com

his wife Erin and Andrew Fawcett) was showing us how they actually reduced 36 of those extra-large bottles of Angostura to stain the birch and mahogany. That is an intense love of bitters.

Arriving in Seattle in 2006 from Canada, Boudreau was behind the bar program at the beloved (and now closed) Vessel. (Scuttlebutt says that Vessel will reopen in 2012.) Since then, Boudreau has come to embrace Seattle and its neighborhoods. "We are trying to be a great neighborhood bar," he says, "where the food and drink is fantastic and the atmosphere lively. All of the barkeeps are trained in classic cocktails, so whether you want beer, wine, or a mixed drink, we can help you."

While showing off the Angostura-soaked bar, Boudreau also showed us his collection of collections: antique glassware, bar books of yore, and dateless bottles decorate the room, along with an immaculate pressed tin ceiling and some 500 bottles of hootch on the wall(s). Like most collectors, Boudreau has some fairly common bottles in his stash, but there are also rarities like a century-old bottle of Tacoma's Cherokee Spring whiskey, plus a bottle reportedly

snagged from the Kennedys' home bar, and several examples of Pro-hibition-era "medicinal whiskey." Some of the rarities are for sale, if you're willing to invest three figures to filter them through your liver and piss them down the toilet. Speaking of which, Canon's bathrooms, complete with a 1940s console radio under the sink, has been a contender for best in Seattle, but let's focus on Canon's skill at getting drinks into your guts, not out of them.

Boudreau also collects recipes. The epic bar menu contains somewhere around 100 of 'em, focusing on classics, but Seattle bartenders seem to prefer taking the bespoke route when possible. "We make all of our own syrups and several liqueurs," Boudreau says. "We also make bitters. Our Boker's bitters are extra special and will be distributed soon." As for seasonality, Boudreau adds, "We don't believe in the latest false 'organic' trend. But we are always on the lookout for fun seasonal ingredients to play with. Figs, heirloom tomatoes, pumpkin, Buddha hand, you name it, we'll play with it!"

Amazing bartenders also seem to be among the accumulations at Canon: joining Boudreau behind the bar is Murray Stenson, one of the most revered bartenders in America. Stenson left his gig at Zig Zag Café in May, 2011 after nearly a decade. Now in his six-ties, Stenson wanted a slower pace. Canon seems like an odd place to find that, but with a capacity of less than 50, the bar is half the size of Zig Zag. Nathan Weber and Brian Lee (both of Tavern Law) and Jared Scarr (of Crush) round out the inaugural team.

Food at Canon is by chef Melinda Bradley. Small plates of finger-friendly food, served in even numbers for easy sharing, are mandated. Pork-belly buns are highlighted on the menu, and also seem to be a customer favorite.

Liberty Bar

517 15th Avenue E.
Seattle, WA
206.323.9898
www.libertybars.com

Of all the cities in this book, only the bars in Seattle would even *consider* opening at 7:00 AM. (although the ones in New Orleans may still be open from last night). The impetus for waking so early has to do with coffee. This is Se-attle, and these people take their coffee rather seriously. Thus, Liberty—espresso by day, scratch cocktails by night. Add maki to the mix, for the win.

Open since April 2006, Liberty is a casual local café, a quintessential Seattleian place for conversation, Wi-Fi, new art on the walls every few months, and Stumptown coffee. At 4:00 PM, the espresso machine shuts down, the sushi bar opens, and it is cocktail time. The environment remains casual, and the Capitol Hill-area bar can get crowded and noisy. "We're a scratch bar," says Liberty owner (and Seattle Bartender's Guild president) Andrew Friedman. "We create all of our own bitters, liqueurs, tinctures, and even things like rhubarb lemon jams." In addition to a list of classics containing the usual suspects, Liberty has several dozen contemporary cocktails on the menu, arranged by base spirit. About half were invented in-house. Cocktails tend to be in the $8–$9 range. We found co-owner Keith Waldbauer's Point of No Return intriguing: gin, green Chartreuse, absinthe, lime juice, rosemary, and fire.

Fire.

Normally, fire and absinthe together don't work for me, but let's give it a whirl.

We were also drawn in by Matt Bailey's contribution, the Catfish Blues (Evan Williams bourbon, blueberries, Nonino amaro, Aperol aperitif). He wouldn't let us order it, however. As Gal Friday Night and I began looking at the menu, he practically grabbed it out of my hands and insisted on making us something custom. There was bourbon involved. Sweet, sweet bourbon.

Speaking of bourbon, Liberty has a nice list of whiskies, with about 50 American brands on hand, and another 60 or so products coming from various islands in the north Atlantic and East Asia. New local distiller Woodinville Whiskey Co. is featured at Liberty, in drinks such as Friedman's Good Dog (Woodinville White Dog, chamomile grappa liqueur, lemon bitters). The bar also offers barrel-aged cocktails in Woodinville casks in the $10–$11 range.

Liberty also uses Voyager gin, another product made in the town of Woodinville, WA, which—as Friedman points out—is a great area for wines. Look for Portland's Aviation gin here, too.

For the hungry, Friedman explains that "Liberty is not a sushi bar; we're a bar that serves sushi." Indeed, food is not the primary focus of Liberty, and those looking for a traditional sushi dinner probably want to head to Maneki or Moshi Moshi (see page 187). But for a rather appropriate snack in a Pacific port town, you can't beat some fresh maki (most $7–$8) with your cocktails.

Rob Roy

2332 Second Avenue
Seattle, WA
206.956.8423
www.robroyseattle.com

As so, it comes to the point in this book where we discuss leather bars. Sorry boys, not *those* leather bars. I'm talking about bars like Rob Roy, which are decorated in enough black leather to provide Rob Halford, Glenn Hughes, Joan Jett, and all of the Ramones with wardrobe options for eternity. In addition to the black leather monster, Rob Roy is all cool gray flagstone, low lighting, and maroon accents. Anu Apte's Belltown cocktail haven is also full of taxidermy, original art, a small (unused) still at the end of the bar, a theft-proof animal hoof lamp, and a killer 1960s hi-fi stereo rig. Added up, it feels classy but slightly pimped, a contemporary take on a late-mid-century lounge, sophisticated but not uptight.

After working there for a few years, Apte and Zane Harris bought the bar from Linda Derschang in August of 2009. Located in Seattle's Belltown neighborhood, an area better known for $6 alcoholic slushies than craft cocktails, Rob Roy is named for a key libation in the classic cocktail canon (essentially a Scotch Manhattan). There are no slushies at Rob Roy, however. Just the opposite, in fact. All rocks drinks get a hand-carved ice ball, shaped to order. Bartender Nathan was on duty when we slipped in; he can be found over at Canon, too. We'd been advised that weekends get

packed and rowdy with the Belltown frat crowd, but our weeknight visit was as calm as can be, with good music on that vintage stereo, and some nice people from Texas next to us at the bar.

As Gal Friday Night (also a Texan) and I began looking at the menu, Nathan practically grabbed it out of my hands and insisted on making us something custom. Is this a Seattle thing? I ended up with a glass full of love, assuming your definition of love equals Cocchi Americano aperitif wine, vintage de Jerez sherry vinegar, green Chartreuse, and Regan's orange bitters. Mine might. "What do you call it?" we asked. "I dunno," said Nathan. It was love. It was also $10, which is a small price to pay for true love. Gal Friday Night, a fan of singer Scott Walker, went for the 30th Century Man (Ardbeg Scotch whisky, Cointreau, crème de cacao, lemon juice, absinthe rinse; $10). It smells, I quipped, like a house on fire. That's the burning house of love, babe.

Back to that menu—there are roughly eight originals and eight classics rotated in seasonally. Every one of the bartenders on staff has contributed at least one drink to the menu. If you must have *just one more*, the Mr. Creosote (reposado tequila, Cynar bitter aperitif, yellow Chartreuse, Angostura bitters) is one to be careful of, but we were too busy drooling over the Scotch selection to think much more about cocktails. We'll save the thinking for a visit to Swig Well, Apte's bartending academy.

A small menu of snacks begins with a bowl of Goldfish ($2) and works its way up to a gruyere-and-tomato grilled cheese sandwich ($8).

Legend has it that the diminutive space that Sambar currently occupies was once owner/chef Bruce Naftaly's residence, and specifically his bedroom. Well,

Sambar

425 NW Market Street
Seattle, WA
206.781.4883
www.sambarseattle.com

no point in discussing details, but his son is named Sam. Adjacent to Naftaly's restaurant, Le Gourmand, is the zinc bar at Sambar, which has exactly four seats with six small tables nearby for a total capacity of less than 30. A seasonal patio adds a few more places to plant your

pants among the plants. Naftaly and his pastry chef wife, Sarah, opened Sambar in 2003 as an adjunct to Le Gourmand (which has been open since the 1980s), presumably forcing them to move their home a bit further away from work. Justin Thain was the inaugural booze slinger at Sambar, but it is Jay Kuehner who has been making drinks there for the bulk of the bar's existence.

The French/Northwest cuisine is always made with fresh, seasonal, locally-cultivated ingredients, and the bar follows suit. "Sam goes to a school who have their own farm for students, and we source a lot of our ingredients from them," Keuhner says. "We also forage, visit local farmers' markets, call upon local purveyors, and even grow many herbs and fruits on site. We have figs, fennel, shiso, mint, lavender, strawberries, grape leaves, apples, rosemary, lemon balm, edible flowers, bay leaf, and more growing on the premises, sometimes quite unintentionally. Often, if a customer requests something, I literally leave and come back a few minutes later with ingredients for their drink."

As Gal Friday Night and I began looking at the menu, Kuehner practically grabbed it out of my hands and insisted on making us something custom. This is indeed a Seattle thing!

Keuhner got to work with the dozens of seemingly unlabeled bottles behind his bar; we asked what was in them, and that was my first mistake. These Seattle people like to make things. Keuhner sent us a list: ginger syrup, cinnamon-ancho-chile syrup, tamarind water, pumpkin water, campari sorbet, Tahitian vanilla bean syrup, poached Seckle pears, smoked apple purée, barley water, jicama-lime-chile foam, sage bitters, tomato water, black-peppercorn-infused tequila, crushed raw cane in cachaça, yuzu marmalade, raspberry shrub, cachaça infused with apricot kernels, rose petal syrup, macerated Montmorency cherries in bourbon and brandy, lemongrass syrup, horchata, long pepper syrup, saffron syrup, preserved lemons, Morrocan black lemon syrup, Jamaica (Senegalese jus de bissap), coffee-rum-cocoa nib tincture, and ginger beer. Keuhner concluded with the statement that the bar is of "modest origin but ambitious to a fault." We haven't detected any faults yet, and we're not inclined to search for them.

Of course they can't make *everything* on-site, but the booze in your drink will probably be made within a few hundred miles. To wit: Clear Creek eaux de vie, Ransom Old Tom gin, Oola gin, Ebb and Flow gin from Sound Spirits, Woodinville whiskey and Voyager gin, Marteaux absinthe, Krogstad aquavit, and Aviation gin.

All right, stop drooling. Here's what Keuhner might be doing with all of this liquid awesomeness: the Le Mystère (Voyager gin, tarragon, sugar, Pacifique absinthe), the Barbato (Ransom Old Tom gin, rhubarb syrup, amaro, tonic), or the Belem (Clear Creek pear brandy, tamarind-infused cachaça, lime juice, orange bitters, Cointreau). All are $10, and none contain more than four ingredients. That, my friends, is a sterling example of restraint. We all know that the best drinks are the simplest ones; Keuhner has a whole lot of fresh and unique ingredients to play with, but he still keeps his recipes simple.

"The goal," he says, "is to be pushing our medium of the cocktail into unexplored realms without too much science, but rather with a recognizable bar of simple tools, honed skills, and acute attention to detail."

We say, go drink at Sambar.

———◆———

There are two types of bar in the world: those with their own distillery on the premises, and those without. Sun Liquor has one of each. Co-owner Michael Klebeck opened the original Sun Liquor location in May 2006, just steps away from his well-regarded doughnut shack, Top Pot. The bar (and doughnut shop) are on a residential street at the north end of the Capitol Hill area. Sun Liquor falls firmly

Sun Liquor Distillery

514 E. Pike Street
Seattle, WA
206.720.1600

Sun Liquor

607 Summit Avenue E.
Seattle, WA
206.860.1130
www.sunliquor.com

into the category of casual neighborhood bars that just happen to have a focus on solid cocktails made with fresh ingredients.

The doughnut shop's name comes from the vintage neon sign that once lured diners into the Top Spot Chinese restaurant. When transporting the sign, the "s" fell off, and the owners stuck with the name Top Pot. They've got eight locations around Seattle now, but the first one was the Summit Avenue store, right next to the original Sun Liquor. Sun Liquor actually shares more than just an owner with Top Pot. Both businesses have a mid-century retro energy to them, with a strong influence of Chinoiserie—bamboo furniture in the bar, wallpaper with Asian patterns, and a vintage firecracker ad used as a mural. Monkeys with explosives. As it should be.

The cocktail menu is focused on classics, some slightly retooled. (As in their Mai Tai, which fatally adds grenadine. Sorry, we have a deep-rooted disposition, almost at a genetic level, against that.) Required by law to serve food, Sun Liquor has TV dinners for sale ($20).

Sun Liquor Distillery is nine blocks away on the busier Pike Street. Opened in 2011, they have the distinction of being the first bar in Seattle legally entitled to serve their own house-distilled spirit. (A third-party source told us that they have to sell it to the state and then buy it back at a mark-up!) The bar's Hedge Trimmer gin is made in a big custom-built brass still, visible to bar customers behind a big glass wall. Erik Chapman is the distiller and head bartender. He's been discussing a seasonal gin for the winter holidays, as well as apple brandies for the future. This bar also has a bit of mid-century fun going on, with an ancient television embedded into the wall, a display case full of antique badminton accoutrements, a collection of aviation-themed vintage cocktail shakers, a wonderful world map mural by Tina Randolph, and another

firecracker ad, this time a big sunburst of diodes advertising Lady Fingers explosive amusement.

Food here is a basic selection of sandwiches (cheeseburger, BLT, grilled cheese) with paprika shoestring fries ($8).

As Gal Friday Night and I began looking at the menu, bartender Cale Green practically grabbed it out of my hands and insisted on making us something custom. This is definitely a Seattle thing! We ended up with a Bourbon Renewal (bourbon, crème de cassis, lemon juice, simple syrup, Angostura bitters; $9) and, when we asked for "booze-forward and with Chartreuse," we got a standard but always welcome Bijou (gin, green Chartreuse, sweet vermouth, orange bitters; $9). We would have preferred for a bartender insisting on making a bespoke cocktail to go a little further off the map, but it was fine. By the by, this one dates from the 1890s and was featured in Harry Johnson's *New and Improved Bartender's Manual* of 1900. Bijou is French for jewel, and the recipe uses gin to represent diamonds, vermouth for rubies, and Chartreuse for emeralds.

◄─◄►►─

Tavern Law is an upscale lounge a few blocks away from the raucous Pike and Pine intersection in the Capitol Hill area. The bar was opened in the autumn of 2009 by Brian McCracken and Dana Tough, the duo responsible for **Spur** (113 Blanchard Street; 206. 728.6706; www.spurseattle.com).

Tavern Law

Needle and Thread
1406 12th Avenue
Seattle, WA
206.322.9734
www.tavernlaw.com

Located in the renovated 1919 Trace Lofts building, Tavern

Law is decorated with shelves of old law books, a vintage type-writer, wood paneling, a lovely mural of a woman in 1920s garb with a crowned bluebird, and an antique roulette wheel (non-functioning; it's mounted on the wall). A fun numbering system embedded in the wood of the bar recalls, more than anything else, a vintage bowling alley. The bar was named after the Pioneer Inn and Tavern Law of 1832, which allows hotels, inns, and taverns to sell alcohol to people not necessarily renting a room for the night.

Tavern Law serves some of the better bar food we've tried, courtesy of McCracken and Tough. Really, calling it bar food almost seems unfair, as there are certain connotations inherent in that term, and the food here far exceeds the expectations of "bar food." Around 10 items are listed on a blackboard, at about $6–$15. An oxtail banh mi seemed interesting, but we went for a piece of salmon ($15) that has become the stuff of legend, and some fried chicken that redefines expectations of fried chicken ($10). Thusly fortified, it's time for further fortification.

The menu at Tavern Law is about three dozen cocktails strong, and is supported by a shorter list of tropical drinks. It also contains a table of contents, a manifesto, and a fair bit of history (properly MLA-cited, in fact). All cocktails are made with freshly-squeezed juices and house-made syrups and tinctures, and often use local or small-batch liquors.

As Gal Friday Night and I began looking at the menu, bartender Philip Thompson practically grabbed it out of my hands and insisted on making us something custom. This is *most* definitely a Seattle thing! Our first glass was blessed with Martin Miller's gin, passion fruit purée, lemon juice, and strawberry syrup, while the second glass soon contained local Pacifique absinthe, Broker's gin ("a higher proof gin to cut the sweetness of the absinthe," says Thompson), Cocchi Americano aperitif wine, and orange bitters. These drinks were met with a large degree of approval.

Thompson wanted to play more, and we wanted him to play more, so he ended up serving a half-and-half combo of Laird's bonded applejack and Bulleit rye, enhanced with green Chartreuse, maraschino liqueur, and Demerara sugar. We noted the always exciting Seelbach on the menu, and almost had to insist upon ordering Tavern Law's take on this classic. We were also intrigued by a few of the listed house drinks, such as former bar manager Nathan Weber's the Birchwood (rye, cognac, Cynar bitter aperitif, Punt e Mes vermouth, Licor 43, cucumber garnish).

You may also spot an antique telephone next to a heavy old iron bank vault door within Tavern Law. Using the phone to call Needle and Thread, the bar upstairs, may or may not get you access, depending on capacity (weekends are predictably packed). Reservations are recommended. Custom cocktails are the only option up there, and base spirits are generally of an even higher caliber than the very good stuff being poured downstairs. Among antique tables, crystal chandeliers, and brocade sofas, you'll hear jazz on the sound system, and see photos of jazz-era cuties along the staircase walls.

As soon as you start talking about drinks in the Pacific Northwest, the conversation will inevitably turn to Zig Zag. Maybe this is because they've been mixing like they mean it since 1998, putting them pretty far ahead of the curve, or maybe it's because of the skill of longtime bartender Murray Stenson (who departed in 2011 after a decade of service), or maybe it's due to their astounding collection of spirits, ranging from the standard to the obscure. If nothing else, Zig Zag is the place where a beloved lost cocktail was reborn, after Stenson plucked the Last Word out of Ted Saucier's 1951 book *Bottom's Up* and added it to the menu. This fantastic forgotten tipple—which was already three decades old when Saucier wrote of it—is now considered a standard. (It is equal parts gin, green Chartreuse, Luxardo maraschino liqueur, and lime juice. You're welcome.)

Zig Zag Café

1501 Western Avenue
Seattle, WA
206.625.1146
www.zigzagseattle.com

Zig Zag Café is located at the edge of Seattle's Pike Place Market, somewhat hidden among the foliage halfway down the Pike Street Hill Climb, one of those massive stairways that are found all over hilly Seattle. Inside is a casual bistro, with about 10 seats at the bar, a bunch of tables beyond that, and a tiny patio among the shrubbery. Decor is rather minimalist, with tile floors and plain cinder block walls, and quiet jazz playing in the background. Food at Zig Zag is sourced from Pike's Place Market, and includes lighter fare such as a cheese plate, bruschetta, flatbreads, salads, and sandwiches, plus seafood including gumbo and seared albacore tuna in a wasabi crust. Food is served late.

Zig Zag is owned by Ben Dougherty and Kacy Fitch. One can find five-year veteran Erik Hakkinen or Benjamin Perri behind the bar most nights. As Gal Friday Night and I began looking at the menu, Hakkinen practically grabbed it out of my hands and insisted on making us something custom. This is *absolutely* and *most* definitely a Seattle thing!

What we ended up with was a glass containing Wild Turkey and Bonal Gentiane-Quina aperitif wine, and a second vessel blessed with Giffard apricot brandy, dry vermouth, lemon juice, and Angostura bitters. The simplicity of the ingredients in these drinks should not obscure the care with which they were prepared; we were once again reminded that flashy menus full of unlikely combinations are never a substitute for skillful barcraft. That's why a simple Manhattan or Martini works so well in the hands of a master.

Admiring the spirited yet adult group of regulars—some dressed in mid-century vintage style, another quietly and unselfconsciously reading Hemingway at the bar—we had a conversation with Fitch. "The thing that I am the most proud of," he said, "is that we stuck to our initial concept since the beginning and it seems to have caught on. I think our consistency is what sets us apart. We have been doing the same thing since day one, but our customers have become more discerning and adventurous, so our 'house drinks' program has evolved."

We moved forward, gleefully, to another pair of unnamed improvisations: Pampero Aniversario rum (a product not served in nearly enough bars), Campari, and Giffard crème de cassis definitely did the trick, but a promising mix of calvados, lime juice, Giffard apricot, and house-spiced habanero tequila ended up just a tad *too* spicy. Naturally, Hakkinen was only too happy to swap it out for something more to taste.

In addition to the habanero tequila, Zig Zag Café also makes their own ginger beer, falernum, Swedish punsch, pimento dram, bitters, and grenadine. They also include local spirits such as Aviation gin, Pacific absinthe, Marteau absinthe, Clear Creek eau de vie, and others within their encyclopedic spirits collection.

LAST CALL!
More Destinations to Explore in the Seattle Area

Bars owned by musicians are not uncommon, but it is a bit rare to see a cocktail bar owned by a consortium of bass players. In the case of **Hazlewood** (2311 Market Street; 206.783.0478), the bass players are definitely not Mick Karn, Charles Mingus, or Geddy Lee, but they may or may not be Drew Church, Steve Freeborn, and Ben Shepherd, along with Keith Bartolini.

The small bar is located on a bustling street full of nightlife in Seattle's Ballard area. They opened in 2006 with four seats, a bench, an even smaller upstairs room, a seasonal patio in front, and a menu of about 40 cocktails. It is all wrapped in a vibe that aims to be part Lee Hazlewood and part Vincent Price, firmly planted in the home of grunge

rock. Bartender Jessica Levey handed us an appropriately crusty menu and reported that Hazlewood was the second bar in Seattle to do classic cocktails. She is also the artist behind a blog full of cartoons that mostly take place in a bar. Is bartoon a word? The characters are all sort of pathetic, reminding us of a legion of alcoholic hipster Ziggys. As we sipped her skillful take on the Last Word, a bass player came over and told us that they "aim to keep the bar accessible, with fewer barriers to people new to [drinking well]." Done.

Knee-High Stocking Co. (1356 East Olive Way; 206.979.7049; www.kneehighstocking.com) is just starting to gain some attention. Seattle's entry into the "hidden bar where you must text message for a reservation" paradigm, Knee-High offers sandwiches, cheese plates, vegetarian bruschetta, lumpia, and other bites to compliment its cocktails. Divided by spirit, the three-dozen-ish drinks available include classics like the Hemingway Daiquiri and the Sazerac, plus modern favorites like a crème de cassis Bramble variant (Bombay gin, lime juice, simple syrup, Briottet crème de cassis). Another dozen drinks rotate in; the classic Preakness (Elijah Craig 18-year bourbon, Carpano Antica Formula vermouth, Bénédictine, bitters) is always nice to see on a menu.

This one falls into the "early influences" category: **Maneki** (304 Sixth Avenue South; 206.622.2631; www.manekirestaurant.com) is a Japanese restaurant that has the distinction of being the oldest restaurant in Seattle, the first to serve sushi, and the only one with a bartender—Fusae Yokoyama—who has been there for more than 50 years (she is over 80 years old). She has been cited as an inspiration by everyone from Murray Stenson to Jay Keuhner. Maneki is also the only Japanese restaurant in the world whose dishwasher went on to become prime minister of Japan (Takeo Miki).

Very close to Hazlewood is **Moshi Moshi** (5324 Ballard Avenue NW; 206.971.7424; www.moremoshi.com), a solid sushi bar with very nice cocktails by Erik Carlson. His Fluted Barrel (gin, Sauternes sweet wine, dry vermouth, hibiscus bitters, grapefruit bitters; $11) is tasty, as is the West India Regiment Punch (Trinidad rum, black-tea-infused Batavia arrack, tawny port, lime juice, pineapple gomme, orange juice, orgeat, nutmeg; $11). We also liked the Hell's Wind Staff Cocktail (bourbon infused with Fuji apple, cachaça, green Chartreuse, demerara syrup, Peychaud's bitters, lime zest; $11). The menu of around 16 Carlson creations is supplemented with a rather exhaustive glossary on the back.

The well-loved **Vessel** (www.vesselseattle.com) has closed, but is slated to reopen in 2012. Keep your eyes and livers open for that one.

West 5 (4539 California Avenue SW; 206.935.1966; www.westfive.com) is on a fun street in remote West Seattle, with an antique mall across the street and a bona fide record store on the corner. Solid and tasty comfort food like Reubens and mac and cheese compliment the 1950s bowling alley decor: leather bucket barstools, blond wood, black velvet paintings, patterned Formica tabletops, and custom swizzle sticks. The menu elaborately espouses the virtues of Chartreuse, but the cocktails that we ordered in this comfortable, spacious, and fun bar could have been pulled up a notch.

PORTLAND

Portland is divided by the Willamette River into an east side and a west side. The east side seems more residential and a bit more laid back. The west side is home to the downtown area, most of the museums, and a large concentration of nightlife in the Pearl District. Some (not all) of the Pearl District businesses can get a bit pompous. You've been warned.

Beaker & Flask

727 SE Washington Street
Portland, OR
503.235.8180
www.beakerandflask.com

There are bars in this book that serve a full menu of food, and there are restaurants that happen to have great cocktail programs. Beaker and Flask is ostensibly a bar first, but it blurs the line more so than most, as its menu of food has been earning high accolades in foodie publications, too.

Beaker and Flask was opened in June 2009 by Kevin Ludwig, the former manager and bartender at Park Kitchen and an alumnus of Paley's Place, too. You'll note that all of these are restaurants. Ludwig brought in his Paley's Place pal Ben Bettinger as the chef at Beaker and Flask, and it's safe to say that Bettinger has embraced his work enthusiastically. From the tiny open kitchen come small plates such as grilled pork cheeks ($12), as well as larger entrees like grilled beef shoulder tender ($24). Snacks like crispy pig ears ($4) and smoked trout deviled eggs ($4) pair nicely with cocktails. The bartender known as Young James advised us that these two snacks work particularly well together, and he was correct. When we commented on the music playing—semi-obscure tracks from Echo and the Bunnymen, OMD, and Duran Duran—Young James commented that they have a new mix every night.

Looking around, the 1980s music isn't the only pop culture piled behind the bar. Ceramic beer steins, piles of classic cocktail books, Coco Joe tiki figures, a brass turtle, an array of beakers, flasks, cocktail shakers, and random vintage glassware, plus at least two (count 'em) plastic Jabba the Hutts battling a plastic frog dressed as a Jedi knight. And a weird fuzzy rat-bear thing. It's all about the weird fuzzy rat-bear thing. Zooming out, the long bar dominates the room, which is filled with wine barrels turned into cocktail tables, and circular booths under big picture windows that offer a fantastic view of distant downtown Portland. This is a fun and casual place. Let's get a drink.

Ludwig is joined behind the bar by Tim Davey (former bar manager of Clyde Common) and Brandon Wise (former bar manager of In Fine Spirits in Chicago). Wise got busy mixing up two songs named after drinks—wait, strike that and reverse it—two drinks named after songs: the White Overalls (Wild Turkey rye, honeyed Campari, Bonal aperitif wine, orange bitters; $9), named for the 1978 tune by Krautrockers La Dusseldorf; and the Mandolin Rain (English Harbor five-year rum, sweet vermouth, Averna amaro, Fernet-Branca amaro, Old-Fashioned bitters; $9), which is named after a Bruce Hornsby tune. The latter, according to a sheepish Wise, was named "on a dare." The honeyed Campari is blended in advance for efficiency; after being mixed with the liqueur, the honey will remain liquid. Gal Friday Night (who once played steel drums in a reggae band) was drawn to the Kingston Crusta (rhum agricole blanc, Clement Creole Shrubb, lemon juice, grenadine, bitters; $9), and then the Salt & Pepper (gin, grapefruit juice, Peychaud's bitters, salted rim; $8).

Also on the menu: the Brazillian Firing Squad, the Killer Crossover, the Two Dollar Pistol, the Bitter End, and the Devil in a Boot. This could get dangerous. Are Jabba's minions after us? No, but the Sal's Minion might be (aged rum, pineapple gomme, coconut water ice cubes; $8).

Behind Beaker and Flask, in the same building (but accessed from a door on the other side), is **Rum Club** (720 SE Sandy Boulevard; 503.467.2469; www.rumclubpdx.com). This new spot by Kevin Ludwig and Mike Shea opened in July 2011. Even more sharply cocktail-focused than Beaker and Flask, Rum Club was designed to appeal to the service industry. Decor by designer Mark Annen includes low ceilings, dim lighting, Asian bird-of-paradise wallpaper, and lots of wood, all in an effort to differentiate Rum Club from the industrial spaces that are so trendy in Portland. Bartenders David Shenaut and Emily Baker have moved from Beaker and Flask to the tile-fronted African mahogany bar at Rum Club. Well-regarded drinks include a variant on the Pedro Martinez (Ron Matusalem rum, Cocchi di Torino vermouth, maraschino liqueur, orange bitters, B. G. Reynolds' falernum bitters; $8), originally by Bryan Schneider of Brooklyn's Clover Club, and the Avondale (cachaça, Cynar bitter aperitif, pineapple gomme, egg white, lemon juice, Agnostura bitters; $8). Snacks (or "American continental cocktail cuisine") include deviled ham sandwiches ($6), shrimp cocktail ($8), and pickled eggs ($1), all designed to further evoke a mid-century lounge feel.

Clyde Common

Ace Hotel
1014 SW Stark Street
Portland, OR
503.228.3333
www.clydecommon.com

Clyde Common is a restaurant first, but it has also been embraced in the spirits world. In contrast to Beaker and Flask, Clyde Common (near the southern edge of the Pearl District) is billed as a restaurant, but it is by no means unheard of to treat it purely as a cocktail destination.

Opened in May 2007 by Nate Tilden and Matt Piacentini, Clyde Common is adjacent to the Ace Hotel. They describe the restaurant as a "European-style tavern serving delicious food and drinks in a casual and energizing space." Ace Hotel mainstays Jack Barron and Natasha Figueroa chose an industrial decor of canvas tarps, metal stools, bare bulbs, folding wooden chairs, concrete, and exposed ducts. A few large Douglas fir branches in a glass vase remind us that we're in the Pacific Northwest.

Bartender and blogger Jeffrey Morgenthaler has earned some notice for kicking off the barrel-aged cocktail trend in the U.S. He got the idea after learning of Tony Conigliaro's experiments

with aging cocktails in glass at London's 69 Colebrooke Row. Clyde Common acquires used Tuthilltown bourbon casks, fills them with sherry, and ages it for a month. Then they empty the barrels of sherry and add the pre-mixed cocktail, which they age for a further six weeks. Libations subjected to this process have included classics like the Remember the Maine (rye, vermouth, house-made cherry brandy, absinthe), the Chrysanthemum (dry vermouth, Bénédictine, absinthe), and the Deshler (rye, Dubonnet aperitif, Cointreau, Peychaud's bitters). However, it is the Negroni, that cornerstone of classic cocktails, that seems to work the best. The drink comes out of the barrel mellower and more round, with just the vaguest hints of the sherry and, just maybe, the whiskey that lived in the barrel first. Morgenthaler points out that the time in the barrel subjects the drink to a lot of oxidization and "softinization." He prefers good ol' Beefeater gin and Cinzano sweet vermouth, and indeed, it is hard to argue that using a more complex gin or a richer vermouth (such as Carpano Antica Formula) would improve the drink in this case. Barrel-aged cocktails are $10.

The other bartenders, such as Shannan Shute and Junior Ryan, should not be underestimated. As we bellied up to the zinc bar, Ryan hooked us up with a Nasturtium (Dolin Blanc vermouth, Domaine de Canton ginger liqueur, Bonal Gentiane-Quina aperitif wine, lemon peel; $8). Named for the national flower of Japan (and yet the drink has no sake, yuzu, or Japanese whiskey?), it is sweet, smooth, and feels great on the tongue. The One-Trick Pony

(Pelinkovac, maraschino liqueur, house-made tonic water, lime juice) is intriguing for its use of Pelinkovac, a wormwood-based bitter liqueur popular in Bosnia, Croatia, and Serbia (and, apparently, Portland). We also liked the St. Steven's Sour (Hennessey VS cognac, Appleton VX rum, lemon juice, B. G. Reynolds' orgeat; $8). Portland resident Blair Reynolds (also known as Trader Tiki) is the man behind that orgeat. "Blair is a good friend of [Clyde Commons]," Morganthaller says. While it is great to see the large number of bars in the Pacific Northwest (and beyond) supporting Reynolds, Clyde Commons do make some of their other syrups in-house, including quinine syrup, ginger beer, raw ginger syrup, gewurztraminer wine reduction, and honey syrup.

The communal tables in the loud dining room are serviced from an open kitchen run by chef Chris DiMinno. A smaller balcony is home to just a few more private tables. The menu changes daily, and usually includes choices of large or small portions for each dish. Noting the restaurant's logo—a butcher's carving diagram of a pig—it isn't a surprise that one of their signature dishes is Clyde Common pig. Salted pork belly, shredded pork shoulder, and pork sausage are served with braised cabbage in a shallot vinaigrette. We were also drawn to the prosciutto-wrapped trout ($24). Cheeses are $5, served with local honey, summer jam, and walnut bread.

Kask

1215 SW Alder Street
Portland, OR
503.241.7163
www.grunerpdx.com

There are two types of bar in the world: the Black Lodge bars and the White Lodge bars. Fans of of the classic television series *Twin Peaks* will recognize the black-and-white lodges as places where good and evil spirits of the Pacific Northwest woods reside. One might think that Seattle bars would milk their fair share of *Twin Peaks* references, but maybe they're over it by now; all of the *Peaks* fans seem to be in Portland.

Kask was opened in July 2011 by Kurt Huffman with chef Christopher Israel. This tiny bar is adjacent to Huffman's alpine restaurant, Grüner (there is an additional bar within the restaurant).

Upon first glance, Kask might indeed resemble a set from the *Twin Peaks* television series. Ten seats at the dark, cozy, woody bar are joined by 16 more at a banquette along the opposite wall. All of the wood originated in the Pacific Northwest and was reclaimed and installed by Dylan Chace, who took inspiration from the great designer George Nakashima, among others. We liked the Carpano Antica Formula vermouth tins in the front window, and the vintage poker chip carousel holding bottles of bitters. There's always music in the air; in this case, it was the dulcet tones of Leonard Cohen, who fit the atmosphere perfectly.

So, what kinds of spirits reside in a White Lodge bar? Good ones, of course. The spirits program was put together by Drew Putterman and bar manager Tommy Klus, who has been tending bar in Portland since 2000. Klus remarked that Kask "is very, very, very focused on small brands and family-owned products." He pointed to the bottles of Roi Bene cherry liqueur and Combier Liqueur d'Orange. "The company who makes these products predate Cointreau by 40 years," he said, "but the products are virtually unknown in the U.S. because of Cointreau 'bullying' them."

Naturally, we had to give these a try, and of the eight drinks on the menu, we were (of course) drawn to the Log Lady, named (of course) after the *Twin Peaks* character. Klus steered us away from that, however, and suggested that we try his updated take on it, which he has dubbed . . . wait for it . . . the Black Lodge. Natch. It consists of Rittenhouse rye, Carpano Antica Formula vermouth, Cynar bitter aperitif, Roi Bene Rouge cherry liqueur, and orange bitters ($10). We let Klus improvise the second one (perhaps he was guided by Tibetan spirits, as *Peaks* agent Dale Cooper often was). We ended up with Springbank 100-proof single malt Scotch whisky, Clear Creek Oregon brandy, Carpano Antica Formula vermouth, Fernet-Branca amaro, Angostura bitters, Peychaud's bitters, and just a little bit of Laphroaig Scotch whisky ($9). For good measure, the ice was rinsed with Herbsaint. So, essentially, this was a ridiculously complex Manhattan, but we were completely on board for it. If we're still on *Peaks* here, let's call that one the Leo Johnson, because it will kick your ass.

Kask also offers just a bit of charcuterie and cheese (but no cherry pie). If you want to eat a full meal, head next door to Grüner.

Laurelhurst Market

3155 E. Burnside Street
Portland, OR
503.206.3097
www.laurelhurstmarket.com

Sometimes our vegetarian and vegan friends just have to understand that not every eatery on earth is meant for them. I mean, it's nice when meateries have options for your buddy's pain-in-the-ass date, but expecting every restaurant to cater to *everyone's* eating preferences just isn't realistic. You can't please all of the people, all of the time.

We are not going to try to guess at Laurelhurst Market's take on this statement, and the above paragraph is not meant to express their views. But we will say that failing to ingurgitate a big mass of animal flesh at Laurelhurst is like going to any of the bars in this book and ordering a Busch light beer. If you do want a killer steak, freshly killed no less, you're in the right place.

Chef-owners David Kreifels, Jason Owens, and Benjamin Dyer opened their butcher shop (by day) and restaurant (by night) in the space that was once a convenience store called Laurelhurst Market. Fascinating. A large cooler right by the door greets you with charcuterie, patés, and further European variants on manipulated mammal products. Once seated, it's all about American steaks. A large blackboard with a diagram of a cow on it shows what's available that night (compare with Clyde Common's pig). Any of the pasture-raised beef cuts shown are also available for sale to go.

Ah, but what of the bar, you ask? It's cool. To say that they take their ice program seriously might be an understatement. The most famous drink in the house is the Smoke Signals (Jack Daniels whiskey, Amontillado sherry, chopped pecans, lemon juice; $10), which utilizes smoked ice. To get the smoked ice, a giant block of ice is melted over smoke, and the big vat of resulting water is then refrozen and chipped by hand into cubes. Unsurprisingly, the drink tastes like a smoky whiskey sour, and that is by no means a bad thing. Would using a good smoky Scotch be too much of a good thing, or would it cut a step out of the process? We would ask creator Evan Zimmerman, but he's already departed Laurelhurst Market. He popped in for a stint as bar manager after a few years at Teardrop (see page 197) before opening his own place, Woodsman Tavern (page 205). Rather, bartendrix Mae improvised a drink of Bulleit rye with house-made cherry shrub ($8), while my unflappable companion went for the classic Deshler (rye, Dubonnet aperitif, Cointreau, bitters; $8).

───── ◄►► ─────

It's no secret that we're on board with businesses that embrace the whole local/seasonal thing. In *some* cases, bars that claim a commitment to locally-sourced ingredients do little more than pull wild mint for garnishes from the backyard before calling it a day. If you want the real deal, however, look no further than this pair of taverns from owner-chef Scott Dolich.

Dolich opened Park Kitchen in 2003, in a historic building across the street from a cozy urban park at

Park Kitchen

422 NW 8th Avenue
Portland, OR
503.223.7275
www.parkkitchen.com

The Bent Brick

1639 NW Marshall Street
Portland, OR
503.688.1655
www.thebentbrick.com

the east edge of the Pearl District. Committed to being "as local as possible," they use meat, seafood, and produce from local sources and feature a continually rotating menu of dishes. Entrees from the kitchen of Dolich and chef de cuisine David Padberg might include monkfish ($26), roulade of lamb ($26), and "pork three ways" ($26).

The bar area has a half dozen seats, and is divided from the restaurant by a long wall. A blackboard showcases works of art by John Q. Porter. When we visited, a tiny chalk farmer stood atop one of many giant chalk wine bottles, brandishing a chalk corkscrew like a chalky farm tool. That just about sums this place up (no, it's not chalky—we mean farmers and wine and hard work).

Mary Bartlett took over as bar manager in 2011, having arrived at Park Kitchen after two years at Teardrop. She set us up with a St. Elizabeth Sour (Beefeater gin, lemon juice, ginger syrup, St. Elizabeth allspice dram, Aperol aperitif; $9). Served neat in a rocks glass, the ginger came through on the finish. Somehow, the conversation turned to the herbal liqueur Becherovka (maybe it is because Gal Friday Night is Czech), so Bartlett took our challenge and improvised a glassful of VSOP cognac, Cynar bitter aperitif, Becherovka, and celery bitters ($11). "A lot of our drinks are designed as aperitif-based," she explained, "since we're primarily a restaurant." We also liked the possibilities within the Black Magic (Cruzan white rum, Cruzan blackstrap rum, Fernet-Branca amaro, cinnamon syrup; $9). Fernet and cinnamon . . . hmmm.

From the bar's food menu, assistant manager (and cheese expert) Jenny Cook suggested salt cod fritters with malt vinegar ($11 for three) as a bar snack. Super light and fluffy inside. A good choice. That just about sums this place up: *a good choice.*

In June 2011, Dolich opened the Bent Brick. Park Kitchen alumni working in the Bent Brick include chef Will Preisch, bar manager Adam Robinson, and interior designer Mark Annen. Robinson landed in Portland in 2009 after a stint at David Chang's Momofuku Ssäm Bar in Manhattan. The striking foyer was inspired by Dolich while watching his son stack firewood in an awkward way that reminded him of a Jenga game. A curving banquette adds to the unbalanced feeling. Things resolve once inside the tavern (their preferred term). The bar counter connects directly to an open kitchen, providing physical solidification of their philosophical merging of the two. The bar seats about 11 people, with another 50 or so seated for meals.

Even more so than at Park Kitchen, Bent Brick is where Dolich and company get serious about local ingredients. All the wines are from Oregon and Washington. There is no Parmesan cheese (they use domestic hard cheese like Juniper Grove's Tumalo Tomme), and Italian prosciutto is replaced with country ham from Virginia. Yes, Virginia is a bit of a drive from Oregon, but it is a heck of a lot closer than Italy. At the bar, *all* of the spirits are made in the United States of America. Those of you looking for Carpano Antica Formula vermouth, Scotch whisky, Bénédictine, or Brazilian cachaça

are going to be out of luck.

Wait, no Fernet? Well, we do like to be challenged, right? Deep breath. We can do this. To replace these ingredients, Bent Brick uses American substitutes, or employs a variety of house-made tinctures and infusions to emulate the key flavor notes of your favorite amaro or genever. The result is an exciting cornucopia of unfamiliarity when gazing at the bottles lined up on the back bar. It is almost impossible to stay in one's comfort zone; nearly every cocktail will have at employ at least one brand unfamiliar to even the most experienced cocktailian.

Interestingly, the menu doesn't ever list brand names. This is a curious choice, as it would be easier to turn people on to potentially exotic local spirits if their names were listed. Of the concise selection of eight drinks, we liked the looks of the Long Overdue (rye, cherry shrub, cider, bitters; $8) and the Border Crossing (apple brandy, beet shrub, smoked tea, black pepper; $9). Other drinks such as the Room with a View (spiced rum, orange, lemon, orgeat, anise, bitters; $8) might inspire a bit of a trivia game: how many American spiced rums are worth drinking? That's a pretty short list. No fair peeking at those bottles. Let the debate ensue.

———— ◄●► ————

Teardrop is one of the very few 21st-century bars you'll see that has been carpeted. I mean, who carpets a bar anymore? Is this 1971? But carpeting is actually really

Teardrop Cocktail Lounge

1015 NW Everett Street
Portland, OR
503.445.8109
www.teardroplounge.com

good, because it absorbs noise and helps the bar feel much more quiet. How many great lounges are ruined by poor acoustics that make them uncomfortably loud, even when an intrinsically mellow crowd has gathered?

Yes, we are going there. Quit your crying. We are opening the profile of Teardrop by discussing the carpeting. Perhaps you thought we would lead with Teardrop's lofty position in the Portland cocktail community, specifically its status as the bar by which all others in town are measured. Or the idea that it seems to be a training ground for Portland's greatest mixologists—witness the fact that virtually every other Portland bar in these pages is exploding with ex-Teardroppers. Or the fact that it constantly makes lists of the nation's top bars. No, all of this pales in comparison to the calm-inducing cerulean carpeting.

In addition to the wall-to-wall goodness, Teardrop sports a cobalt-colored bar lined with a rack full of matching bottles containing a humbling variety of house-made tinctures and bitters. A lucite teardrop shelf is suspended above the bar, holding more booze. A few small booths orbit the round bar, and a projector shows old films on a billowy white sheet. A skylight among the vintage wood-beam ceiling lets in some natural light (hope it doesn't fade the carpet), and there may be a few tables al fresco on the sidewalk when the weather allows for it. Sadly, the sidewalk isn't carpeted. All in all, Teardrop feels sleek, modern, clean, and bright, a fitting vibe for the very trendy and affluent crowd so often seen in the center of the Pearl District.

Daniel Shoemaker and Ted Charak opened Teardrop in 2007, after a decade-long stint in San Francisco. The bar prepares its own specialty liqueurs, syrups, digestifs, vermouths, tonic water, bitters, and tinctures, as well as an Amer Picon substitute (also see In Fine Spirits in Chicago, page 91), all are made from local produce and natural sugars. They even make a Kina Lillet substitute. Today's Lillet Blanc used to be called Kina Lillet. The old Kina was closer to a quinquina (or quinine-forward aperitif). In the 1980s, with tastes drifting away from the bitterness of quinine, Kina was made sweeter and rebranded as Lillet Blanc. So, Teardrop is able to come closer to reproducing classic drinks that call for Kina Lillet than those using off-the-shelf Lillet Blanc. Formidable cocktail geekery is de rigueur at Teardrop, but don't panic—a glossary is included on the drink menu so the newbs can keep up.

Let's get to that menu. It is divided into sections for classics, house drinks, and "friends." Friends, of course, are drinks created by other bars around the world.

Teardrop does dig deep for its classics; nothing so common as a Sidecar will be seen on its list. For example: the Continental Apple-jack Sour (Laird's applejack, lemon juice, sugar, soda, fruits, Bordeaux float; $9) by O. H. Byron from *The Modern Bartenders' Guide* (1884) or the Quarter-Deck Cocktail by Harry MacElhone from *Harry's ABC of Mixing Cocktails*, 1930 (Dubonnet Rouge, Amer Picon, Cointreau; $9). Daily specials always include one classic-era cocktail. We tried the Trilby (Glenmorangie 10-year Scotch whisky, Dolin sweet vermouth, Parfait Amor liqueur, Herbsaint pastis, orange bitters; $11), created in 1940 by Patrick Duffy. Next up was a sweet, fizzy, and balanced Love in the Afternoon (Rittenhouse rye, pluot, lemon-basil-demerara soda, mint sprig; $9). A pluot is a plum/apricot. Apriums also exist.

We'll be darned if there aren't a bunch of drinks on the menu named after movies. The Kessel Run Highball (Elijah Craig 12-year bourbon, yellow Chartreuse, Lillet Blanc, Meyer lemon, pimento dram, soda) is clearly a *Star Wars* reference (but can they make this drink in less than 12 parsecs?), which leads us to wonder if the African Swallow is named for *Monty Python and the Holy Grail*.

Will the bartenders "bring us a shrubbery"? No, but they may use a shrub in the recipe (Martin Miller's Westbourne Strength gin, house Kina Lillet, blood orange shrub, Chartreuse Elixir Végétal, lemon peel). Chartreuse Elixir Végétal is

essentially Chartreuse bitters—awesome stuff and not commonly seen in North America. The Brian's Song (pear brandy, ginger syrup, mezcal, lemon juice) makes the menu, too, while the
Freedonia is clearly a Marx Brothers reference (foie gras armagnac,
coffee, Licor 43, pistachio-balsamic gastrique). We also can't help
but wonder if the Modus Operandi (rye, Nonino amaro, Carpano
Antica Formula vermouth, sasparilla and clove tinctures, bitters)
was inspired by David Lynch's character in *Twin Peaks: Fire Walk
with Me*.

There's no popcorn to go with the movie drinks here, but you
can get hot buttered rum (seasonally). A small menu of food is great
for snacking, but can provide dinner as well. We liked the looks of
the rabbit wrapped in prosciutto with brussel sprouts, but ended
up trying the lasagna. It was tasty enough, but we would have preferred if it weren't served at room temperature. This is nothing to
cry about; there are no tears allowed at Teardrop.

After all, tears might stain the carpeting.

LAST CALL!
More Destinations to Explore in Portland

Portland is absolutely blowing up as a food and cocktail
town. Here are some more destinations in Portland that
you might like. They're opening almost faster than we can
track, research, and visit them! Go Portland!

Hale Pele (2733 NE Broadway; 503.427.8454; www.
halepele.com) is owned by Blair Reynolds, tropical syrup
maker to the stars. Reynolds creates handcrafted tiki drinks
the way you're *supposed* to do tiki drinks—in a tiki bar filled
with tikis. Low lighting, red leather booths pulled from a
classic Armet & Davis Denny's, paintings on black velvet,
tiki carvings from Stephen Crane's legendary Kon-Tiki
Ports (via Portland's defunct Jasmine Tree), and a sunken
bar. Drinks include all of the usual tiki canon at $7–$9,

including the Mai Tai, the Scorpion, the Zombie, the Tonga Punch, the Fogcutter, and a special top-shelf Mai Tai ($15) created for the annual Northwest Tiki Crawl. Snacks are in keeping with the expected mid-century Polynesian-Chinese fare found at the classic-era tiki bars, and are divided between tidbits ($6–$10) and entrees ($11–$14), such as fried shrimp, egg rolls, meat skewers, and crab rangoon. The mandatory pu-pu platter includes all six of their tidbits choices, plus fire, for $28.

We tend to like quiet bars. The word "quiet" can have a few connotations, though. Portland visitors will doubtlessly be directed to Clyde Common or Teardrop first, but don't let the less hyped, less hyper, and less high-volume places slip under your radar. One good example is **June** (2215 E. Burnside Street; 503.477.4655; www.junepdx.com). June was launched in August 2010 (two months late?) by chef Greg Perrault, formerly of the revered DOC, with architect/manager Matthew Peterson. The cozy and diminutive restaurant has all of nine tables, plus six seats at the bar, for a total capacity of about 35. Decor is simple, almost ascetic, with homey earth tones and lots of wood. Perrault's market-driven menu is the focus at June, which has Portland food critics raving. However, it's those six seats at the bar that we're eyeballing. Kelly Swensen (of the defunct Ten 01) is

the man behind the stick. His spirit-driven cocktails are familiar but adventurous, and keep within the realm of new takes on old favorites. The Marigold Old-Fashioned, for example, is made from Old Charter 10-year Kentucky whiskey, local Mt. Adams honey, and five small marigolds muddled in the glass ($9), while the Wild at Heart is tequila, Barolo Chinato spiced wine digestif, Campari, and a float of Cointreau ($9). Perhaps the most revered of the five drinks on Swensen's notably concise menu is the P.S. I Read Your Diary (New English gin, fortified Moscato d'Asti sparkling wine, orange bitters, absinthe; $9). Swensen also improvised for us: Junipero gin, lime juice, celery bitters, a dash of powdered sugar on top, and a soda fill ($9). Crisp, refreshing, and summery.

Speaking of crisp, refreshing, and summery, **Mint** and **820 Lounge** (816/820 North Russell Street; 503.284.5518; www.mintrestaurant.com) are the restaurant and adjacent bar by Lucy Brennan. As a veteran of Portland's bar community for over 20 years, London-born Brennan is often credited as being among the first in Portland to bring the kitchen and the bar closer together, particularly in her early work with fruit purées. Mint, her American bistro, opened in spring 2001. Housed in the historic Frederick Torgler Building, Mint's cuisine by Brian McElmeel focuses on Pacific Northwest, Mediterranean, and Latin American influences. The more cocktail-focused 820 followed in spring 2003. The 18-foot bar is all about the fruit, so you ought to treat yourself to a Splash (gold tequila, mandarin purée, lemon-lime juice, float of amaretto; $8) or the innovative Avocado Daiquiri (light rum, gold rum, avocado, cream, lemon-lime juice, sugar; $9).

In Montavilla, the southeastern extremity of Portland, is Kate Duncan's **The Observatory** (8115 SE Stark Street; 503.445.6284; www.theobservatorypdx.com). Nineteenth-century booze ads are juxtaposed with photos of earth and space, plus an antique brass astroglobe and a telescope, validating the restaurant's name without being too theme-y. The cocktail menu contains about a dozen spins on classics, such as the Stellar Mojito, the Fresh-Fashioned, and the Blood Orange Negroni. Friendly bartender Dusty mixed us a Ruby Rye Manhattan (rye, balsamic cherry ruby port, Fee Brothers Aztec chocolate bitters, cherry bitters; $8).

Reasonably priced food includes Carlton Farms pork ragu ($12), Idaho trout piccata ($11), and a generous cheese platter bargain-priced at $12.

Contrary to its name, **Secret Society** (116 NE Russell Street; 503.493.3600; www.secretsociety.net) isn't playing up to the speakeasy fad. In fact, it is named for something much cooler. The 1907 building was originally the home of the fraternal group Woodmen of the World, before housing the Prince Hall Freemasons for about 50 years. The tiny second-floor bar was opened in June 2008 by Matt Johnson. "We strive to conjure the feel of an early-'20s era hotel lobby bar," Johnson says. Indeed, it is decorated with old black-and-white photos, framed paintings of Pacific Northwest themes, a taxidermy kudu, and cozy maroon walls under dim lighting. Secret Society shares the building with Toro Bravo restaurant, the Wonder Ballroom, and a recording studio. The menu focuses on classics courtesy of Michael Sellers, but upon our visit, we were greeted by Chelsea McAlister, who poured us her best attempt at an Old-Fashioned. We asked about local products and were rewarded with quite a list: Aviation gin, Krogstad aquavit, Temperance Trader whiskey, Smalls gin, Ransom Old Tom

"A bartender, in the classic sense, performs many duties beyond making drinks. He or she is host, server, conversationalist, local tour guide, shrink, DJ, cab-caller, crowd controller, and teller of jokes, among many other roles. The act of tending the bar is a broad and varied role."

—MATT JOHNSON, Secret Society

gin, Ransom grappa, Voyager gin, Trillium absinthe, Imbue vermouth, Clear Creek cassis liqueur, Glory Bee honey, cocktail olives and onions from the Garlic Lady, and Columbia Gorge Organic juices.

There's a catch-all profile of the **Trader Vic**'s empire in the San Francisco/Bay Area section of this book, but while we're on the subject of tiki, we want to give a shout-out to the new Portland store (1203 NW Glisan Street; 503.467.2277). Some of the neo-Vic's that have opened in the last 15 years or so have been really great, and some haven't. This one is fantastic. Bartender Courtney practically begged us to show her how to make a classic Victor Bergeron drink that isn't on Portland's menu, so perhaps she'll now make a Tortuga (three rums, three citrus, sweet vermouth, crème de cacao, grenadine; $11) for you as well.

Vintage (7907 SE Stark Street; 503.262.0696; www.vintagepdx.com) is just down the street from the Observatory. Dark wood and Belle Epoch posters on maroon walls give it a cozy feeling. Forty drinks on the menu are half classics and half originals. The bartender, named Cross, tells us that Vintage is 98 percent booze and 2 percent food. We'll take that booze, thanks. He mixed us a Hammer Thyme (Hendricks gin, citrus, cucumber, thyme tincture, Fee Brothers orange bitters, simple syrup; $8).

Wafu (3113 SE Division Street; 503.236.0205; www.wafupdx.com), opened in August 2011 as a late-night stop for small plates, noodles, and a short list of classic, modern, and Asian-inspired cocktails. Whiskeys, shochus, and an obsessive ice program are in the hands of bar manager Alan Akwai. The Ginza-school influence shows in his thorough attention to detail when crafting his Saz variant, the Sriracha Sazerac (Russell's Reserve 6-year rye, simple syrup, Peychaud's bitters, Brooklyn Hemispherical sriracha bitters, Herbisant rinse, lemon zest).

Woodsman Tavern (4537 Southeast Division Street; 971.373.8264; www.woodsmantavern.com) was opened by Duane Sorenson in October 2011, virtually next door to his popular Stumptown Coffee. The Tavern is decorated in reclaimed wood, flannel on the waiters, and a wall filled with Pacific Northwest landscape paintings. Cuisine by chef Jason Barwikowski (of Olympic Provisions) consists of Northwest tavern food, seafood including a raw bar, and plenty of pork. Cocktails by Evan Zimmerman (of Laurelhurst Market) focus on elegance and simplicity, and are mainly twists on classics. To wit: the Gold Rush (bourbon, lemon juice, honey; $8). Most notable—and first on the menu—is a take on the Old Pal, called the Hunting Vest (Old Overholt rye, dry vermouth, Fino sherry, cedar-steeped Campari; $9). Inverting Clyde Common's vaunted barrel-aging process, Zimmerman chars cedar chips, stuffs them in a jar, fills it with Campari, and leaves it to sit for two weeks. The Campari is then triple-strained before serving. We were also drawn to the Kentucky Special (bourbon, lapsang souchong smoked tea, Cherry Heering, bitters).

SAN FRANCISCO BAY AREA

San Francisco and its satellite towns to the north and east boast more Michelin-starred restaurants than any other metropolitan area in North America. With this culinary excellence comes great drinking (yay!) in a style that defines the West Coast. Although many of the bars in this book strive for seasonal, sustainable, local, organic, or all of the above, these things seem to be de rigueur in the Bay Area, and that's a very good thing. Not too many Manhattan bars have their own forager on staff (and if they did, we're not sure we'd want to consume the results). On the West Coast, it's a completely different scenario.

Absinthe Brasserie & Bar

398 Hayes Street
San Francisco, CA
415.551.1590
www.absinthe.com

While some houses of liquid worship make serving absinthe their mission, there are bars that simply use the word "absinthe" to evoke a time, a place, or a mood. San Francisco's Absinthe Brasserie & Bar is in the latter category. Bill Russell-Shapiro opened his upscale eatery in 1998, along the then-nascent Hayes Valley restaurant row. When Absinthe opened, absinthe was still illegal in the United States, but the very thought of this forbidden firewater has always been quite effective at conjuring up images of Belle Époque Paris. Thus, it's a fitting name for a restaurant serving high-end southern French cuisine (by chef Adam Keough) paired with a Eurocentric 50-page wine list (topping out at $3,600 for a 2003 Petrus Grand Cru, from Pomerol).

Certainly, the plush and cozy restaurant feels every bit a part of the era it is conjuring, and the festive murals featuring guest appearances from a devilish green fairy definitely help push the vibe.

While absinthe is certainly available at Absinthe, it doesn't seem to be a focus. Rather, Russel-Shapiro and bar manager Carlos Yturria seem more focused on cocktails at their bar.

That, my friends, is never a bad thing.

The High Cotton (rye, Pimm's, Dubonnet rouge, peach bitters, mint bitters, lemon peel, mint leaf) is a classic-style, three-ingredient (plus bitters and garnish) wonder, simple and elegant, conjuring up images of Antebellum porches on hot Georgia afternoons. The Real Maria (celery-and-peppercorn-infused tequila, fresh heirloom tomato juice, peppered sherry gastrique, olive) is a tipple that Bloody Mary fans might find to be an interesting alternative. Naturally, we wanted to try some drinks that actually make use of the green stuff. Absinthe gets its name from a key ingredient, *artemisia absinthium*, or grand wormwood. This is added to a base spirit, usually grain alcohol, along with fennel, anise, and other herbs. The bar puts it to good use in the Lawhill (rye, dry vermouth, absinthe, maraschino, Angostura bitters, flamed orange peel). The absinthe reveals itself as the drink progresses, but is more subtle in the Sacred Heart (La Pinta pomegranate tequila, absinthe, limoncello, splash of citrus, twist of lemon). All cocktails on the list of nine house creations are $11. A completely separate bar (food) menu contains another 18 cocktails, mostly standards (Sidecar, Corpse Reviver #2, Martinez) in the $9–$11 range. In 2006, Jeff Hollinger and Rob Schwartz, a pair of Absinthe bartenders, collected some of the bar's best recipes for their book *The Art of the Bar*.

Gal Friday Night was excited to bring her French boyfriend to Absinthe, and while it was hard to impress him with the coq au vin and cassoulet that we thought were quite good, he couldn't deny the quality and selection of cheeses. California lamb shank and oysters from the raw bar are also hard to resist.

A BIT ON ABSINTHE

For the uninitiated: Absinthe has been legal in the United States since 2005 and does not make you hallucinate. The reason 19th-century poets flipped out on this stuff is simply that they were drinking *way* too much of it. Wormwood, a plant containing thujone (the ingredient that supposedly causes the psychedelic effects), is found in greater quantities in many vermouths than in absinthe.

Absinthe is most commonly consumed after having cold water dripped into it from above, one drop at a time, giving the liquor a beautifully cloudy, milky appearance. Sometimes that water is dripped through a sugar cube placed on a special spoon atop the edge of the glass. The spoon has slits carved into it, allowing the sugar water to pass through. If the sugar cube is on fire, please leave the bar immediately; you're dealing with amateurs. Flaming drinks are exclusively for the tiki bar.

Alembic

1725 Haight Street
San Francisco, CA
415.666.0822
www.alembicbar.com

We like being served astounding drinks, but we don't like feeling like we're unwelcome in a bar if the valet didn't just take the Bentley off to be washed. Save the fancy stuff for people sober enough to care. The mood of a bar, like the cocktails (and like life), is all about balance. Alembic is your Haight Street destination for great cocktails in a casual environment. It does a nice job of bringing a somewhat more refined vibe to the Haight without feeling like it is at odds with the neighborhood's uniquely grubby atmosphere.

Perusing an exhaustive whiskey list and a menu divided into "the canon" and "the new school," with eight drinks on each side, we went for a Vieux Carré (a fine rendition of the classic), a Bee's

Knees (a fine rendition of the classic), and a Clover Club (a fine rendition of the classic, featuring locally-made raspberry syrup).

Moving on to the new school, we went for something so new that it hadn't been named yet (Batavia arrak, lemon juice, lime juice, crème de pêche, Peychaud's bitters, simple syrup, shaken with a mint sprig in the shaker). Next were two of bar manager Daniel Hyatt's creations: the Procession (Espolón tequila blanco, white crème de cacao, ruby port, hibiscus tea, orange bitters) and the simple but surprising Golden Spike (Tennessee whiskey, yuzu, honey, Chinese hot mustard). All cocktails are priced at $11.

Since 2008, the last Sunday of each month has been devoted to Savoy Cocktail Night, hosted by Erik Ellestad of Heaven's Dog. The normal cocktail menu is replaced by complete copies of Harry Craddock's mandatory 1930 recipe compendium, *The Savoy Cocktail Book*. Ellestad and another Alembic bartender do their noble best to make any requested recipe from among the 800-ish listed in the book. In 2007, Ellestad began working his way through the book, page by page, systematically making every single drink as he went. At press time, he was just about to finish. Obsolete ingredients? He'll make 'em. And we'll drink 'em.

A concise menu of food from Ted Fleury begins with the bar's notorious pickled quail's eggs ($2), as well as plates like miso-grilled trumpet mushrooms ($17), flat iron steak ($23), and pork belly sliders ($5 each).

If you're coming to Alembic as a tourist, you're not going to be able to avoid/resist walking up Haight Street at least once. You'll still encounter all of the counterculture stereotypes that have haunted the Haight since the 1960s, but with maturity has come certain pockets of elevation. **Club Deluxe** (1509–1511 Haight Street; 415.552.6949; www.sfclubdeluxe.com) has long been a destination

Bar Agricole

355 11th Street
San Francisco, CA
415.355.9400
www.baragricole.com

This book is all about bars that are extremely dedicated to making you a good cocktail. But then there are the ones that are nothing short of *obsessive*. In this context, "obsessive" is not to be used derisively. Just the opposite, in fact. If we are going to pay upwards of 10 bucks for a few sips of liquid, then we want the people making it to put as much care as possible into our tipple. It is also key to note that part of any obsession with quality and freshness means sourcing things locally. This has the residual effect of being good for local economies and good for the environment. Everybody wins. Pay attention, kids, this is the future.

Bar Agricole was opened in August 2010 by Bay Area bartenders Thad Vogler (of Heaven's Dog) and Eric Johnson (of Bourbon & Branch) with Andreas Willausch. The bar is named after rhum agricole, Vogler's favorite spirit. *Agricole* is also French for "agriculture," so the name is doubly fitting.

In-between the bar and the street is a fence of redwood and corrugated zinc that hides a courtyard and a 500-square-foot biodynamic garden. Here, Bar Agricole grows dill, hyssop, fennel, and citrus fruit. The idea of growing your own limes right outside the door is completely foreign to most of the big city bars in this book, but Agricole takes full advantage of the California climate, cutting out the need for industrialization in the process of bringing fruits and herbs to your cocktail. This attention to both quality and sustainability (funny how those things go hand in hand) continues with Bar Agricole's partnerships with local farms and distilleries. Local distillers are helping the bar develop their own spirits, such as a farmhouse curaçao and multiple biodynamic brandies. Of course, America's first agricole rum, Agua Libre, is made just over the Bay Bridge in Alameda, so you'll find that on the menu as well. A pair of farms in Ukiah and Fresno provide Bar Agricole with chickens, eggs, and lamb.

Inside Bar Agricole, two bars put all of this good stuff to use in drinks such as the Moonraker (Marian Farms biodynamic brandy,

Leopold Bros. peach brandy, Cocchi Americano aperitif wine, absinthe), an update of a lost treasure from the *Savoy Cocktail Book*, and the El Presidente (Haitian rum, farmhouse curaçao, grenadine, orange bitters). The bar's namesake spirit shows up in the Rhum Dandy (white agricole rum, sweet vermouth, lemon juice, absinthe). We also liked Vogler's hot Castle Dip (calvados, simple syrup, absinthe, sprig of mint, boiling water, lemon twist) and the Bellamy Scotch Sour (Scotch whisky, lemon juice, orange juice, honey, egg white). All cocktails are $10. Among five kinds of ice, house bitters, and all of the farmyard action, it goes without saying that "a few" of the syrups and other ingredients behind that bar are house-made.

Food by Brandon Jew changes nightly, but may include selections such as rabbit saddle ($32), smoked duck breast ($12), antipasti ($14), and country-style pork paté ($10).

The building is LEED-certified, and won Best Sustainable Structure from *California Home + Design* magazine in 2010, as well as the James Beard Award in May 2011 for best restaurant design. Wood strips reclaimed from whiskey barrels and century-old oak barn beams support the farm-to-table theme, but otherwise the space looks quite modern. Three very cool glass sculptures resembling curtains blowing in the wind (by Nikolas Weinstein Studios) enhance a trio of skylights, but add no warmth. That comes from the bourbon.

Bourbon & Branch

501 Jones Street
San Francisco, CA
415.346.1735
www.bourbonandbranch.com

Several bars have used the term "speakeasy" in the 21st century because it was good trendy marketing in 2007, but others can back the term up with some history. Brian Sheehy's Bourbon & Branch is part of a very, very short list of so-called speakeasies that can boast of being housed in a building that has continually been a tavern since 1865, including a stint as a *real* speakeasy. It was called the Ipswitch—A Beverage Parlor from 1921 to 1933. Pioneering the speakeasy fad on the West Coast, and supporting it with some of the best drinks in California and a complete commitment to the concept, Bourbon & Branch is to San Francisco what Teardrop is to Portland, what the Violet Hour is to Chicago, and what Milk & Honey was to New York—the defining craft cocktail bar in a town swimming in them.

Make your reservation online, and then make your way through the seedy Tenderloin District to 501 Jones Street. Once inside, the vibe at Bourbon & Branch is dark, warm, woody, and potentially romantic. We noted fresh roses at either end of the bar, a vintage-style tin ceiling, backbar shelves built right into the brick walls, velvet damask wallpaper, friendly hostesses, 1930s jazz records playing just loud enough to be audible, lighting almost exclusively from candles, and cloth cocktail napkins.

The Main Bar area is in the front, and contains cast iron stools bolted to the floor opposite a series of small booths. Up a few stairs are further booths in a reserved-seating balcony that overlooks the Main Bar. Hidden behind a large bookcase, the Library is a noisier and less interesting space held aside to corral those without reservations.

The exhaustive tippler's tome contains a good balance of classics, variations of classics, and new creations. We were impressed by a whole page devoted to the precious Havana Club rum (see page 287). That stuff is hard to source in the United States.

All drinks are $11. Our bartender wasn't initially as warm as the hostess had been, but after a few minutes we were speaking the same language, and the magic began to happen. After a complimentary amuse-bouche, we went for a Rudy Boy (Appleton rum, Campari, Cointreau, lime, grapefruit bitters, splash of soda water), which was borrowed from Trailer Happiness in London. The conversation soon turned to Chartreuse (that happens), and VEP in particular. VEP, or Vieillissement Exceptionnellement Prolongé ("exceptionally prolonged aging") sits in oak casks longer than the standard Chartreuse, and retails for about three times as much. We sorta had to try a VEP Last Word, which was . . . well, Gal Friday Night's notes say that I cried. There are no photos, therefore it didn't happen.

This was followed up with a Clermont Affair (rye, Nonino amaro, whiskey-barrel-aged bitters, clove tincture float) and a Laphroaig Project (Laphroaig Scotch whisky, yellow Chartreuse, green Chartreuse, maraschino, lemon juice), because there is no such thing as too much Chartreuse (or too much Laphroaig, for that matter).

In order to escape raiding lawmen, the original incarnation of the speakeasy was equipped with five tunnels that eventually surfaced as far away as Leavenworth Street. While the tunnels are not open anymore, there are further mysteries to explore at 501 Jones Street, such as the Wilson and Russell's Room.

The Wilson seems to draw inspiration from Dashiell Hammett, author of so many San Francisco-based detective novels (including *The Maltese Falcon*), and creator of the incomparably cool Nick and Nora Charles (if you haven't seen the 1934 film *The Thin Man*, stop reading and go do so—*now.*) Near the restrooms is a locked door labeled Wilson & Wilson Private Detective Agency. A password, different from the one required for admission to Bourbon & Branch, is required to gain admittance. Inside, you'll enjoy a three-cocktail prix fixe menu ($30) or à la carte drinks at $12 each. Three bartenders are on hand to cater to only 22 customers, so personal attention is nearly guaranteed. Russell's Room is named after the JJ Russell Cigar Shop, which was once the front for the original speakeasy on these premises. The room is smaller and more intimate than the Main Bar.

Four bars under this roof aren't nearly enough, however. Bourbon & Branch offers weekly cocktail classes as **The Beverage Academy** (www.beverageacademy.com), with a rotating curriculum of topics.

You may also want to visit **Cask** (17 Third Street; 415.424.4844; www.caskspirits.com), the bar's retail source for artisanal and rare hootch, quality bar tools, California wines, and books for boozers (including vintage and rare ones). Finally, there is a new bar called **Tradition** (441 Jones Street; 415.474.2284; www.tradbar.com), which was briefly a dive bar called Mr. Lew's Win-Win House and Grand Sazerac Emporium.

Cantina

580 Sutter Street
San Francisco, CA
415.398.0195
www.cantinasf.com

Raise your hand if your first exposure to the word "cantina" was the crazy Mos Eisley cantina in the original *Star Wars*. The Cantina in San Francisco, hometown of Lucasfilm, opened just one day before the 30th anniversary of the release of *Star Wars*. Too many coincidences for you? Well, cool it, kid, because that's where it ends. It's safe to assume that Chewbacca wasn't drinking a Caipirinha in the *Star Wars* cantina.

Cantina was founded in May 2007 by owner/bartender Duggan McDonnell with Kristina McDonnell, Aaron Prentice, and Christene Larsen. The idea of the bar was to provide a community destination for art, music, and cocktails in an environment that pays homage to the Latin American influence in San Francisco. New artwork, mainly from Bay Area artists, is rotated in every six weeks or so. The art tends to focus on the bar's themes of San Francisco and Latin America (and Dagobah). Disc jockeys provide Latin, techno, and pop music for a crowd that can get quite noisy later in the evening (especially after those freaky alien musicians with big heads start playing). There's no proper signage announcing Cantina from the street; look for the Jolly Roger logo on the window (or R2-D2 outside).

In addition to handcrafted libations from McDonnell and his bar staff, Cantina offers wines from Latin America, plus local beers. Of course, all cocktails include house-made bitters, syrups, and infusions, plus hand-squeezed citrus and a preference for premium spirits. Citrus—including Meyer lemon, grapefruit,

Palestinian lime, kumquat, and Mandarin orange—is sourced from the bar's own grove of trees in the Santa Clara Valley, which is harvested by Ewoks.

Of course, cocktails veer strongly toward the Latin end of the spectrum (all are $9, and are available by the pitcher for $28). Gal Friday Night used the Force to guide us to the popular Five-Spice Margarita (Tres Agaves tequila, Combier Liqueur d'Orange, lime juice, five-spice-infused agave nectar), followed by the Blackberry and Cabernet Caipirinha (Cabana cachaça, muddled limes, Driscoll's blackberries, Carlos Basso cabernet), and finally Cantina's take on the Pisco Punch (Campo de Encanto pisco, crushed pineapple, citrus, Angostura bitters, "secret sauce"). The "secret sauce" is gingery, but we won't spoil it.

A bit further down the menu is a section of "Cocktails de Culinaire" (that's French, not Spanish, but who's complaining?). These are $11 and include house creations such as the Old Gringo (Don Amado mezcal, Pimm's, dry vermouth, lemon juice, agave nectar, Castillo Perelada Reserva Spanish cava).

Salud, cheers, and may the Force be with you.

◄◄►►

When discussing the Bay Area's commitment to sustainability, Camino in Oakland is the East Bay outpost that most gives San Francisco's Bar Agricole a run for their honey. We're talking about a bar that keeps bees on its roof to produce

Camino

3917 Grand Avenue
Oakland, CA
510.547.5035
www.caminorestaurant.com

honey for its cocktails. Is there room for a joke here about catching a buzz?

Opened in May 2008 by Russell Moore and Allison Hopelain, Camino has strict standards for their purchasing: no artificial anything, no industrial products, no big distributors—only traceable grain or fruit for base spirit, and no genetically-modified foods.

We stopped in for dinner and drinks, and were pleased with the friendly service while enjoying a nice ragu of lamb, a salad made with rockfish and salted lingcod, and good bread. Menu items range from around $8 for starters to about $27 for entrees.

Moving on to the cocktails, it is interesting that none of the libations on the menu have names. Instead, drinks simply reference the base spirit. Choices on our visit were: gin, armagnac, gin (again), rum, and "pisco-style brandy." We went for the gin (with Spätlese Riesling, peach, hibiscus bitters, and three tiny wine grapes on the stem at the bottom of the glass), the armagnac (Chateau de Pellehaut, gomme syrup, absinthe, house-made bitters, and a fat twist of lemon peel), and the pisco (Marion Farms pisco, lemon juice, house-made vermouth, raspberry syrup, and a bay leaf garnish). Drinks are $9–$10. The gin drink was interesting, but we are never quite convinced by Riesling in a cocktail. The armagnac tipple was a stronger offering, with a carefully achieved balance. The pisco cocktail used the vermouth with pleasant subtlety, and even more so with the raspberry.

It goes without saying at this point that a lot of the ingredients are made in-house. A short list includes: honey, ginger, grilled fig leaf, blood orange, and peach syrups. Bitters include hibiscus, peach, orange, "Angostura-style," "Peychaud-style," and coffee. Camino makes their own version of Nocino (a walnut liqueur originating in Italy), and have vintages from several recent years available. They make sour cherries as well, by infusing brandy with quince, apple, and peach. Seasonal ingredients may include grilled fig leaf, cucumbers, pluots, grapes, anise hyssop, wild fennel, savory, and pomegranate. Citrus is always California-based organic, except for a few Texas grapefruits. Is it considered cheating at this point to confess that they get gomme syrup and orgeat from Small Hand Foods?

Yes indeed, they are busy bees at Camino.

The building that now houses Comstock Saloon was built in 1907, the year after the great earthquake of 1906 leveled much of the Barbary Coast, San Francisco's notorious red light district. In keeping with the seedy aspects of the neighborhood at the time, a ceramic trough was built into the floor, right along the front edge of the bar. This may or may not have been for relieving one's self in, or it may have been a spitoon. We'll never know. In any case, there are proper plumbing facilities on the premises today.

Comstock Saloon

155 Columbus Avenue
San Francisco, CA
415.617.0071
www.comstocksaloon.com

During the past century, the building has continually been used for a succession of restaurants and watering holes. In April 2010, Jonny Raglin and Jeff Hollinger partnered with the Absinthe Group to launch the space's newest incarnation, named for silver baron Henry Comstock.

Tired of the over-complexity they perceived in the cocktails at Absinthe and aware of the history of the building, Raglin and Hollinger decided to get back to the basics with Comstock. The drinks are riffs on ones that might have been served at the turn of the century (although probably not in a bar with a spittoon-trough), and the decor has been restored to something that is period-appropriate but presumably somewhat nicer than what 1907 visitors to this space encountered. The bar itself was restored, and in some ways this has dictated the menu; since there isn't room for many bottles on the small, century-old backbar's shelves, the liquor selection has been tightly curated. Leather-coated liquor flasks contrast damask wallpaper, while velvet booths stay cool under original vintage electric fans. The lucky or the early might score a seat at the cozy fireplace alcove in the back, and live jazz players will be stationed in a private mezzanine. A mid-19th-century absinthe fountain and a collection of other bar-related antiquities round out the decor.

The short menu of 10 drinks draws heavily from classics (Martinez, $12; Pisco Punch, $10; Blood and Sand, $11), but also contains lesser-known selections from the Harry Craddock canon, such as a heavily-modified Hop Toad Cocktail (Jamaican rum, apricot brandy, lime juice, bitters; $11) and lighter fare such as the

Bamboo Cocktail (Oloroso sherry, dry vermouth, bitters; $9). The renowned bar staff is capable of much more than this, of course. In fact, their best-selling drink is "all the rest," in the form of Barkeep's Whimsy ($10).

Chef Carlo Espinas updates and expands recipes from the same era as the drink menu. From the wood-burning stove in his kitchen comes a weekly three-course prix fixe, plus options like the Fishermen's Breakfast (seared trout, hash browns, broccoli, bacon vinaigrette, sunny side up egg; $20), chicken-fried rabbit (with "rabbit toast," celery, and fennel salad; $16), or the picnic platter (roasted pork sausage, smoked trout salad, pretzel, cheddar mayo, mustard, pickles; $19). You also won't want to miss his lauded beef shank and bone marrow pot pie ($18.50).

Forbidden Island

1304 Lincoln Avenue
Alameda, CA
510.749.0332
www.forbiddenislandalameda.com

Contemporary tiki bars like to make excuses. They half-ass the drinks because (as they tell us, continually) people don't want to wait for (or pay for) drinks done properly (plus, it's too much work for the poor suffering bar stewards to manage). They install televisions, pool tables, and hip-hop jukeboxes because (as they tell us, continually) these are necessary in order to keep their bar doing brisk enough business to stay open. These things are crowd-pleasers for those who don't get the tiki concept, we are told. We are told this a lot.

So why do it at all? Open a sports bar.

On the flipside, the craft cocktail nobility have finally deemed tiki drinks worthy of inclusion on cocktail menus. But very few slow bars that *specialize* in well-made tiki drinks are willing to go the distance with the entire tiki concept.

Exceptions to all of the above statements are few, but we do have a small elite of businesses getting all of it right, including Alameda's Forbidden Island.

This is a tiki bar.

Mahalo.

Forbidden Island was founded in 2006 by Michael Thanos, Mano Thanos, and Martin Cate. Cate has since sailed across the bay to create Smuggler's Cove. The menu features over 60 cocktails by Donn Beach, "Trader" Vic Bergeron, and various other classic Cali-tiki institutions, as well as new drinks created by the staff.

It goes without saying that you'll be able to get a proper Mai Tai here, not to mention a Suffering Bastard (brandy, gin, lime juice, ginger beer, Angostura bitters), or a Missionary's Downfall (rum, peach brandy, lime juice, pineapple juice, simple syrup, mint). Those who believe that tiki drinks are too sweet and lack complexity should be directed toward a Test Pilot (rum, rum, rum, lime juice, grapefruit juice, cinnamon syrup, falernum, Angostura bitters, absinthe). Now, on the other end of the spectrum, we are indeed looking for experience here. Go for the Makalani Bowl (dark rum, El Dorado 5-year rum, Luxardo maraschino liqueur, maple-apple-cinnamon reduction, vanilla-cinnamon syrup, St. Elizabeth allspice dram, lime juice, grapefruit juice) served in a custom ceramic bowl (that you

may keep) with fresh orchids and a real pearl. That ought to do it.

In 2010, Forbidden Island expanded their horizons with 20 classic cocktails, often with an added tropical spin. Traditional favorites such as such as the Aviation or the Blood and Sand join the new Rose Sazarac (Black Maple Hill small batch bourbon, St. George absinthe, rose syrup). Longtime bar manager Suzanne Long, who departed in January 2012, is particularly excited about the St. George products. "We have an excellent partnership with the illustrious St. George Spirits, including sharing a staff member," she says. "In addition to several cocktails on our main menu featuring their spirits, we also frequently feature their spirits in seasonal specials throughout the year."

Long also launched multiple ongoing events at Forbidden Island, such as Black Orchid Sessions, during which a specialty ingredient is announced (usually a house syrup or cordial). Each guest has the opportunity to taste the specialty ingredient and work with the bartender to use it in a bespoke libation. The resulting cocktail recipes are logged in personalized notebooks. Guests may come to Forbidden Island at any time, ask for their notebook, and have their specialty cocktail prepared for them. The best of these recipes have become part of Forbidden Island's permanent menu.

The bar also holds an annual luau, plus the famous Forbidden Island parking lot sale, packed with vintage and Hawaiiana vendors. Scheduled DJ nights feature tiki illuminati such as Dean "The Jab" Curtis's International Flight Lounge, Otto von Stroheim of Tiki Oasis, plus Will "The Thrill" Viharo's movie night.

Wait, who was it that was telling us a tiki bar can't thrive unless it's compromised? Oh yeah, it was the guy whose other bar *is* a sports bar.

Flora

1900 Telegraph Avenue
Oakland, CA
510.286.0100
www.floraoakland.com

If you want to see a sterling example of an elegant art deco-influenced bar, look no further than Flora. But really, calling the bar "art deco-influenced" isn't going quite far enough. Flora is housed in the amazing Oakland Floral Depot building. Designed in 1931 by Albert Elvers and decorated in cobalt blue tile and silver terra cotta, the building achieved landmark status in 1983. The small neon sign saying "Flora" is original and clearly inspired the name of the current business, which opened in November 2007. Owners Thomas Schnetz and Dona Savitsky have frosted the windows and retrofitted the interior of Flora with a deco decor in keeping with the exterior.

Oakland's Uptown neighborhood is in the midst of a revitalization that echoes Brooklyn's rebirth, especially if one were to contrast Oakland's relationship with San Francisco and Brooklyn's relationship with Manhattan. The Fox Theater (across the street from Flora) hosts music concerts, and the amazing Paramount Theatre is down the block. There are plenty of other restaurants and bars in the area, some of which are owned by Schnetz and Savitsky (including Mexican eateries Doña Tomás, Tacubaya in Berkeley, and Xolo, two doors down from Flora). Next for Schnetz and Savitsky is a plan to take over the space between Flora and Xolo, offering a more casual bar than the classy Flora. Hopefully some of the Fox Theater rock show crowd will spill over into that environment; Flora can get chaotic on gig nights.

Erik Adkins (of Slanted Door and Heaven's Dog) helped to set up the cocktail program. Twenty recipes, mainly classics (French 75, Pisco Sour, Pimm's Cup), are all $10, except for two that use sparkling wine ($12). Of the originals present, Gal Friday Night was most intrigued by the Jake Walk (Don Amado reposado mezcal, Bénédictine, Fernet-Branca amaro, orange bitters), while I was drawn to the Creole (Buffalo Trace bourbon, Cointreau, bitters, absinthe). Another Adkins creation is the Filibuster (rye whiskey, lemon juice, maple syrup, Angostura bitters, egg white).

We were also eager to sample the well-regarded Montego Bay (Smith & Cross rum, grapefruit juice, lime juice, honey, allspice dram, absinthe, Angostura bitters). This was adapted by Adkins from Jeff Berry's indispensable recipe compendium, *Beachbum Berry's Intoxica!*. Berry, in turn, uncovered this 1940s Donn Beach recipe from the Sahara Hotel in Las Vegas.

The spirits list is long, with a whole lot of whiskies present and accounted for. Flora's art deco absinthe fountain can be put to good use as well, perhaps with some of the local St. George absinthe, made one town over in Alameda. Of course, selected syrups and bitters are made in house.

Food at Flora is American comfort food, reinvented California-style. After some chef shuffles in 2010, Rico Rivera seems to have landed the gig for now. Entrees from his menu include fish and shellfish stew ($24), half-chicken cooked under a brick ($25), and grilled confit pork shoulder ($26).

Heaven's Dog

1148 Mission Street
San Francisco, CA
415.863.6008
www.heavensdog.com

The Slanted Door

1 Ferry Building #3
San Francisco, CA
415.861.8032
www.slanteddoor.com

Here's a capital idea: base the bulk of your cocktail menu on the recipes contained within a seven-decade-old, booze-infused travelogue. Sounds right up our alley, but there is a caveat—Charles H. Baker Jr., author of the 1939 tome *Gentleman's Companion, or: Around the World with Jigger, Beaker and Flask,* wasn't always diligent about printing the recipes in a precise and easy-to-read format. Erik Adkins, bar manager at Heaven's Dog, explains their approach to updating the sometimes vaguely described recipes. "This was fun for us because most of the drinks needed a lot of work," he says. "We also like the travelogue, because unlike other cocktail books of the time, which were compiled from other cocktail books, the *Gentleman's Companion* was a snapshot of drinking around the world in the 1930s. Each drink [in the book] was served to Charles Baker at a specific bar on a specific day."

With this manifesto firmly in place, owner Charles Phan opened Heaven's Dog in January of 2009, as a sister establishment to Slanted Door. "We are really proud of our bar at the Slanted Door," Adkins says, "but because of the crush of business and the focus on pairing German rieslings with the food, we felt that the bar didn't have as much of a chance to shine. We opened Heaven's Dog to focus more on cocktails."

Although the full menu of food at Heaven's Dog is strongly Asian-influenced, there is a decidedly San Franciscan ethic at work when it comes to the bar. They use Marian Farms' biodynamic, California-style pisco (made in Fresno) in the Pisco Apricot Tropical, (Marian Farms California-style pisco, Small Hand Foods pineapple gomme, apricot brandy, lime juice, Angostura bitters; $11), a drink created at the Lima Country Club in the 1920s. They also support "some of the better farmer spirits, regardless of where they come from. The idea that the still is a way to diversify the farm still exists in some places."

Naturally, in-house products include fresh-pressed ginger juice for bucks and mules, as well as fresh-pressed pineapple juice (from a hydraulic press) for fixes, slings, and tiki drinks, complemented with house-made marmalades, coconut crème, local honey, and organic maple syrup. Heaven's Dog and Slanted Door also use orgeat, pineapple gomme, gomme syrup, grenadine, and raspberry gomme made by Small Hand Foods, which is owned by Slanted Door bartender Jennifer Colliau.

The succinct cocktail menu is swayed more toward rum than you'd expect, but this is by no means a bad thing, given the choices at hand. Adkins's take on the Montego Bay (described above, as served at Flora) makes an appearance, and we also like the looks of the Cap Haitian Rum & Honey ("Clairene au Miel") made with Barbancourt 15-year rum, local organic honey, and Angostura bitters, served over a hand-cut ice cube. Including the Barbancourt 15-year rum in a cocktail when most people would be happy with the 8-year or less is truly living the dream, my friends, and that's why we're here. For the indecisive, Heaven's Dog offers the Freedom From Choice (is that a Devo reference?): "Tell us your spirit and let us know if you want your drink to be citrus driven or spirituous." All cocktails are reasonably priced at $10.

The Slanted Door opened in 1995 and moved into its current digs in 2004. Check out the great views of the bay, a result of the restaurant's location in the historic Ferry Building. Chef Charles Phan's updated take on Vietnamese food include organic chicken claypot ($19), spicy Monterey squid ($18), and grass-fed Estancia shaking beef ($36).

"We are all proud bartenders. Some of us study old cocktail books in our spare time."
—Erik Adkins,
Heaven's Dog & The Slanted Door

Jardinière

300 Grove Street
San Francisco, CA
415.861.5555
www.jardiniere.com

Some people were so clearly born to cook that their very names prohpetically reflect this. Case in point: Traci Des Jardins, two-time James Beard Award winner, and chef/co-owner of Jardinière. In French, *des jardins* means "gardens," and *jardinière* can mean "gardener" (feminine form), or a sort of plant stand, or a dish cooked with a mix of vegetables. In any case, fate has been quite kind to bestow this name upon the owner of a restaurant. Imagine, for instance, if her name had been Des Poubelle. Doesn't really work, does it? Ms. Des Jardins is also an activist and philanthropist working with hunger relief organizations. And guess what? Hunger relief (not to mention sobriety relief) is exactly what we had in mind when Gal Friday Night and I entered the elegant Jardinière.

Opened in 1997, the restaurant is within a vintage brick building in the ritzy Hayes Valley area, close to the Louise M. Davies Symphony Hall and also very near Absinthe (see page 206). Built after the 1906 earthquake, the space is notable for once having housed venerable jazz club Kimball's West. The current interior was designed by co-owner Pat Kuleto. A circular mahogany bar with a massive marble top is the centerpiece of the room. Tiffany-style lamps rest atop the bar, which in turn sits below a big dome dotted with sparkly lights, meant to resemble an inverted champagne glass. There are tables orbiting the bar, but the place to sit for dinner is on the circular balcony. In keeping with the room's jazz heritage, there's live jazz every night at 7:30.

Much of the drink menu was designed by Brian MacGregor, who has since moved on to the new Locanda (see page 237). The nocturnal Gal Friday Night put her faith in the house creation, the Midnight Prayer (G'Vine Floraison gin, crème de violette, St. Germain elderflower liqueur, Regan's orange bitters; $14), the Pony Express (Sazerac six-year rye, Qi white tea liqueur, lemon juice, maple syrup; $12), and the Shadow of El Cero (Ranchero tequila, Campari, Vieux Pontarlier absinthe, lemon juice; $11).

You may have noticed the preference for French spirits: the Vieux Pontarlier absinthe and the G'Vine Floraison gin both come from France, and the St. Germain uses elderflowers harvested from the foothills of the French Alps. This carries over to the kitchen, where Des Jardins' hybrid of French and California cuisines are prepared. Craig Patzer's house-made charcuterie ($18) and cheese from Jardinière's walk-in cheese cave are available at the bar, but those seated for dinner might prefer to order delicately-portioned entrees from the changing daily menu. Hoffman Ranch hen ($34), loin of cervena venison ($44), and potato gnocchi with local Dungeness crab ($21) were on the menu recently, along with wine pairings and a chef's tasting menu ($120).

More than a few slow drinks bars put their drinks on a pedestal, making damned sure you know how special they are. Others are just neighborhood bars that happen to serve amazing drinks. It might be argued, in the second decade of the 21st century, that the former begat the latter.

Rickhouse

246 Kearny Street
San Francisco, CA
415.398.2827
www.rickhousebar.com

The latter, however, might be the wave of the future. This welcome evolution is clearly illustrated in the pair of bars owned by Brian Sheehy, owner of both Rickhouse and Bourbon & Branch.

Located near Union Square, Rickhouse opened in July 2009. A rickhouse is a warehouse where whiskey is stored as it ages, sometimes for decades. In keeping with the name, Rickhouse feels woody and rustic; if a bar could look like bourbon, it would look like this. One wall is brick, and is a survivor of fires related to the 1906 earthquake. The others are all wood, including the ceiling a full 20 feet up, which is covered in the remains of 300 Kentucky whiskey barrels. There are two bars on the ground floor, plus a balcony providing a bird's eye view of the amazing collection of booze behind the front bar. Stacked all the way up to that high ceiling—on backbar shelves salvaged from an Ozark nunnery that made "medicinal" hootch during Prohibition—is a rather impressive collection of spirits. Edison light bulbs, swinging doors separating the backbar area from the front bar, and just a few tables make the cozy, financial district Rickhouse feel much more like a casual neighborhood spot than its brother bar Bourbon & Branch does.

The encyclopedic cocktail menu contains nearly five dozen drinks ("classic cocktails and contemporary variations"), a selection that is only dwarfed by a list of 200 whiskeys. Short explanations provide insight into each of the libations, which of course are focused on fresh ingredients, local produce, and natural syrups.

Among the most popular creations is Eric Castro's Kentucky Buck (strawberry-infused bourbon, lemon juice, simple syrup, ginger beer, Angostura bitters). Gal Friday Night never forgets a drink, nor the sensation of holy Chartreuse mixed with a very smoky Scotch, so she wanted to try Owen Westman's take on the Laphroaig Project (Laphroaig Quarter Cask Scotch whisky, green Chartreuse, yellow Chartreuse, Luxardo maraschino liqueur, lemon juice, Fee Brothers peach bitters). You'll recall, as she did, that they're working on this project over at Bourbon & Branch, too. That is a project worth finishing, and then ordering again. Bartender Kelli Bratvold has contributed to the house recipe library as well: the Noble Savage (Sombra mezcal, Dolin Blanco sweet vermouth, Bénédictine, Regan's orange bitters, strip of orange peel) made me feel like conquering Granada. Or drinking grenadine.

Into the realm of less acrobatic selections, we liked the looks of the Rye Maple Fizz (rye, lemon juice, maple syrup, egg white, soda, Angostura bitters), and the La Bonne Vie (Plymouth gin, lemon juice, grapefruit juice, fresh basil, bitters). All cocktails are $8.

It is key to note that the quality of the libations at Rickhouse is nearly identical to that at Bourbon & Branch. Bartenders employed by Sheehy rotate between both bars. The lower prices at Rickhouse balance the more personalized service at Bourbon & Branch. Rickhouse also features live music on Monday and Saturday nights. Although the bands aren't particularly loud, the bar does get a bit noisy, even on non-music nights.

If your goal is to visit a tiki reviv-alist bar done properly, the ones you want to visit first are those conceptualized by San Francisco's Martin Cate. Being a California native, he's got a decided advantage over the places serving tropical drinks in New York, London, and

Smuggler's Cove

650 Gough Street
San Francisco, CA
415.869.1900
www.smugglerscovesf.com

elsewhere: he's spent decades immersed in the state that spawned tiki. He gets that tiki isn't just a drink style, it's a *lifestyle*. The man lives it. He has been *macerated* in it.

Cate left his previous bar (Forbidden Island) to open Smuggler's Cove in December 2009. He cast a somewhat wider net with his new bar, preferring to celebrate the entire history of rum. "Tiki was my entry into rum," Cate says, "and it will always be my first love in terms of cocktails, but tiki drinks represent about 35 years of a 350-year-old spirit." That's a small window indeed, but one that Cate agrees is "glorious and magical."

Thus, the nautical-themed (as opposed to tiki-themed) Smuggler's Cove *can* be your place for excellent tiki drinks, but you can also get Prohibition-era Havana drinks like Mojitos, Daiquiris, and Mary Pickfords, and even pirate grogs or colonial tavern rum punches, whose recipes date back hundreds of years. Cate has even contemplated the integral importance of rum to Caribbean lifestyles—after all, this is where much of the world's rum is pro-duced—and has dug up endemic recipes from many Caribbean na-tions, serving them with location-correct products.

The bar's current menu contains 75 rum drinks, requiring 29 different rums. Staunchly committed to serving only the finest and most authentic brands, Smuggler's Cove only carries premium products. You won't often see Ron Zacapa 23 in a speed rail, but you will at Smuggler's Cove! The bar carries a total of about 315 brands; none are artificially flavored and only two are spiced (Cru-soe and Chairman's Reserve). Cate personally vetted the spiced rums to ensure that they were made with actual spices. He calls Chairman's "dynamite, the absolute market champion." Smug-gler's Cove also carries most of the California-made rums: Agua Libre, Sergeant Classick, Charbay. Plus, they've got a house brand,

exclusively distilled in three varieties by St. George Spirits of Alameda. Sorry, kids, you'll have to belly up at Smuggler's to try these, since they aren't bottled commercially.

Naturally, Smuggler's Cove make their own orgeat, grenadine, Don's mix, hot buttered rum batter, Jamaican jerk spiced syrup, and other ingredients, but the bar *does* use commercial falernum. "I'm happy with the John D. Taylor's," Cate says. "It's a Bajan product made with Bajan sugar, with Bajan rum, by Bajan people in Barbados with real Dominican limes. It's a very honest product."

Smuggler's Cove also hosts a Rumbustion Society, a club with three levels. Disciples of the Cove have sampled 20 different rums. "You're going to love some of them and you're going to hate some of them," Cate says, "but there is a rum for everybody." After taking a quiz, Disciples may sample 80 more rums to become a Guardian of the Cove. But wait, there's more! The truly courageous may sample 100 *additional* rums (that's 200 in total) to become a Master of the Cove. As of late 2011, seven people have become Masters, and two of them have gone off the map and sampled *another hundred rums*, bringing their total to 300. "The amazing thing here," Cate points out, "is that even after rejecting the cheap rums, the artificially-flavored ones, and the mass-mass-produced ones, there are still over 300 solid rums on the market."

Masters of the Cove get to go on a distillery visit with Cate; Disciples get a merit badge, a certificate, and a plaque in the bar.

Disciples just get drunk. But hopefully they learn something about rum.

"It is the most complicated spirit to understand," Cate says. "I can tell you about tequila very easily. It is made in one state, within one country, out of one raw material. But my biggest fear is when a consumer sees a recipe that calls for 'dark rum' and goes into a store and sees something *very* dark, like a Whalers, and then something like an Appleton V/X, and is confused. They don't get the results they want, their drink doesn't taste good, and they give up on drinking rum altogether."

———◆———

There are two bar franchises that have defined tiki: Don the Beachcomber, and Trader Vic's. They both began in the 1930s in California, and both went on to open locations all over the world. Trader Vic's, however, has remained in business continually for nearly 80 years, and has lived to see the demise of the original

> **Trader Vic's**
>
> 9 Anchor Drive
> Emeryville, CA
> 510.653.3400
> www.tradervics.com

Don the Beachcomber stores, not to mention the complete evaporation of second-tier chains like Stephen Crane's Kon-Tiki Ports and Marriott Hotels' Kona Kai, plus the quietus of literally hundreds of one-off imitators.

Trader Vic's currently has five U.S. locations (Atlanta, Emeryville, Sarasota, Portland, and Los Angeles) and 19 more worldwide. Their flagship restaurant is the Emeryville location. As far as defining the tiki aesthetic is concerned, the ones in Tokyo, Munich, Emeryville, Portland, and Atlanta are probably the most impressive. They're all chock-full of as many giant Polynesian fertility figures and pufferfish lamps as you can reasonably cram into a restaurant. But you, my friends, are here to drink, so let's get to it. The giant wooden phalluses will come into play later, trust me.

One fine day in 1944, "Trader" Vic Bergeron was entertaining Tahitian guests. He mixed some J. Wray and Nephew 17-year-old rum, fresh lime juice, orange curaçao, a dash of simple syrup, and a mint sprig garnish. His guest supposedly remarked, "*Mai tai!*

Roa a'e!" which, (according to the Trader) means "The best! Out of this world!" in Tahitian. In reality, that's not an accurate translation, but these things don't matter when we're discussing tropical drinks. After all, the Suffering Bastard was the result of some forgotten lush slurring, "Suffering bar steward." (I swear it wasn't me.) Anyway, *matai'i roa* is Tahitian for "very good" (not necessarily "the best"), while *a'e* means either "separate" or "more."

Close enough. Sixty-eight years later, "Mai Tai" has become shorthand for any slop of well rum, sugar, and random quantities of canned fruit juice . . . unless you're at Trader Vic's, which still serves its signature cocktail with surprising consistency from location to location, although it is usually made with their house-branded mix. Ask for your Mai Tai "the old way" or "San Francisco-style" in most Trader Vic's, and you'll get something fresher and closer to what the Trader intended. Or, just go to one of the many craft bars in this book that have finally become hip to the idea that tiki drinks can rock, and ask 'em for a Mai Tai: many of them now do this drink a fair bit of justice.

In addition to the Mai Tai, most of the Trader Vic's locations (save some of the ones in the boozeless Middle East) serve a broad selection of tropical drinks, including many designed by Victor Bergeron: the Samoan Fog Cutter, the Tiki Puka Puka, the Scorpion Bowl, the Kamai'ina, the Shingle Stain, and our fave, the Tortuga. Interestingly, the preparation of these drinks doesn't always parallel contemporary craft cocktail standards. Many Trader Vic's bars still hand-squeeze juice, but they also still use pre-bottled syrups. Seeing some of the Vic's locations making their own passionfruit syrup or orgeat would be amazing.

The food at Trader Vic's in the 21st century is also not fundamentally different from Bergeron's original intentions. His faux-Polynesian dishes have expanded in scope to include cuisine from around the Pacific Rim. The menus generally contain a mix of contemporary selections paired with the classics for which the chain is known. Smaller plates attributed to Vic Bergeron—bongo bongo soup and crab Rangoon—are just the set-up for entrees prepared in Trader Vic's signature Chinese wood-fired ovens.

LAST CALL!

More Destinations to Explore in the San Francisco Bay Area

There are so many fantastic places to explore that we couldn't list them all in more detail. All but the Hotsy Totsy Club (Albany) and Prizefighter (Emeryville) are in the city of San Francisco.

15 Romolo (15 Romolo Place; 415.398.1359; www.15romolo.com) is a North Beach-area bar hidden down an alley off of Broadway (near Columbus), an area of seedy strip clubs and Beat Generation history. Originally opened in 1998, the place got a facelift from owner Aaron Gregory Smith and reopened in early 2009. Prior to that, for nearly a century, the space was the bar for a Basque hotel. This casual saloon offers nice cocktails in the $9–$10 range, a jukebox, and small plates of food. Drinks can be adventurous, such as the Spaghetti Western (rye, Campari, organic tomatoes, splash of pilsner), the Ferdinand's Famous Fizz (St. George absinthe, strawberry-thyme shrub, cream, egg white, seltzer), and the Nautilus Flip (Kraken black spiced rum, Port Brewing Santa's Little Helper imperial stout, Bonal aperitif, honey syrup, chocolate bitters, egg, nutmeg). We can't resist a shout-out to Port Brewing. Their Old Viscosity is a fantastic beer for those whose tastes run toward beer as black as midnight on a moonless night, with a palate of coffee and burnt motor oil. Look for it seasonally. Food at 15 Romolo includes pork sliders ($7), jambalaya croquettes ($6), and platanos fritos ($7).

When you think of a beretta, what springs to mind? A muscle car? A gun? A funny hat worn by Roman Catholic ecclesiastics? We think of a bar. **Beretta** (1199 Valencia Street; 415.695.1199; www.berettasf.com) was opened in April 2008 by Deborah Blum, Adriano Paganini, and chef

Ruggero Gadaldi. This Mission District eatery, sparsely decorated with stenciled filigree, earth tones, and worn wood tables, gets a little raucous on the weekends. They serve traditional Italian-style pizza and an extensive list of antipasti served in portions that suggest tapas-style sharing. Food and cocktails (from lead bartender Ryan Fitzgerald) are fresh, seasonal, sourced from local farmers, and served until well after midnight. Fitzgerald may shake up a house specialty Rattlesnake (rye, lemon juice, maple syrup, Peychaud's bitters, egg white; $10) or a Square Root (house-aged rum, brandy, vermouth, falernum, bitters; $9).

Burritt Alley is notable to film noir fans as the scene of Miles Archer's murder in the 1941 film version of *The Maltese Falcon.* Today, the alley lends its name to **The Burritt Room** (Crescent Hotel, 417 Stockton Street; 415.400.0500; www.crescentbh.com), a cocktail lounge and music venue within the Crescent Ho-

tel. Avoid Burritt Alley by entering the hotel around the corner on Stockton Street, and head up a narrow staircase to the Burritt Room. The 1910 hotel became the Crescent relatively recently, and they opened the bar in May 2010. The large bar retains much of the feel of the era in which it was constructed, decorated with red velvet cushions on the bar stools, vintage tile on the floors, dim chandeliers, a white piano, exposed brick, a long wooden bar, and distressed wood wainscoting. Joel Baker (of Bourbon & Branch) oversees a menu of about 18 cocktails, divided between classics, modern favorites, and house creations.

Detailed descriptions of each drink are provided within a menu that includes a Kerouac Cocktail (reposado tequila, Aperol aperitif, Cointreau, grapefruit juice, lemon juice; $10), and a Kurosawa Cocktail (single malt whiskey, Oloroso sherry, Aperol aperitif; $10). Will they do a Kandinsky next? Bites include duck confit and mango strudel ($12) and Southwest beef empanadas ($12).

E&O Trading Company (314 Sutter Street; 415.693.0303; www.eosanfrancisco.com) is Southeast Asian grill with very cool Asian-modern decor inside, and (if smells may be trusted) some quite good food (it smelled really, really good in there). E&O was once a microbrewery. They pulled all of the beer equipment out, expanded the restaurant seating space, and started a cocktail program. We were drawn to the Asian-influenced Apple of My Eye (cinnamon rooibos-infused shochu, apple brandy, honey, lemon juice; $10) and the Ex-Pat (Bulleit bourbon, fresh ginger, yuzu, soda; $11).

Elixir (3200 16th Street; 415.552.1633; www.elixirsf. com) was opened in November 2003 by H. Joseph Eh-

rmann. The space has continually operated as a saloon since 1858, making it San Francisco's second-oldest bar. It was also the first certified green bar in San Francisco. Located in the Mission Dolores area, Elixir is as casual as it gets, with sports on television, dart boards, a jukebox, and regular pub quiz nights. Conversely, velvet curtains, maroon accents, and a beautiful mahogany backbar preserve the feel of Elixir's historic legacy. As stated elsewhere in these pages, we see the development of basic corner pubs serving well-crafted cocktails as a positive thing; this should be the rule, not the exception. Classics like the Pisco Sour, the Sidecar, and the Bronx will set you back $8–$9 at Elixir. Looking at their house cocktails, we're excited about the Homecoming (Ron Zacapa 23-year rum, Warre's 10-year tawny port, pumpkin butter, lemon juice; $10). Any cocktail bar that pours Zacapa and still brings the drink in at 10 bucks is worth a visit in my book. And guess what? *This is my book.*

Last time we visited Albany's oldest bar, **The Hotsy Totsy Club** (601 San Pablo Avenue, Albany, CA; 510.526.5986; www.hotsytotsyclub.com), they were a divey local bar with an awesome vintage neon sign. Now, co-owner Jessica Maria is featuring a drink of the week from Ted Haigh's compulsory *Vintage Spirits and Forgotten Cocktails,* and house specials such as the Redlands (Sino reposado tequila, cinnamon vermouth, jujube syrup, cranberry bitters; $8). Classics include a Brandy Alexander (Osocalis brandy, Tempis Fugit crème de caçao, half & half, ground nutmeg; $9) and a barrel-aged Negroni ($10). Tempus Fugit is based in Petaluma, and produces a wonderful line of liqueurs that includes a fernet, a crème de violette, a quinquina, a gin, several absinthes, and their storied Gran Classico bitters.

New gastropub **Jasper's Corner Tap and Kitchen** (401 Taylor Street; 415.775.7979; www.jasperscornertap. com) opened mere days after our most recent visit to San Francisco. The buzz on this one is massive. Drinks by bar manager Kevin Diedrich, such as the Black Cross (black-tea-infused Smith & Cross Rum, Dubonnet Rouge, Belle de Brillet pear liqueur, Angostura bitters) and the A Harlot's Progress (Bols Genever, St. George absinthe, honey, peaches, lemon) make us want to visit as soon as possible. So do a very solid wine list, cocktails made with beer (a rapidly emerging trend), and house-made sausages from the kitchen of chef Adam Carpenter. The kitchen starts serving breakfast very early in the morning, but unfortunately you'll have to wait until lunchtime to get a cocktail.

Locanda (557 Valencia Street; 415.863.6800; www.locandasf.com) is the newest Mission District restaurant from Craig and Anna Stoll. Opened in April 2011, the osteria features a heavy Roman influence prepared with a California sensibility. White walls, a sleek black bar, shiny wood floors, and diamond-shaped tiles in geometric patterns set the mood for food by James Beard Award winner Craig Stoll and chef Anthony Strong. House-cured charcuterie and an extensive offal menu (brains, anyone?) contrast a Jewish-style artichoke ($6) that is so popular they used it as the restaurant's logo. Brian MacGregor (formerly of Jardinière) and lead bartender Michael Sager claim the city's largest selection of amari. We like their Negroni flight ($20), which spotlights the history of gin by using Bols (genever), Beefeater (London dry), and Aviation (new Western). Recipes are kept simple and seasonal, and take full advantage of the amari on hand: the Apothecary (mezcal, Cynar bitter aperitif, Carpano Antica Formula vermouth, Cocchi Americano aperitif wine) and the Nonna del Diavolo (rye, Strega herbal liqueur, ginger, lime, seltzer). All cocktails are $10.

Prizefighter (6702 Hollis Street, Emeryville, CA;

510.428.1470; www.prizefighterbar.com) was opened in November 2011 by John Santer of Bourbon & Branch and Dylan O'Brien of Bloodhound. Bartenders Carlos Yturria (Absinthe), Patrick Brennan (Prospect), and Lucia Gonzales (Flora) help to keep the hometown of Pixar and Trader Vic's well-lubricated. A shuffleboard table, exposed brick, dim lighting, shelves made of industrial metal pipes, a worn walnut bar, and a poster-sized photo of Muhammad Ali make this place feel masculine, but there's also a lush patio for you lady lushes. Adult beverages include simple classic cocktails like the Jack Rose (calvados, lime juice, grenadine; $9), punches such as the eponymous Prizefighter (rum, lemon juice, port, porter beer), carbonated cocktails from a soda fountain (the jury is still out), and three sangrias, all served over ice (Kold-Draft or chipped from a 300-pound block). Did we really just write about this bar without resorting to terms like "punch drunk" or making puns about getting knocked out by the drinks? That's discipline.

Why should you visit **Quince** (470 Pacific Avenue; 415.775.8500; www.quincerestaurant.com)? Perhaps to meet Jason "Buffalo" LoGrasso, who has also worked at Flora, Alembic, Beretta, Rickhouse, and Bourbon & Branch (errrm, maybe he should have guest authored this San Francisco chapter of *Destination: Cocktails*?). Owners Michael and Lindsay Tusk moved their venerable Michelin-starred Mediterranean restaurant into the current location in November of 2009. Their house drink is the simple Quince Martini (chamomile-infused gin, Dolin dry vermouth, bergamot tincture when in season, or the Bitter Truth lemon bitters).

Mission District spot **Trick Dog** (3010 20th Street) aims to be a neighborhood bar with excellent cocktails (if you don't see that as the way of the future, you aren't reading carefully enough). Their pedigree backs up their ambition, so we look forward to a visit. The room also houses a large collection of vintage bar paraphernalia.

LOS ANGELES

The City of Angels is known for a lot of things: earth-quakes, movies, smog, and fake boobs—but cocktailing isn't usually first among them. This is changing, and fast. Although it's lagging a few years behind London, Tokyo, New York, Chicago, and San Francisco, La-La Land seems to be making up for lost time, with a veritable epidemic of great bars popping up since 2008. Given this progress, we'll forgive this town for being the birthplace of the Harvey Wallbanger (great name, lousy drink) and the White Russian (sorry, Jeff Lebowski).

1886 Bar

The Raymond Restaurant
1250 South Fair Oaks Avenue
Pasadena, CA
626.441.3136
www.theraymond.com

Sometimes when you walk into a bar, the first thing you think of is a stegosaurus. The Pasadena spot 1886 Bar in no way remind-ed us of a stegosaurus, but we did notice several things that are star-tling in their implications. The hotel (torn down in 1931) was built by Walter Raymond in 1886, the year Pasadena was incorporated, and also the year the stegosaurus was first discovered. It seems that one of these may be a coincidence and the other may not.

The original building burned to the ground in 1895, was re-built, and then fell victim to the Depression in the 1930s. Raymond and his wife retreated to the caretaker's cottage, which now houses the restaurant and bar. Opened by Rob and Leslie Levy in 1975, the Raymond restaurant has recently been revamped, adding the 1886 Bar in November 2010. Designed by David Poffenberger and

Derrick Flynn of SO|DA, the space retains its Craftsman-style roots, with mismatched wooden tables, low tin ceilings, soft lighting emanating from behind the bar, and damask-style wallpaper.

Food at the Raymond is courtesy of chef Tim Guiltinan, and may include dishes like angus beef short rib ($34), lamb in the style of Morocco ($35), and Lake Superior whitefish with crispy skin ($33). Guiltinan also provides a smaller bar menu such as chilled foie gras torchon ($12) and crispy Szechuan fish ($10). As of now, they are not serving stegosaurus.

Conceived by Liquid Assets (consultant Aidan Demarest and his partner Marcos Tellos, who have previously contributed to Seven Grand and the Edison, among others), the cocktail menu at 1886 Bar takes inspiration from the era in which the hotel was first built. Many of the recipes on the list only require three ingredients or so, and are made with hand-chipped ice and house-made syrups, as they would have been made in 1886. Punches, swizzles, and smashes appear on the menu regularly. Just a few of the older drinks deviate from the mission and are given a more contemporary spin. For example, the Vintage Caprice (Beefeater gin, dry vermouth, Bénédictine, orange bitters) is barrel-aged for up to eight months. In a show of transcontinental solidarity, drinks from East Coast bars such as Clover Club and Mayahuel appear as well.

Things veer away from the 19th century and get more inventive with creations like the Chic(ory) Flip (chicory-coffee-infused rye whiskey, Yeti stout, whole egg, caramelized chicory coffee sugar). Yep, that's whiskey, a whole egg, and stout beer in one glass. Lead bartender Garret McKechnie invented the Per-Sin-Amen Cocktail (mezcal, persimmon, house-made cinnamon bark syrup, lime juice, chocolate-creole bitters). Gal Friday Night, who was born in China, was excited to try Tellos's creation, the Saladito (mezcal, lime juice, honey, salt, chile). *Saladito* is the Mexican name for a Chinese sweet made from dried plums; in Mexico, they're dropped into soft drinks to enhance the flavor. You'll get one as a garnish with this cocktail. During the summer months, the locally inspired portion of the menu may give a nod to Donn Beach with careful renditions of his Zombie and QB Cooler, both of which date from the mid-1930s.

Tellos is also responsible for the Sporting Life, an organization he founded in March of 2008 (with Christine England, Eric Alperin, and Damian Windsor) to promote classic cocktail culture in Los Angeles.

So, you're wondering about the stegosaurus. Or the yeti. Or China. Or where you can get saladitos. I can only help you with the booze, my friends. You're on your own for the rest.

Rum. The noble spirit is often disdained by uninformed booze newbies who don't consider it to be on par with the best whiskeys or cognacs. This is largely due to the fact that the four rums most commonly seen behind American bars are all mass-produced swill.

Caña Rum Bar

714 W. Olympic Boulevard
Los Angeles, CA
213.745.7090
www.213nightlife.com

However, it takes only moments to introduce someone to one of the hundreds of extremely varied and extremely delicious rums out there. General manager Allan Katz of Caña in downtown Los Angeles is out to do just that. "We seek to prove rum is worthy of a cocktail bar that uses it accordingly," he says.

Caña was opened in early 2010 by Cedd Moses ("the Willy Wonka of downtown Los Angeles inebriation," according to Allan Katz) as a direct response to L.A.'s growing cocktail surge. Caña occupies the space formerly held by L.A. cocktail pioneers the Doheny, a members-only bar that required dues of $2,200 to join. Caña also requires membership, but their much more reasonable $20 fee includes a free cocktail, invitations to rum tastings, and allowance for members to bring three guests per visit. Look for the entrance on Flower Street, behind the building's parking garage, or just follow the huge pink neon sign.

Inside, Caña has a cozy and warm feeling, with wood-paneled walls, leather booths, a mish-mash of Caribbean-influenced paintings, and DJs spinning music at reasonable amplitude. The bar proudly serves local-ish rums by Charbay, Solomon Tournor's, St. George, and Prichard's (which Katz counts as "local," since "the rum world is so vast that Tennessee ain't that far"). Of course they do their own syrups and cordials, not limited to orgeat, curaçao, grenadine, canela, and "*many* bitters," but Katz also says that he buys from Portland's B. G. Reynolds "as much as possible to support him." Of seasonal ingredients, Katz points out that everyone makes all kinds of claims on seasonality. "It's really gotten pretty lame, so I try to keep it as real as I can," he says. Noted and appreciated. When we spoke in the late summer, he enthused: "Right now zucchini, cherry tomato, and peaches are in their glory," resulting in the Jewel of the Nile (agricole rum, zucchini juice, Galliano L'Autentico). Katz was also excited about ripe peaches "soaking in a threeway of Tennessee whiskey, cognac, and tequila. It's gonna be a SoCal take on all of those old Fish House-style punches."

Most of the drinks on the menu are Katz's creations, though he shares credit with John Coltharp (of Seven Grand), and senior bartender Danielle Crouch. "Dani made this absolutely sick punch called Jitterbug Perfume with fresh jasmine blossom-infused rye," Katz says. "Wish to hell we'd infused five times as much! I sorely miss that drink. [We're] hedonists who have a knack for noting where flavors in anything overlap, and we'll whip a tasty drink outta it. There are way too many cats using savory stuff and pairing odd spirits for the sheer sake of it. That ain't experimental! It's just attention-starved."

Further cocktails consumable at Caña (mostly $12–$13) include the Happiness (is a Warm Gun), which "features Luxardo's fernet, which beats up Fernet-Branca and takes its lunch money."

There is no food at Caña, but they will sell you a cigar ($14–$19). Smoke those outside, under a mirror painted by Shepard Fairey.

Located near the Beverly Center in West Hollywood, David Myers's cozy but high-energy brasserie serves bistro cuisine in an environment that is more casual than the neighborhood or the prices might suggest. Butcher paper

Comme Ça

8479 Melrose Avenue
West Hollywood, CA
323.782.1104
www.commecarestaurant.com

on the tables is contrasted by dark wood wainscoting, plenty of mirrors, photos and paintings of Parisian street scenes, and a chalkboard spelling out the boîte's daily specials (and/or Hemingway quotes).

Traditional dishes by executive chef Kuniko Yagi include oysters ($29/dozen), paleron of beef bourguignon ($26), crispy skate grenobloise ($25), and mushroom risotto ($14–$21). We like the daily cheese selection, too, all expertly paired with fruits or honey ($15). Comme Ça's "bistronomy," a seasonal prix fixe option "inspired by our travels," is inspiring in itself ($45/three courses; $65/five courses).

The original bar menu was assembled by Sam Ross of New York's Milk & Honey. The scant four drinks on the list included Milk & Honey classics like their influential Penicillin (blended Scotch whisky, Laphroaig Scotch whisky, lemon juice, honey, ginger). With just a little bit of Laphroaig added to another less smoky Scotch, the smoke doesn't overwhelm the ginger. Ross's concise menu stood from Comme Ça's October 2007 opening until 2009, when bar man Joel Black added 18 more drinks to the list. The list itself has been dubbed "18A," after a Paris–Los Angeles flight, and has been paired back to 10 drinks plus a Cocktail du Jour (their term for bartender's choice).

We like the straightforward inventions such as the Doe-Eyed Doll (cognac, Aperol aperitif, lemon juice) and the Hundred Years' Fizz (cognac, lemon juice, egg white, soda, Pernod). Bartender David Mupchinski is responsible for the neighborhood-appropriate Fashionista (Martin Miller's Westbourne-Strength gin, tarragon, Luxardo Marasche cherries, Banyuls vinegar mixture, sugar cube, Peychaud's bitters, flamed orange twist). The Banyuls vinegar is infused with toasted white pepper, juniper berries, and coriander seeds. All cocktails are $12.

Copa d'Oro

217 Broadway
Santa Monica, CA
310.576.3030
www.copadoro.com

Copa d'Oro is exactly the sort of bar you're *not* expecting to find along Third Street Promenade in Santa Monica, so close to the Santa Monica beach— it is neither beach bar nor tourist trap nor corporate franchise. Instead, the dark and cozy Copa d'Oro ("glass of gold") is all about dim lighting, few windows, exposed brick walls, rusty-gold tones, candles in the booths, and enough Spanish touches to justify the bar's name. Copa d'Oro opened in early 2009. The vibe is quiet early in the night, and a louder, clubbier crowd takes over when the DJ starts.

Bar chief Vincenzo Marianella (of Providence) is all about fresh ingredients from the Santa Monica Farmers' Market, right across the street. In fact, while so many bars in this book offer a bespoke/omakase/bartender's choice option, Copa d'Oro takes this paradigm a step further by listing all of their available herbs, fruits, vegetables, and juices on the menu. The idea is to build your own drink, sort of like Mongolian Barbecue, but with booze. Want a Matusalem rum-basil-cranberry-lychee-celery-tini? Well, that's up to you, but if you order it, Marianella will happily suggest a way to edit that down to something palatable, and then he'll make it work. The ingredients on hand are lined up in full view along the lengthy bar (along with a notice that this salad is not for snacking on). Actual snacks include a short menu of paninis, grilled cheeses, charcuterie, and a cheese board.

For those looking for a bit less adventure in their drink order, the menu also lists nearly 50 cocktails, divided up into the Fast, the Furious, Because You Can . . . , and Classic Cocktails from a Drunk Italian Bartender. Naturally. The deviants include an Aviation reimagined as a Navigation (bourbon, maraschino liqueur, lemon juice), a Clover Club now called a Clover Pub (Scotch whisky, house-made raspberry syrup, lemon juice, egg white), and a bourbon Negroni called a Barboni (bourbon, Campari, Martini Rosato vermouth, orange bitters).

The Because You Can . . . section adds top-shelf booze to familiar classics, such as the 5th Ave. Manhattan (Rittenhouse 25-year rye, Carpano Antica Formula vermouth, Angostura bitters) and the Gold-Plated Sidecar (Hennessey XO cognac, Grand Marnier Cinquantenaire, lemon juice).

Salut!

—◄●►—

Some bars are based in cities so multicultural that they don't neeed no steeenking Eeenglish. La Descarga, for those keeping count, is the fourth consecutive bar listed in this book whose name is either French or Spanish (translation for this one: "the discharge"). This is

La Descarga

1159 N. Western Avenue
Hollywood, CA
323.466.1324
www.ladescargala.com

also the second of these bars that call on rum as a spirit guide.

You'll want to make a reservation for La Descarga. Upon arrival, the doorman will guide you to a seedy second-floor hotel room, where a receptionist will lead you into the wardrobe. Upon emerging from the other side, you will definitely not find yourself in Narnia, but you may believe that you're in Havana. You'll be on a wrought-iron balcony overlooking the small bar room below.

Under iron chandeliers, a 19th-century-styled backbar is stacked five shelves high with rum, while more shelves nearby are stacked with old books. We'll be darned if there aren't some Havana Club bottles on those shelves; those are basically mandatory to complete this place's intended vibe, but not easy to get in quantity 'round these parts. A small Afro-Cuban combo does a short set of music four times a night on weekends, accompanied by a fire-breathing burlesque dancer, performing right on the marble bar top. Cocktails are served at this bar when the dragon lady isn't working it. A smaller bar room in the back is for cigar smoking and for taking your rum neat. It all feels very much like Havana (although Havana's classic 1939 Tropicana nightclub stops just short of featuring fire breathers).

The most authentic detail, however, might be the ceiling: simulated rotting plaster revealing exposed wooden slats. Havana *is* all it's cracked up to be, with a dazzling array of architecture from the 1880s to 1958 still standing, and American cars from the 1940s and 1950s still making up something like 40 percent of all traffic. But Havana is rotting, it's decaying, it's all falling apart. So the broken patches in La Descarga's ceiling? That's a real indication that one of the designers has actually done his homework. But this is Hollywood, after all, and La Descarga is far from the only bar in town decorated via the expert craftsmanship of a moonlighting big-budget set decorator.

Speaking of craftsmanship, the handy Gal Friday Night was eager to get a drink after a long night of language lessons. General manager Steve Livigni and startender Pablo Moix designed the original cocktail list for the bar's February 2010 opening. By the end of 2011, the 16-beverage menu also contained recipes by head bartender Kenny Arbuckle, with an assist from Meghan Malloy and Armando Conway. The rum list is now up to over 100 brands.

The best place to start navigating this menu is with a visit to the Cartographer (El Dorado 12-year rum, Cynar bitter aperitif, Angostura bitters, superfine cane sugar), which was designed as a rum Old-Fashioned variant. The Blood & Samba (cachaça, Carpano Antica Formula vermouth, Cherry Heering, orange juice) does the same to the classic Blood & Sand, substituting cachaça for the traditional Scotch whisky. The menu recognizes L.A. as the birthplace of tiki drinks with the La Passoã (Ron Matusalem rum, Passoã passion fruit liqueur, lime juice, orange juice, orgeat, falernum).

There are a few drinks on the menu that aren't rum-based, such as the Arbuckle's Onbeat (House Spirits 100 Percent Barley White Dog, mango-basil syrup, lemon juice, Bitter Truth lemon bitters). That white dog (white whiskey) is usually only available in the House Spirits tasting room in Portland, so it's cool to see it here.

Twin owners Mark and Jonnie Houston also own two other heavily experiential bars, the New Orleans-inspired **Piano Bar** (6429 Selma Avenue; 323.466.2750; www.pianobarhollywood.com), which opened in 2009, and the new neo-nouveau **Pour Vous** (5574 Melrose Avenue; 323.871.8699; www.pourvousla.com). The Houstons also own a little bar called Harvard & Stone that we may tell you about some time.

If you love high-concept experiential bars, Los Angeles is the place to find them. After all, this is the town that gave us Hollywood and its endless artifice, plus Disneyland, where everything is manufactured, right down to your happiness. Nighttime entertainment can be just as fabricated in a land with an endless supply of craftsmen producing every imaginable environment. Among other things, Hollywood is the home of the theme bar. When Don Beach opened the first tiki bar in 1934, the term "tiki bar" was still a ways off, but he was following a legacy of nightclubs themed after every place on earth, from Asia to Zanzibar. His South Pacific beachcomber decor was just the latest schtick, and it was by no means the last. There is a direct evolutionary path from Don the Beachcomber to Planet Hollywood. The bars of Mark and Jonnie Houston come from a common ancestor, even if the family tree branched off into a slightly different species a few generations back.

Harvard & Stone

5221 Hollywood Boulevard
Los Angeles, CA
323.466.6063
www.harvardandstone.com

After launching La Descarga in February 2010, the twins got to work on Harvard & Stone (named for a nearby East Hollywood/Los Feliz intersection) for a February 2011 launch. The theme here is not so different from the Edison (see page 257), with 3,500 square feet on two floors designed to look like a mid-century factory, perhaps something Rosie-ready for World War II, mixed with a steampunk influence.

All manner of salvage is used effectively here, as tractor seats become bar stools, old rusty baskets suspended from the ceiling become booze shelves, jacks support tables, and it seems that rivets were bought by the truckload. Antique sewing machines and chicken feeders are now haute decor under the exposed ducts and terminally distressed brick. Shadow boxes house period flotsam. Naturally, there is roving entertainment here, too. This is all the rage in Los Angeles these days; full immersion is hot. A small stage for impromptu live music is separate from support infrastructure right above the bar for acrobatic dancers. DJs and a celebrity-curated juke provide music.

Steve Livigni and Pablo Moix are behind the menu once again (see La Descarga, page 245), heavily focused on American distilleries in general and American whiskeys in particular. Head bartender Matt Wallace (of Seven Grand) crushes his ice in a Lewis bag when needed, and makes drinks with cheeky names like Baby's First Bourbon (Bulleit bourbon, orgeat, lemon juice, Angostura bitters; $10) and Teacher's Pet (applejack, Combier Liqueur d'Orange, maple syrup, lemon juice, egg white, peach bitters; $10).

A small room in the back of the upper level is known as the R&D (research and development) Bar, and is decorated like the factory boss's office. One spirit is featured per month; staff and guest bartenders make new inventions on the fly, based on that month's spirit. Many are forgotten, some will be future classics. Events with brand ambassadors or distillers are also held in the 25-seat room.

Providence

5955 Melrose Avenue
Los Angeles, CA
323.460.4170
www.providencela.com

We know of a lot of bars where knowing the difference between "on the rocks" and "neat" might help you order, but the advanced drinkers among you might be ready for bars at which a familiarity with terms like "immersion circulator" are mandatory vocabulary. Opened by chef Michael Cimarusti with Donato Poto in 2005, this

Michelin-starred seafood restaurant has been called, by some, the best eatery in Hollywood. The subdued atmosphere is decorated in earth tones, but includes unexpectedly whimsical touches like table lamps that resemble coral and barnacles clustered together in ceiling corners. Providence offers tasting menus in five-, nine-, and thirteen-course variants, or à la carte fare such as wild Spanish octopus ($21), farm-raised sustainable caviars ($130-$180 per 30 grams), wild Quinault river king salmon ($48), and charcoal-grilled wild French turbot for two ($51 per guest).

Inaugural bartender Vincenzo Marianella (now at Copa d'Oro) shared Cimarusti's vision of maintaining the same level of craft in the bar as in the kitchen. Some of the first molecular-style bartending in Los Angeles was performed at Providence, using interesting foams, drinks served in gel sacs, and experiments with the sous vide techniques of immersion cooking. The gelled (or "spherical") drinks are a signature amuse-bouche at Providence. Classic cocktails like the Margarita are served encapsulated in an edible gel on a silver spoon, looking like a Dalinian take on a fried egg. These are sometimes complimented with gelée cocktails, such as a Mojito, molded into a little brick that you can bite into or just pop into your pie hole all at once. Kind of like alcoholic sushi. One of these days, someone is going to start doing this with sake, shochu, and Suntory recipes, and will open a gelée cocktail sushi bar. Just you wait and see.

Further molecular offerings come from London-born Zahra Bates, who took over the cocktail program in 2009. An oyster-inspired creation from her "protein series" is made from Manzanilla sherry, lettuce, Japanese cucumber, and celery, all sealed with a Cryovac and then subjected to an immersion circulator before being released and doused in Tanqueray gin.

Pairing your dinner with cocktails (as opposed to wine) has long been a Providence specialty. Bates carries on the tradition with creations such as the Opium Den (tamarind-infused Buffalo Trace bourbon, apple juice, sesame-kombucha dry vermouth) and the Il Padrino (Bertagnolli Grappino grappa, Luxardo maraschino liqueur, Cointreau, house-made crème de violette, lemon juice, Regan's orange bitters, egg white). Bartender Laura Lindsay came up with the Cider Mill (Laird's bonded applejack, Sapling maple liqueur, vanilla sugar syrup, lemon juice, St. Elizabeth allspice dram, Angostura bitters, fresh cinnamon). All standard cocktails are $15.

◀━▶

The Roger Room

370 N. La Cienega Boulevard
West Hollywood, CA
310.854.1300
www.rogerroom.com

We can't promise you that the bartenders at the Roger Room will know what you want to drink before you order it, but the two big neon tarot cards in the front window suggest that they might. Aside from the rarefied gasses hinting at prognostication, there are no other indications that a business may be operating within the corner space next to the Largo (a concert club). Use your cosmic awareness and visualize cocktails in your future, and you'll find the Roger Room (or just show up at 370 N. La Cienega Boulevard).

The tiny, press-shy Roger Room was launched on June 1, 2009 by Jared Meisler and Sean MacPherson. The interior decor recalls something like a circus in a train car in the 1920s, with a mirrored ceiling, vintage photos, a circus-themed menu, an antique mahogany bar, murals on the walls, and mohair booths. The dozen seats at the bar and the handful of rust-colored booths will be filled with a younger, trendier crowd (and we do mean *filled*).

Meisler and Damian Windsor are responsible for many of the cocktails at the Roger Room, including the Japanese Maple (Yamazaki whiskey, lemon juice, maple syrup, egg white, and a mist of their 151 rum/Angostura bitters mixture; $13) and the Grifter (Mata Hari absinthe, pressed mint, simple syrup, club soda, crushed ice; $16). Gal Friday Night was longing for her hometown in Mexico, so we went with the Tijuana Brass (Tres Reyes blanco tequila, lime juice, agave syrup, cucumber foam; $13) and a Fresa (Avión blanco tequila, crushed strawberry, lemon juice, agave nectar, allspice dram; $13). We liked Mata Hari's reappearance in Roger Room's take on a Pisco Punch (Gran Sierpe pisco, Mata Hari absinthe, lime juice, pineapple syrup, pineapple juice, crushed grapes; $14). Finishing up with both themes (absinthe and "south of the border") intact, we liked the looks of bartender Jason Bran's South of the Border (Don Julio añejo tequila, agave nectar, Fee Brothers grapefruit bitters, Regan's orange bitters, absinthe; $14).

There is no food at the Roger Room, but you may get a garnish held in place by the sort of plastic monkey you're used to seeing in bars by beaches or on Bourbon Street. Despite the Hollywood address and secret location, the Roger Room aims to keep things friendly and low-key. Ask them for one of those beachy drinks, and they'll do their best to accommodate (and perhaps elevate) it for you.

Many bartenders will tell you a bit about the spirits you're drinking if you happen to ask, but we especially admire those who consider education a priority. Sharpen your pencils and pack a lunch—we're going to visit Seven Grand.

The bar was opened in 2007 by 213 Nightlife (which also own the Varnish, Caña, and half a dozen others). Chief mixologists are Angus McShane, Andrew Abrahamson, and Leo Rivas. McShane is the one who clued us in to Seven Grand's intellectual pursuits. "Our emphasis is education," he said. "We have a Whiskey Society curated by our Spirit Guide Pedro Shanahan which promotes sharing information from master distillers and international brand ambassadors on a regular basis. We host three to four events every month, and aim to dispel the myths surrounding brown spirits."

Seven Grand is located on the second floor of the vintage Jewelry Mart building (home of Clifton's Silver Spoon). The staircase

Seven Grand

515 W. 7th Street, 2nd Floor
Los Angeles, CA
213.614.0737
www.213nightlife.com

you'll have to climb to get to the whiskey goodness is decorated in plaid. On the way up, you'll encounter a vitrine filled with wax-covered Maker's Mark bottles, a mannequin hunter loaded with bottles of whiskey in his pockets, and an unsettling number of deer skulls. And you're not even inside the bar yet. The interior is not substantially different, but you'll also find pool tables, leather sofas, and perhaps a band set up in the corner. Dark wood, whiskey, and taxidermy. Not unlike a hunting lodge, but much warmer-feeling and not nearly as theme park-ish as the rather fun **Bigfoot Lodge** over in Silver Lake (3172 Los Feliz Boulevard; 323.662.9227; www.bigfootlodge.com).

Seven Grand is a whiskey bar. Their cocktail menu is whiskey-focused, offering vintage and original whiskey cocktails that are changed every spring and autumn. Their global whiskey library contains at least 350 products from the U.S., Canada, India, Australia, Japan, Ireland, and Scotland. Seven Grand also promotes West Coast distilleries whenever possible, including House Spirits, Rogue Ales, Fog's End, GreenBar Collective, Bitter Tears, and Ballast Point.

With this fabulous collection comes a wide array of cocktails, but the good old Old-Fashioned never goes out of fashion; McShane estimates that they serve between 400 and 500 of them every week. Perusing the concise 10-drink menu, we were drawn in by some favorites, such as the vintage 1920s Boulevardier (Old Weller 107 bourbon, Campari, Carpano Antica Formula vermouth; $13). Looking toward house originals, the liberal Gal Friday Night was hesitant about the unfortunately-named Dagny Taggart (Glenlivet 12-year Scotch whisky, Aperol aperitif, and Torani liqueurs; $14). Naturally, it's the most expensive drink on the menu. The Torani liqueur was unidentified, but we were thinking it was their Amer liqueur.

Looking toward the future, McShane says the bar is experimenting with dehydrated seasonal fruits like figs, apples, pears, tangerines, pomegranates, and spices. They're also making their own syrups (not limited to ginger, grenadine, vanilla riesling pear, balsamic fig, and "whatever we pick up at farmers' markets").

Just be careful navigating back down those stairs, you don't want to trip and get impaled on an antler after a few nips of firewater.

There are two types of bar in the world: the ones named after Aesop's fables, and the ones named after Bukowski poems. Surprisingly, we are not aware of any bars named after Bukowski poems, so let's talk about the Aesops. There aren't too many of

Thirsty Crow

2939 West Sunset Boulevard
Los Angeles, CA
323.661.6007
www.thirstycrowbar.com

those either, and of the bunch, we can only think of one that is *also* named after the owner's race car: Thirsty Crow.

Opened in April 2010 near the Silver Lake area's hip Sunset Junction, Thirsty Crow's name was indeed inspired by *The Crow and the Pitcher* (in which a crow, after failing to tip over a pitcher of water, fills it full of pebbles so as to be able to bring the water inside to a reachable level). An apt enough name for a tavern, we suppose, but what of this race car? Co-owner Bobby Green's car was originally dubbed "Old Crow" (after the whiskey) but was re-dubbed when gasoline consumption was tallied. Along with Green, the bar is co-owned by Dimitri Komarov and Dima Liberman.

The trio's love for whiskey is evident not just in the name of Green's car, but also in the bar's philosophy. The woody room with the horeshoe-shaped marble bar is definitely whiskey-focused, filled with small batch bourbons, whiskeys from around the world, and seasonally-rotated craft cocktails.

House-made products are tricky for the Thirsty Crow. "We don't have a kitchen, so we've had to get creative with what we can make in-house," explains bar manager Cooper Gillespie. "We

just gained access to a space to begin producing more house-made syrups and infusions, so they're on the horizon. Our menu changes quarterly, so seasonal ingredients are everything to our bar program. We work closely with a local organic produce supplier to determine what fruits and vegetables are best used at different times of the year. All of our produce comes from local farms."

Perusing the menu, we were drawn to the Thirsty Crow Cocktail ($12), one of Gillespie's own creations. "It is hugely popular," she told us. "It consists of rye whiskey, ginger beer, citrus, and magic, all served in an adorable mason jar. People can't seem to get enough of it." The rest of the concise menu is made up of a short list of Manhattan variants ($12), classics ($12), and a few prosecco creations ($10), including the classic Death in the Afternoon (prosecco and absinthe).

Tiki Ti

4427 Sunset Boulevard
Los Angeles, CA
323.669.9381
www.tiki-ti.com

It seems as though all of the best surviving vintage tiki bars in the world are those opened by former Don the Beachcomber bartenders, and are usually still run by their descendants. Tiki Ti is a tiny tiki bar in Hollywood. Six very small booths and 15 seats at the bar mean that you should show up early, or you will wait in line.

Ray Buhen, the man responsible for Tiki Ti, was a local legend among Los Angeles tikiphiles. Ray was hired as a bartender at the original Don the Beachcomber in Hollywood as far back as 1934. He also worked at legendary tiki power points like Seven Seas, Stephen Crane's Luau, the Tropics, and the Beverly Hills Trader Vic's. Buhen opened Tiki Ti in 1961 and maintained it until his death in September 2001. His son and grandson (Mike and Mike Jr.) have steered the ship through the bar's 50th anniversary (in 2011) and beyond, with no signs of stopping.

The decor of the cozy bar is strictly old-school beachcomber mixed with an imprint left behind by more than 50 years of regular customers. Martin Denny and other Exotica artists often provide the soundtrack, as is properly befitting any good tiki bar.

Like his early mentor, Donn Beach, Ray kept many of his best recipes secret, choosing to mix from a variety of unmarked bottles and leaving the patrons bewildered by his mixing magic. As his son and grandson share his zeal, these recipes are sure to remain safe for years to come. The menu features 42 rum cocktails, including the Penang, the Shark's Tooth, the Tuba Cola, the Never-Say-Die, the Sumatra Kula, the Blood and Sand, and what is perhaps the bar's most famous drink, the Ray's Mistake. They also offer a variety of libations made from gin, tequila, and other mysterious potions.

Okole maluna!

There are two bars in Cole's restaurant. The one you'll notice first is in plain sight within the vintage 1908 eatery, which is locally famous for its French dip sandwich. This bar pours a perfectly respectable cocktail. The bar you'll want to make an extra effort to find, however, is the Varnish. It's the one

The Varnish

118 E. Sixth Street
Los Angeles, CA
213.622.9999
www.213nightlife.com

hidden behind a door at the back of Cole's dining room, marked only by a tiny icon of a cocktail glass.

Launched in February 2009, the Varnish is a partnership between Eric Alperin (formerly of Osteria Mozza), Sasha Petraske (owner of Milk & Honey in New York), and Cedd Moses (owner of Cole's and "just a few" other Los Angeles night spots). Alperin describes the Varnish succinctly: "We are a classically-focused cocktail bar." Indeed, upon entering, you'll find a short bar with no stools and a dozen or so booths surrounding an old upright piano. Vintage tile floors, wood paneling, dim lighting. The pianist was happy to take our request for a favorite Prohibition-era standard,

Irving Berlin's "Blue Skies," and the bartenders were happy to take our request for a favorite cocktail from a slightly earlier era.

As necessitated by the limited space behind the bar, the Varnish's booze selection is carefully curated. "We have spirits from around the country and the globe," Alperin says. "Our 'well'—or, we like to say 'house'—spirits are what we find work well in our classic repertoire of drinks. We also must stand behind each spirit that we have selected as our house or on our back bar." Naturally, the bar makes their own honey, ginger, and raspberry syrups, plus violet and curaçao liqueurs.

Aspiring actress Gal Friday Night made a beeline for the Talent Scout (bourbon, curaçao, Angostura bitters). We are in Los Angeles, after all. Being drawn to bright, shiny things, we also went for the Emerald (Red Breast Irish whiskey, Carpano Antica Formula vermouth, orange bitters), and then finished with an Army & Navy (gin, lemon, orgeat) and a Fish House Punch (peach brandy, cognac, Jamaican rum, lemon juice, sugar). That last one is a recipe that may date as far back as 1732. It is usually attributed to the Schuylkill Fishing Company, a club of gentlemen that did, on occasion, go fishing when not smoking cigars, drinking whiskey, and escaping their wives. Cocktails are $13.

Bartender's Choice can also be a great idea when at the Varnish, and will of course vary based on who is serving your drink. Alperin isn't worried about consistency, however. The team here have a solid synergy, key to the vibe of the bar. "I am proud of the people I work with," Alperin says. "We're all on this machine together."

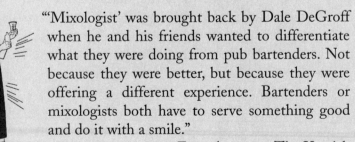

"'Mixologist' was brought back by Dale DeGroff when he and his friends wanted to differentiate what they were doing from pub bartenders. Not because they were better, but because they were offering a different experience. Bartenders or mixologists both have to serve something good and do it with a smile."

—ERIC ALPERIN, The Varnish

LAST CALL!

More Destinations to Explore in the Los Angeles Area

Don the Beachcomber (16278 Pacific Coast Highway, Huntington Beach, CA; 562.592.1321; www.donthebeachcomber.com) was born Ernest Raymond Beaumont Gantt in 1907, and spent the Prohibition years running illegal rum from the Caribbean. In 1934, Gantt launched a more legitimate version of the business he knew so well: selling rum. While inventing the Zombie, the Missionary's Downfall, and many others, he mentored the men who opened the two best remaining vintage tiki bars in the world, Mai-Kai in Fort Lauderdale, and Tiki Ti in Los Angeles. Beach lost control of his restaurant empire to an ex-wife and moved to Hawaii, where he lived the lifestyle he'd helped popularize: laying on the beach with a cocktail.

The 20-odd Don the Beachcomber stores had all more or less vanished by the end of the 1980s. Today, there are two new ones in Hawaii and one in Huntington Beach, within the space that formerly housed Sam's Seafood, a sprawling, multi-room pretend paradise. Tiki fans will love that the restaurant is still playing Martin Denny records over the muzak system, and will also adore the dozens of tikis scattered among the labyrinthine restaurant complex. Fans of Beach's most famous drinks need look no further than here to discover nearly 20 of his best recipes. Former bar manager Marie King built the bar program with great success; reviews have been mixed since her departure. King can now be found at North Hollywood's **Tonga Hut** (12808 Victory Boulevard, North Hollywood, 818.769.0708; www.tongahut.com).

Although we were served two shockingly bad drinks at the highly-regarded **Edison** (108 W. 2nd Street #101; 213.613.0000; www.edisondowntown.com) it's worth mentioning for a few reasons. First, it may have been the template for the huge L.A. trend of steampunk-influenced experiential night clubs, cavernous spaces filled with rusting iron machinery and live entertainment drawing equally from the not-unrelated arenas of burlesque and circus. How many of these are in the city now? We lost count. Second, the Edison also hosts the Radio Room, an occasional promotion wherein the club is visited by guest bartenders who work their magic, accompanied by fresh oysters and live jazz. That's the night you'll want to visit.

Pablo Moix (of La Descarga and Harvard & Stone) has beefed up his resume further by creating a new menu for **Elevate Lounge,** within the well-regarded Takami restaurant (811 Wilshire Boulevard, 21st floor; 213.236.9600; www.takamisushi.com). His Serrano Kiss (Oxley gin, serrano chile, basil leaves, lime juice, simple syrup; $12) may or may not be a nod to the day that he and I were in a taxi cab with Eric Alperin, Brad Bolt, and Jeffrey Morganthaler (see the Varnish, Bar DeVille, and Clyde Common) that was being driven by a one-armed Pakistani midget, who

pissed off a Manhattan motorcyclist wearing snakeskin leather from head to toe, and almost got us all shot. True story. All right, maybe the drink has nothing to do with that, but I had to mention that somewhere in this book.

In spite of its location in the most touristy part of a touristy town, **Eveleigh** (8752 W. Sunset Boulevard; 424.239.1630; www.theeveleigh.com) is well worth a visit. The rustic-feeling restaurant has a peaked roof, reclaimed wood everywhere, barn doors leading to the patio, a fireplace, and greenery both inside and out (including citrus trees and an herb garden). Owners Nick Hatsatouris, Nick Mathers, and Lincoln Pilcher all hail from Australia, as does chef Jordan Taft, whose kitchen produces comfort food dishes like roasted half jidori chicken ($25) and polenta and hen of the woods ($14). Not-Australian bar manager Dave Kupchinsky (of the Tar Pit and Comme Ça) took over in December 2010. From their concise menu of farm-fresh cocktails, they're best known for their Pisco Punch (pisco, fresh pineapple juice, house-made pineapple syrup, lemon juice, lime juice, vanilla, black pepper; $12), but we also like the looks of their eponymous tipple, the Eveleigh (Hendricks gin, rose and lavender Rooibos tea, dry vermouth, Barolo Chinato; $12). Barolo Chinato is a digestif made of Barolo wine. We were also intrigued by a Suffering Bastard variant, the Sad Bastard (bourbon, gin, clove, ginger, lime, soda, Angostura bitters; $12).

For those of you that like both books and cocktails (cough, cough) try **The Library Bar** (Hollywood Roosevelt Hotel, 630 W. 6th Street, Suite 116-A; 213.614.0053; www.librarybarla.com). Once upon a time, the libations were literary in inspiration (the Earl Grey Hemingway, the Scarlet Letter, the Tequila Mockingbird, the Catch-22, etc.). The A Clockwork Orange tastes like a creamsicle. Welly welly well my droogs, your friend and humble narrator was expecting more of a kick to the gulliver with this one. But the Korova Milkbar this is not (that was in Manhattan and closed a few years back). Bar chief Matthew Biancaniello might have dispensed of the menu altogether to offer nothing but bespoke seasonal cocktails. Has it happened? Pay him a visit and find out. We're not going to spoil the ending for you. We will say that a glance over the bar will reveal that Biancaniello has probably been at the farmers' market lately. Since the lil' bar only has room for one bartender at a time, Biancaniello might serve you a Jamaican Waiting Punch (Smith and Cross rum, Batavia arrack, Meyer lemon peel, sugar, blood orange juice, nutmeg; $5 or less), which you'll sip as you wait for something even more spectacular. The tiny bar is filled with plush couches, low tables, rugs, bookshelves, and a bit of zebra skin, all surrounding the bar. A disproportionately giant television might spoil the library vibe, but it is helpful for their Sunday movie nights. Snacks include pork belly skewers and cheese fries with asiago and bleu cheeses.

Like liquid comfort food, **Musso & Frank Grill** (6667 Hollywood Boulevard; 323.467.7788; www.mussoandfrank.com) will serve you a Martini, and they will do it exactly as they have been doing it since your great-grandparents ate and drank here (the restaurant has been open since 1919). Ignore trendy Hollywood Boulevard outside, and step into a time warp. William Faulkner mixed his own mint juleps here, and the bar was also frequented by Bukowski, Hemingway, and Fitzgerald (wait, are we still discussing Library Bar here?). It is Manny Aguirre's Martinis, served in tiny flasks, that give the place its reputation among cocktailians. They'll also make you a Ramos Gin Fizz or a Brandy Alexander. Swillsters might be further fortified with Welsh rarebit, an invention of cheese infused with beer, seasoned with paprika, and melted over toast. Fennel cakes are a specialty as well. Diners looking for more substantial fare may sit in either the dining room or at an incongruous lunch counter, where they'll enjoy pricey old-school fare like steaks, lobster tail, or sea bass, each served with a green salad, dinner roll, and potatoes. That's the kind of place this is, temporally flummoxed, stuck in a past decade, and proud of it.

Owner Ferris Wehbe opened **Next Door Lounge** (1154 N. Highland Avenue; 323.465.5505; www.nextdoorhollywood.com) in June 2011, next door to his low-key restaurant, the Corner. With 4,000 square feet of space inside, Wehbe wants Next Door Lounge to be a casual community hangout. Decorated in wood tables, old movies projected onto brick walls, maroon accents, plush vintage-style sofas, and even some 1940s barware from the Beverly Hills Hilton, it is comfortable with a classic feel. To lure in the locals (and international travelers—this means you), Wehbe stripped out existing Edison-style waterfalls and fire pits, but brought in Edison bartender Joseph Brooke (also of Copa d'Oro). Brooke is keeping things simple with classics, some as envisioned in the golden age, and some slightly updated. The bar's signature cocktail is the Dame Next Door (Canadian Club 12-year whisky, dry vermouth, clove-infused pineapple gomme syrup, pineapple juice, egg white, Angostura bitters). A big neon key marks the building, and a stencil of this logo is used to shape a spray of nutmeg onto the foamy top of the drink. We also liked the looks of the Volstead & Vice (Illegal mezcal, Pernod absinthe, cucumber water, agave nectar, lime juice). Most cocktails are $12. By the time you read this, their "secret" basement bar may also be open, and there may be musicians taking advantage of their upright piano. Light snacks include fried spaghetti, flatbreads, and bruschetta.

The de-luxe **Tar Pit** (609 N. La Brea Avenue; 323.965.1300; www.tarpitbar.com) opened in December 2009 but looks at least 80 years older than that, in the very best way possible. Decorated in white leather banquettes, a black marble bar, chandeliers, etched glass room dividers, and iron palm fronds between private booths, this convincing recreation of a classic deco-era supper club is elegant and streamlined. Mark Peel (of Campanile) opened Tar Pit with his wife, Nancy Silverton, and Audrey Saunders of New York's Pegu Club. Saunders has since departed, but her influence is still felt on the cocktail menu with her Jamaican Firefly (dark rum, house-made ginger beer, lime juice, simple syrup, crystallized ginger) and its relative, Saunders's signature Gin Gin Mule (gin, lime juice, simple syrup, house-made ginger beer). There aren't many whiskey drinks at Tar Pit; gin and rum seem to take center stage here, such as in the Palm Frond (lemon-myrtle-infused gin, green Chartreuse, apple-infused fino sherry, Bianco vermouth, muddled mint, simple syrup). All cocktails are $12. Peel's food menu keeps things surprisingly affordable, with options topping out at $17. Look for live music and burlesque shows on selected nights.

The Tasting Kitchen (1633 Abbot Kinney Boulevard, Venice, CA; 310.392.6644; www.thetastingkitchen. com) was opened by chef Casey Lane, formerly a resident of Portland, in mid-2009. The farm-to-table restaurant serves half a dozen French- and Italian-inspired dishes that change every night. Wild bass ($36), branzino ($40), and duck & luciana spiedino ($29) were on the menu when we looked. Bar manager Justin Pike, also of Portland, learned a few things while working at Clyde Common; his Whiskey Paddle (Bulleit bourbon, Luli Chinato fortified wine, Becherovka, Kübler absinthe) is aged in a rye barrel for seven weeks. Most cocktails at the Tasting Kitchen are $11–$13, including the Golden Ticket (pisco, passion fruit, honey, bitters) and the English Garden (gin, fennel dram, cucumber, lime juice). They also offer a short Gentlemen's List of tipples, utilizing premium spirits at about $20.

Usually, when I walk out of one of these bars, I've got a menu covered with hand-written annotations so that I stand some semblance of a chance of remembering what I drank (unless Gal Friday Night is with me, in which case she's already uploaded all recipes, ingredients, tasting notes, and photos to her database in the cloud before the tab is even paid). At the Tasting Kitchen, both of our methodologies were proven obsolete, since their menu of about 11 cocktails is already whimsically annotated with scribblings, details, and doodles in the margins. Of course, the next morning I thought I'd drank so much that I'd permanently altered my handwriting, so I proceeded to celebrate by committing a wide array of activities that turned out to be felonies. Who knew? Fortunately, my Gal Friday Night is an attorney.

SAN DIEGO

Given San Diego's proximity to the exploding cocktail scene in Los Angeles, it was only a matter of time before some rather fine cocktails started showing up in America's Finest City.

Craft & Commerce

675 W. Beech Street
San Diego, CA
619.269.2202
www.craft-commerce.com

El Dorado Cocktail Lounge

1030 Broadway
San Diego, CA
619.237.0550
www.eldoradobar.com

Noble Experiment

777 G Street
San Diego, CA
619.888.4713
www.nobleexperimentsd.com

Arsalun Tafazoli and Nate Stanton seem to hold a near-monopoly on San Diego's craft cocktail community. With their three bars comprising most of the San Diego cocktail destinations in *Destination: Cocktails*, they're clearly doing something right.

Craft & Commerce opened in August 2010 as the third of the duo's four businesses (in addition to the three bars profiled here, they also own Underbelly, a Japanese noodle house with a bar). Probably the busiest of the bunch, the Little Italy-area restaurant has also won interior design awards from the San Diego Architectural Foundation. Indeed, the graffiti-covered chartreuse booths, black subway tiles, long shelves of haphazardly arranged books, a mirror that is supposed to make the room look bigger than it actually is, and exposed brick with big slogans carved into it ("DEMAND LESS") give the place a striking look.

Executive chef Craig Jimenez isn't beholden to the area's Italian surroundings, preferring to also take inspiration from the city's Filipino and Mexican populations, while crafting a cuisine of distinctly American comfort food. The menu begins with a manifesto explaining their "demand less" philosophy, and ends with "Dinnertime" selections such as fried chicken ($14), a farmer's plate (vegetables and grains; $14), and mussels with fries ($12). Smaller plates include fried pickles ($7), and bacon Cracker Jacks ($4). That last one is exactly what you're thinking it is, and also includes marcona almonds, hominy, sea salt, and a toy surprise.

Let's move on to something more adult. The cocktail list was designed with an assist from Philip Ward of New York City's Mayahuel, and has received attention for its beer-based cocktails. We liked their Dark and Stormy variant, the Darkest Storm (Port Brewing Old Viscosity ale, Gosling's Black Seal rum, ginger beer, lemon juice, candied ginger; $10). Another intriguing "beertail" is the Up in Smoke (Allagash Curieux barrel-aged tripel ale, Laphroaig Scotch whisky, Fuji apple juice, lime juice; $10). Moving away from the beer, Gal Friday Night was drawn to a beverage inspired by her homeland called the Dutch Flower (genever, St. Germain elderflower liqueur, Cointreau, lemon juice, absinthe; $10).

Much clubbier than Craft & Commerce is **El Dorado,** which opened in November 2008 and was recently retrofitted with a Kold-Draft ice machine, punch service, and new glassware to bring it more into line with Tafazoli and Stanton's other businesses. Ward and Sam Ross (of New York's Milk & Honey) got the bar program up and running at El Dorado. Craft cocktails coexist with divey beers here, as DJs spin techno tunes for a busy dance floor. The sparse decor facilitates the younger and more festive atmosphere of the Gaslamp District, but it does give one just enough cues to link the gold rush name to the surroundings, including paintings of Old West scenes and a giant taxidermy bison head named Otis perched over the jukebox. A short menu of selected cocktails is

rotated seasonally. Try the Night Creature (rye, mezcal, Averna amaro, Bénédictine, orange bitters; $9).

Oft-cited as the top of the heap in San Diego's burgeoning craft cocktail scene, **Noble Experiment** was named after president Herbert Hoover's terminology for Prohibition. Tafazoli and Stanton's Prohibition-themed bar opened in February 2010, and is accessed via a gastropub called Neighborhood. A stack of kegs near Neighborhood's restrooms is actually a hidden door leading into one of the more uniquely decorated bar rooms on record. We're talking about 2,000 bronzed skulls covering a wall, reminding the Parisian Gal Friday Night of the catacombs of Paris. The skulls are complemented by video monitors on the ceiling that display continually changing works of art, all juxtaposed with crystal chandeliers, creamy leather, and bottles of booze stacked up to the high ceiling. You'll need to make a reservation via text message before being admitted by one of the young and well-dressed hostesses. The small bar only has room for about three dozen tipplers, so

plan appropriately.

The cocktail menu here is roughly the same as at Craft & Commerce, which is no surprise since the bars share not only ownership, but bartenders as well. The most notable difference is that you'll see fewer beer cocktails at Noble Experiment than at Craft and Commerce. The sharp-eyed Gal Friday Night did spot a bona-fide bottle of Amer Picon on the shelf, and promptly ordered a cocktail inspired by her hometown: a Brooklyn (rye, maraschino liqueur, dry vermouth, Amer Picon). Bar manager Anthony Schmidt might mix up a Holiday Gold Rush (bourbon, lemon juice, honey, allspice liqueur, bitters, muddled orange) with a block of hand-carved ice in it. Bartender Eric Johnson created the Mescao (blanco mezcal, white crème de cacao, Barolo Chinato digestif, Bittermens xocolatl mole bitters, flamed orange peel). But either man, or any of the other bartenders on staff, will also be happy to deliver a bartender's choice, usually with solid results.

There is no food at Noble Experiment, but you can get some chow at its parent pub, Neighborhood (619.446.0002). They'll do small plates like jalapeño mac and cheese ($7), plus sandwiches like venissimo grilled cheese sliders ($9), seared albacore tuna ($10), and a black bean burger ($9), to be paired with the contents of impressive beer and whiskey lists.

LAST CALL!
More Destinations to Explore in San Diego

Ave 5 (2760 5th Avenue; 619.542.0394; www.avenue5restaurant.com) opened in the Banker's Hill area in August 2007. Owner and chef Colin MacLaggan focuses on farm-to-table cuisine, such as grilled wild salmon ($19) and filet mignon ($27), all harvested in what he says is a sustainable manner. At the bar, things can veer toward the molecular, as with their Cotton Candy Cuban (dark rum, mint, sparkling wine, lime juice, cotton candy). The liquid mixture is given to the customer in a little beaker, along with a glass of cotton candy that dissolves as the drink is poured over it. Sounds like a perfect way to introduce your kids to the joys of rum. Or, if you'd prefer that they eat their vegetables, try P's & Carrots (tequila, peach, passion fruit, carrot, lime juice; $10).

At the **Grant Grill,** within the U.S. Grant Hotel (326 Broadway; 619.744.2077; www.grantgrill.com), Jeff Josenhans is experimenting with bottle-conditioned cocktails. His cocktails are prepared *sur lie* (Gal Friday Night tells us that is French for "on dregs," or "on scum," but the gist is "rested in yeast"). The drinks ferment and carbonate in a bottle, resulting in libations with the texture of champagne. The already complex Smokin' Pumpkin (pumpkin-infused rum, allspice dram, applewood-smoke coconut sugar, Laphroaig Scotch whisky, saffron, vanilla) is bottled with ale yeast. Further upscale creations from Josenhans include the Cinnamon Basil French Julep (Pierre Ferrand cognac, orange blossom sugar, muddled pink lavender, cinnamon basil, Moët Chandon champagne) and the Walnut Rocks (High West whiskey, walnut liqueur, lemon juice, simple syrup, egg whites). All cocktails are $12. Chef Chris Kurth's kitchen is joining the bar in serving inventions containing ingredients grown in the century-old hotel's new rooftop terrace garden. His tasting menu of three to five courses runs $40–$80. The restaurant and lounge opened in 1951 and were retrofitted in 2006 with deco-inspired decor, which has since been updated once again.

Prohibition Liquor Bar (548 5th Avenue; www.prohibitionsd.com) is another speakeasy-themed bar, this time disguised as the law office of "Eddie O'Hare, Esq." in the trendy Gaslamp district. Use their website to get on the guest list and acquire a password. Although the drinks are comparable to some of the places listed above, the advantage of visiting Prohibition over, say, Noble Experiment, is jazz. Prohibition hosts live music three night per week, with an emphasis on the jazz and excursions into funk and bossa nova. The half dozen cocktails on the menu are mixed by bartenders like Levi Walker and Dustin Haarstad. Selections are split between classics including a Brandy Crusta (brandy, Cointreau, Luxardo maraschino liqueur, lemon juice, Peychaud's bitters) and house inventions like the Risky Fizziness (Islay Scotch whisky, cinnamon syrup, egg white, ginger beer). Most cocktails are $12.

Midtown's **Starlite** (3175 India Street; 619.358.9766; www.starlitesandiego.com) has a pleasing contemporary-yet-mid-century-influenced design by Barbara Rourke & Jason St. John. A hexagonal entryway leads to a sunken rectangular bar under a modernist steel chandelier, all surrounded by flagstone walls. Chef Kathleen Wise keeps the chow in season with dishes like pan-roasted jidori chicken ($20), their much lauded burger (with Brandt beef and gruyere cheese; $13), and their popular sausage board ($13), featuring house-made sausages. Cocktails are $9 (always nice to see 'em under 10 bucks these days) and include the Kentucky Colonel (Buffalo Trace bourbon, Cock 'n' Bull ginger beer, lemon juice, house-made cherry vanilla bitters) and the Gunga Din (Montecristo 12-year rum, Earl Grey tea, cardamom syrup, Meyer lemon juice, mint).

INTERNATIONAL

It's a beautiful world we live in, and there are a whole lot of cocktail bars in it. This section represents the very best destinations within nations that your humble scribe and his constant companion have visited during the past five years or so.

VANCOUVER

The craft cocktail movement is flourishing in the Pacific Northwest. The sudden variety of worthwhile places to visit in the Vancouver area is wonderful to see (and taste), and the undeniable talent on display is impressive.

There are two types of bar in the world, and the one that tickled us the most had a giant quote painted on a wall covering all three sides of a secluded alcove. It began: "There are two types of people in the world . . . ." The past tense is appropriate here, since Boneta has recently moved from its location on West Cordova to newer digs. The new

Boneta

12 Water Street
Vancouver, BC
604.684.1844
www.boneta.ca

Boneta near Blood Alley is slightly deeper in the now-thriving Gastown nightlife zone that the restaurant helped create. Ultra-locavore touches include a water filtration system on-premises (no wasteful bottles needed), tables made from solidified recycled paper, and a commitment to buying from area farmers.

Food by chef Ben de Champlain includes poutine, smoked bison carpaccio, octopus chips, and crispy pork ear frites. Small plates are $9–$15, and larger portions go for $24–$26. The poutine is served with crispy fries, and makes good use of local Okanagan cheese curds. Gal Friday Night describes our poutine as "more honest" than some of the other poutines we have sampled in Vancouver, and she never lies.

Barman Mathieu Faure was in a creative mood when we planted our pants at Boneta. He may have been taking a cue from his neighbors down in Seattle when he decided we were going to get bartender's choice all night. El Jimador Blanco tequila, Aperol aperitif, Cynar aperitif, and Fernet-Branca amaro filled the first glass that landed in front of us, and then an Old-Fashioned variant happened: Maker's Mark bourbon, Redbreast Irish whiskey, and a wash of Ardbeg Islay Malt Scotch whisky. Sure, why not blend

Scotch, bourbon, and Irish whiskies in one glass? A worthy take on the cocktail formerly known as "the Cocktail."

Also behind the bar is Simon Kaulback, serving drinks from a concise menu of about eight house creations (all $10) and three "classics" (all $12), which are actually recipes from revered contemporary bartenders like Chris Hannah (Arnaud's in New Orleans) and Eric Castro (Rickhouse in San Francisco). We were also drawn to the Green Eyed Devil (pear and green tea liqueur, sake, lemongrass rose water, lime cordial, soda) and the Gaoler's Sour (Wild Turkey bourbon, Forbidden Fruit liqueur, rooibos syrup, lemon juice, egg, grapefruit bitters).

Apparently, there are two kinds of people in the world: stop into Boneta and find out what they're drinking.

Chambar

562 Beatty Street
Vancouver, BC
604.879.7119
www.chambar.com

Plenty of bars talk about sustainability and environmental commitment, but how many back that up with a manifesto on their website? We don't want to spoil your dinner appetite or diminish your thirst by talking about the hip Chambar's trash, but before jumping in, take a look at their specs: the restaurant and its sister businesses (Café Medina and the Dirty Apron Cooking School) aim to exceed their green certification requirements in order to become completely carbon-neutral. They reuse or recycle everything possible (right down to making their own notepads), food waste is composted, cleaning products are certified green, no plastic or styrofoam is used in their to-go containers, and even the bottles from their Chambar Ale are cleaned and reused. In spite of this, the restaurant doesn't feel rustic or come across as an especially good place for hippies to hang out. Just the opposite, in fact. With dark wood, exposed brick, maroon accents, and candlelight, the large bar area in the front of the contemporary space feels warm, and just bit masculine. The dining area toward the back is a bit brighter and . . . stripier (if we may).

Owner-chef Nico Schuermans was trained in Belgium, so his Franco-Belgian cuisine, bolstered with North African and Middle Eastern influences, comes naturally. Expect dishes like l'omble de l'Artique niçois ($28), entrecôte de boeuf ($33), and various moules frites variants ($22). Poutine à la belge ($9) appeared in front of us; the poutine is becoming a Vancouver theme. This one utilized blue cheese and pink peppercorn to great effect.

With quiet jazz playing during an early evening visit, an amuse-bouche materialized as bartender Derek Granton suggested an off-menu Death-Proof (Beefeater gin, green Chartreuse, sake, citrus, apple juice, egg white, simple syrup; $12). Quentin Tarantino did not show up to serve it to us. Gal Friday Night, who is a descendant of Lewis Carroll, ordered the Mad Hatter ($14). Let's just say that, for the first and only time ever, she was too preoccupied with gustatory joy to write down what was in it. We were also drawn to the Los Altos (blanco tequila, fig syrup, port wine, lemon juice; $9) and the Bitter Saint (rum, La Chouffe Belgian pale ale, passion fruit, Fernet-Branca float; $11). Also found behind the bar are friendly general manager Justin Tisdall and bar manager Jacob Sweetapple (who recently took over from Wendy McGuinness). When a restaurant unleashes the GM behind the bar, you know their cocktail focus is serious.

The Diamond

6 Powell Street
Vancouver
www.di6mond.com

Just around the corner from Boneta, and also an easy walk from L'Abattoir (has your evening's itinerary taken shape yet?), the Diamond was launched by bartenders Mark Brand (of Boneta), Josh Pape (of Chambar), and Sophie Taverner (of Boneta and Cascade Room). Located in a second floor space with big windows overlooking Maple Tree Square, right on the corner of the most festive part of Gastown, the Diamond is a great place to spy on the crowds below. Perhaps a bar with as much local pride as the Diamond deserves this exceptionally good space. Their business cards carry the same quote you see as you (carefully) descend the steep staircase: "I live in Gastown by choice. Those unfamiliar with its particular allures are entitled to wonder why." That, of course, is an appropriation of a Truman Capote quote about Brooklyn, but the Diamond makes it their own.

Tables scattered throughout the bright room, a mere seven seats at the bar, exposed brick, and kelly green accents give the place a slightly pub-ish feeling. Don't mistake their name as being an indicator of elegance; this is a very casual spot. The crowd is on the younger end, and the bar will get a bit loud on the weekends.

Food is at the Diamond is Vietnamese fusion with a few Japanese influences, served mostly as smaller plates to be shared. Go for the stuffed baby squid ($12), betel leaves ($10), gyoza ($7) or rock cod ceviche ($12).

The cocktail menu is delivered on a clipboard with a thick slab of leather covering the pages. About two dozen drinks are divided up as Delicate, Proper, Boozy, Refreshing, Notorious, and Overlooked, with about four libations in each category. Each is labeled with the date and place they were invented, and about half of them list the Diamond as their place of origin. We liked the inclusion of the intense Widow's Kiss

(calvados, green Chartreuse, Bénédictine, bitters; $12) in the Over-looked section. This classic and others are served in Japanese-sized portions, and in fact, the menu does disclaim that "all cocktails are 2 oz." The glassware was striking, however—an elegant bit of vintage stemware. On tracking this stuff down, head barkeep Ron Oliver confided, "We each have our own secret spot to score" ("we each" being the various Vancouver bars, which all seem to favor an eclectic mix of classic glassware).

While praising the strong sense of community in the Vancou-ver cocktail scene and musing on the challenges inherent in main-taining quality in a high-volume bar like the Diamond, Oliver got started on a house original, the Parliament (cachaça, Fernet-Branca amaro, lime juice, honey; $11). The bar staff, he said, had worked hard to develop the drink, and we could tell; Gal Friday Night found it to be well-balanced, with each ingredient standing out distinctly.

Want to learn to make your own cocktails? The Diamond of-fers their Preparatory School for All Things Drinks for enthusiasts and future professionals alike.

There are bars that serve drinks that make you *think* you feel bet-ter after drinking them, and there are those that serve drinks that just might make you feel better for real. At the Keefer Bar, manager and mixolo-gist Danielle Tatarin invents potions that draw heavily from the bar's Chi-natown location. Raiding the local apothecaries, Tatarin makes drinks using astragalus, ginseng, and yunzhi—and that's just for starters. Not only does this add a whole new world of flavors and textures to the drinks at the Keefer Bar, but it also reminds us of the earliest days of the cocktail, when bit-ters were sold and used medicinally. The Chinese have been using these herbs for medicinal purposes for *millennia*, and its hard to deny that this back-to-basics approach to healing makes a lot of sense. If we can combine Eastern medicine with a cocktail, says

The Keefer Bar

The Keefer Suites
135 Keefer Street
Vancouver, BC
604.688.1961
www.thekeeferbar.com

part-time acupuncturist Gal Friday Night, then count us in.

Tatarin tells us that nearly every drink on the "List of Remedies and Cures" contains some sort of root or tea. The Dragonfly (dragonfruit-infused gin, Momokawa Pearl sake, lemon juice, ginger syrup, magnolia bark tincture) is the bar's best seller. We were also amused by the Corpse Reviver #135, which adds Lillet blanc infused with lychee and lavender to the traditional Corpse Reviver #2 recipe. The Sweet Intentions mixes bourbon and tea with vanilla-infused green Chartreuse (because, you know, Chartreuse just isn't complex enough on its own). The Chinatown Sour (Wild Turkey 101 bourbon, Fernet-Branca amaro, lemon juice, astragalus orgeat) hit the spot, with the Fernet coming out subtly on the finish. Cocktails are $9–$12. "Essences" are available for $1 each. These are tinctures that can be added to any drink to "balance emotional and mental disharmonies." Wait, isn't that what *all* cocktails are for?

The Keefer Bar is a small and narrow space, but is strikingly decorated. Very low lights from bare Edison bulbs are accented in red, contrasted by backlit plastic panels covered with X-ray photos and Chinese text. Ancient-looking hand-labeled bottles are filled with tinctures and infusions, coexisting on high shelves with mysterious old brass gadgets (scales, perhaps) and a collection of vintage glassware. There's at least one skull in the place, and a library ladder that we watched Tatarin scampering up more than once to reach bottles filled with plant life and alcohol.

The bar happens to be on the property of the chic and trendy Keefer Suites, but it has its own entrance and feels like a completely separate entity. Seldom have we encountered a hotel bar that felt less like a piece of corporate real estate and more like the brainchild of an indie cocktail nerd ("indie cocktail nerd" being a term of deep endearment in this book). There's no food at the Keefer Bar, but you may feast your eyes on burlesque performers fairly regularly, and live music from time to time. That's good for what ails ya'.

***

There are bars that inspire thoughts of bunnies, and there are bars that inspire thoughts of slaughterhouses. Within Vancouver's no-longer-totally-danger-ous Gastown district,

L'Abattoir
217 Carrall Street
Vancouver, BC
604.568.1701
www.labattoir.ca

you might stumble across Blood Alley or Gaoler's Mews ("gaol" is the British spelling of "jail"). Between them is a bustling bistro called L'Abattoir. That's French, as you know, for the Slaughter-house. Jails? Blood Alley? Slaughterhouses? What kind of drinks do they serve here? Bloody Marys and Corpse Revivers? Widow's Kiss? No, nothing so macabre. In reality, the updated 19th-century building is indeed Vancouver's former jail, and the slaughterhouse was next door. No further comment shall be offered on the urban planning methodologies of Vancouver's founding fathers.

Opened in July 2010, the upscale L'Abattoir makes some of the best cocktails in the region, and serves delicious food courtesy of co-owner/chef Lee Cooper. His excellent French-meets-West-Coast menu might feature leg of lamb in Indian spice ($23), pan-fried fillet of steelhead ($24), or steak Diane ($27). The rabbit canelloni ($17) is a nice smaller plate. A smaller plate of bunnies. The bread basket placed on the table is almost worth the price of admission by itself.

The space makes use of its history but feels contemporary, too. The 15-seat bar is right at the front of the room as one enters, while seating for food is in the rear and on a balcony. We like the intricate black-and-white tiles on the floor, the complex driftwood sculpture filtering the sunlight from an atrium ceiling, and the accommodat-ing staff, from co-owner/manager Paul Grunberg right down to the friendly hostess, Tara.

Cocktails from head bar-man Shaun Layton come from a menu bolted to a solid metal plate. We went for the barrel-aged Hanky Panky (gin, sweet vermouth, Fernet-Branca; $10), served in a cool vintage glass with a gold band around the rim. Those mismatched vintage glasses are definitely a Vancouver trademark. The drink was very forward on the Fernet. Our bartender, David, agreed: "The Fernet really beat the barrel!" Said barrel comes all the way from New York's Tuthilltown distillery.

Gal Friday Night, a vegan except for when there is charcuterie, hot dogs, sushi, barbecue, quail, bacon, or any form of meat or cheese involved, went for a variant on the classic Red Hook called the Meat Hook (bourbon, maraschino liqueur, Punt e Mes sweet vermouth, Ardbeg 10-year Scotch whisky; $11). This is served in the shaker, which is wrapped in a custom-made koozie. The cocktail is well-balanced, with the ubiquitous Ardbeg deep in the background, adding a hint of smoke. We did not detect the presence of meat in this drink, but we were hooked, for sure.

West

2881 Granville Street
Vancouver
604.738.8938
www.westrestaurant.com

Within 10 minutes of our arrival at West, lead bartender David Wolowidnyk was enthusing over his visit to Japan, telling us about an impromptu bartending master class given to him by none other than Kazuo Uyeda. Within a day of returning from Japan, Wolowidnyk had whipped up his first Kakkoii (plum wine, G'Vine gin, cinnamon

syrup, lemon juice; $12) in honor of his visit to Tokyo. This is (of course) served over a sphere of hand-carved ice, Japanese-style. It doesn't stop there: Japan isn't the only country to inspire Wolowidnyk. The Passage to India (Havana Club añejo blanco rum, lemon juice, Orchid mango liqueur, chili, cilantro, curry) also conjures up images and tastes of travels to destinations in far-off lands.

The bulk of West's cocktail menu is made up of about two dozen classics, all pulled directly from the classic cocktail catalog, including the Brown Derby (Bulleit bourbon, grapefruit juice, honey syrup, lemon splash; $11), the Brandy Crusta (Torres five-year brandy, Cointreau, lemon juice, maraschino liqueur, Peychaud's bitters; $10.50), and the Kir Royale (Sumac Ridge Stellar's Jay brut champagne, crème de cassis; $15). The menu also lists the year each recipe was created (in this case: 1930, 1852, and 1841, respectively). Always looking to discover something new, we also went for Wolowidnyk's Four O'Clock (Maker's Mark whiskey, Grand Marnier, old-fashioned bitters, lemon juice, Navan orange blossom foam; $13).

Often cited as among the very best of Vancouver's bartenders, and working within what are often cited as among the very best of Vancouver's restaurants, Wolowidnyk presides over a long, polished cherrywood bar, in front of a huge wall storing West's massive wine collection. An art deco absinthe fountain is one of the few extraneous decorative touches in the sleek, bright, and modern restaurant. Located along the trendy South Granville shopping corridor, West opened a bit over a decade ago.

Quang Dang is the current executive chef, sourcing local ingredients to create a concise list of about five main courses, including Haida Gwaii sablefish ($36) and organic grain-fed veal chop ($49). These are to be complimented with a lengthy list of small plates ("Elements"), including Vancouver Island octopus ($11.50), Oyama prosciutto ($13), and foraged mushrooms ($11). West also offers a pair of "chef's tables" (where diners can get personal with the chef and interact with the creation of their meal), as well as tasting menus that include sea ($76), land ($68), and vegetarian ($58) options. The Top Table Group also owns three other Vancouver restaurants: CinCin, Blue Water Café, and Araxi.

LAST CALL!

More Destinations to Explore in Vancouver
(Note: The first bar is located in Victoria, about 60 miles from Vancouver)

Named after Clive Piercy, owner of one of Victoria's few remaining independently owned hotels, **Clive's Classic Lounge** at the Chateau Victoria Hotel (740 Burdett Avenue, Victoria, BC; 250.361.5684; www.clivesclassiclounge.com) has been nominated as the best hotel bar in the world (by the Spirited Awards). Clive's "mixology mantra" states that they only use juices squeezed to order, refrigerate their vermouth and other wine-based products, chill all glassware, make some of their bitters in-house, and hand-make their garnishes. Clive's also offers a swell selection of absinthe, barrel-aged cocktails, spirit flights, and a drink made by infusing rum with a cheese sandwich (!), plus themed seminars and workshops. Gal Friday Night was reminded of her childhood home in Kansas by the Click Your Heels Thrice (Bornholmer aquavit, Martini & Rossi Bianco vermouth, house-made hibiscus liqueur, Seville orange bitters, lemon juice; $10), but instead opted for a drink from her hockey player husband's hometown: the Saskatoon Julep (Forty Creek Barrel Select whisky, house-made Saskatoon liqueur, mint; $11). We were also hot for the Sophie & Audrey (El Jimador reposado tequila, Lillet Blanc vermouth, Esprit de June liqueur, barrel-aged peach bitters; $12). Esprit de June is a sweet liqueur made from the vine flowers of several French wine grape varietals.

The Rosewood Hotel Georgia first opened in 1927, and featured visiting talent such as Duke Ellington and Marlene Dietrich. In 2011, the hotel was renovated, resulting in a fresh take on the restaurant and bar, **The Hawksworth** and **1927 Lobby Lounge,** respectively (801 W. Georgia Street; 604.673.7000; www.hawksworthrestaurant.com; www.rosewoodhotels.com/en/hotelgeorgia). The hotel boasts some 200 works by Vancouver artists, and you'll find further creativity at chef David Hawksworth's restaurant. His locally-focused, Asian-influenced menu might feature chestnut and black truffle agnolotti ($25) or Yarrow Meadows duck breast ($36). At the 1927 Lobby Lounge, manager Brad Stanton has made sterling use of Ted Saucier's fantastic (and expensive) *Bottom's Up* (1951), resurrecting a published cocktail recipe invented at this very hotel: the Hotel Georgia Cocktail (Plymouth gin, lemon juice, orgeat, orange blossom water, egg white, nutmeg; $12). Also, 1927 was the year that the first talkie was released, and so it is fitting that the Jazz Singer is the name of one of barman Robyn Gray's cocktails (Plymouth gin, lemon juice, simple syrup, maraschino liqueur, black cherries, prosecco; $12). The hotel's **Prohibition Lounge** is slated to open in 2012, featuring a jazz-era theme.

The Polynesian Room in the Waldorf Hotel (1489 East Hastings Street; 604.253.7141; www.

waldorfhotel.com) was listed in *Tiki Road Trip* (2007) as being a spectacularly decorated, multi-level, mid-century tiki lounge that was closed for business but immaculately preserved, as if encased in rummy amber. New ownership restored the 1947 hotel (and the 1955 Polynesian Room) prior to reopening in November 2010. The ground floor section has been dubbed the Tiki Bar, with all-vintage bamboo trim, moody blue lights, wooden tikis, and authentic Edgar Leeteg paintings intact. We wandered in, expecting to be served a second-rate Mai Tai, and stumbled out thoroughly impressed with their carefully prepared selection of classic cocktails. The adjacent Leeteg Room is a larger space where the hotel's chef-in-residence program is conducted. Killer diller.

Don't let the dive bar name fool you; **Pourhouse** (162 Water Street; 604.568.7022; www.pourhousevancouver. com) is a stylish restaurant and lounge opened in late summer 2009, run by head bartender Jay Jones and executive chef Chris Irving. Maroon and gold trim accent a room that recalls art nouveau somewhat, giving the Pour House a feeling akin to fin-de-siècle Europe. Irving, an alumnus of

West, has filled his menu with elevated takes on traditional comfort food, including spaghetti and meatballs ($19), foil-wrapped campfire trout ($26), Cornish hen ($30 for two), grilled cheese with soup ($12), and pork croquettes ($9). Barkeeps Daniel Pitt and Emily Shulze pour from a very short menu of cocktails, but are fully up to the task of taking advantage of the vast array of bottles behind them. Pour House also features live jazz on Sunday nights.

Located among the raucous nightclubs, music venues, and partying collegiates of Granville Street, **The Refinery** (above Sip Resto Lounge, 1115 Granville Street; 604.687.8001; www.therefineryvancouver.com) is a completely different type of venue. Sip was designed by Marilou Rudakewich and May Cheng of Vancouver's M-Studio Design to be a fully green dining and drinking environment. The Refinery carries this concept to the upstairs bar. Their well-regarded cocktail program is maintained by mixologist Graham Racich, whose cocktails pair with a relatively large food menu by chef Kirk Morrison. Simple entrees like roasted halibut ($17), gnocchi ($15), and beef carpaccio ($11.50) are complimented by flatbreads ($14) and a cheese board ($17). All seafood is certified by Ocean Wise. Racich is responsible for the bar's house-made bitters, vermouths, grenadine, vegetable waters, juices, purées, preserves, sodas, and powders, plus local products like Victoria gin. He'll put all of this to good use in tipples like the My Marma-Lady (Plymouth gin, yuzu marmalade, lemon juice, peach bitters, float of rosé wine; $10) and his Rich Manhattan (Alberta premium rye, house chocolate vermouth, house sweet vermouth, house coffee bitters; $10). We also did a double-take at the Last Word First (tea-infused gin, maraschino liqueur, lime juice, house-made green Chartreuse pop; $10). House-carbonated green Chartreuse? Nice!

HAVANA

Oh, Havana.

During Prohibition, this was America's playground. Located only 90 miles from Key West, Havana was a place for swilling rum and losing oneself in the sweaty beats of Afro-Cuban rhythm, giving in to the lust this music was meant to inspire. Somehow, Cuba soon became a communist pain in the keister, and let Russia point a bunch of nuclear missiles at Washington. Who let *that* happen?

Gal Friday Night wants *fun Cuba* back, and I'm not arguing. Someone has to make this happen, and Washington isn't doing it.

We went there.

A silly little thing like international politics wasn't going to get between us and the Cradle of the Daiquiri. Cuba is not a country where the locals have much cash to spend on things like fine dining/drinking. There are almost no bars in Havana outside of the tourist zone. People take in their rum (daily) on the verandas of their crumbling 19th-century colonial mansions, usually in the company of a few friends and neighbors playing some music.

Thus, we're going straight to the Last Call here.

LAST CALL!
Destinations to Explore in Havana

Perhaps an entire book could be written just about the bars that claim Hemingway drank in them. Only one has erected a bronze statue of the man in place of his favorite bar stool. **Bar La Floridita** (Obispo No. 557 esq. a Monserrate;

867.1299; www.floridita-cuba.com) is a seafood restaurant at the edge of Habana Vieja, the touristy part of Havana. About the Havana bars, Papa says, "My Mojito in La Bodeguita, my Daiquiri in El Floridita." Indeed, the daiquiri was said to have been invented in this very room, which is often called "La Cuna del Daiquiri" ("the cradle of the daiquiri"). For that reason alone, you must visit this bar, which opened in 1817 as La Piña de Plata (the Silver Pineapple). Choke down one of their awful Daiquiris, pay your respects, and then go mix some much better drinks of your own with some of the insanely cheap Havana Club rum that you'll be able to get here (see page 287).

A block from there is the amazing art deco **Bacardi building** (Monserrate 261), built in 1925. Bacardi was kicked out of Cuba after the revolution (December 31, 1958), and moved to Puerto Rico, where they proceeded to corner the global rum market with their heavily advertised, mass-produced firewater. Truly, Bacardi is the McDonald's of rum. But the building that Mr. Bacardi left behind? Spectabulous. On the second-floor balcony is a small café that was once the Bacardi family's private bar. When we visited, the wizened old bartender, Alberto, wasn't shy about his skills, claiming to be "the only person who could make them [cocktails] properly." We have little doubt that he thought he meant what he said, and we admire his dedication to his craft. *Properly*.

Next door to the entirely skippable Havana Club distillery tour and gift shop is **Bar Dos Hermanos** (San Pedro 304), which claims to be the oldest bar in Havana. Steeped in history, they've remodeled and are back open as of 2009. Hemingway preferred the Mojito at **La Bodeguita del Medio** (Empedrado 207). Opened in 1942 by Angel Martinez, this is where the drink may or may not have been invented. Pablo Neruda, Nat King Cole, and Marlene Dietrich are said to have been regulars at the perpetually-packed little bar, and apparently Ernesto Garcia Lorca, Marlon Brando, and Errol Flynn drank here, too. But that doesn't mean their Mojito is all it's cracked up to be. Every single bar in Havana will tell you that a Mojito is "a special drink in Cuba that you cannot get anywhere else in the world." Such is the price of isolationism.

The grand finale of a Havana trip is a visit to the **Tropicana Nightclub** (72 Street between 41st and 45th, Miramar; 267.1717). The Tropicana is a time warp, a piece of 1939 transported into the 21st century. If this old-style supper club (without the supper) has ever been updated, that renovation cannot have happened any sooner than half a century ago. Surrounded on all sides by a lush jungle, visitors to the Tropicana will enjoy an old-style cabaret show under the stars. An elaborate stage, itself a marvel of mid-century design, is home to performers in elaborate costumes singing, dancing, and performing music during a two-hour show that would have made Desi Arnaz weep with pride. We love the conga soloist on his own hydraulic-lift platform and the giant chandelier moving over the audience on a track, followed by girls in chandelier dresses. Chinese-style acrobats (but Cuban, of course) balance on tall objects to the sound of "Flight of the Bumblebee." It is a rather steep $70 to get in, but the price includes a glass of champagne, and rum is free. Cola is not. *Cuba Libre*, indeed. After the show, the venue stays open for dancing, but most of the audience will leave immediately (the tour buses are a-waiting).

A BIT ON CUBAN RUMS

Rum is dirt cheap in Cuba. If you have a fetish for Havana Club, who have a near-monopoly on rum in Cuba, then Havana is rummy heaven. A bottle of Havana Club 7-year and the younger but better 6-year Añejo Reserva are less than 10 bucks each. The vaunted Cuban Barrel Proof is now out of production, having been replaced by the new Selection de Maestro, which should set you back about $30. Havana Club also sells an Añejo 15-year and a Máximo Extra Añejo for $150 and $1,700, respectively. Perspective: the average Cuban will require about six years to earn $1,700. Don Jose Navarro, master blender for Havana Club, asserts that the Máximo is the most expensive currently-produced rum in the world. Most of the 1,000 bottles made per year are exported to Europe. The locals are all drinking the frankly mediocre Añejo Blanco, Añejo 3 Años, and Añejo Especial, which can be bought for about $5 each. The problem is that fresh produce and soft drinks are not cheap. So if it is Mojitos, Cuba Libres, or Daiquiris you're looking for, then your limes, soda, and mint leaves will get you into money. Just be careful of the ice, *mis amigos*—it's made from the local water.

Some other Cuban rums that Gal Friday Night had the presence of mind to take note of are: Ron Mulata (at least four varieties), Ron Santero (Añejo Blanco, Aguardiente, and Palma Superior), Arecha (Elixir de Ron), Ron Añejo Legendario, Brandy Torres Perfecto, Ron Añejo Santiago de Cuba (Blanco and Añejo), and Ron Varadero (Palma Superior and Añejo 7). All are about $4–$8 per bottle. On the higher end, Mulata has a Solera for about $46, and a Palma Reserva for about $38. Stop drooling.

LONDON

London has been called the cocktail capital of the world by many well-traveled tipplers. New Yorkers, San Franciscans, and *Edokko* (Tokyoans) might disagree, but we know one thing for certain—you don't have to look very hard to find an excellent Martini in the town of beefeaters, Banksy, and the Clash. London's calling, so let us begin at one of its most famous addresses (other than 10 Downing Street).

69 Colebrooke Row

69 Colebrooke Row
London
754.052.8593
www.69colebrookerow.com

There are bars (and men) with names, and there are bars (and men) with no names. The "Bar With No Name" is located at 69 Colebrooke Row, near Islington's bustling Upper Street. Clint Eastwood has yet to be spotted there. For a bar with no name, this bar has made quite a name for itself. So has its owner, Tony Conigliaro, who shares a name with a certain 1960s Boston Red Sox outfielder. There are no Red Sox at 69 Colebrooke Row, but there are red leather banquettes opposite ebony chairs. The room is otherwise entirely black and white, and seems to somehow share a design aesthetic with the *New Yorker* magazine. Forty thirsty drinkers are enough to make the bar feel crowded, so you'll want to make a reservation if you'll be visiting during peak hours. Those who have to wait might visit co-owner Camille Hobby-Limon's nearby pub, Charles Lamb, for ales and pub chow.

Conigliaro has a deep interest in the deconstruction of the cocktail, to the degree that his laboratory on the upstairs floor of 69 Colebrooke Row had to be moved to a larger building (Pink Floyd's old recording studio, no less). All of the lab gear—the Soxhlet extractor, the bain-marie, the homogenizer, and the Rotavapor—mean little next to the elegant simplicity of Conigliaro's most notorious contribution to modern mixology: the aged cocktail.

Although he has worked with barrel aging, Conigliaro prefers glass. This allows for longer aging, since glass won't continually alter the flavor of a drink like wood would. He began bottling cocktails in 2004 after he opened an 80-year-old bottle of Dubonnet (a wine-based aperitif) and found it to be excellent.

Most selections, such as the signature Manhattan, are aged for six months, but in 2010, the bar did pour a Manhattan that had been aging for six years. We were intrigued by the El Presidente (Havana Club Barrel Proof rum, triple sec, Martini Rosso vermouth, house-made grenadine; £12.50), which is aged for six months.

When not aging cocktails or subjecting them to a centrifuge, Conigliaro is designing custom spirits. The Spitfire (69 house cognac, crème de peche, lemon juice, sugar, white wine) contains a cognac that Conigliaro created specifically to use in this drink. This house cognac has notes of apricot and peach so as to work with the crème de peche and the chosen white wine.

But can you get a plain ol' cocktail at 69 Colebrooke Row? Natch. Bartenders in lab coats will serve you a Barbershop Fizz (pine-infused Beefeater gin, birch and vanilla syrup, patchouli-infused mint, lime juice, soda) or a Honey Suckle (pollen liqueur, champagne) for £9 each. All right—those are not so plain after all. By the way, that liqueur is made with pollen gathered by Transylvanian monks, plus honey and honeysuckle.

Sip your tipples to the sound of quiet jazz, which is performed live a few nights a week (what, no Pink Floyd?). The bar also offers cocktail master classes on selected Saturday afternoons for you aspiring mixologists with no name (yet).

Following 69 Colebrooke Row, Conigliaro and Hobby-Limon opened the new bar at **Zetter Townhouse** (49–50 St. John's Square; 020.7324.4545; www.thezettertownhouse.com) in April 2011. Designed to evoke the parlor of some fictional mad Englishman's wealthy and eccentric relations, the aspadistras, dark wood, maroon accents, taxidermy, and endless bric-a-brac are in precise opposition to the clean white lines at 69 Colebrooke Row. What the two do have in common is Conigliaro's inventive sensibility. Try a Fig Leaf Collins (Beefeater gin, lemon juice, sugar, fig leaf tincture, soda) or the Richmond (Chivas Regal 12-year, apple honey, Lillet blanc). Libations are £8.50–£9.50.

Academy

12 Old Compton Street
London
207.437.7820
www.labbaruk.com

There are bars for the learners and there are bars for the masters. And then there are the ones where the learners *become* the masters. Since 1996, Academy (formerly LAB, or London Academy of Bartenders) has been a place for bartenders to hone their skills before moving on to some of London's best watering holes.

The 1970s pop decor at this bi-level Soho spot is the precise inverse of the endless upper-crust hotel bars you will stumble into (and out of) all over London. The crowd of partiers shaking it to the DJ is young and the place gets pretty loud, but there's some solid mixology happening here.

But we must wonder—who is doing the learning here? Most of the twentysomething crowd may themselves be just on the verge of discovering the joys of well-crafted cocktails, if not on the verge of being able to afford them. Is the Academy a training ground for drinkers just as much as it is for bartenders? Quite possibly. The pours are affordable (for London) at around £7.50–£9.50. This gives the trendy crowd an opportunity to try new flavors while giving the bar staff more chances to experiment, create, or just practice.

The front cover of the menu, which is designed to look like a 1970s magazine, reminds us of the bar's "no ties" policy (again, the opposite of the posh hotel bars). The document lists over 100 cocktails, contrasting house creations with classics. As expected, there are some really solid creations here, and a few that may seem questionable. This is one of the only bars in this book (if not *the* only one) mixing with Jägermeister, but on the other hand, we're seeing things like Ardbeg Islay Scotch whisky and Fernet-Branca amaro in the mix, too.

Those especially enamored with Academy may attend the Lab Experience, which costs £40 per two-hour mixology lesson. Food at Academy is provided by Taro, the Japanese restaurant next door. They'll hook you up with gyoza (£4.80), a sashimi platter (£10.50), yakisoba (£6.90) or teriyaki don (£6.90–£9.80).

***

At some bars, you're likely to get punch, and at others, you're likely to get punched. The latter usually happens at Fight Club, but we can't talk about that. The former is quite likely to happen at any of London's three Hawksmoor steakhouses. Before cocktails, and even before flips, juleps, or mules, there was punch. Like so many other categories of intoxicating libations, the humble punch has devolved to the degree that it is now viewed by many as a sickly-sweet soft drink served at high school dances. Its roots, however, go back to the very beginning of Western drinking culture; alcoholic

Hawksmoor Guildhall

10–12 Basinghall Street
London
207.397.8120
www.thehawksmoor.co.uk

Hawksmoor Seven Dials

11 Langley Street
London
207.420.9390

Hawksmoor Spitalfields

157 Commercial Street
London
207.426.4850

punches were an evolutionary ancestor of the modern cocktail.

Barman Nick Strangeway is widely credited with bringing punch back into style, while working at Hawksmoor Spitalfields (which opened in 2006). When David Kaplan and Phil Ward of New York's Death & Co visited London, they brought Strangeway's passion for punch back to North America with them. Many of the best craft bars are now offering punch service. Some of them are spotlighting punch as a key part of their program, while others keep a batch handy to placate guests waiting for more time-consuming bespoke cocktails.

Strangeway has moved on to other ventures, but Pete Jeary (formerly of the Lonsdale, and current head barman at Hawksmoor Seven Dials) has maintained the historical aspects of Hawksmoor's cocktail program. The cocktail menu (nearly identical at all three Hawksmoor locations) features a History of the Cocktail in 10 Drinks, which begins with the 1672 recipe for Hannah Wooley's Punch and ends with the 1970s Piña Colada.

Hawksmoor is also featuring a revival of "bridging drinks," an Edwardian-era style of cocktail meant be served after lunch, but before the first pre-dinner aperitifs appear. Gal Friday Night liked the looks of the Dandy (cognac, maraschino liqueur, Bénédictine, champagne, sugar). Another neglected category of 19th-century libations that Hawksmoor spotlights is the Anti-Fogmatic, a drink to be consumed immediately after awakening. The famous Corpse Reviver No. 2 is on this list, as is Jeary's creation, the Shaky Pete's

Ginger Brew (gin, house-made ginger syrup, lemon juice, Fuller's London Pride ale).

Owners Will Beckett and Huw Gott launched Hawksmoor Seven Dials in November 2010. The Covent Garden restaurant is within the erstwhile Watney-Combe brewery space. The spacious interior features a

heavy focus on reclaimed materials in its eclectic decor: chemistry lab table-tops, a vaulted brick ceiling, old doors from train stations and hotels, Victorian cast iron columns, and tiles from the firm that supplies replacements for the London underground.

Cocktails at Hawksmoor Seven Dials may only be consumed with food (due to their license), but steak lovers will not mind. Executive chef Richard Turner prepares large cuts of beef, sourced directly from a herd of Longhorn cattle raised in North Yorkshire, and cooks them simply in a charcoal grill.

The third Hawksmoor location is the largest of the three. Hawksmoor Guildhall opened in October 2011. Bar manager Liam Davy and his team will get you started with cocktails as early as you like; their license begins at 7:00 AM, and compliments the restaurant's breakfast menu.

Incidentally, "punch" comes from *paanch*, the Hindi word for "five." The original punches had five ingredients, and—perhaps not coincidentally—knuckle sandwiches do, too. Those aren't on the menu here; you'll have to get them at Fight Club.

L ondon seems to be a town with more respect for its own gustatory history than any other. Just one of the places where we've discovered this is Hix. Mark Hix spent 17 years work-

Mark's Bar

(at Hix Restaurant)
66-70 Brewer Street
London
207.292.3518
www.marksbar.co.uk

ing for a variety of respected London restaurants before opening Hix Oyster and Chop House in 2008. He opened his next restaurant, simply called Hix, in 2009, and recruited Nick Strangeway of

Hawksmoor to develop the cocktail program for the restaurant's basement bar, Mark's Bar. Like the trio of Hawksmoor restaurants, Hix has now expanded into multiple locations and has seen the eventual departure of Strangeway, although his contributions are still strongly felt.

The food at Hix is heavily influenced by traditional British cooking, and the drinks at Mark's Bar adhere to the same philosophy. Looking over the cocktail menu, Strangeway's well-known devotion to spotlighting British cocktail history is clear. The menu sections detailing Early British Libations and London's Golden Age showcase this.

Dating from around 1820, the Punch à la Regent (PX sherry, rum, brandy, curaçao, pineapple syrup, lemon sherbet, citrus, green tea, champagne; £11) is just one example of Strangeway's enthusiasm for punches. On to the golden age—the Jo's Special (house-made Beefeater sloe gin, dry vermouth, orange liqueur, lemon juice; £9.75) was created by W. J. Tarling of Café Royal, a key spot for British nightlife from the 1890s through the 1930s. The house-made Beefeater sloe gin is further proof of the British devotion to local products. Although it is strange for most people to consider a large brand like Beefeater to be "local," it is made just a few miles from Mark's Bar, and is used as the base in the bar's quince, rhubarb, sloe, and lovage gins, as well as in other house infusions.

The zinc bar counter was once a sushi bar; now the built-in refrigerator is used to chill cocktail glasses and ingredients. The cozy basement is decorated with Oriental rugs, aged mirrors, a New York-style tin ceiling, and a British billiards table from the 1930s.

As is the case with many London destinations, ordering food with your cocktail is required by law. Fortunately, you'll probably want to anyway. Small plate versions of several dishes from Hix are available at Mark's Bar, such as chips and curry sauce (£3.50), Scotch quail's eggs (£6.25), and Blythburgh pork cracklings (£3.25).

Upstairs at Hix restaurant, the bright spacious room contrasts with the more intimate space below. Decorated with custom-designed mobiles by a variety of artists, the restaurant features dishes like chargrilled Shetland Isles halibut (£29.50), roast Woolley Park Farm free-range chicken (£55.00), and hanger steak with baked bone marrow (£19.25).

This is starting to get a bit repetitive, but we'll say it again: here is a London steakhouse that creates classic cocktails, always mindful of the history of British tippling.

The Lonsdale

48 Lonsdale Road
London
207.727.4080
www.thelonsdale.co.uk

Make no mistake, there are no complaints here. If the steak and cocktails combo is your bag, head to London.

The Lonsdale opened in 2002, and was given a bit of a rethink when new ownership took over in June 2010. The Notting Hill bar owes its new look to Dtwo, a design team that took the existing science-fiction-influenced decor and added more of a mid-century flair. As a result, the bar (in the front) is decked out in red leather stools, small chandeliers above the bar, and semihemispherical indentations in the ceiling resembling some sort of meteor craters. The restaurant (in the back) is all about the red leather banquettes, a parquet floor, and a big dome overhead. A smaller space upstairs, used for private parties, has a less trendy look, with dark curtains over off-white wood paneling. The stylish crowd of locals that has discovered the Lonsdale within the quiet residential neighborhood will be digging the DJs, who spin records a few nights per week.

The 13-page cocktail menu contains individual sections for sours, punches, bucks, and cups—all of which are old-school cocktail categories—but it also honors London Contemporary Classics, and even features two pages devoted to Dick Bradsell. This famous London barman worked at the Lonsdale from 2002 to 2004. Though famous for his Bramble (gin, sugar, lemon juice, float

of crème de mure), we liked the looks of his Rose Petal Martini (Bombay Sapphire gin, Lanique rose liqueur, lychee juice, Peychaud Bitters; £9).

Further famous London bartenders of yore are paid tribute with the Whiz-Bang (Bailie Nicol Jarvie Scotch whisky, Noilly Prat dry vermouth, house-made pomegranate syrup, absinthe, orange bitters; £9), which was created by Tommy Burton in 1920, and the Golden Dawn (Henry de Querville calvados, Beefeater gin, Cointreau, apricot brandy, orange juice, pomegranate juice; £9.50) as published by the legendary Cafe Royal in 1939. The family of drinks called "bucks" are worth a mention, too, as they were invented in London, probably in the 1920s. We liked the looks of the Lonsdale Buck (Beefeater gin, elderflower cordial, Poire William eau de vie; £7.50) and the Winter Buck (Hennessy cognac, Pimm's winter cup, tawny port; £7.50). Gal Friday Night says: "Now is the time to pass the buck!"

In order to keep recipes authentic to the period from which they hail, the Lonsdale doesn't stock any brands introduced after 1960, and they use the earliest possible variant of any given recipe.

Steaks are provided by Allens of Mayfair, which has been in the butcher business longer than any other in Britain. They raise free-range cattle in the Cairngorms National Park in Scotland. Steaks range from onglets (£16.90) to filets (£29.50), or feast upon a duck breast (£16.90) or sea bass (£17.50).

◀·◆·▶

Milk & Honey

61 Poland Street
London
207.065.6840
www.mlkhny.com

One cannot discuss the arc of the cocktail revival without referencing Milk & Honey. Mastermind Sasha Petraske's original Manhattan location opened well ahead of the curve in 2000, with an unmarked door, constantly shifting phone number, and decor influenced by the 1920s.

More importantly, it was among the first of many lounges to truly spotlight a sorely needed new excellence in mixology.

After getting a load of the pioneering Milk & Honey in Manhattan, Jonathan Downey convinced Petraske to open a second bar in London's Soho area in April 2002. Like the New York bar, the Milk & Honey in London is members only. Non-members may visit before 11:00 PM after phoning for a reservation.

The location just off Oxford Street features three floors of fun, including the Games Room, the Red Room, the Basement Bar, and the main bar on the ground floor (the only area open to non-members). The very large and very dark space might get a little more festive than the tranquil New York location was, but house rules like "No fighting, play fighting, no talking about fighting" and "No hooting, hollering, shouting, or other loud behavior" are still enforced by a friendly staff.

The notoriously secretive bar tends toward omakase tipples and bartender suggestions rather than relying on a menu, but it is said that a house tome has been continually evolving since the bar's inception. This mythical grimoire may or may not be a handbook for all past and present Milk & Honey mixologists. In any case, it's actually cool to imagine *all* bars maintaining this sort of expanding time capsule of their house secrets. Donn Beach did something like this back in the 1930s, but he didn't share it with his people. With the new millennium, more egalitarian methodologies may prevail. Gal Friday Night, who was once shot by Joe Strummer (with a gun made of thumb and forefinger, of course), just had to sample the London Calling (gin, sherry, lemon, sugar, bitters), while I kept it simple for once with the Business (gin, honey, lime juice). That's the thing. We've said it before and we'll say it again: if your cocktail is prepared with a certain level of care and craft, then gin, honey, and lime juice is all you need. Well, until the next drink arrives, that is. Case in point: the Morning Glory Fizz (Scotch whisky, absinthe, lemon juice, sugar, egg white). Cocktails are generally under £9.50. Diverging from the parent location, the Milk & Honey in London offers a small menu of food (£4–£19), including pork pie, oysters, and canapés.

Milk & Honey membership will also get you into other private Rushmore Group clubs, including the Player (also in Soho), the

East Room (Shoreditch, London), the Starland Social Club (Notting Hill, London), Danger of Death (Brick Lane, London), and the Clubhouse (Chamonix, France). Some of these businesses are more cocktail-focused than others.

Montgomery Place

31 Kensington Park Road
London
207.792.3921
www.montgomeryplace.co.uk

When imbibing recreationally around the globe, it is always fascinating to visit watering holes endemic to whatever culture they're in, but it is also interesting to consider the global phenomenon of businesses that bill themselves as an "American bar," no matter where on earth they may be. Many nations helped influence the development of the modern cocktail, and England is most certainly one of them. But the cocktail (like jazz and skyscrapers) has become synonymous with America's great early modernist achievements. Thus, we find "American bars" all over Europe.

Although Montgomery Place doesn't advertise itself as such, it certainly fits the bill, being in a stand-alone building (as opposed to a hotel) and serving a menu of classic libations complimented by American-influenced small plates. Their basement kitchen creates riffs on everything from burgers (£7.50), to tuna sandwiches (£6.50), to buffalo wings (£6.00), which are elevated into tapas-style offerings designed to pair well with one or more cocktails (we like the "more" part).

We tried one or more cocktails from a lengthy menu of classics ("traditional") augmented with a few house creations ("inspired"), such as Ago Perrone's Kentucky Apple (Buffalo Trace bourbon, smashed apples, cinnamon sugar, ginger beer; £9.25) and Thrilla in Vanilla (Santa Teresa Gran Reserve rum, smashed cranberries, lime juice, mint leaves, soda; £8.95). In a town as Martini-obsessed as London is, every bar has its preferred ratio, and they all seem to be in competition to see who can get away with using the *least* vermouth. With a 15:1 gin/vermouth mixture, Montgomery Place's Martini (£9.50) may be in the lead.

Ago Perrone has departed Montgomery Place for the Connaught Bar, and has been replaced by bar manager Ales Olasz (a collector of vintage absinthe tools). Jack Hubbard of the Academy and Deborah Cicero can be found behind the stick, too. Olasz is working with barrel-aged Jensen gin in the house Martinez (£9.50).

Opened in April 2006 in the trendy Notting Hill neighborhood, the small and dimly lit bar attracts professionals in a musical environment realized in wallpaper depicting antique string instruments under lamps fashioned from old horns and gramophone speakers. Photos of American barflies Frank, Sammy, Dean, and the boys hang above banquettes.

Some bars are named for beverages you've heard of, and some are named for beverages that you haven't heard of. Until now. See what happens when you read books? Keep going.

Purl was named for a Dickensian street beverage made of warm ale, gin, and spices. The house has, of course, created its own take on the Purl (Hendrick's gin, Doom Bar bitters, hops, cinnamon, anise, wormwood). It is fair to say that this bar can deliver just a bit more than that, however. Its concise menu of a dozen drinks is delivered on a bookmark tucked into a back issue of *Blackwood's* magazine (which began publication in 1817, and first serialized Joseph Conrad's *Heart of Darkness*). At £8.50–£10, the drinks range from classic (Negroni, Hemingway Daiquiri), to innovative and theatrical.

Purl

50/54 Blandford Street
London
207.935.0835
www.purl-london.com

To wit: the Champagne and Caviar is made of Veuve Clicquot brut champagne augmented with little spheres of house-made mango and pine caviar. The bottle-aged Rob Roy comes in its own little bottle that is also quite aged-looking. The What's Your Poison . . . ? includes two little blue pills, plus a prescription and dosage directions. Adding the pills to the drink transforms it both visually and gustatorily. The Mr. Hyde's Fixer Upper is an elevated rum and coke, made with Ron Zacapa 23 rum, house-made cola reduction,

and orange bitters. It is also served in its own bottle, with Lapsang fog adding to the scent and to visual appeal. Even the Martini, that London staple, is made with a scientist's attention to detail. Cooled by liquid nitrogen, it is stirred with a probe to monitor the exact temperature. A minimal amount of vermouth comes from a spritzer. Ice at Purl is lavender-infused (of course). Bar snacks are limited to olives (£4), nuts and parsnips (£4), charcuterie (£10), and a cheese board (£10).

Opened in May 2010, Purl combines the techniques of molecular mixology with the requisite jazz-era New York vibe. Owned by the quartet of Tristan Stephenson, Thomas Aske, Matt Whiley, and Bryan Pieterson, the Marylebone-area bar occupies the cozy basement of a Georgian house. It's decorated in exposed brick, dim lighting, tables hidden in little alcoves, fireplaces, vaulted ceilings, and an anachronistic phone booth. Put that to good use when your mobile needs attention. Best of all is the antique globe that splits open to reveal a small bar inside. *Want.* Jazz music may give way to more contemporary sounds on the weekends, but the upright piano is put to good use on Sundays.

Salvatore at Playboy

Playboy Club
14 Old Park Lane
London
207.491.8586
www.playboyclublondon.com

One can find very few bars that will offer you a cognac distilled in 1788, served by a girl in a bunny outfit. Here is one of them: Salvatore at Playboy Club, the new bar by Salvatore "the Maestro" Calabrese that opened in June 2011 (or 223 years after that cognac was bottled). Calabrese's previous venue, Salvatore at Fifty, vanished when its parent casino shut down in November 2009.

Located among the ritzy hotels of Park Lane, the members-only club embodies the anachronistic fantasy lifestyle that Playboy works so hard to preserve. The eponymous bar's conspicuous opulence is defined by scantily clad waitresses and the showy attire of the patrons. This is all eclipsed by the main draw for booze-hounds—Calabrese's astounding vintage spirits collection.

Displayed for inspection in hexagonal cells within long glass cases, the bottles date as far back as the 18th century, as does Calabrese's collection of bar tools and shakers. There are brands here that you'll never see again, and all of them are available for consumption—at a price. The "vintage cocktail" concept may also be done elsewhere, but Calabrese is one of the few bartenders who can make you a cocktail invented at nearly any point in the past two centuries, mixed entirely with ingredients authentic to the original recipe's period of creation. The absolute rarest of them may set you back as much as £3,000, but if you're at the Playboy Club, you're the sort who likes to throw money around anyway, right? Want to take a nip from the oldest bottle of rye known to exist? Served by a dame in a bustier, stilettos, and bunny ears? Calabrese has that handled for ya, big spender.

For the proletariats who have snuck into the club incognito (author raises his hand), a menu of Calabrese variants on classics will set you back less than £20. Gal Friday Night was actually once a Playboy bunny herself, so she used her connections to get us a seat in the lounge. After all, how often does one have the chance to have "the Maestro" wheel his personal copper-and-glass Martini cart up to your table to mix for you personally? It was Calabrese who in-augurated this concept while at Dukes Hotel (see page 306). His souped-up cocktail hot rod has a nine-hour battery to keep your gin chilled at minus 18 centigrade (that's just about zero degrees Fahrenheit).

Calabrese began his "liquid history" concept when he was working at the Lanesborough, London's single most expensive hotel. You'll recall your stay there; you spent £14,000 for a night in the Lanesborough Suite. Calabrese recently stepped down from his post as president of the United Kingdom Bartenders' Guild, but he still gives private bartending master classes and has recently released his 10th book.

The Worship Street Whistling Shop

63 Worship Street
London
207.247.0015
www.whistlingshop.com

WS2 (as it is known) seems to be rooted in the past, while definitely looking toward the future. Eighteenth-century "dram shops" were essentially chemists' shops that sold medicinal gin. Some customers took it to go, others drank it on-site. The bar as we know it today evolved from the dram shop's sales counter. By the 1820s, beer and wine sales had been added, elaborate decor had become common, and the first gin palaces had been born. The term "whistling shop" was Victorian slang for a gin palace. In the late 19th century, the gin palace evolved into the pub.

Opened in April 2011, the newest venture from Tristan Stephenson, Thomas Aske, Matt Whiley, and Bryan Pietersen of Purl is designed as a contemporary update of the Victorian gin palace. The large space is decorated in period style, with exposed brick, candles, plush leather sofas, dark wood, an embossed ceiling, and real gas lamps. The heavily experiential space has a menu of two dozen drinks (mostly under £10), including six aged infusions presided over by head barkeep Ryan Chetiyawardana (of 69 Colebrooke Row). The infused spirits mellow for months and are sold neat, but they can also be used in cocktails. Their Old Tom gin (£8) is infused with sweet spices and sugar before being aged in oak sherry casks, while their rye whiskey starts with Balvenie spirit and is blended with beech, maple, and peat syrup, all aged in new oak (£30).

Classic English cocktails are given a very 21st-century twist in their modern molecular presentation, à la sister bar Purl. The House Gin Fizz (Tanqueray gin, lemon juice, extra virgin olive oil, vanilla salt, orange bitters, soda) is trumped only by the Champagne Gin Fizz, which sees the cocktail bottled, corked, and fermented with champagne yeast. Gal Friday Night's doctorate in radiochemistry allowed her to understand the Radiation Aged Cocktail (Diplomatico rum, house-made chip pan bitters, Campari, Dubonnet aperitif, absinthe, house-made grenadine), but all she could explain to the rest of us Luddites is that it is matured instantly via irradiation in the bar's lab.

Yes, they have a lab. Through smoky vintage glass panes, one can peer into the Fluid Movement lab. It is here that the resident mixos concoct their new tastes and textures. The bar also has a space called Dram Shop, available for parties of up to eight. In a little room with a bathtub in the center and hay on the floor, you're given the key to a cupboard filled with gin. Your party is on the honor system: drink your fill and pay your bill, both as you deem appropriate. WS2 plans to add other themed rooms in this style.

As if that weren't enough, Cocktail Emporium is yet another fully experiential room, where five to eight of your friends can enjoy a tasting menu of five cocktails (at £95 per person). The room is designed so that sound, video, smells, lighting, and mood will change as each new drink is served. The theme in this "fairground ride of cocktail imbibation" changes every few months.

Naturally, the food menu is also Victorian-inspired but ultra contemporary. Look for mock turtle "magic mushroom" soup, fish and chips, crumbled oysters, a British cheese board, mini pork pie, and jellied smoked eels.

THE HISTORIC HOTELS OF LONDON (AND THEIR MARTINIS)

London is a city of dozens of grand hotels. Many of these palatial masterpieces have been catering to bona fide royalty, slurping up gin in their swank bars for decades or centuries. As is the case globally, some of the very finest of them can't seem to muster a decent drink. Here are a handful that most certainly can.

The Artesian Bar at the Langham Hotel (1c Portland Place, Regent Street; 207.636.1000; www.artesian-bar. co.uk) is located in the elegant Marylebone area. The first

of Europe's grand hotels, the Langham opened in 1865, but head bartender Alex Kratena is a much more recent addition. After studying the Ginza style of bartending in Tokyo, Kratena brought Japanese techniques back to London. The bar carries 60 rums, including the rare Havana Club Máximo Extra Añejo (£300), which probably *isn't* one of the rums used in the Artesian Punch (rum, rum, rum, Poire William pear brandy, pineapple, citrus). Most cocktails are £14–£15, including house inventions like the Pink & Gold (Don Julio blanco tequila, lime juice, house-made Chinese white tea/hibiscus flower/rose petal syrup). The Asian influence extends beyond the tea and Kratena's trips abroad. A trio of pagodas top the back bar, and are one of several Asian touches in the otherwise classic upscale British decor. Elaborate garnishes are king here, and are not limited to plant life; discs of ice with the bar's logo etched into them are machine-carved off-site. The Artesian Bar's barrel-aged Cask Mai Tai is made with Appleton Extra and comes with further machine-cut frigid awesomeness—a large, perfectly spherical ice ball with corrugated ridges etched into it. We also like the idea of trying selections from the Artesian Bar's rare mezcal, genever, or rum collections, paired with an appropriate snack for £38. Note their cover charge after 11:00 PM.

The Booking Office at the St. Pancras Renaissance Hotel London (Euston Road; 207.841.3540; www. bookingofficerestaurant.com) was opened in March 2011. Designed by George Gilbert Scott, the hotel opened in 1873, next to the St. Pancras railway station. It was subsequently used as railway offices from 1935 to 2011, but

was renovated and expanded for its 2011 reinstatement as a hotel. The bar might be among the most visually astounding in Europe, with soaring 60-foot-high cathedral ceilings in a modernist gothic revival room that once housed the railway's booking offices. Everything else is built suitably to scale: the bar is *95 feet long*. The cocktail menu has been assembled by Nick Strangeway and Henry Besant. The focus is on updates of 19th-century recipes, as in the simple but effective Gin Fix (gin, sugar, soda water, lemon juice, lemon peel, seasonal berries; £9.00), as well as plenty of punches like the Billy Dawson Punch (cognac, rum, demerara sugar, lemon peel, porter, nutmeg). Punches are served in custom-made copper mugs at £6–£8.50. Head chef Julien Maisonneuve discovered a Victorian-era menu in the building and is using it as inspiration for the hotel's restaurant. The bar features British snacks like haggis bon-bons at £5–£7.

The Connaught Hotel (16 Carlos Place; 207.499.7070; www.the-connaught.co.uk) in Mayfair is home to the **Connaught Bar** (formerly the American Bar). A 2008 renovation by David Collins freshened things up while maintaining the Edwardian-meets-deco interior. Their Martini trolley is trimmed in black leather, and will be pushed to your table by white-gloved barmen offering you a choice of housemade bitters. The bar's elegant formality prohibits seating at the bar counter. Guests are served an amuse-bouche to start their evening, and each of the featured cocktails is accompanied by a card with the recipe printed on it. Head bartender Agostino Perrone (of Montgomery Place) has

created an array of specialties in the
£12–£15 range. Paying homage to his
hometown of Como, Italy, Perrone uses
grappa in the Balsamic Cobbler (Nar-
dini grappa bianco, Galliano balsami-
co, nutmeg sugar syrup, lemon juice,
Taylor's 10-year tawny port, blackberries). Chef Hélène Darroze creates
small plates inspired by the southwest
of France. You'll also find the slightly
more casual (*slightly* being the key
word here) **Coburg Bar** on the hotel

premises. Their exhaustive wine list (which they refer to
as Bacchanology) is augmented by caviar and £12 cocktails,
including London staples like the Bramble and the Lond
Island Iced Tea. Yup, they're trying to elevate that one, too.

Dukes Bar (Dukes Hotel, 35 St. James's Place;
207.491.4840; www.dukeshotel.com) is famous for its
Martinis and for being a frequent haunt of Ian Fleming,
creator of James Bond. It is said that the catchphrase "shak-
en, not stirred" originated at Dukes (although many would
debate that a proper gin Martini is better stirred). Career
waiters in white jackets may mix your Martini (£15) tableside from a silver cart, as you enjoy the works of art hung
salon-style all over the room. Wait, *another* London Martini cart? No, not "another." This is the original, as innovated
by Salvatore Calabrese during his tenure here. Many consider Dukes to be the global departure point for the Martini, and this is certainly the one place in Britain to which
enthusiasts of this cocktail will want to make a pilgrimage.
Lead barman Alessandro Palazzi also mixes from a menu
of house creations, some of which are named for various
Fleming characters. The boutique hotel was first built in
1885 as housing for young aristocrats (possibly illegitimate
sons of Charles II), and became a hotel some 23 years later.

Dukes' other bar, **PJ Champagne Lounge,** specializes in Perrier-Jouët champagne.

Last but not least is the **American Bar** at the Savoy Hotel (Strand, London; 207.836.4343; www.fairmont. com). While paging through this book, you may have noticed a few references to the inescapable *Savoy Cocktail Book* by Harry Craddock, originally published in 1930. Craddock wrote the book while working right here. As head barman at the Savoy from 1925 to 1939, Craddock was the third in a long line of legendary shaker shakers working at this legendary bar. Others included Ada Coleman (from 1903 to 1924), the first female bartender to achieve bona fide legend status, and Erik Lorincz, who has held the post from 2010 to present.

Lorincz's signature recipe is the El Malecón, named for the road that winds along the seaside edge of Havana. Roving cocktail writer Crosby Gaige described an El Malecón cocktail in 1941 (white rum, Swedish punsch, dry gin, peach schnapps), but Lorincz has more or less built a polyseme beverage for his 2007 remix (white rum, Smith Woodhouse 10-year port, Sanchez Romate Hermanos— Don José Reserva Oloroso sherry, lime juice, caster sugar, Peychaud's bitters).

Richard D'Oyly Carte opened the Savoy Hotel in 1889, and it stayed in his family for over a century. As one of Britain's first luxury hotels, the Savoy was a European pioneer in features like electric lights, elevators, private bathrooms, and American-style cocktails. Classic American jazz piano is performed live every night, and the Savoy Grill and Savoy Restaurant also remain open for your dining pleasure. After a £220 million renovation completed in August 2010, the Savoy opened a second bar (for the first time). **Beaufort Bar**'s house tipple is the Winston (Hennessy XO cognac, blood orange purée, quince liqueur, and vanilla syrup, strained through a muddled Romeo y Julieta cigar; £80).

LAST CALL!

More Destinations to Explore in London

Calloph Callay (65 Rivington Street; 207.739.4781; www.calloohcallaybar.com) was inspired by Lewis Carroll's proto-Dada poem "Jabberwocky." Owner Richard Wynne has hidden his bar on a cobblestone street in Shoreditch. With its eclectic furniture and striking lighting by design duo Dtwo, the bar is atypical for scrappy Shoreditch. Mixologist Sean Ware is just as aware of London's drinking history as the other British barmen in these pages are. His menu contains drinks like the classic Avenue (Four Roses bourbon, Laird's applejack, passion fruit nectar, orange flower water, simple syrup), which comes from the legendary Café Royal. Cocktails are £8–£10. A wardrobe at the back of the room is the hidden entrance to a bigger and somewhat clubbier second bar, decorated in mirrors, Astroturf, repurposed cassette tapes, and bathtubs used as sofas. Try a house creation, the Afternoon Twee (Hendrick's gin, blackberries, lavender sugar, maraschino liqueur, apple juice, lime juice, orange bitters). Behind a curtain and up a staircase, you'll need a key to access **Jub Jub Bar,** the members-only *third* bar on-site. Membership is free, provided that the prospective member can "prove their love of drinks to the satisfaction of our team." Jub Jub is where you'll find the premium spirits. They're served by a new guest bartender every week who creates bespoke recipes during a brief tenure at the bar. Chef Marco Schneof's chow menu consists of bar bites and a few entrees.

Dick Bradsell is currently behind the stick at **El Camion** (25–27 Brewer Street; 207.734.7711; www.elcamion.co.uk). Bradsell is as revered in the U.K. as Dale DeGroff is in the U.S., and with good reason—they were both pioneers of the new mixology. During the 1980s, when things were looking pretty grim in the cocktail world, Bradsell began rocking British bars, spending the next few decades inventing modern classic cocktails like the Bramble and Treacle (Havana Club 7-year rum, apple juice, sugar, bitters) while working his way through Zanzibar, Fred's, the Groucho Club, the Lonsdale, MatchBar, and Dick's Bar. Today, you'll find Bradsell at the unassuming Baja Room in the basement of a Soho area Mexican restaurant. Although the brief drink menu lists just a few south of the border classics (Margaritas, Daiquiris, and Cuba Libres at £6.50), do grab a booth or a barstool and let Bradsell go omakase. The food menu contains exactly what you'd expect from a taqueria where almost nothing is over £9.

After opening the trio of bars that gave Paris its much-needed introduction to cocktail culture, the trio of Olivier Bon, Pierre-Charles Cros, and Romée De Gorianoff (now with Xavier Padovani on board) have expanded their **Experimental Cocktail Club** brand into London (13a Gerrard Street; 207.434.3559; www.experimentalcocktailclublondon.com). Opened in December 2010, the London outpost is hidden behind a discreet door in Chinatown. Wanting a spot that could stay open late (a relative rarity for London), the owners found a unique space that had previously housed other after-hours clubs (and was thus licensed to serve late). This comes at a price, however; there is a cover after 11:00 PM, and reservations are recommended at all times. Dorothée Meilichzon (designer of Prescription in Paris) was brought in to fill the two-story bar with exposed brick, tin ceilings, tête-à-tête loveseats, ornate wallpaper, mirrors, and a (non-functioning) piano built into the upstairs bar counter. "Vintage" cocktails, made with authentic 1950s to 1970s bottles of gin or bourbon, sell for as much as £120–£250, but more contemporary creations will set you back £10–£12. We were drawn toward the Turf War (aquavit, maraschino liqueur, Lillet Blanc, absinthe, orange bitters) and the Jamaican Pogo (rum, green Chartreuse, house-made smoked pineapple syrup, Jamaican jerk bitters). The menu also features a few drinks paying homage to North America's best craft bars, like the Smoked Palomino from Mayahuel (New York) and the Havana from L'Abattoir (Vancouver).

Mahiki (1 Dover Street; 020 7493 9529; www.mahiki.com) is a contemporary tiki bar in the Mayfair area. Although it is committed to a casual environment, it still attracts plenty of celebs and other big spenders, who pack the upstairs bar and the basement club as the evening progresses. Nick House and Piers Adam opened Mahiki in 2006, decking it out with a number of private alcoves decorated in black Bamboo, faux-giraffe skin, carved Polynesian-style panels, and murals of island sunsets. As befits any good tiki bar, princess chairs are lit by swag lamps hanging from a ceiling decorated with painted hibiscus flowers. Cocktails range from respectable to ridiculous: the Baron Samedi's Brew (Mahiki Grog, honey cream, lime juice, Angostura bitters, ginger beer, absinthe; £8) gives way to the Sea Pearl (rum, raspberry, strawberry, cranberry, coconut, lemon, champagne; £200), which is served in a clamshell for eight of your closest friends. The honey cream is brown sugar, honey, and butter in equal parts, and Mahiki Grog is a house blend of five rums. In an expansion effort that would make Donn Beach proud, the Mahiki brand now encompasses multiple cities, clothing design, music festivals, and a house branded rum.

Nightjar (129 City Road; 207.253.4101; www.barnightjar.com) opened in November 2010, and is atypical among the pub-ish bars found along Shoreditch's nearby Old

Street. A nightjar is a type of nocturnal bird, and this particular bird makes us think of New York jazz: Charlie "Bird" Parker and the famous Birdland jazz club. The suitably dark basement level Nightjar features live jazz music four nights per week, and cocktails by Marian Beke (of Montgomery Place and Purl). Beke brings a bit of his Slovakian heritage to the BBC Cocktail with his use of Becherovka (Boulard Grand Solage Pays d'Auge calvados, Becherovka herbal bitter, wormwood bitters, apple slice, smoke). Cocktails such as the Morning Glory Fizz (whisky, absinthe, champagne, lemon juice, lime juice) are around £10. Many of the London bars featured in these pages take their British heritage to heart, but with its post-war New York vibe in full effect, Nightjar seems to unabashedly embrace a new era's take on the classic European concept of the American bar. Exposed brick, dim lighting, brass accents, and friezes on mirrors are suitably bebop era. Nightjar reclaims its Britishness with the Tea Punch, which is served in a teapot spiked with dry ice to create cold "steam" shooting out the spout. A small menu of snacks includes beef carpaccio canapés and fried plantains. Resident DJ Jean-Paul Séculaire spins on nights when the bands are taking five.

Karl Marx wrote *Das Kapital* in the apartment above what is now **Quo Vadis** (26–29 Dean Street; 207.437.9585; www.quovadissoho.co.uk). The original restaurant was opened by Pepino Leoni in 1926. Expanding several times, he grew the business over three decades, after which it passed through multiple subsequent owners. Brothers Sam and Eddie Hart (of Fino and Barrafina) revamped Quo Vadis in 2008 as an upscale restaurant with an upstairs private member club. The later-day, prairie-style stained glass windows remain from previous incarnations, but the Damien Hirst artwork is new. Paul Mant is in charge of **QV Bar** next door, which launched in January 2011. His concise menu of about eight cocktails is paired with a short menu of food exclusive to the QV Bar. When someone in London asks you where you are going, tell them Quo Vadis.

Trailer Happiness (177 Portobello Road; 207.065.6821; www.trailerhappiness.com) is a basement bar right on Portobello Road in Notting Hill. It is decorated in what might be best described as a post-1960s bachelor pad theme, with shag carpeting, white banquettes, bean bag chairs, ceramic ducks, cork tile, beaded room dividers, and, yes, *Thunderbirds* wallpaper. British pop culture at it's finest. Most striking of all is a mural-sized reproduction of Vladimir Tretchikoff's *Chinese Girl* at the back of an alcove they call "the den." It isn't hard to miss reproductions of J. H. Lynch's *Tina* or *Autumn Leaves* elsewhere on the premises. With the pop decor and a younger crowd digging the nightly DJs, libations seem appropriately priced in the reasonable £6–£9 range. Trailer Happiness also has an unexpected ace up their sleeve; Dale DeGroff put their cocktail menu together, and the current bar staff have been living up to that honor. A menu emblazoned with a 1970s op-art design is divided into House Favourites, Tiki Classics, and Homage Drinks, with each drink description sporting a little icon of the glass it comes in. Gal Friday Night liked the looks of the Coup D'Akuffo (calvados, Dubbonet, Cherry Heering; £8), while I went for the Fire & Ice (Wray & Nephew overproof rum flamed with cinnamon, Mount Gay XO rum, honey, lime juice, champagne; £8).

Simple food at Trailer Happiness keeps with the casual, retro theme, including sesame shrimp, smokin' sausage salsa, crispy roast duck, and TV dinners, all in the £5–£6 range. Trailer Happiness also offers a monthly rum club and cocktail master classes.

EDINBURGH

Edinburgh, the land of Sir Arthur Conan Doyle, Sean Connery, and loads of good whisky, is home to plenty of places to wet your whistle, but we're just going to introduce you to one. It's killer diller, and this is just a starting point. There are more.

It might be said that the 1980s were among the cocktail's darkest decades in the 20th century. Sure, we had Prohibition in the '20s, but that was just in the United States. The rest of the world spent that decade enjoying their inebriants without interruption. But by the 1980s, highballs and the rise of

Bramble

16A Queen Street
Edinburgh
0131 226.6343
www.bramblebar.co.uk

"flair" bartending—wherein bartenders spent more time learning to juggle than to mix—were dominant. It can't be said that many truly great cocktails emerged from the 1980s, but if there is one exception we're quick to point out, it's the Bramble: gin, lemon juice, and sugar, topped with a drizzle of crème de mûre and garnished with two raspberries. Londoner Dick Bradsell of Fred's Club came up with this one, which is enthusiastically served at nearly every bar in the British Isles, their territories, and as far away as the Antipodes. Jerry Thomas wrote of a similar drink in 1862, the Gin Fix (Hollands gin, lemon juice, powdered sugar, raspberry syrup). It seems that Bradsell relegated the raspberries to garnish status and added the blackberry flavors of the crème de mûre to create his hit tipple.

By 2006, Mike Aikman and Jason Scott had opened a bar named Bramble on Edinburgh's busy Queen Street. It's unfair to say that they're jumping on the speakeasy fad, but the cellar-level bar is nonetheless a bit tricky to find, camouflaged amidst the more pedestrian watering holes in the neighborhood. Inside, you'll discover a comfortable seating area near the bar and a labyrinth of stone and brick alcoves for more intimate rendezvous. The

18th-century stonework and lighting via candles and small lamps make for a romantic atmosphere early in the evening, but later on the DJs and younger crowd will make the room feel considerably more festive.

On the menu—hidden between the covers of old hardback books—you'll discover an emphasis on gin that echoes the namesake drink of this bar, but that seems incongruous to a foreign visitor to Scotland. Shouldn't this bar be about the whisky? Well, that might be too obvious, and there's nothing obvious about Bramble.

Drinks at Bramble are mainly between £6.50 and £8. The Mint 500 (Hendrick's gin, elderflower, apple juice, lime juice, mint, basil, peach bitters, vanilla gomme) is served in a stemware/teacup hybrid that you'll see all over the British isles, but the tea influence is most obvious in the Tea Time Toddy Martini (Hendrick's gin, chamomile flowers, honey, lemon juice, pineapple syrup). Those requiring Scotch can get it, particularly in the New Yorker (Revisited) (Glenglassaugh Blush Scotch whisky, lemon juice, simple syrup, red wine float). The Glenglassaugh distillery has a history, too—first opened in 1875, they've closed and reopened three times, most recently laying dormant from 1986 to 2008. Hmmmm . . . there's that 1980s curse again.

In mid-2011 Bramble joined the barrel-aged cocktail craze, choosing to submit the classic Affinity (Glenmorangie 10-year, byrrh, Noilly Prat dry vermouth) to the process. Byrhh is a blend of red wine and tonic. The cocktail is aged in new American oak barrels for six weeks, and then further aged in little 100 ml bottles. Each bottle is wax-sealed, stamped with a skull and crossbones, and then stored under refrigeration. The drink is served with a chilled glass spritzed with orange bitters, a lemon peel, and a house-made cocktail cherry.

BELFAST

There are plenty of places to get pie-eyed in Belfast, the land of Oscar Wilde, the *Titanic*, and loads of good whiskey. We're going to start you off with just one, but it's a doozy.

If you want a Mai Tai made with original-recipe Wray & Nephew 17-year-old rum, you're either going to have to visit the Bar in the Mer-

The Bar

The Merchant Hotel
16 Skipper Street
Belfast
028.9023.4888
www.themerchanthotel.com

chant Hotel in Belfast, Ireland, or you're going to have to procure the services of a time machine and a trip to San Francisco.

Wray 17-year was the original rum that "Trader" Vic Bergeron used when he created the Mai Tai in 1944. Rum nerds will tell you that the only bottles of this rum known to exist today are the remains of a single case of 12 unearthed about a decade ago at the distillery. There may be as few as three of these bottles left. Are they in the Caribbean, where this rum was made? No. Are they in a Trader Vic's restaurant? No. Are they on some exotic Pacific isle, as befits the storied tiki vibe of the Mai Tai? No. Those that don't remain on Jamaica were sent to Great Britain, where they're all in the hands of private collectors—except for one, which is at the Bar in the Merchant Hotel.

Sampling this rum won't come cheap. *Guinness World Records* awarded the Merchant the title of World's Most Expensive Cocktail (in 2007) for the Mai Tai made with the Wray 17. At the time, you could have had the drink just as Trader Vic intended, for a price he never dreamed of charging: £750. Today, Gal Friday Night's sources within MI5 claim that there's about an ounce left

in the bottle. You'd better hurry if you want to be the one to kill it. Think it over though—there's a lot of air in that bottle, too. That Wray might not be at its best anymore. I have nightmares, with some regularity, involving an octogenarian with a forgotten case of Wray & Nephew 17-year-old rum collecting dust in his basement. I wake up screaming as his heirs throw it in a dumpster while cleaning out the estate.

The *Guinness World Records* title isn't the only award won by the Victorian-meets-deco Merchant Hotel bar. Their cocktail menu, which weighs in at 112 pages, regularly wins accolades within the bar industry. The impressive tome provides a full page of history for each of the major drinks, and then adds a "variants and mixology" section at the bottom where other related beverages are listed. Most cocktails are in the £9.95 range.

Head barman Sean Muldoon—himself a multi-award winner—keeps the menu populated with a list of established classics, but adds his own twists to them, such as in his Champagne Negroni (Plymouth gin, Martini Rosso vermouth, Campari, lemon juice, ruby grapefruit juice, cane syrup, Moët & Chandon champagne; £14.95), the Cincinnati Kid (Hennessy VS cognac, elderberry eau de vie, lemon juice, house-made cinnamon syrup, allspice tincture, seltzer water; £9.95), and the Phoenix (plum-infused poitín, poire eau de vie, lemon juice, local flower honey, pure County Armagh apple juice; £9.95). Poitín is a sort of Irish moonshine made from malted barley grain or potatoes that was completely illegal from 1661 to 1989. Now, of course, two boutique distilleries in Ireland are producing an elevated version of it.

The five-star Merchant has two other bars on premises: the less cocktail-focused Cloth Ear, and the exclusive, members-only Private Members Bar. Although the Bar offers a limited food menu, the sumptuous Great Room within the Merchant is an opulent destination for fine dining, complete with plush velvet seats and an ornate domed ceiling.

PARIS

While visiting Paris in mid-2007, we asked one of our most trusted lieutenants where to get a good cocktail. "There *are no* good cocktails in Paris!" he scoffed. Fortunately, that has changed radically in the past five years, so now "La Ville-Lumière" is just about perfect.

Authentic Mexican taquerias in Paris are almost as rare as good cocktail bars. Actually, they are even more rare—there really is only one. It is Candelaria, and it has the added advantage of having a New York-style secret cocktail bar hidden in the back. Just as Paris has been desperately in need of a good

Candelaria

52 Rue de Saintonge
(3rd arrondissement)
Paris
4274.4128
www.candelariaparis.com

cocktail bar, it has also been in need of a real taqueria for quite some time. Given the North American roots of both the taqueria and the classic-style cocktail, it isn't a surprise that it took a team of Mexicans and Americans to bring Candelaria to Paris.

Owner Adam Tsou, his wife, Carina, and their partner, Josh Fontaine, all hail from Connecticut, but they met in Paris while slinging gin at L'Experimental Cocktail Club and Curio Parlor. They opened Candelaria in March 2011. Chef Luis Rendon is from Mexico City. Together, they've put together a familiar-feeling little restaurant that seats about 15. The walls are white, the bare bulbs are bright, and the minimal decor is accented in primary colors. If you've been to Mexico, you've seen this before; this is solid comfort food from south of the border with few contemporary embellishments. Tacos are around €3. They've even got Jarritos sodas and Mexican beers. But if you're thirsty, head for the discreet door in the back of the little room.

The much larger bar room dwarfs the restaurant, and has a completely different atmosphere—low lighting from candles, colorful mosaics, and stone walls with details of reclaimed wood (some tables and the bar top itself are also rescued wood). A giant wool tapestry above a banquette is made from the hide of a sheep breed that had nearly been hunted to extinction. Although the breed has been nurtured back to safer numbers, at least one of 'em clearly didn't make it. Chairs are upholstered in a similar woolly hide. The crowd of hip young Parisians expands as the hour gets later, and the popular spot can be crowded even at times when you'd expect otherwise.

Cocktails skew toward the South American end of the spectrum, with choices like the Santa Margarita (tequila, agave, hibiscus, vanilla, lime juice) and the Pisco Disco (pisco, Aperol aperitif, house-made orgeat, lime juice, bitters, edible glitter). Wait, edible glitter? You don't see that every day, but take a peek at the sparkly Eiffel Tower after any night after dark and you might glean the inspiration. Cocktails are around €11. Candelaria also stocks a solid selection of uncommon tequilas and mezcals, like El Tesoro de Don Felipe, Centenario, 7 Leguas, Corralejo, and Tapatio. They also carry northern Mexico's Hacienda sotol, which is a tequila variant distilled from the sotol cactus.

Salud!

Olivier Bon, Pierre-Charles Cros, and Romée Goriainoff grew up together in the southern French town of Montpellier. While living in Montréal, they found themselves regularly visiting Manhattan, exploring Death & Co and Pegu Club. Recognizing that Paris had no cocktail bars to speak of, they headed back across the Atlantic and opened their first bar, the Right Bank's **L'Experimental Cocktail Club,** in November 2007, making the trio the pioneers of Parisian slow cocktails. Selecting a quiet cobblestone street very close to the trendy Rue Montorgueil in the swank Châtelet-Les-Halles district was a wise move; they were able to

L'Experimental Cocktail Club

37 rue Saint-Sauveur
(2nd arrondissement)
Paris
4508.8809
www.experimentalcocktailclub.com

Curio Parlor

16 rue des Bernardins
(3rd arrondissement)
Paris
4407.1247
www.curioparlor.com

Le Prescription Cocktail Club

23 rue Mazarine
(6th arrondissement)
Paris
4634.6773
www.prescriptioncocktailclub.com

attract an upscale and trendy crowd that might be receptive to their concept. Suffice to say, it worked.

The single-room space is hidden behind a discreet Haussmann-style door with only a brass nameplate marking the entrance. Invoking a New York vibe—possibly due to the fact that the designer, Cuoco Black, is a New Yorker—the room's focus is a zinc bar opposite black leather banquettes. Exposed brick walls and ancient wood ceiling beams support a trio of "ghost chandeliers" designed by Sander Mulder.

Committed to cocktails, the bar serves no beer or wine, but offers a solid selection of whiskeys, bourbons, and ryes. Their list of about a dozen libations usually lands in the €10–€12 range. It is nice to see that the menu also contains homages to the bar's original inspirations, Death & Co and Pegu Club. The Applejack Rabbit (applejack, maple syrup, lemon juice, orange juice) is an update of the classic Jack Rabbit. The Old Cuban (rum, mint, lime juice, ginger, champagne, bitters) looks tasty as well. Former bartender Carina (now co-owner of Candelaria) is the namesake of the Carina's Experience (cognac, Miller's gin, Carpano Antica Formula vermouth, lavender tincture, Bitter Truth aromatic bitters).

In a town where people usually claim that hard alcohol ruins the taste buds, the unlikely success of L'Experimental Cocktail Club inspired Bon, Cros, and Goriainoff to open a second bar. In another audacious maneuver, they put their new bar near the Latin Quarter, on the unfashionable Rive Gauche. They also went with a two-story layout and nearly quadrupled the total size. **Curio Parlor** has an awesome "cabinet of curiosities" theme, with taxidermy animals all over the room and a display case full of mounted butterflies, seashells, and fossils right next to a case full of silver cocktail shakers. It seems likely that some of this organic bric-a-brac comes from the famous taxidermy shop Deyrolle (46 rue du Bac; 4222.3007; www.deyrolle.com), which was first opened by Jean-Baptiste Deyrolle in 1831. Curio Parlour's hidden alcoves behind thick curtains, green velour davenports, green jacquard wallpaper, and further green-and-black accents give the space a mysterious

and sexy vibe. The downstairs bar has a curved ceiling like some sort of Quonset hut, additional fossilized animal life, and more of a party vibe when the late night DJs get going. The entrance to Curio Parlor is almost as nondescript as that of L'Experimental; look for the ex-raccoon in the window.

Try the Copa Verde (tequila, honey, avocado, lime juice) or the amusing Lynchburg Lemonade (Rittenhouse 100-proof rye, Cointreau, Angostura Bitters, lemon juice, Fever Tree lemonade). Fruit and other produce for cocktails is procured from either Place Maubert market along nearby Boulevard St. Germaine, or at Marché d'Intérêt National de Rungis, a market in the Parisian suburbs recorded as the largest in the world. Open for nearly a millennia (!) it moved to its current location in 1969. It operates from 1:00 AM to 7:00 AM daily, catering to the restaurants and grocers of Paris.

The third Bon, Cros, and Goriainoff venture is **Le Prescription Cocktail Club** (23 rue Mazarine; 4634.6773). Opened in November 2009, the bar is on the Left Bank, but in the sixth arrondissement (Curio Parlor is a walkable journey). Like L'Experimental and Curio, Prescription attracts a young and cool crowd who appreciate each other's stylish glad rags and the DJs spinning at reasonable volume (in the early hours). The two floors of the bi-level bar are joined by a grand staircase illuminated by lights shaped like bowler hats. A bookcase on the upper level hides an additional secret bar; one section of the fake books can be moved to form a window, with

the bartenders working on the other side. The overall space has even more square footage than Curio Parlor, and is accented with antique side tables, exposed brick walls, and plush armchairs. These touches are courtesy of designer Dorothée Meilichzon, who also chose the Japanese-inspired wallpaper design.

Go for a North America Sour (Rittenhouse rye, absinthe, maple syrup, lemon juice, muddled orange, egg white, spritz of Borghetti coffee liqueur), or an Evening Glory (Appleton VX rum, Havana Club Anejo Especial, fresh ginger, vanilla, bitters). Cocktails are €10–€12. Unlike its sister bars, Prescription has food, such as a burger with Comté cheese and truffle mayonnaise.

Did we say that Bon, Cros, and Goriainoff had three bars? Actually there are five now, but three of 'em are in Paris. New York and London now have Experimental Cocktail Clubs, too! Cool to see the New York influence on the original Parisian L'Experimental Cocktail Club come full circle with the opening of the New York branch. Need more? The (shall we say) motivated trio is opening a straight-up wine bar in Paris next.

Harry's New York Bar

5 rue Daunou
(2nd arrondissement)
Paris
4261.7114
www.harrys-bar.fr

Who said Paris had no good cocktail bars before 2007? Harry's New York Bar is as good as they come. Check out this pedegree—it is said that the White Lady, the French 75, the Sidecar, and the Monkey Gland were all invented at Harry's, although some of these claims are disputed. However, even if just one member of this million dollar quartet of cocktails was invented here, it would be reason enough to venerate the place. The bar also lays claim to other famous (and not-as-famous) inventions.

In 1911, an American named Tod Sloan bought the existing bistro, hoping to attract expatriates (conflicting sources, however, say Milton Henry was the original owner). In any case, Harry MacElhone of Dundee, Scotland was hired as chief barman.

MacElhone eventually moved on to other bars (including Ciro's) and wrote some books (*Harry of Ciro's ABC of Mixing Cocktails* in 1921 and *Barflies and Cocktails* in 1927), but came back to Paris a decade later to buy the bar he started in, renaming it after himself. Between the wars, it was *the* gathering place for the English-speaking populace of Paris. Of course, Hemingway and Fitzgerald were regulars. The basement piano bar is supposedly where Gershwin composed *An American in Paris*. Vintage swag from Harry's I.B.F. (International Bar Flies, "a secret fraternal organization devoted to the uplift and downfall of serious drinkers") now sells for big bucks. Lady members were "butterflies."

Harry's granddaughter, Isabelle MacElhone, and her son, Franz-Arthur, are still running the business. They released a book in November 2011 to commemorate the 100th anniversary of what they claim is the oldest cocktail bar in Europe. There are also franchises all over Germany and Switzerland, but the Harry's Bars in Amsterdam, Singapore, San Francisco, and elsewhere are unrelated.

The wood-paneled walls are filled with framed photos, as well as a collection of pennants from nearly every college in the United States. Other sections of the bar are filled with a century of memorabilia, yellowed and layers deep. A cultural anthropologist or urban archeologist's dream come true. Friendly but efficient barmen in white vests and aprons will be happy to mix any of the classics said to have been invented here, or will pour you a taste from the bar's collection of 300 whiskeys. There's no craft-style invention going on here—they did all that a century ago.

Opened in 1901, the Hôtel Ritz Paris is a bastion of excess and conspicuous wealth. You can't get into the place for under $800 per night, and that is for a Tuesday in January (we checked). The only conclusion we can draw is that they charge this kind of cash to keep the riff-raff out.

The Hemingway Bar

Hôtel Ritz Paris
15 Place Vendôme
(1st arrondissement)
Paris
4316.3365
www.ritzparis.com

Falling into that very category, we snuck in for a drink.

The hotel's original art deco bar was opened in 1921. Across the hall, a smaller room was opened where women could wait for their men, as they weren't allowed in proper bars at that point in history. This waiting area, or *salon de correspondence,* became a second bar when the larger one began admitting women in 1936. Ernest Hemingway liked to drink here (who knew?), and the hotel named the bar after him in 1995.

The Hemingway Bar is more cozy and less opulent than the rest of the building, with a fireplace, wood paneling on the walls, and a small bar that seats about eight. There are a handful of tables in the room and a small balcony with four more tables. The walls are decorated with Hemingway memorabilia, including two dozen photos personally made by him on his travels. The menu, curated by highly regarded barman Colin Field, looks like a newspaper, with each "article" describing a drink or a group of drinks.

Gal Friday Night joined me on the upper level as our waiter brought over little silver dishes full of nuts (what, no paté?) and potato chips (what, no caviar?) and glasses of water (what, no champagne?).

Although many cocktail historians credit the creation of the classic Sidecar to Harry's New York Bar (see page 322), the Ritz has been known to take credit as well. They offer an appropriately ritzy version of this classic tipple. For approximately €350, you can upgrade to a version containing the extremely rare 1865 Ritz Reserve cognac. The grapes used to make this cognac predate the notorious 1860s phylloxera blight, making it some of the last great cognac made before spirits production was temporarily crippled across Europe.

Gal Friday Night had the purse strings sealed tight that night, so we skipped the opportunity to sample a Sidecar that cost more than my car, and instead sampled house creations Mach 2 (whiskey, green Chartreuse, house-made ginger) and Doghouse (gin, green Chartreuse, etc.) instead. These drinks were both tasty and made with care, but there was nothing noteworthy about them in either ingredients or preparation to justify a price tag of €30 each. *Le ouch.* This is one of those destinations to hit because of its history, but we'll go back for another round when *you're* buying.

The vintage cocktail bars of Paris seem to fall into pairs: the Hemingway Bar (see page 323) and Bar 228 (page 326) provide the plush pair; now we'll hook Le Forum up with Harry's New York Bar (page 322) for a classic-era duo. Opened in 1918 as Salon du Thé, the bar Le Forum has been family-

Le Forum

4 Boulevard Malesherbes
(8th arrondissement)
Paris
4265.3786
www.leforumparis.fr

owned since 1931 (it is currently run by Josianne and Joseph Biolatto). Le Forum claims to be the oldest American bar in Paris. Harry's chronology seems to contradict Le Forum's claims, but we're not going to start a debate when there are drinks a-waitin'.

The decor at Le Forum is all about wood paneling sharing wall space with stucco, plus tan armchairs, low lighting, and unexpected artwork—it's on the ceilings rather than the walls. When you're flat on your back, ceiling art inspires great epiphanies that you'll forget when you're sober. No one at Le Forum gets quite to that state, however (at least not publicly). The crowd here is made up of American embassy employees and financiers from the local firms, mixed with young trendy Parisians, perhaps from the fashion trade. All are taking one of the bar's house rules to heart: "We have a sense of elegance—and you as well?" Music may be classic jazz, or it may be disco hits from one (or both) of the vintage jukeboxes flanking a doorway.

The bar seems to take their old-school mixology seriously, and the 65-odd classic drinks that make up their list are made with precision. We like the idea of the Mojito Shakerato, which comes with a little sidecar of champagne as a palate cleanser. Their basic

Martini is made with the uncommon Plymouth navy-strength gin. Similar attention to detail is paid to the Sazerac, which uses Sazerac-brand rye and Un Emile absinthe; the little metal stirring spoon is a nice touch, too. The bar's house drink is the Forum Cocktail, a 1929 Martini variant using gin, Noilly Prat dry vermouth, and Grand Marnier. The bar carries no beer on tap and just a pair of wines, but it offers a fine array of champagnes. Le Forum also holds Bar School workshops on Saturday afternoons and conducts whiskey-tasting events.

Right around the corner from Le Forum is Place de la Madeleine, your Parisian go-to spot for the best (and priciest) couture grocers. The square is surrounded by shops selling caviar, exotic fruits, truffles, and wine.

LAST CALL!
More Destinations to Explore in Paris

If you liked the Hemingway Bar, you're going to *love* this one. **Bar 228** (Hôtel Le Meurice, 228 rue de Rivoli, 1st arrondissement; 4458.1055; www.lemeurice.com/bar-228) is the watering hole within the palatial five-star Hôtel Le Meurice. Since 1835, Le Meurice has defined excessive opulence and consumptive extravagance. Located opposite the Tuileries Garden and between the Louvre and the Place de la Concorde, there are few better addresses in Paris. Eat at Restaurant Le Meurice (which rocks three massive murals by Claude Lavalley) or Restaurant Le Dalí, which was named for Salvador Dalí (who spent one month in the hotel each year for three decades). Bar 228 is about leather armchairs, mahogany, and crystal decanters. In 2007, the whole space was subtly updated by Philippe Starck, who commissioned his daughter Ara Starck to paint the huge canvas covering the ceiling at Le Dalí. Starck's mannequin-ish bodies floating among painted draperies are sufficiently ersatz Dalí. Bar 228 serves 50 whiskeys and over 300 cocktails, including 17 house inventions (€24–€28). They have a menu of small plates and feature live jazz duos every night.

Another of our Parisian agents (one can never have too many) says that **Le Bar du Plaza** (Hôtel Plaza Athénée, 25 Avenue Montaigne; 5367.6600; www.bar-plaza-athenee-paris.com) is equally lavish and equally expensive to Bar 228, but has better bartenders. The 1911 hotel is near the Eiffel Tower and Champs Elysées, and is where Mata Hari was arrested. Maybe she didn't pay her bill?

Opened in 2010, **La Conserverie** (35 bis rue du Sentier, 2nd arrondissement; 4026.1494; www.laconserveriebar.com) translates as "the Cannery"—as in, a place where fruit preserves are prepared. Eric Bulteau and Richard Azarnia's bar was once a textile factory, and the decor takes the room's industrial history to heart. Ductwork is painted bright silver and puts anything seen in Terry Gilliam's *Brazil* to shame. These are some *serious* ducts. Warped glass cannery jars are now lamps, and the backbar looks like something designed by Joseph Cornell. This is all contrasted by bright blue walls and plush furniture in primary colors or black-and-white stripes. Add a pastoral tapestry, and you've got a cool vibe in a spacious room near Le Sentier, the garment district. Cocktails run from €12 to €14 and contain a balance between classics and house creations. The Du Maurier (rum, lemon juice, champagne, whole raspberries) is meant to be sipped with the rock candy garnish on the tongue.

L'Entrée des Artistes (8 rue de Crussol, 11th arrondissement; 5099.6711) was opened in late 2011 by Fabien Lombardi of Prescription and Edouard Vermynck, once the sommelier for Hôtel Murano. Vermynck and Lombardi man the bar themselves, with Lombardi making the cocktails and Vermynck choosing and pouring the wine. Lombardi has helped to accelerate the Parisian drinking scene toward contemporary standards by introducing barrel-aged or "vintage" versions of the Negroni and Vieux Carré (€14/€15). The majority of the cocktail list is in the €10–€11 range. The six-table L'Entrée des Artistes likes to call itself "bar à manger," or "bar (at which) to eat." Keeping the operation small and tight, the concise food menu is all prepared by Vermynck's mother.

Here's another family operation: Gal Friday Night's pals from her Venice period swear that **Grazie** (91 Boulevard Beaumarchais; 3rd arrondissement; 4278.1196; www.graziegrazie.fr) is a must-visit. It was opened by Julien Cohen, whose mother, Marie-France Cohen, owns a string of interior design shops called Merci. The space within the hip Marais district is decorated in a rusty corrugated bar, tin ceiling, and metal stools that give it an industrial vibe, in keeping with the reused/recycled feel of Merci's wares. (Merci has to be the world's hippest Goodwill; they sell interior decor and clothing in addition to housing a library and café. All of their profits go to charity!) Pizza and cocktails as a combo isn't hard to turn down, especially with a cocktail menu heavy on amari and drinks named for Fellini films. Drinks in the €12 range include the Pimms Italiano, the Basil Honey Martini, and the Aperol Spritz. The stuffed peacock above the bar is not on the menu.

There is no way we are going to cover the Paris bar scene without mentioning **Silencio** (142 rue de Montmartre; 2nd arrondissement; www.silencio-club.com) which is the club opened in August 2011 by painter, musician, and film director David Lynch. Lynch envisioned the space as a retreat and showcase for all artists in any medium. Styled after a scene in Lynch's film, *Mulholland Drive*, Silencio is members-only until midnight, but the hoi polloi may queue up to frolic from then until 6:00 AM (standard memberships are €780). The multiple rooms in Silencio contain a live music venue, an art library, a sitting lounge, a cinema, and of course, cocktails.

AMSTERDAM

In Amsterdam, the land of windmills, Piet Mondrian, and storefront prostitution, people like to have a good time. All the time. This is a town that has legalized pot and installed urinals right on the street (in certain areas), and enjoys (or tolerates) perhaps the most tourist-skewed ratio of tourists to locals in Europe. But still, in this bastion of decadence, there is refinement; look no further than Door 74, for starters.

There are bars that define order and there are those that define chaos. A short walk from Rembrandtplein (Rembrandt Square) along a quiet street, and just

Door 74

Reguliersdwarsstraat 74
Amsterdam
0634-045122
www.door-74.com

around the corner from one of Amsterdam's many raucous party zones, you'll find Door 74. But, you'll have to look carefully. You're looking for a plain black door with the number 74 on it. Can you remember that? Do so, because behind that door is a contender for the best classic cocktail bar in Amsterdam.

After visiting Le Lion in Hamburg and Milk & Honey in New York, cocktail consultant Phillip Duff was inspired to open a parallel bar in Amsterdam. Partnering with Sergej Fokke, who owns Feijoa just down the block, the pair opened Door 74 in November of 2008. Duff has since departed to continue building his consultancy firm.

Beyond a thick black curtain, you'll find a room decorated with polished wood stained to near-black, matching leather sofas, a New York-style stamped tin ceiling, and contemporary touches that give Door 74 a sleek and trendy feeling. The bar seats 40 in a series of booths on the left. Seating is by reservation only (call before 8:00 PM), but walk-ins may be accommodated at the bar's 10 stools along the right. The process is . . . orderly. Door 74 won't allow standing patrons, as per their requisite house rules list. This checklist contains the usual items about keeping your voice down and behaving like a grown-up, but our fieldwork CFO Gal Friday Night got really mad when she had to keep paying for my violations of the bar's "no nerd" rule. It seems that if a customer engages the bartender in mixological boozetalk beyond a certain reasonable level, the nerd alert goes off and the customer must forego the next cocktail until a rather proletarian shot-and-beer combo has been quaffed. These shots are never quite so cocktailian chic as Fernet-Branca, either. Good thing they don't have Malört in this country (see Chicago's Bar DeVille). In any case, no more questions were asked about the 30-odd house-made bitters lined up on the bar. Cocktails were ordered.

The menu is updated four times a year and frequently includes a theme. Their Charles H. Baker Jr. theme is reminiscent of Heaven's Dog in San Francisco, which uses its Baker-inspired menu more or less perpetually.

We went for a Nuclear Daiquiri (overproof rum, lime juice, green Chartreuse, simple syrup; €10), and were also impressed with the Zena con Humphrey (Campari, champagne, rose jam, thyme liqueur; €12.50).

When in Rome, goes the adage, one must do as the Romans do. So, when in Holland, it follows, one must sample the classic Holland Gin Cocktail (genever, simple syrup, maraschino, Angostura bitters, absinthe). This is unless one can find the equally-vintage Improved Holland Gin Cocktail (genever, simple syrup, orange curaçao, orange bitters). At Door 74, however, the order and chaos go hand in hand—ask for the Depraved Holland Gin Cocktail (genever, mezcal, honey-ginger syrup, agave syrup, Peychaud's bitters). The thematic inclusion of the curaçao in the Improved variant (the islands of Curaçao are a Dutch colony) was a nice touch, but that's what too much depravity will get you—your colonies start to vanish.

The only food you'll see at Door 74 are Bella di Cerignola olives and a custom-made assortment of nuts by Amsterdam-based and family-owned Gotje Nuts. These are served on a small platter that will be refilled during your stay. We actually enjoyed this little touch, which many craft cocktail bars seem to ignore. Perhaps it is considered too pub-ish, or perhaps the more spendy bars would rather you ponied up for their foie gras, but it's just nice to have a little something to crunch on while enjoying a cocktail.

Feijoa (39 Vijzelstraat; 0653.726137; www.feijoa.nl) is about half a block down the street from Door 74, and rests right on the border between orderly Reguliersdwarsstraat and the chaotic party zone around the corner. Owned by Door 74's Sergej Fokke, the bar is named after a fruit grown in New Zealand that inspired Fokke during a trip to Aotearoa. Feijoa is the darker yin to Door 74's yang, the chaos to the more upscale bar's order. The crowd is younger, drunker, and more likely to go home with you (if you are under 30). House rules shift from Door 74's rule against hats on gentlemen to a more pragmatic "no whistling at the bartenders." We sampled a Papa Doble Daiquiri (triple shot of white rum, grapefruit juice, lime juice, Luxardo maraschino liqueur, sugar; €11.50) and a Basil Bramble Sling (gin, basil leaves, lemon juice, sugar, crème de mûre; €8.50). Neither were prepared with the care found at our previous destination; this is clearly just a different sort of bar. However as chaos settles into order (as is the very nature of the universe) the Feijoa patrons may find themselves simmering down, growing up, and wandering over to that orderly black door just up the block.

LAST CALL!
More Destinations to Explore in Amsterdam

House of Bols Cocktail and Genever Experience (Paulus Potterstraat 14; 020-5708575; www.houseofbols.com) is a museum/distillery tour sponsored by Bols, which has been making liqueurs and genever since 1575. This makes them the oldest continuously operating liquor brand in the world. For €11.50, you get a tour through the Hall of Taste and the World of Cocktails, and you also get to taste a cocktail. The multimedia extravaganza won a Dutch design award for "best exhibition and experience." It is located at the Amsterdam Museumplein, meaning it is easy walking distance from the Van Gough museum and the epic Rijksmuseum. Now you've got a plan for your afternoon. You're welcome.

Unrelated to the similarly named bar in Paris, **Harry's Bar** (285 Spuistraat; 020.6244384; www.harrysbaramsterdam.com) is few minutes' walk from Door 74. This classic American-style bar gets pretty crowded, but the white-jacketed bartenders will shake up a by-the-book Sidecar or Negroni (€8.80 each) from a long menu containing all of the usual suspects. Our Sidecar was a small pour, a tiny lil' Japanese-portioned thing, but it tasted the way a Sidecar ought to. The Negroni was served on the rocks, but at least the cubes were big and very cold so they didn't melt and water the drink down.

Our local lieutenant was raving about *bitterballen,* some sort of delicious deep-fried gravy balls that are served as pub snacks around these parts, and was also discussing *kirenwijn,* a high-malt variant of genever (the Bols brand is called Corenwyn). Both kirenwijn and bitterballen can be had at the ancient **Café Hoppe** (Spui 18–20; 420.4420; www.cafehoppe.com), just down the block from Harry's. We liked the old tile floor and the sense of history in the place. Above the ancient woody bar is an ancient oil painting of a man on a horse toasting a woman in a frilly dress, with an Asta dog jumping around as another man looks on approvingly. We also approved. Café Hoppe has been a bar continuously since 1670.

Vesper Bar (Vinkenstraat 57; 02 0846.4458; www.vesperbar.nl) had the nerve to open right after our reconnaissance mission to Amsterdam, but local intelligence says it is within mixological striking distance of Door 74's greatness. The bar is named for Vesper Lynd, James Bond's love interest in the very first Bond adventure, the 1953 novel *Casino Royale*. After Lynd broke Jimmy's little heart, he avoided emotional connections with women until *On Her Majesty's Secret Service*, 10 novels later, when Contessa Teresa di Vicenzo warmed 007 up to marriage. And now a bar, complete with just a few bits of Bond memorabilia scattered about the place, serves Miss Lynd's namesake tipple in Amsterdam's arty and residential Jordaan area. The neighborhood bar vibe is combined with acclaimed cocktails (from a menu of a dozen classics and a few house creations) to make Vesper one to watch. Just like its namesake.

BARCELONA

There are countless destinations at which one can become ossified in Barcelona, the land of paella, Joan Miró, and Antoni Gaudí, but the great Boada's is a good starting point.

Boadas Bar

Carrer dels Tallers 1
Barcelona
933.189.592

There are two types of bar in the world: those that hire venenciadors as shaker monkeys, and those that have to look the word up in the dictionary. In a city known for having at least three solid tiki bars—Kahiki, Kahala, and Aloha—finding a really solid cocktail is more challenging than you'd think. Yeah, Salvador Dalí was born and worked very close to here, but if that man had a fault, it was that he was something of a teetotaler. Bullfighters don't drink much, either. You can get solid sangria just about anywhere, but where does one get a cocktail in Barcelona? At the corner of Tallers Street and La Rambla, that's where. Tallers is a tiny street that runs from La Rambla (the mile-long pedestrian mall that is always packed with tourists) to the nearby college area.

Boadas was opened in 1933 by Mr. Miguel Boadas Parera (1895–1967), who came to Barcelona after spending the Prohibition years getting American tourists loaded on Daiquiris at Havana's La Floridita bar. Extra bragging rights: he was reportedly *the first* bartender at La Floridita. Ever. Boadas Bar is now owned by Parera's daughter, Maria Dolores Boadas. The tiny Barcelona lounge seats about eight people, and there is standing room for another 20. The water closet is literally the size of a closet. There is a fantastic painted portrait of Parera shaking a cocktail on the wall, as well as tons of other framed memorabilia from his life, going all the way back to the turn of the (last) century. A great backlit mural behind the bar shows people in the 1940s enjoying themselves at Boadas.

The old-school bartenders are all dressed in tux jackets, and can make any traditional cocktail you may want. They are all suave older gentlemen, and are first and foremost service-minded, never snooty. Each of them has their own schtick that stops just short of being a little bit too "flair." One guy, for example, mixes drinks in the manner of a venenciador (the traditional manner of aerating sherry). He pours the drink back and forth between two shakers: one held way above his head and the other by his waist. Another fella has mastered the art of a certain prestidigitation involving liquor bottles. But none of it feels corny or overly showy; these guys just have natural style. It's the real deal. It's all presented almost as an afterthought, very nonchalant.

The drink of the day is always listed on a small chalkboard. Upon our most recent visit, it was the Nelson (whiskey, sweet vermouth, bitters). The Nelson is one of those cocktail names that has been applied to a dozen completely different recipes over the years; the Boadas Nelson is a sort of rebalanced Manhattan. We also had excellent versions of a Sidecar, a Kir Royale, and a good old Cuba Libre. Figured we'd take advantage of the chance to drink some Cuban rum while paying homage to Parera's Havana years. Cocktails are reasonable, at around €6.

LAST CALL!

More Destinations to Explore in Barcelona

Bar Marsella (Carrer de Sant Pau; 934.427.263) is located a block or two up St. Pau from La Rambla. It has been operating since the dawn of the 19th century, and the owners claim to run the oldest bar in Barcelona. Based on the inch-high stacks of dust on the chandelier, we believe it. The substance on the 200-year-old bottles decorating the upper shelves goes beyond dust, beyond patina, and crosses fully into the category of unidentified sentient life form (deceased). The centuries-old woodwork has barely been maintained; the marble bar is cracked. There is a feeling of age here, and a slightly sinister edge that recalls Poe or Lovecraft. However, of famous writers, it was Hemingway (natch) who is said to have haunted this bar when in Barcelona.

Bar Marsella is known for its absinthe. They keep an army of snifters full of the green fairy lined up behind the bar, poured and ready to serve. Absinthe is not usually served via the traditional fountain here, but you do get a tiny fork, a bottle of water with a tiny hole punched in the cap, and a sugar cube. Put the cube on the fork, and drizzle water over it as slowly as you can manage, so that the sugar veeeerrry slowly seeps down into the drink. Doing it properly results in the sugar-water mixing gently with *la fée verte*, forming a cloudy mixture. With €5 glasses of absinthe—and given the rowdy crowd of tourists, locals, and hookers—this is just your basic 19th-century, absinthe-based Spanish dive bar.

Unmissable on an Eixample district corner, **Dry Martini** (Carrer d'Aribau 162–166; 932.175.072; www.drymartinibcn.com) is connected to the Dry Martini Academy and to Speakeasy, all of which are operated by Javier de

las Muelas. Speakeasy is a restaurant hidden in Dry Martini's former warehouse, and themed after 1920s Chicago, while the Academy is "a professional training centre for new cocktail talent." All three businesses share a kitchen that will keep your belly full of tapas. In a room filled with Martini-themed art (by Keith Harring, Mel Ramos, and others), bartenders mix up a variety of carefully prepared classics, and many of de las Muelas's own creations. The latter are numerous, and tend to gravitate toward the candy-colored realm of the fruity, the smoothic, the gelatinous, and the frappé. If there was one place where the "-tini" can be justified, it might be here. Javier de las Muelas is also behind the circa-1979 bar **Gimlet** (Carrer del Rec 24; 933.101.027; www.gimletbcn.com).

Within the Gothic Quarter is a maze of dark little streets festooned with tiny cafés. One of them is **Las Cuevas del Sorte** (Carrer d'en Gignàs, 2; 932.954.015; www.lascuevasdelsorte.com). Dimly lit and a bit decadent-feeling, the small restaurant is quintessentially Barcelona. In their basement, one finds a much larger and much more sparsely decorated cavern of debauchery. This could be Gaudí's basement, with blue glass tile all along one wall and curved shapes wherever possible. All of the hipsters, musicians, and poets in town seem to come here.

They serve Caipirinhas (cachaça, lime juice, sugar) and Caipirisimas (rum, lime juice, sugar) for €5 each. Wander around the Gothic Quarter a bit; there lots of little hidden gems like this one.

BERLIN

If we must choose the one nation in continental Europe that has most enthusiastically embraced the American cocktail, it might be Germany. Berlin is clearly the cocktail capital of Deutschland, but Hamburg and Munich are also home to at least two world-class watering holes each.

Becketts Kopf

Pappelallee 64
Berlin
0162.237.9418
www.becketts-kopf.de

Naming bars after authors is not unheard of (one word: Hemingway), but how about naming your bar after a specific part of an author's body? Becketts Kopf is meant to translate from German just how it seems: "Beckett's Head." A small illuminated portrait of Irish author (and Berlin resident) Samuel Beckett marks the door to this cozy bar. Tucked away in an unassuming part of the Prenzlauer Berg borough, just northeast of the central Mitte neighborhood, Becketts Kopf opened in late 2004. The dark and quiet bar seats about 10, and a small seating area accomodates 10 more. A seasonal patio and a back room handle the overflow.

Owner Oliver Ebert is passionate about cocktails, but he could not find a bar that he was satisfied with in Berlin. Thus he decided to open his own place, with his Portuguese wife, Cristina Neves. The combination of the location and the lack of a sign keeps the bar both exclusive and affordable. They want people in there who understand good cocktails, but they want to keep prices manageable. We like the way these people think.

Becketts Kopf prides itself on its seasonal menu. A small company on the outskirts of Berlin grows mint exclusively for bar, so drinks requiring mint are only served between June and September, the months that mint grows best in these parts. They also have their own cocktail cherries custom made, which take two months per batch to create. These cherries are put to good use in the house specialty, the Lusitanian (Antiquissima aguardente velha brandy, Guignolet de Dijon cherry liqueur, Rosso Antico red vermouth, Tropfen bitters, house-made cherry; €8.50), which was named for the nation also known to some as Portugal. Aguardente velha ("old burning water") is a style of Portugese aged brandy, distilled from vinho verde wine.

Wanting to continue with local flavors, Ebert suggested his Herbarium (Scotch whisky, Guignolet de Dijon cherry liqueur, Löwentor kräuter bitter; €8.50). The drink is dry, with a big bite of licorice from the Löwentor kräuter (translation: Lion's Gate herbal). It is served with a skillfully sculpted iceberg in a classy vintage glass. Becketts Kopf uses antique glassware almost exclusively. All ice (except crushed) is cut by hand, and is stored in a freezer kept between 15 and 25 degrees Fahrenheit. The Guignolet de Dijon is made by Gabriel Boudier, which has been producing about 15 liqueurs since 1874.

Kräuter bitters are interesting to discuss. Germany has about 180 distilleries scattered among small towns all over the country, each making micro-regional herbal liqueurs, or *kräuter*, collectively. Every town has its own local brand, and many of these aren't available more than a few kilometers outside of where they are made. A few are mass-produced, but many are made in quantities of only a few hundred cases or less each year. Some of them are quite good, and range from very sweet to very bitter. In a country known for beer, these kräuter liqueurs are considered by many Bavarians to be the true traditional German beverage. Thusly educated, Ebert accommodated us with three further samples.

Der Feldapotheter (the Field Apothecary) has been made since 1870. The name refers to an apothecary on a battle site. Each bottle comes with a reproduction 19th-century document from field generals prescribing this to soldiers. It is more viscous, with more licorice and less chocolate than the Löwentor. Bachmann (from Dortmund) has a Jamaican rum base, and is medium-thick compared to the others. Sweet with notes of chocolate, but with a slightly questionable finish. Killepitsch (from Dusseldorf) has been made since 1858. It is also thicker than Löwentor, much less like licorice, and sweeter and fruitier. As one of the mass-produced brands, it is also closer than any of the other three to Jägermeister, the most famous—and most dreaded—of the kräuter produced for export. Killepitsch is *much* better than Jägermeister, however. Those with fond memories of blacking out at frat parties after too much Jäger might want to graduate to Killepitsch, which is now being imported into the U.S.

The only food served at Becketts Kopf are small cheese and cured meat plates. A few beers and wines are available, though Ebert reports that 95 percent of the customers are into the spirit of the cocktails on offer, and come here for these drinks.

Green Door

Winterfeldtstraße 50
Berlin
030.215.2515
www.greendoor.de

Green Door is surprising for Germany, in that it has the feel of a Midwestern American dive bar, as if it has made the trip from Wisconsin to Berlin. This is not a criticism. Green Door is not a trendy place trying to be ironic; somehow it manages a divey vibe in a completely uncontrived way. When we visited, they were playing various 1960s U.S. lounge kitsch pop music, followed by Martin Denny's "Quiet Village." Weird old bric-a-brac decorates the place; we saw straws stored in an old Trader Vic's bowl, and a 1930s-era mechanical "negro" bartender coin bank. Green Door also has a cool guest book full of writings and drawings from all over the world. Gal Friday Night notarized it. Look us up when you visit. The mural behind bar looks like the result of Van Gogh drinking too much absinthe, staring at a piece of wood for 10 hours, then tracing what he observed. The only hint we're in Germany comes from homey Bavarian curtains and a bit of old blue gingham wallpaper . . . or are those from Kentucky?

Owner Fritz Müller-Scherz—also a screenwriter, actor, reporter, and trumpet player—calls himself "an amateur" (the term "amateur" as used in Europe is more akin to "hobbyist" than the

North American usage of the word) and says he was a bar customer for years, but no one was doing what he wanted to see happen with a bar, so he opened his own place. Didn't Oliver Ebert of Becketts Kopf say the same thing? The two resulting bars are so different, and both are worth a visit.

The menu is full of cool 1920s and 1930s vintage graphics reminiscent of those in the indispensable *Savoy Cocktail Book* (1930). This menu includes the Lufthansa cocktail, as seen at Christiansen's in Hamburg (see page 348), but we chose the Modest (Tabu absinthe, Gilbey's gin, apricot brandy, orange juice, lime juice, mandarin syrup; €9). It was free-poured, which always gives us pause, but it ended up just fine—tart with an anise bite. Next up was Harry Johnson's 1906 creation, the Whiskey Daisy (Rittenhouse rye, yellow Chartreuse, simple syrup, lemon juice, lime wedge; €10). Here's a Berlin thing: the bars all put a wood skewer in the drink as a swizzle stick. I kept thinking they were straws, but Gal Friday Night collected them and used them to fight off bandits as we crossed the Black Forest.

Prost!

When "1700" manifests itself in your consciousness, what do you think of? The year that Western Europe adapted the Gregorian calendar? The date of American witch hunter John Cale's death? How about a bar with 1,700 brands of booze on hand? No, it isn't a dream, it is real, and it is called Lebensstern.

Lebensstern

Café Einstein
Kurfürstenstraße 58
Berlin
030.2639.1922
www.cafeeinstein.com

Lebensstern's insane collection of booze is housed in display cases spread over several rooms. The cases are lit from within and are more or less organized by theme; we saw large concentrations of rum in one room, whiskey in another, and gin in another. Bar manager Ricardo Albrecht estimates that of the 1,700-ish spirits available, they've got 600 rums plus 200 gins and genevers. If you were just to assume that they've got "one of everything," you'd be

on the right track. Lebensstern adds to their stockpile by buying collections from other aficionados.

This elegant bar is located on the upper floor of a ritzy restaurant called Einstein, which is in turn located in a huge old mansion. Albrecht and owner Peter Kowalczyk tell us that Lebensstern was opened around 2006, as one small room on the upper level of the mansion. At the time, the room contained four small tables and seven seats at the bar. Restoring the wood as they went, the bar expanded into the adjacent room, and then the next room, and then the next. Lebensstern now takes up most of the second floor (or first floor if you're European) of the mansion. A very small back patio is open seasonally.

The layout of Lebensstern is such that the individual rooms can be closed off for private parties. The bar is also unique in that it doesn't play any music, preferring to keep things tranquil. Also missing are coffee, tea, and food—those can all be had below, at Einstein.

Lebensstern makes its own line of spirits, including a Caribbean-style rum for mixing, a higher end blended rum for sipping, and two gins. One is an artisanal pink gin produced in Austria for the bar (since 2010) which has both sweet and bitter notes. The other has been produced in southern Germany since 2008, and is a straightforward London dry gin.

Gal Friday Night wanted to start with one of Ricardo's drinks, the Trafo (Maker's Mark whiskey, Grand Marnier Cordon Rouge, lime juice, D'Arbo holunderblütensirop, Wilken's orange bitter marmalade; €9.50). Holunderblütensirop is elderflower syrup. We also sampled a Karthäuser Martini (Booth's gin, green Chartreuse, Dolin dry vermouth, Elixir Vegetal), which was created at Lebensstern by Bernhard Stadler. The free-poured cocktail tastes exactly like what it is: a standard Martini with added Chartreuse. You can't go wrong with that. In fact, it seems that you can't go wrong at all at Lebensstern.

Sometimes bar customers appreciate their favorite bar so much that they end up buying the place. Rum Trader was opened in 1976 by Hans Schröder, a former Trader Vic's bartender who was name-checked by Ian Fleming in his travelogue *Thrilling Cities*. After the demise of the Berlin Trader Vic's, Schröder absorbed a few tiki trinkets to use as decor, and spent a few decades selling rum at Rum Trader. The bar was purchased in 2001 by the dapper Gregor Scholl, who also seems to be the sole employee. Scholl says that if he hadn't bought the place, it would have closed.

Scholl is a proper gentleman, polite if a little aloof, and dressed in a tailored vest and bow tie, but not in a self-conscious hipster way. One gets the feeling that this is how he always dresses. A gold chain strung between vest and shirt has a little cross on one end, and probably has a pocket watch on the other. His English is accented in the manner of London's upper crust. His Victorian costume is matched by his musical choices. Classical music fills the small room, emanating from compact disc transfers of old 78 rpm records, with all scratches and pops intact.

The tiny Rum Trader, which bills itself as an "institute for advanced drinking," seats about eight at the bar and four more at the sole corner table. We liked the ancient Revox reel-to-reel tape machine and a 1930s Cuban tourism poster depicting a flapper girl. Also cool are the very nice (if well-worn) menus featuring textured paper, lithographed with old-style illustrations not unlike those seen in *The Savoy Cocktail Book* (this, along with wooden garnish skewers and free-pours, seems to be a Berlin theme). Seemingly blank pages open up gatefold-style to reveal the drinks listed on the inside. Drink prices are filled in with pencil.

"Rum is the most variable spirit," Scholl asserted as we examined the impressive rum collection. "There is always something new to discover. Even whiskey gets predictable, but with rum, there is always something new." Gregor is also a fan of gin, but he has no plans to open a Gin Trader quite yet.

Scholl started us with a rum Manhattan made with OVD (Old Vatted Demerara) rum and Noilly Pratt vermouth. It's always a bonus to try a liquor that isn't available in the U.S. when traveling.

Free-pouring the cocktail with a dangerously generous quantity of OVD, Scholl topped the drink off with a bit more happiness from the shaker after we took a sip. A Fog Cutter, a Mai Tai, and an Elephant Hunter were up next. Although all of these drinks are borne of the tiki canon, and although there are just enough tiki accoutrements in the bar to make them worthy of note, these drinks were prepared and served more like traditional cocktails. They're strong and rum-forward. Fruity garnishes, and even fresh fruit juice other than lemon or lime aren't something that there is much room to deal with behind the tiny bar. This is definitely a rum bar, and any resemblance to tiki is purely coincidental.

We've also heard good things about **Die Bar** (the Bar, Fasanenstraße 47; 030 8850464), just a bit down the block from Rum Trader.

———————◆▶·————————

Stagger Lee

Nollendorfstraße 27
Berlin
030 2903.6158
www.staggerlee.de

Stagger Lee was a St. Louis taxi driver, a pimp, and the killer of William "Billy" Lyons in 1895. In subsequent years, Lee became a folk figure, credited with having magic powers, of making a deal with the devil, of causing the San Francisco earthquake, and of once having dueled with Jesse James. A song written about Lee has been performed by dozens if not hundreds of musicians over the past century. Nick Cave wrote an all-new song about Lee for his 1995 album *Murder Ballads*. We wondered if the bar owners were fans, and soon noticed a Cave quote on menu.

Wait, are we dealing with a high-end cocktail bar inspired by Nick Cave—once himself a Berliner?

Why, yes, we are.

The bar opened in September 2009 by Maureen Reichl, who co-conceptualized the space with lead bartender Jake Etzold, he of the cocktail shaker tattoo. Stagger Lee is designed to look like a 19th-century Western saloon, but a nice one—if that isn't an oxymoron. Textured red wallpaper with a black floral motif covers the walls that surround a very dark wooden bar. An ancient brass cash register (not used) rests on the bar, next to a single old brass beer tap. The only beer coming from this tap is Pilsner Urquel; this is a cocktail bar.

"Drinking 19th-century drinks is better in a place that looks like it," Etzold said as he started us off with their house specialty, a Stagger Lee Julep (Maker's Mark bourbon, maraschino liqueur, black cherry jam; €9.50). It is served in a little shaker packed with ice and mint, placed on a small silver platter. The strainer is left on top of the shaker, with the idea being to drink it through the strainer. Three maraschino cherries are served on a wooden skewer placed on the platter, next to the drink. The cherries are of Stagger Lee's house-made variety.

Speaking of houses, or homes, Reichl has managed to make Stagger Lee quite a cozy place. It feels relaxed and casual there; we liked the Skatalites records that were playing for most of our visit. "I wanted a place that felt like my living room," Reichl told us. Sans murderers, we assume.

Flexing his bartending skills a bit, Etzold improvised a libation made of Buffalo Trace bourbon, Campari aperitif, Killepitsch kraüter, Punt e Mes vermouth, and Bitter Truth German-made bitters. It was served over a big ice ball and garnished with a lemon peel. Two German ingredients, two Italian ingredients, and one American. If the whiskey were Japanese instead of American, this drink could be called the Axis.

The array of libations unique to Germany is . . . staggering. We have already discussed the 180-odd kraüter liqueurs made all over the country. Southern Germany is of course known for an equally impressive variety of *kirschwassers* (cherry brandies). Etzold took things to the next level (down) by introducing us to korn, Germany's moonshine. This is a liquor that can be made from rye, corn, barley, or wheat, and is typically consumed by the working class, usually as a shot chased with a beer. He also pulled out Schinken Häger, a liqueur made to be consumed with *schinken* (ham). There are pictures of meat on the bottle. How often do you see meat on a booze bottle?

Getting excited about showing off local tradition, our barman soon appeared with an apple-shaped wooden platter covered with sliced pickles, wheat bread topped with *schmaltz*, and bread with

ham on it. This was joined by a small glass of beer (about four ounces) in a gold-rimmed glass, and a healthy shot of Schinken Häger (at least two ounces), each of which had its own place on the platter. A true German drinking experience in a bar named after an American killer, as sung about by an Australian musician.

Good stuff.

LAST CALL!

More Destinations to Explore in Berlin

Listing retail shops is a bit out of the scope of this book, but we wanted to mention **Big Market** (Buckower Damm 86; 030.604.5686; www.big-market.de), a liquor store in the Britz neighborhood that boasts of the largest whiskey selection in Europe. It is organized as a "museum" with 4,000 bottles, all for sale. Hans-Jürgen Horn opened Big Market in 1965 and retired in July 2011, leaving the market in the hands of Jürgen Laskowski.

The brand-new **Buck and Breck** (Brunnenstraße 177; www.buckandbreck.com) might be named after American president James Buchanan and vice president John Breckinridge. Of course, the president of vice is always a great person to name a bar after, but Buck and Breck is more likely named for an 1860s intoxicant (cognac, bitters, absinthe, champagne) that was named after these two leaders of men (they led us, incidentally, into the Civil War). Bar owners Gonçalo de Sousa Monteiro and Holger Groll have hidden their 14-seat bar behind the facade of an art gallery. Inside, all of the seats gather around a big rectangular bar that looks like a grand dining room table. If you've remembered to make a reservation, you'll receive personal service in an intimate and stylish environment.

Reingold (Novalisstraße 11; 030.2838.7676; www.cms.reingold.de) is a lounge sporting plush black leather booths, gold leaf details, a huge J-shaped banquette, and an elegant walnut bar that recalls art deco. Bartenders sport attire in keeping with the same era, and pre-war jazz completes the vibe. A mural of Erika and Klaus Mann (daughter and son of German novelist Thomas Mann) dominates one end of the space, and is painted upon pages of Mann's book about them. The connection? They used to hang out at Berlin's original 1920s Reingold bar. A young and fashionable crowd drinks from a fairly comprehensive selection of classic cocktails as a DJ keeps things lively.

It is probably our duty to drop additional hints about **Trio Bar** (Motzstraße 19; www.triobar.de) as well. This "institute for applied bar culture" is run by a true cocktail nerd (that's a compliment) who has moved Trio Bar all over Berlin, opening for business as (and where) he wants to. His collection of rare spirits is amazing, and he shares the same passion for rum that the rest of Berlin seems to have. Go find it.

Günter Windhorst's tiny, chic, eponymous bar, **Windhorst** (Dorotheenstraße 65; 030 2045.0070) is located near the American Embassy. Clearly operated as a labor of love, Herr Windhorst and bartenders such as Holger Groll mix classics and house creations from a 52-page cocktail menu. All juice is pressed to order. Jazz and Latin music come from a collection of vinyl visible along the back wall. Given the location in an upscale neighborhood, you may want to stop in here after the theater or the opera. Paintings of musicians on the wall complete the musical theme.

HAMBURG

Although not as festooned with great saloons as edgy Berlin, historic Hamburg, home of the Reeperbahn, the early days of the Beatles, and ships aplenty, is also home to a few excellent bars.

Christiansen's

Pinnasberg 60
Hamburg
040.317.2863
www.christiansens.de

Hamburg's Fischmarkt (Fish Market) was once exactly what the name implies, but this famous Hamburg spectacle now offers a wider range of goods beginning at 5:00 AM every Sunday morning. If you need a reason to stay up all night in order to get there on time, try Christiansen's. The eponymous bar owned by Uwe Christiansen has been open since 1997. Christiansen's is also near enough the seedy Reeperbahn to draw in business, but far enough away that they don't need bouncers to deal with fights.

Christiansen wanted a small classic bar where he could interact with his customers in a quiet environment. Dark wood, red trim, and a huge booze selection do indeed make for cozy environs. The bar seats about 15, and there are plenty of booths and tables, too. The eight-foot-long aquarium is kind of old school, in a good way. You just don't see many new bars with aquariums. Maybe they're too much of a headache to maintain. Why not gaze upon some fish while drinking like one? Now the bars all have televisions. We'd rather watch fish.

Christiansen has tended bar in places such as South Africa and Greece, and likes to represent his travels in his liquor collection, which features spirits from all over the world. Getting to these places requires airfare, of course, so it is apropos that Christiansen has resurrected the famous Lufthansa cocktail. This orange-apricot tipple was created decades ago as a signature beverage by the eponymous airline, but was eventually discontinued. The idea of an airline having a signature drink defines the 1960s jet-set, does it not? Christiansen had a precious few examples of the original, via a dusty handful of those tiny airline bottles, which he used to reverse-engineer the flavor profile. He brought it back as a modern pre-bottled liqueur, which can be mixed with gin, rum, or whiskey. The drink begins a bit tart, but is sweet on the finish. His product line also includes a surprisingly well-balanced coffee liqueur that we found superior to Tia Maria or Kalua.

In his efforts to keep things accessible, Christiansen focuses on classic cocktails, but he will not shy away from contemporary mainstream favorites. The bar uses antique 90-year-old glassware for selected classic cocktails. They bought six cases of these glasses at auction a decade ago, and have only lost two to date; one was broken and one stolen. No one knows if the same person is responsible for both.

We began with an East India (Viel cognac, Chambord raspberry liqueur, Angosura bitters, orange curaçao, maraschino liqueur), a cocktail first printed in Harry Johnson's *Bartender's Manual* (1882). That version contained pineapple, which is replaced with raspberry syrup when it later appears in the *Savoy Cocktail Book* (1930). Christiansen adds Chambord to his variant, upgrading the raspberry syrup. Next up was the Club Cocktail from 1919 (gin, dry vermouth, sugar, orange bitters, yellow Chartreuse). Attributed to F. J. Beutel, this is probably the root of the Karthäuser Martini mentioned in our profile of Lebensstern in Berlin (see page 341).

Bartender Eyck Thormann has created a beautifully illustrated recipe book (in German only, alas) consisting of 60 original recipes and 30 classics. All share a common ingredient: Samova tea. Uwe Christiansen's other tavern, **Bar Cabana** (Fischmarkt 6; 040 8000.7114; www.barcabana.de) is just down the block, and is properly within the Fischmarkt area. The Cuban-tiki hybrid bar has a hefty rum selection, a cigar room, and a wide array of tropical-Carribean-tiki drinks. This one is larger, brighter, younger, and louder than Christiansen's, and veers toward the cartoon-y end of the tiki spectrum. Also look for Nina Hagen's daughter's bar just across the street!

Le Lion

Rathausstrasse 3
Hamburg
040.33475.3780
www.lelion.net

Jörg Meyer opened Le Lion in 2008, and promptly won a nomination for best new cocktail bar (from the Spirited Awards). The bar is located in the center of Hamburg, just steps away from the rathaus, the heavily ornamented traditional city hall. The small, dark, and intimate lounge is camouflaged by an unassuming facade along a street that thousands of tourists traipse by each day. Admission to Le Lion is achieved via doorbell and a little bit of patience.

Once warmly greeted by bartenders Mario Kappes and Torben Bornhöft, we started with one of Le Lion's two house specials, the Gin Basil Smash (Tanqueray 10, simple syrup, basil, muddled lemon; €12), made with special red basil. This basil is very fragrant; we could smell it from across the bar. A solid, fresh-tasting drink. The other house drink is the Le Coquetiez du Lion (€9.50), which is a reverse Martini, with the ratios between the gin and the Lillet swapped. A dash of Peychaud's gives it dimension. We opted for a Manhattan variation called Green Point (Old Overholt rye, Punt-e-Mes sweet vermouth, yellow Chartreuse, orange bitters, Angostura bitters; €12). We were also impressed with the Ranglum (named for

Jamaican ska guitarist Ernest Ranglin). This is a rum sour containing Gosling's rum, Forgotten Flavors falernum (while supplies last!), Wray & Nephew 151 overproof rum, lemon juice, lime juice, and sugar. It was created by the former head bartender at Le Lion (now living in Berlin) while he listened to Ranglin and experimented with falernum. We finished with a Cardenal Mendoza brandy de Jerez, a beautiful brandy from Andalusia. Sweet and peppery.

Bornhöft and business partner Philipp Jäckel had been making rather good falernum, Swedish punsch, and pimento dram under the name Forgotten Flavors until 2011. It's sad to see them cease production, but never fear—Germany has more than its share of local products to boast of.

The libertine Gal Friday Night firmly believes that the best places to drink are the bars where the bartender will hook you up for a threesome involving members of his family. Dreiling ("threesome" in German) is made by Jörg Meyer's cousin. The name was inspired by the trio of flavors used to make it: fennel, dill, and caraway. There is a whole category of liqueurs collectively called kümmel that use the caraway flavor, making them taste like liquid rye bread (the most popular brand is called Gilka—look for the penguin on the label). Dreiling also contains notes of carnation, coriander, ginger, lemongrass, bitter almond, iris root, and chamomile. Lovely stuff. Mario called Dreiling an aquavit, which is another category of liquors altogether. As kümmel-ish as it tastes, this product definitely says "aqua vitae" on the label. In any case, Dreiling is extraordinary. Too bad it's unavailable outside of Germany. Booo!

We also sampled Mirabellenbrand, a brandy made out of a yellow plum (Mirabellen is the name of the plum) by a cousin of Kappes's father. Distilling brandies from various fruits is a tradition along the Moselle River. Kappes's grandfather began distilling this brandy to use as barter goods after World War II. They couldn't get enough grapes to make wine, so they made plum brandy. They upped the alcohol content in later years to make it more valuable to barter with, usually trading it for bread. The village has one distiller, and all of the fruit growers come to that distiller to make their hootch.

The take-away lesson here is that, whether we're dealing with brandy or threesomes, it's best to keep it in the family.

LAST CALL!

More Destinations to Explore in Hamburg

Absinth (Schanzenstraße 99; 176 2362.1956; www. absinth-bar.com) is located in the festive Sternschanze neighborhood, just steps away from the Schanzenstraße U-bahn (subway) station. Sternschanze is safely north of the seediest parts of dockside St. Pauli, but still south of ritzy St. Georg. The area is full of hip 20- and 30-somethings and endless restaurants, bars, cafés, and clothing shops. Owned by a slightly gothy couple, the stark Absinth is all about bare-bones white walls, just a few tables, and minimal decor. Behind the bar is an astounding collection of absinthe, including Nouvelle-Orléans, Vieux Pontarlier, and Marteau. To the sound of jazz standards (what, no Einstürzende Neubauten?), we sipped a Verte de Foug-erolles (€6.50), prepared carefully via a drip from a vintage absinthe fountain.

In the microscopic **Jahreszeiten Bar** (Seasons Bar) at the Fairmont Hotel Vier Jahreszeiten (Neuer Jungfernstieg 9–14; 040.3494.3360; www.hvj.de), Santo Pupillo holds court over the lucky few who might get a seat in his smoky little cavern of awesome. Sequestered within this former cloakroom since the 1980s, the Sicilian barkeep continues to serve some of the best cocktails in Hamburg. When the 1897 hotel was renovated in 2010, hundreds of antiquities (including the hotel's hallmark Flemish tapestries) were also restored, but the little Seasons Bar doesn't seem to change, no matter the season, the year, or the decade.

MUNICH

Bavaria, the southernmost and most traditional part of Germany, is where the bulk of the kräuter and kirschwasser mentioned in the Berlin and Hamburg sections comes from. It is also home to dirndls, radler, Oktoberfest, and at least two excellent contemporary cocktail bars.

Schumann's American Bar

Odeonsplatz 6–7
Munich
089.229.060
www.schumanns.de

Most bars make the bulk of their income on Saturday nights. There is just one, in our experience, that is run by a man who is, shall we say, so self-assured that he has been known to close on Saturday nights, if for no other reason than to avoid dealing with the large crowds of tourists, amateurs, trendies, and posers who may come out on Saturdays. Located just south of Marienplatz in the very center of Munich, and directly across the street from an Aston Martin dealership, Schumann's American Bar is the very definition of exclusivity. Indeed, this part of town attracts both the wealthy and the tourists (and the wealthy tourists), not to mention plenty of celebrities, but Charles Schumann doesn't seem to be impressed with any of them.

As if running his bar since 1982 and being the author of *American Bar: The Artistry of Mixing Drinks* (1995) and *The Tropical Bar Book: Drinks and Stories* (1989) wasn't enough, Schumann is a spokesmodel for Amber (a cologne by Baldessarini). When we asked what inspired him to open his bar, he pragmatically replied, "To survive." Thinking this over a bit longer, he told us that in 1982, the idea of opening a stand-alone cocktail bar (outside of a

restaurant or hotel) was professional suicide. But he had the idea, and was determined to make it work. Thirty years later, even a cursory glance though this guide will reveal that many of the best cocktail bars in the world right now are stand-alone places, created by visionaries with an idea of how to do things properly. Do they all owe their existence to Schumann's vision?

Speaking of doing things properly, the cocktail menu at Schumann's is vast, with about one hundred recipes printed in a bound leather book. Schumann's own creations are labeled with the date he invented them. Many look intriguing, such as the Amber, named after the Baldessarini fragrance (2006; bourbon, honey, lemon juice, sherry, star anise). Some drinks that carry Schumann's pedigree sent us off into a flurry of research; his claim to have invented the Royal Bermuda Yacht Club Cocktail in 2008 must be in reference to a *variation* on this classic 1940s cocktail. We tried it, and the combo of Goslings Black Seal rum, lime juice, Cointreau, and John D. Taylor's Velvet Falernum definitely follows the traditional recipe, but don't let's quarrel about it. No matter who invented it, this is a damned fine drink. And here's another shocker: all of the drinks at Schumann's are free poured, as is the custom in Germany. This is something that might raise eyebrows in some parts, but the white-jacketed bar staff (each with their name custom-embroidered in red) make this perilous and potentially inconsistent methodology work. Cocktails are mostly €9–€12.

Naturally, Schumann's has an extensive collection of booze behind the bar, but perhaps the most impressive thing, especially for any Italian pirates who may be reading this, are the 75 bottles of Campari on the wall. They're all lined up like Roman columns, except that they're red and made of glass, and are relatively small from an architectural point of view. And guess what—this is one of the only places in the world where you may be served a drink containing the out-of-production and increasingly rare *other* Campari product, Campari Cordial. Schumann's report: 14 bottles left in his stash.

Go. Now. And try this: the Due Campari (Campari, Campari Cordial, Bruno Paillard champagne, lemon juice).

Schumann is also a man of exquisite taste when it comes to food—he called Chicago "the number-one dining town in the world." A bold statement, especially coming from a cultured European. Food at Schumann's is tasty, Italian-inspired, and drawn from a short menu of small plates.

◆━▶◆

M ost of the bars in this book will sell you their rendition of the classic staple, the Corpse Reviver #2, but not

Bar Tabacco

Hartmannstrasse 8
Munich
089.227.216

too many will hand you a book-sized menu with pages dedicated to the rest of the forgotten drinks in the Corpse Reviver clan. Want a Corpse Reviver #1 or #3? Bar Tabacco is your place.

The warm-feeling bar is located in the pedestrian zone in the center of Munich, near the famed Frauenkirche. Although very close to a lot of the tourism and high commerce, Bar Tabacco might be the antithesis of the endlessly fashionable Schumann's. The sign is discreet, and the trendy set aren't necessarily flocking to this bar. But they should be. As should you. Bar Tabacco was founded by a pair of former Schumann's bartenders more than a decade ago, and they serve cocktails that are every bit up to the standards of their former mentor.

Working through the truly epic menu, we sampled a Carabineri (tequila, Galliano liqueur, lime juice, orange juice, egg yolk; €8.50), a Millionaire (bourbon, Cointreau, lemon juice, egg white, grenadine, absinthe wash; €8.50), and a bartender improv (Havana Club 3-year, lime juice, orange juice, Amer Picon; €8.50). Of course, we asked for the Amer Picon to be worked into that one due to the sheer novelty value (it is not imported into the U.S.). See the profile of In Fine Spirits (page 91) in Chicago for more on Amer Picon. Gal Friday Night finished with a Porto Flip (port, brandy, egg white, cream, and nutmeg; €9).

Bar Tabacco is decorated in rich wood paneling, with sconces and chandeliers providing soft light. A row of tables is lined up opposite the bar, which seats about 15. Although primarily a bar, a full menu of food is available from the kitchen of chef Rodney Lockwood. When we visited, Gal Friday Night was far from the only person tackling a full steak dinner right at the bar.

LAST CALL!

More Destinations to Explore in Munich

Opened in 1998 by Mauro Mahjoub, **Negroni Bar** (Sedanstrasse 9; 089.4895.0154; www.negronibar.de) is impressive for its menu of 140 cocktails, including a list of Negroni variants. We may be even more impressed by Mahjoub's collection of a reported 2,000 cocktail books. (We're hoping he's made a space for *Destination: Cocktails* as number 2,001.) This relaxed bar is not as swanky as some, but it is a notch nicer than some others, landing comfortably in the center of the scale. We enjoyed a Negroni Magnifique (gin, Campari, dry vermouth, absinthe; €8), which swaps the sweet vermouth for dry vermouth and adds absinthe. We then sampled a classic Americano (Campari, sweet vermouth), the precursor to the Negroni. It was indeed Count Camillo Negroni who suggested adding gin to an Americano in 1919, and making us all happier for it. The bar also serves a short menu of tasty food.

Pacific Times (Baaderstrasse 28; 089 2023.9470; www.pacifictimes.de) is not far from the opera house, on a street filled with antique stores and shops selling designer dirndls

(traditional Bavarian costume) for upward of €1,000. Andy, the bartender/owner of Pacific Times, opened the restaurant in 1997. The bright and spacious room feels like a colonial home on a French Tahitian plantation. We'd been instructed by local filmmaker Jochen Hirschfeld to ask for a Rum Runner "Jochen's way" (St. James Royal Ambre rum, Havana Club Barrel Proof rum, dashes of Appleton rum and Bacardi Dark rum, Tia Maria coffee liqueur, pineapple juice, Fee's aromatic bitters, orange bitters, garnished with a lil' orange peel, a lil' lime peel, a whole cherry, and some mint). We were glad we did. The free-poured drink was a pretty solid take on a tiki classic, and it definitely fit the theme of the room. The out-of-production Barrel Proof has probably been replaced with the new Selection de Maestro by now.

We also discussed Berlin's bartending styles with Andy. "Munich is stuck on the standards and doesn't experiment or move forward," he said. Conversely, he added, "Berlin walks before they crawl, jumping in to making their own syrups, bitters, etc. before learning the basics of how the classics are constructed." Of course, the topic of Chartreuse came up as well. Andy quipped, "We like Chartreuse, too," and proceeded to pour the Pacific Times variant on a Mary Pickford (Hayman's Old Tom gin, green Chartreuse, soda water, over a muddle of pineapple, sugar, lemon). Yum.

An impressive-looking appetizer platter sets the stage for entrees in the €10–€20 range, which originate from all around the Pacific Rim. Cocktails are €7–€9. The beautiful menu is illustrated with maps of the Pacific.

Speaking of tiki, **Trader Vic's** (Bayerischer Hof Hotel, Promenaderplatz 2–6 München; 089 2120.995; www.bayerischerhof.de) is located on the lower level of the ultra ritzy Bayerischer Hof (Bavarian Court) Hotel, which is often thought of as among Munich's very best flophouses. A fuller look at the Trader Vic's phenomenon can be found in the San Francisco section of this book (see page 231), but we wanted to draw your attention to this particular island in Vic's global archipelago, since it is one of our very favorites (along with Atlanta, Emeryville, and Tokyo). It is about half a block from Bar Tabacco.

VIENNA

Vienna, the land of Mozart, Beethoven, and Ultravox, is home to plenty of places to wind up spiflicated. Barfly's is first among them as a conspicuously copacetic starting point.

Barfly's

Hotel Fürst Metternich
Esterházygasse 33
Vienna
01.586.0825
www.barflys.at

Can any one bar emphasize quality and quantity equally? Barfly's in Vienna makes a case for a resounding affirmative. Just off of the congested shopping street Mariahilfer Straße, among a quiet row of Viennese houses, you'll find the Hotel Fürst Metternich (Prince Metternich), built in 1897. Inside the fin-de-siècle edifice is a bar that stocks a reported 1,200 whiskeys and 480 rums. Those are put to very good use in the cocktail menu, which contains about 250 selections sorted by base liquor, with historical commentary provided for the bulk of them. Cocktails run €7–€11 and consist mainly of classics. Given the hootchtopia at your fingertips at Barfly's, it almost seems like a shame to order a cocktail when there are so many unique opportunities available for sipping uncommon and rare spirits neat.

Rat-pack era jazz commonly fills the air in the deco-inspired bar room, and photos of Frank Sinatra and Dean Martin adorn the walls near a humidor full of Cuban cigars. The only food served at Barfly's are small warm sandwiches referred to as "toasts" (€5).

Long-time barman Mario Castillo, who had been at Barfly's since it opened in 1989, died unexpectedly in 2010. His widow, Melanie Castillo, now runs the urbane bar.

COPENHAGEN

Copenhagen, the land of Legos, Vikings, and King Diamond, is home to plenty of places to explore the possibilities within your glass, but we're just going to introduce you to one. It's the cat's pajamas, and this is simply a place to begin. There are others.

Ruby

Nybrogade
1203 København
(45.33) 93.12.03
www.rby.dk

Many bars will try to make you feel at home, but what we really like are bars that are *in* someone's home. Or could be, anyway. No, we're not talking about your buddy's basement rec room here, but we may as well be. Ruby takes up two floors of an apartment block in central Copenhagen. The rest of the building is home to private residences and to the Georgian embassy. The front door of the 18th-century townhouse is unlocked during business hours, so you won't need to ring the ambassador's doorbell to get in.

The ground floor of Ruby is decorated in a manner befitting the Georgian ambassador's neighbors, with gilt-edged mirrors, oriental rugs, Chesterfield sofas, taxidermy, and fresh flowers. Big windows provide a great view of the Bertel Thorvaldsen museum and the Folketinget (national parliament). Essentially, Ruby feels as though you're hanging out in your wealthy pal's wealthier uncle's place. Gal Friday Night, who was born on a goat farm near Tbilisi, tried to visit the Georgian ambassador, and reports that his pad is decorated in Lucite furniture, shag carpeting, op art, and lava lamps, but we haven't confirmed this. We can confirm that the basement level of Ruby was once a bank vault, has just three seats at the bar, a few small booths, and wingback chairs around glass-fronted cabinets full of firewater.

The bar was opened in autumn of 2007, and is considered a forerunner of the emerging Copenhagen cocktail community. The menu changes four times a year, and is big on classics like the Blood and Sand, the Martinez, and the Silk Stockings. House creations include the Rita & Ruby (house-infused licorice root tequila, lime juice, house-made rhubarb syrup), the Devil's Apricot (Sagatiba Velha cachaça, apricot brandy, lime juice, apricot pureé, Old Decanter's bitters), the Muircock (Black Grouse whisky, yellow Chartreuse, sage, honey, lemon juice, Chartreuse Elixir Vegetal, orange zest), and the Burnt Fig (Hennessy VS cognac, Peter Heering coffee liqueur, muddled with caramelized fig and fig syrup, topped with cream and nutmeg).

Ruby also hosts Spirit Sessions in the basement, a combination of alcohol appreciation classes and mixology school. Rumors that the Georgian ambassador was down there learning about Fernet are wholly unsubstantiated.

LAST CALL!

More Destinations to Explore in Copenhagen

Working with partner Morten Drastrup, British mixologist Gromit Eduardsen opened **1105** (Kristen Bernikows Gade 4; 45.33.93.11.05; 1105.dk) in 2008, after running the bar at the Hotel Fox and a tiki bar that didn't last. Their house cocktail is the Number 4, which is a classic Bee's Knees with added cardamom and black pepper. Eduardsen also won a competition sponsored by Peter Heering in August of 2009. The goal: Use Peter Heering cherry liqueur (made in Denmark since 1818), to create the Copenhagen, a cocktail that might define the city (as in a Manhattan or a Toronto). Eduardsen's winning combination is Bols genever, Cherry Heering liqueur, lime juice, simple syrup, and Angostura Bitters.

You should also visit **The Union** (Storstrandstraede 18; 45.41.19.69.76; www.theunionbar.dk). In keeping with the theme of Brits opening American-style cocktail bars in Denmark, Newcastle native Paul Muldowney has mandated that no post-1940 music be heard in his bar. After finding the bar and buzzing the doorbell for admission (no sleeping ambassadors here!), you'll find vintage maps sourced from France, and a New York-style tin ceiling. From a menu packed with 1920s American slang, try gangster cocktails like the Double-Cross (cognac, apricot brandy, Amaretto almond liqueur, lemon juice) and the Bootleg (champagne, burbon-infused gunpowder tea).

ZURICH

There is no shortage of places to tie one on in Zurich, the land of yodeling, shipwrecked Georgian-era families, and Arnold Böcklin. Here's your best place to start. It's the bee's knees, and there are more.

The Widder Bar

The Widder Hotel
Widdergasse 6
Zurich
44.224.2411
www.widderhotel.ch

Many lounges will hire a designer to supply decor, but the Widder Bar outdoes them all; the room is like a who's-who of 20th-century design. Opened in the 1970s, the Widder Hotel is made up of nine government-protected historic houses, stitched together and connected within. Strewn throughout the 42 rooms are furnishings by unknowns like Mies ven der Rohe, Charles and Ray Eames, Frank Lloyd Wright, Adolf Loos, and Le Courbusier. Y'know, no one important. And who is this Warhol guy? The five-star hotel caters to the bankers and art dealers arriving in central Zurich on business, or wealthy tourists, typically in their thirties or older.

Translating the name and address into English, we have the Ram Bar in the Ram Hotel on Ram Lane. Naturally, there is a big wooden statue of an anthropomorphized ram in the bar. Sure it's armless and female, but if you're gonna put an animal's head on a human body, who are we to argue if you want to go all Venus de Milo on us? This is Zurich, after all, birthplace of Dadaism. Marcel Duchamp would approve. Doctor Moreauisms aside, the beautiful space is decorated with walnut tables, a lovely curved bar, and amazing carved ceiling beams that are centuries old. You'll also see—and hear—a grand piano that is used for live jazz, ranging from notable touring jazz artists each spring and autumn, to

lounge-kitsch acts singing bossa nova and 1960s light pop tunes.

But you're here for the firewater, and you will not be disappointed. The bar has somehow crammed one thousand bottles of hootch onto their back wall. Comprising a quarter of those thousand bottles, the Scotch collection is one of the best in Europe. Sample an Ardbeg 1965 for $815, if you dare. House cocktails include the Hellboy (Islay single malt Scotch whisky, Frangelico hazelnut liqueur, chili-honey syrup) and the Garden & Tonic (gin, mint, cucumber, maraschino liqueur, celery bitters, tonic water).

The sophisticated traveler gets just as hungry as the hoi polloi; a menu of bar snacks includes a burger with foie gras. The bar is also a popular spot for the cigar set.

LAST CALL!
Another Destination to Explore in Zurich

You must also hit the bar at the **Restaurant Kronenhalle** (Rämistrasse 4; 262.99.11; www.kronenhalle.com). A masterful art deco bar sits opposite a wall displaying original works by Miró and Klee, hung along mahogany panels above plush black leather banquettes. Giacometti designed the lamps and tables. The restaurant dates from 1862 and rocks more art by Picasso, Chagall, Hodler, and Matisse in the various dining rooms. Do you think the contemporary painters and writers of Zurich chill here? Only the ones who can afford it. We sampled the Kronenhalle Spezial (gin, Cointreau, apricot brandy, grapefruit juice). Cocktails run €18–€20, and you can't afford dinner.

MELBOURNE

The bars of the entire southern hemisphere are probably best represented in the two island nations of Australia and New Zealand. Let's begin our exploration of this region in Melbourne.

Black Pearl

304 Brunswick Street
Fitzroy
613.9417.0455

We have it on good authority that a lot of the slow cocktail bars in the world get pretty sick of continually being asked if they serve Coors beer or Cosmopolitans. For the most part, they don't. But we wonder whether or not it is even more tedious for a bar to be continually asked if they're named after a fictional pirate ship. Black Pearl is on Brunswick Street in the Melbourne suburb of Fitzroy. As far as we know, you will not find Keira Knightley there. The bar is just one of many on the busy nightlife strip, but it is the leader of the bunch when it comes to cocktails. Plush and cozy seating around low tables give Black Pearl an intimate vibe during the week, but on weekends, when all of Brunswick Street gets swamped with revelers, Black Pearl may be as raucous as any of the other bars on the strip.

There is some food available here, but Black Pearl is a bar first and foremeost. In fact, it is two bars. After the decade-old business underwent a 2011 renovation, the main bar on the ground floor was joined by a second space upstairs. Called the Attic, this space is quieter and more relaxed than the main room downstairs. For admission, you'll need to ring a doorbell at the end of a hallway. Once inside, you may be greeted by Chris Hysted. His Diversity Cocktail (Bowmore's 12-year Scotch whisky, yellow Chartreuse, Suntory Lena banana liqueur; $22) juxtaposes the solid Scotch selection with the potentially cheesy banana liqueur and makes it work. The Lena banana liqueur is infrequently seen in North America, and is made by Suntory, who are also responsible for the more common

Midori melon liqueur, as well as other fruit liqueur flavors. Suntory also distills a substantial profile of whiskeys, including Yamazaki, which became the first-ever Japanese whiskey in 1924.

But back to Australia here. Ground-level barmen include Rob Libecans and Cristiano Beretta, who created the Finsbury Cocktail (Tanqueray 10 gin, Domain de Canton ginger liqueur, pink grapefruit juice, lemon juice, mango simple syrup, egg white). We also like their take on the classic Zombie, which they call a Whisk(e)y Zombie, served in a huge rum bucket decorated Maori-style. The traditional blend of rums has been replaced by several whiskeys that less skilled shaker monkeys have no business even putting on the same shelf, let alone in the same shaker.

Der Raum

348 Church Street
Richmond
613.9428.0055
www.derraum.com.au

Calling something, anything, "the best" in its idiom is a bold statement, and the person making it had better be ready to back it up. The Bowery in Brisbane (see page 370) has been called the best bar in Australia several times, but Der Raum, near Melbourne, has been offered the title of best bar in the *world* (by a website coincidentally called "World's Best Bars"). Of course, this makes us wonder why it isn't also the best bar in Australia (sorry, Bowery), but we'll leave that puzzle to the Aussies.

This begs the question: what makes a bar "the best"? We know people whose local shot 'n' beer corner pub is the best bar in the world, as far as they're concerned. Their buddies are there, the bartender is cute, and they get a free round now and then. For other people, the best bar in the world serves an absolutely immaculate traditional Manhattan, and for others, the best bar in the world is doing mind-blowing "molecular mixology," presenting their cocktails as popsicles or something. If molecular is your bag, then Der Raum (who don't especially like being pigeonholed as "molecular") might indeed be the best bar in the world (although Grant Aschatz of Chicago's Aviary might disagree).

Der Raum currently requires a membership for admittance,

although non-members are admitted if capacity allows. Visitors might choose to order one of the bar's *dégustation* menus, either the Tour de Force ($140 for eight drinks) or Tourist Route ($80 for five drinks). À la carte cocktails are generally $20–$22. In any case, Bunsen burners, beakers, and smoke machines might be involved, and you may or may not end up sampling a cocktail called Pharmacy. Brought to you on a silver tray, this one is made with pear and roasted capsicum gin, served in a bottle along with a syringe filled with Aperol aperitif, and a pill made of citrus sherbet. Inject the Aperol, pop in the pill, shake it up, and you've got a drink. Capsicum, by the way, is the plant that provides cayenne pepper.

Along the same lines of presentation is the Jamaican Blackstrap, served in a bottle within a paper bag. The Bax Beet Pinot comes in a wine bottle, but is actually a cocktail of Carpano Antica Formula vermouth, Fernet-Branca amaro, and smoked beetroot. Another "molecular" style drink is the Toreador (Ocho blanco tequila, lime, apricot liqueur, agave nectar). This is essentially a Margarita, but with the addition of a ladle of liquid nitrogen, the drink is flash-frozen into a sorbet. Der Raum is capable of keeping things simple, however, such as in their classic Crusta Reserva (Pampero Seleccion 1938 rum, maraschino liqueur, lemon juice, pineapple juice).

The bar's creativity and commitment to serving the best product possible extends to the ingredients themselves. Der Raum makes their own gin, an array of bitters, all of their syrups and cordials, and their own vermouth. Any drinks containing fruit juices are only available when the fruit is in season. On the flipside, they've got a blacklist of ingredients that they absolutely won't use, such as cream, Malibu rum, Red Bull energy drink, and Southern Comfort whiskey. For the most part, we're solidly in agreement, but their no-cream rule does sort of rule out the Ramos Gin Fizz, does it not?

Der Raum ("the Room" in German) was opened in 2001 by owner-bartender-artist Matthew Bax, who also owns the Tippling Club in Singapore. The decor is fairly simple, perhaps so as not to draw attention away from the striking presentation of the drinks themselves. The most unique visual feature in the room is the arrangement of the actual booze bottles. They're all hanging from the ceiling, suspended on bungee cords. Similarly, the menus are chained to the bar, but that's probably to curtail souvenir collectors.

So, is Der Raum really the best bar in the world? Gal Friday Night, daughter of a bona-fide Zen master, reminds us to always be present in the moment. All you need is now. If there is a solidly made cocktail, a decent atmosphere, and a good friend with us, we're pretty happy to be wherever we are. So, during your time at Der Raum, it may indeed be the best bar in the world.

LAST CALL!
More Destinations to Explore in Melbourne

Joining Black Pearl in the Fitzroy area are some other bars that we have heard good things about, including **The Everleigh** (150–156 Gertrude Street, Fitzroy; 9416.2229; www.theeverleigh.com), **Kodiak Club** (272 Brunswick Street, Fitzroy; 3194.7910; www.kodiakclub.com.au), and **I Know A Place** (451 Brunswick Street, Fitzroy; 1503.0974). At the latter, ask bartendrix Sarah Miller for the classic Morning Glory Fizz (Scotch whisky, absinthe, lemon juice, sugar, egg white). First mentioned in print in George Kappeler's *Modern American Drinks* (1895), you can chase it with one of the seven styles of gourmet hot dogs available on the bar's back patio.

Back in Melbourne proper (as opposed to suburban Fitzroy), you'll definitely want to visit **1806** (169 Exhibition Street; 9663.7722; www.1806.com.au), which is named after the year the word "cocktail" was first mentioned in print. In keeping with the theme, their fantastic menu lists at least one cocktail from every decade of the past two centuries, and provides some historical perspective about each. The elegant bar also has a short menu of snacks. Don't let the brevity of this blurb fool you. Go there.

Your best bet for daytime drinks is **Madame Brussels** (59–63 Bourke Street, Level 3; 9662.2775; www.madamebrussels.com), where you'll want to play croquet on a fourth-floor rooftop's AstroTurf lawn. The real Madame Brussels was born in Prussia in 1851, as Caroline Baum. She went on to own a string of brothels on British soil, eventually finding herself in Melbourne. The bar named in her honor serves food like cucumber sandwiches, cupcakes, fondue, and macaroons, with a cocktail menu that is conspicuously focused on Pimm's. Pimm's Cup is sold by the pitcher, in fact. We were told that they go through 40 cases of Pimm's per month. With tongue fully in cheek, the feminine space is decorated in cast iron patio furniture, a preppy male staff in white shorts and polo shirts, and a trellised and hedged bar.

Madame Brussels is an English garden party happening full-time and presided over by one Miss Pearls. Ladies will want to wear their vintage 1950s sundresses. The gentlemen of Madame Brussels's era would have needed a den to retreat to; look for the more private Parlour, where the rare hootch is kept. They focus on the brown stuff, with 20 rare rums featured.

BRISBANE

The capital of Queensland, temperate and booming Brisbane is home to plenty of places to discover the cause of, and solution to, all of life's problems. Here is the first of many; it's a doozy, and it's just a starting point.

The Bowery

676 Ann Street
Fortitude Valley
617.3252.0202
www.thebowery.com.au

After returning to Australia from working in Japan and New York, respectively, Cam Birt and Stephanie Canfell opened the Bowery in October of 2003. They wanted to give Brisbane a true classic-styled cocktail bar, serving recipes from the pre-1930s canon prepared to the highest standards, but in a casual and friendly atmosphere. We like the way these people think. At the time, Brisbane's trends were in the same place as many other global cities—bars were doing Caipirinha and Mojito variants, and the odd infusion. No doubt inspired by Canfell's experiences in New York, the pair opened the Bowery, more or less launching the craft cocktail movement in Brisbane. In the ensuing years, many Queenslanders have followed in the footsteps of Birt and Canfell, going on to open their own bars, or to elevate the cocktail programs in existing bars. The Bowery, then, is very much akin to the Violet Hour in Chicago or Pegu Club in New York; it's a place that tends to innovate while inspiring the city's cocktail community, acting as a breeding ground for new talent like alumni Mathew Hewitt, Shay Leighton, and Daniel Gregory.

Drinks at the Fortitude Valley-area bar average $16, and may be selected from an exhaustive four-volume menu. Of course, all juices are pressed daily, but the Bowery is also proud of its policy of using only premium spirits in all cocktails, and of using the oldest and most original version of any given recipe. All of its bar staff are full-time employees, guaranteeing a commitment to the quality and consistency of an experience at the Bowery.

The bar hosts live jazz on weeknights, and features DJs on Fridays and Saturdays. The crowds you'll find in the bar tend to be in keeping with the music; weekends will be younger and more festive, whereas early on a weeknight, you may find people reading, or regulars chatting with the bartenders.

Birt and Canfell opened their second bar, the **Sky Room** (234 Wickham Street, Level 2, Fortitude Valley; 3852.6337; www.skyroom.com.au), in January 2009. Cocktails by Mathew Hewitt and Barry Chalmers ($16–$22) are served in a casual room filled with retro 1950s-style furniture. We like the chartreuse upholstery, the dark polished wood, the lil' indoor palm trees, and the stylish young customers grooving to techno. Gal Friday Night went for the Lemongrass Lassie (pisco, lemongrass, lemon sugar, condensed milk, egg white, bitters). Like the Bowery, Sky Room serves no food, but the Buffalo Club restaurant is on the ground floor, right below the bar. Chow at Buffalo Club is from none other than chef Ryan Squires of French Laundry, San Francisco's perennial holder of three Michelin stars.

LAST CALL!
More Destinations to Explore in Brisbane

Canvas (16b Logan Road, Woolloongabba; 3892.2111; www.canvasclub.com.au) is a stylish bistro with a solid menu of tapas and cocktails, such as the Vasquez (Ron Zacapa 23-year, maraschino liqueur, Tagliatella, coconut water ice sphere; $19). Tagliatella is a grappa-based liqueur that shouldn't be confused with the type of pasta that shares its name. Don't miss Thursday Absinthe Hour, and Tapas & Tequila Tuesday.

Whiskey fans will want make a stop at **The Lark** (1/267 Given Terrace, Paddington; 3369.1299; www.thelark.com. au). Owner-bartender Perry Scott keeps at least 50 whiskies on hand, and offers flights. The cheeky menu labels drinks as "org." or "clas." and offers pronunciations for drinks like the Sazerac ("saz-er-rack") and the Lark Mimosa ("lark-memo-sa"). Cocktails are $13–$20. Lark also serves dinner selections, including dukkah spiced chicken skewers ($23) and quail saltimbocca ($18).

SYDNEY

Boomerangs, Vegemite, and a certain opera house. Forget these clichés; forward-thinking Sydney is joining Melbourne and Brisbane to make Australia the best place in the southern hemisphere to grab a tipple.

A ustralian bars seem to like to accumulate awards; the Bowery and Der Raum have been deemed either the best in the country or the best in the world, depending on

Eau de Vie

Kirketon Hotel
229 Darlinghurst Road
Darlinghurst
614.2226.3226
www.eaudevie.com.au

whom you choose to listen to. Eau de Vie, hidden deep in the recesses of the Kirketon Hotel, continues Australia's winning streak. It has been called the best *new* bar in the world by both *Gourmet Traveller* and *Bartender* magazine in 2010 and 2011, respectively.

Owners Sven and Amber Almenning opened the bar in early 2010. You'll have to wander through a lobby labyrinth to find it (watch out for the minotaur; he's been drinking tequila), but you'll be glad to have made the effort. The bar is decorated in a comfortable manner that befits a secluded hotel lounge: candles, antique crystal decanters, a few art deco details, Royal Doulton tumblers, Chesterfield lounges, teacups perched atop stemware, and globes of the Old World. Yeah, that's plural: *globes.* Flanking a grandfather clock. If you think you got lost looking for the place, these will remind you of your position in both time and space, and in both cases they're telling you that you're in the past.

While they do serve examples of the family of fruit brandies for which Eau de Vie is named (*eau de vie* also translates literally to "water of life"), the bar is happy to serve from a lengthy menu of classic cocktails. The good old Southside (Tanqueray No. Ten gin, mint, lime juice, simple syrup; $17) is always dependable. Sticking

with the gin theme for the moment, bartender Luke Redington's nod to Australia's love for beer is the popular Bloomsbury Bitter (Tanqueray No. Ten gin, amaro, yellow Chartreuse, white grapefruit juice, "beer" syrup, egg white, soda, grapefruit zest oils, dandelion bitters). Redington is joined behind the stick by a welcoming and service-oriented bunch, including Barry Chalmers (of Brisbane's the Bowery and Sky Room), Elle Wormald, Max Greco, and Calum Lawrie.

We thought we heard at least one Scottish accent among that crew, so it might explain the Scotch cocktails that keep appearing. Scotch can be hard to mix with, but Eau de Vie's staff seem to like the challenge, coming up with inventions like the Robbie duh Sprung (Glenfiddich 12-year Scotch whisky, thyme, Peychaud's bitters, quince liqueur, wormwood, lemon zest, rosemary) and the Grounds for Divorce (Talisker 10-year Scotch whisky, walnut liqueur, crème de cacao, James Squire porter beer).

The rest of the menu is subdivided into cocktails for sharing, edible cocktails, famous cocktails from other Australian bars, and just a little bit of food.

Rockpool Bar & Grill

66 Hunter Street
Sydney
612.8078.1900
www.rockpool.com

You've got your places styled after 19th-century saloons, you've got your sleek trendy lounges, you've got your hip dives, and you've got your mid-century modern jet-age rocket fuel depots, but there's always just an extra layer of awesome at play when you're sipping a perfect cocktail surrounded by art deco environs. If you're picking up what we're laying down, then Rockpool in Sydney wins the awesome award. The runner-up, by the way, is the bar in the **Hilton Cincinnati Netherland Plaza** (35 West Fifth Street, Cincinnati, OH; 513.421.9100; www.cincinnatihilton.com). Seriously. But their drinks aren't as good as Rockpool's.

Chef and co-owner Neil Perry opened his first deluxe steakhouse in Melbourne before expanding to Perth and then to an amazing 12-story green marble building in Sydney. When architect Emil Sodersteen put up this wonder in 1936, it was the tallest building in town. In some ways, it still is. Check out the ceiling: Benzoni's *Flight from Pompeii* as rendered in relief by Rayner Hoff. The building was erected as the City Mutual Life Assurance Society, but what we can assure you now is that Perry will sell you a $110 wagyu sirloin steak, a bacon-Gruyère wagyu cheeseburger, or a variety of small plates for sharing. The restaurant also has a reported nine million dollars worth of wine (a reported 3,800 labels), and 45 seats at the bar. When I stumbled in, Gal Friday Night was saving me one of those seats. We got busy with mixologist Linden Pride's cocktail menu.

Call me a Dick, but I had to order an A Schooner Darkly (Trumer Pils beer, Amer Bière beer, Aperol aperitif; $15), while my companion went for the Almond Sidecar (fat washed Hennessy VSOP, Cointreau, orgeat, lemon juice). This one was created in Gal Friday Night's hometown by Eben Freeman of New York's fondly missed Tailor. From the selection of classics, the Manhattan Deluxe (Tuthilltown Hudson Manhattan rye, sweet vermouth, Angostura bitters) might have provided another taste of home, but at $55, we opted to taste the Tuthilltown on thriftier shores at a later date. We were relieved to see our old pal Jack Rose (Laird's applejack, house-made pomegranate syrup, lime juice; $17), who as you may know was once a Peruvian Shoe Maker (Peruvian pisco, plum pisco, Steve's falernum, citrus, sparkling wine; $17).

WELLINGTON

New Zealand, the Land of the Long White Cloud and home of tuataras, moko, and Split Enz, is also home to one jim-dandy Wellington classic. This is your starting point. There are more. Just pay careful attention when planning your Australia/New Zealand pub crawl; there's the small matter of 1,500 miles and the Tasman Sea to navigate between them. Taxis are hard to get out there.

Matterhorn

106 Cuba Street
Wellington
4384.3359
www.matterhorn.co.nz

New Zealand is a special kind of place. The bottom of the world. One of the last major landmasses on the earth to be settled. No stranger to conflict, this is the kind of place where the bartenders infuse their rum with gunpowder. Yeah, seriously, let the puns fly—this drink will blow your mind. We are sure that former co-owner Ben Simpson has heard it all, but still, this man infuses his own Man o' War gunpowder rum. That's rum with tobacco, chilies, and real gunpowder. The gunpowder is what gives it that kick. Right. This is New Zealand, mister.

Matterhorn was opened in 1963 in a modernist building owned by two Swiss brothers who were the first to bring espresso and fondue to New Zealand. The business was then sold to a Polish family, which then sold it to a Greek family. The venerable restaurant teetered between iconic and kitschy status until it was finally bought and revitalized by a team of four investors in 1997. By 2007, Matterhorn had begun racking up mixology awards, and was sold again in 2011 to another quintet: Sam Ansley, Simon Ansley, Mark Keddell, Matt Bould, and Kate Prangnell. Although redecorated several times over the years, Matterhorn still maintains some original mid-century touches, such as Danish modern-style room dividers

and simple wooden chairs that might have been in the room since 1963. Live music includes jazz, soul, and funk, plus DJ nights.

Matterhorn boasts 300 wines from the Old and New Worlds, plus a collection of 200 spirits, passionately sourced from around the world by the bar staff. Liqueurs, bitters, and infusions are all made in-house. Around 70 cocktails make up a list divided into preprandial, classics, smokers', mentors', and other categories.

Always a fan of the classic Death in the Afternoon, the well-read Gal Friday Night wanted Matterhorn's take, the Blackberry Death in the Afternoon (blackberries macerated in La Fée absinthe, Duval Leroy 96 champagne; $22). The Sazerac (Proprietary Style) looked good, but at $32 for the combo of Sazerac brand 18-year rye, La Fée absinthe, Peychaud's bitters, and sugar, we opted instead for the Smoked Peach Rob Roy (Ardbeg 10-year Scotch whisky, peach liqueur, Rosso Antica vermouth, peach bitters; $17).

While we're thinking of drinks invented by authors (in theory, we heartily approve) the mentors' list contains Gary Regan's DAM aka the Reluctant Tabby Cat (Dolin sweet vermouth, limoncello, Laphroaig 10-year Scotch whisky; $16) and Robert Hess's Petrucio (Beefeater gin, Aperol aperitif, the Macallan 12-year Scotch whisky; $16). Always with the Scotch . . .

There is no doubt in our minds that there are a whole lot of other bars to explore in Wellington, not to mention in Auckland, Christchurch, and elsewhere. But if you need further diversion after a visit to Matterhorn, we've heard good things about **Motel Bar** (2 Forresters Lane; 4384.9084; www.motelbar.co.nz), and are intrigued by the Asian-themed **Ancestral** (31–33 Courtenay Place; 4801.8867; www.ancestral.co.nz).

TOKYO

Do not miss cocktails in Tokyo. The recipes there are usually based on the American classic canon, but are scaled-down in size; most drinks end up around two ounces or so in total, as opposed to three or four ounce pours in the West. The bulk of the best bars are in the flashy Ginza area, but in a city of 13 million, there's going to be a few other zones where a restorative can be found. To really understand the Japanese bars, flip ahead a few pages and begin by reading about Tender Bar.

Bar High Five

26 Polestar Building, 4th floor
7-2-14 Ginza
Tokyo
81-3/3571.5815

Ginza was once known for "hostess bars," where a wealthy gent might find an elegantly dressed female companion. Today, the Asian ladies of Ginza are far more respectable, but visitors may still enjoy the company of a White Lady. You see, at Bar High Five, owner and bartender Hidetsugu Ueno (formerly of Star Bar Ginza) has made the classic White Lady, a gin-based Sidecar variant (London dry gin, Cointreau, lemon juice), his house specialty.

Like all Japanese bartenders, Ueno maintains a focus on precision and presentation. One really has to visit Japan to truly understand how much their sense of aesthetics matters. When presented with a gift, the wrapping may be of equal importance as the contents. *Ikebana* (flower arranging) is a highly-regarded art form, and the color of a cocktail is as important as the taste. The ideal Japanese cocktail is a pastel shade; more saturated colors are less revered. So, at Bar High Five, your White Lady will arrive presented perfectly, with everything from the hard shake (see Tender Bar, page 383) to the napkin placement carefully considered and meticulously executed.

The cozy Bar High Five seats about a dozen at the bar, with one small booth available. As is the case with most of the Tokyo bars, the close environs mean personal service, often from the owner. Exploring the cocktail options at Bar High Five a bit further, we see that Ueno has a penchant for fresh fruit. Classics like the Piña Colada and the Singapore Sling (traditionally: gin, Cherry Heering, Bénédictine, pineapple juice) are always made with fresh Sarawak pineapple, while their classic Bellini (peach purée, prosecco, sometimes lemon juice or peach brandy) uses the freshest peaches. A further popular favorite at Bar High Five is the aperitif-style Bamboo (sherry, vermouth, orange bitters). There's a bit of Spain in this bamboo; the sherry is aerated by a bartender who is also a bona-fide venenciador (a practitioner of sherry aeration who pours it into a glass from another vessel held much higher). High five!

L et us discuss the kings and let us discuss the peasants. Small and grubby Kinguramu may seem like one of the peasants at first glance, but after perusing their rum collection, you'll

Kinguramu (Bar King Rum)

Otaya Building, 1st floor
2-9-1 Ikebukuro
Tokyo
81-3/3980.2903
www.kingrum.jp

understand why they're cheeky enough to declare themselves king.

Kinguramu has the unusual advantage of being on a major avenue in young and hip Ikebukuro, with a street-level entrance all its own. The gritty bar contains just one small booth and seven bar stools, providing a total seating capacity of about a dozen. It is almost completely free of anything that might point to the past or present presence of a decorator. But Bar King Rum is where rums go to die. There are so many bottles here that they don't all fit behind the bar, so they rest in clusters on the bar counter itself. Right in front of us on the bar top was an ancient bottle of St. James, a Trois Rivieres 1953, a Saint Etienne, and a bottle with a hand-printed label on it: "Rhum Vieux dans Reserve, Albert Go-defoy, 50cl, 45°." Godefoy makes good rum, but we're not sure what this one was . . . or if we could *handle* knowing. Their Damoiseau 1953 was tucked away more securely elsewhere.

We settled on an XYZ, a popular choice in Japanese cocktail bars, made here with Havana Club rum (the unaged blanco, unfortunately), Cointreau, and lemon juice. It was mixed a little on the tart side (and I generally like my drinks like I like my women—tarty and boozy), but with a hair less lemon and a bit better rum it could be a winner. The only thing for it after that would be to try some Japanese rums. Bar King Rum has five of them: Rurikakesu, King Rum, Cor Cor, Cor Cor Agricole, and Omiki. There is also a rum from India called Old Nonk, as well as the expected array of Caribbean and Central/South American products. The bar's namesake rum seemed to be the one to try (¥735, or about $9.50 for a 1 oz. pour), while Gal Friday Night sampled the Cor Cor Agricole (¥945, or about $12). This is made in Okinawa (South Borodino Island, Minamidaito) by three women who make all of the product themselves.

Most of the bars in Tokyo levy a "seating charge" (or variant thereof), often equal to the price of a drink; our bill at Kinguramu was padded with the sketchy ¥500 seating charge. Some bars *also* add a questionable sliding-scale tax that *gaijin* (outsiders) only seem to be hit with; we were often charged 5, 10, or 15 percent "tax," but it was always less when we were with locals. At Kinguramu, it was 10 percent. Fortunately, you are not usually required to tip.

◆━━━◆━━━◆

Kuroitsuki (Black Moon)

33-10, Udagawacho, 3rd floor
Shibuya
Tokyo
81-3/3498.2089
www.kuroitsuki.jp

Forget those trendy American "speakeasies." Tokyo has thousands of tiny, hidden cocktail bars that no cop (or customer!) could ever hope to find. In fact, they almost seem to dare you to find them. For every Bar High Five or Tender Bar, there are 15 little holes

in the wall making perfectly worthy cocktails completely under the radar. And we mean *completely*.

Kuroitsuki is our case-study example. The contact who sent us there described it as being on the third floor of an otherwise completely generic office building, and told us that the door to the bar had no signs on it whatsoever. After stumbling around the same block for an hour, we discovered an unmarked copper door in a cramped and tiny cinderblock hallway on the third floor of another of Tokyo's endless identical office buildings. That's Tokyo for you, folks. Get used to it. Hint: it is across the street from the Tokyu Honten department store in Shibuya.

All of the walls are untreated concrete, cold and industrial looking. Only the bar top and some concealed storage areas are made of any other material—the same copper sheeting that covers the door. When we arrived, there was one customer in the place, as well as owner and bartender Nitta Rikako with her dog, Koshu. A small stereo in the corner was softly playing some music that we later realized was the 1960s lineup of King Crimson. On vinyl. *This* we did not expect.

Rikako is a real cocktail aficionado, and from her tiny, dim, coldly decorated cave, she pours from a solid little selection of whiskeys and a carefully curated assortment of gins, rums, and tequilas. Rikako does not speak a word of English, but she does speak Negroni. Ours was perfectly presented in an intricately-etched vintage glass (¥1,000 or about $13). Gal Friday Night had red wine, which was served with 1848-brand 86 percent cacao French chocolate. A very nice pairing.

How do these places stay open? How can anyone even know they are there? No one would ever choose this nondescript building, wander up three flights of stairs at random, and then decide to pull open an unmarked door just to see if there happened to be a cocktail bar in there.

And yet, places like this are all over Tokyo. Go find 'em!

Star Bar Ginza

Sankosha Building, Basement 1
1-5-13 Ginza
Tokyo
81-3/3535.8005
www.starbar.jp

You know you're in for a serious liquid treat when your bartender is also the director of technical research for the Nippon Bartenders Association. *Director of technical research.* For a bar. Let that sink in. Some people might say that the ability to properly mix a cocktail is not exactly rocket science. Hisashi Kishi, owner of Star Bar Ginza, might disagree. From ice temperatures to stirring angles, the Japanese obsession with precision is quantified to ever deeper degrees, to more decimal places if you will, as the minutiae of their craft is recorded, refined, and repeated.

Hisashi Kishi opened Star Bar Ginza in 2000, and the subterranean hideaway is perhaps second only to Tender Bar in its international notoriety. Like so many other Ginza bars, cocktails here are lil' versions of Western classics. Each Ginza bar seems to have staked a claim on one recipe in particular to be recognized as the house drink. In the case of Star Bar Ginza, they're known for the venerable Sidecar (¥2,100 or about $27). Invented some time before 1922 (possibly during World War I), several institutions take credit for the drink, including Harry's American Bar in Paris. This simple blend of cognac, Cointreau, and lemon juice is a perfect vehicle for Japanese deconstruction and reconstruction. Note that when Hidetsugu Ueno left Star Bar Ginza to open High Five Bar, he went on to perfect the White Lady (as discussed above), which is essentially a Sidecar with gin instead of cognac.

Most other cocktails (including the Gimlet, the Mojito, and the Martini) will set you back ¥1,575 to ¥1,875 (about $20.50 to $24), including an array of seasonal fresh fruit-based libations at ¥1,785–¥2,835 ($23 to $37).

Another swell Japanism is at work at Star Bar Ginza—when mixing a drink, the bartender (such as lead drink slinger Hidetsugu) will always place the bottles for all of the ingredients right on the bar, labels carefully turned toward the customer for inspection. It is always fun to see details like this (not to mention techniques like the hard shake; see Tender Bar, page 383) make their way over the Pacific to North America. This is becoming more common, but there's nothing like seeing this species of bartender doing their thing *in situ*—on their home turf.

Snacks at Star Bar Ginza include handmade chocolates, cheese (a rarity for Japan), and a Japanese form of charcuterie, which is sometimes the result of Hidetsugu curing the meat himself. Seating charge is ¥1,000 (about $13).

Associated with Star Bar Ginza is **Land Bar** (1st floor, 6-4-7 Ginza, Tokyo; 81-3/3571-8090). This tiny (surprise) bar is presided over by Ito Daisuke.

There are two types of bar in the world, those owned by living legends, and those owned by mere mortals, simple proletariats with delusions of grandeur at best. Thus forewarned, I'd like to introduce you to the former, one of the best cocktail bars in the world: Tender Bar. This one is right on Sotobori-dori, the main road in the heart of spendy Ginza. As is the case with even the most high-profile businesses in Tokyo, this one is way up on the fifth floor of an office building. Their sign, also sticking out of the building on

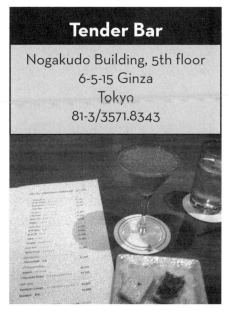

Tender Bar

Nogakudo Building, 5th floor
6-5-15 Ginza
Tokyo
81-3/3571.8343

the fifth floor, is easy to miss. Inside, the bar is diminutive but relaxed, plush, and quiet.

The owner is the distinguished Kazuo Uyeda, winner of a dizzying array of world bartending trophies, some of which are displayed behind his bar. Inventor of the Japanese "hard shake" technique, he is truly the lord of this room, a bona-fide *sensei* (honored master) held in awe and respect by his underlings. During our visit, two guys in their thirties were occasionally allowed to make a drink when the master deemed them worthy, while a younger guy (perhaps college age) was the new apprentice. He had been working at Tender Bar for four years, and has yet to serve a single drink to a customer. He told us that he practices making drinks at home every night, using the lessons he has learned at work each day to improve his skills. He doesn't drink a drop of it. While perusing a menu of 16 house original cocktails, we asked the lad if he had ever invented a drink of his own. He looked shocked, taken aback, almost afraid. No, he said, wide-eyed and shaking his head—he is nowhere near ready for that. Just to be sure, we clarified the matter: not even at home, not even just for his own fun?

Never.

This patient lad's *sensei*, the stoic Uyeda, is committed to a culturally ingrained dedication to detail, to pride in his craft, presentation, and customer service. Uyeda began bartending in 1966, and spent the darkest days of cocktail culture deconstructing and reinventing the art of the cocktail. Likening the preparation of a cocktail to the precision of the Japanese tea ceremony, each vital step in the ritual is conducted with the utmost care.

Beginning with the rum-based Maria Elena (¥1,600 or about $21), we witnessed the legendary Ginza hard shake in action. Ice chilled to exactly minus 4 degrees Fahrenheit is placed with tongs into a three-part shaker, followed by free-poured ingredients (more on the free-pour below). With the shaker held horizontally, the left hand supports the bottom and lifts the shaker up and down from belly-height to head-height. The right hand, at the top of the shaker, simultaneously guides it towards and away from the bartender. The impossibly aggressive abuse of the metal shaker gradually decelerates to a more modest motion, and then eventually eases off to a nearly motionless jiggle. This technique is said to make the drink a full 10 degrees colder than other methods, maximizes aeration, and mellows out the ingredients, all without over-dilution. Want to learn how to do this yourself? Of Uyeda's four books, only *Cocktail Techniques* (2000) is available in English.

An uncharacteristically impressed Gal Friday Night proceeded to make me order two more Uyeda creations, the whiskey-based King's Valley (bourbon, lime juice, Cointreau, blue curaçao; ¥1,700 or $22), and the Pure Love (gin, framboise, lime juice, ginger ale;

¥1,600 or $21). All told (and including table charge), we dropped well over $80 for our three drinks at Tender Bar, but if there is one pilgrimage cocktail destination in Tokyo where you'll want to splurge, this is it.

———◆▶——

L et us never underestimate the use of ice in our cocktails. Whether our drinks are shaken and strained, or stirred around a hand-carved ice ball, ice is a bartender's equivalent to a chef's stove: it controls temperature, dilution, and ultimately plays a big part in texture and flavor.

Y&M Kisling

7-5-4 Ginza, 7th floor
Tokyo
81-3/3573.2071

Many bartenders pay close attention to their ice programs. Others *define* ice. Just around the corner from Tender Bar is Y&M Kisling, another upscale lounge with bartenders in cream-colored cocktail jackets shaking things hard. The atmosphere is comfortable, spacious, and better designed than most of the other Ginza bars. Nobuo Abe's bar is one of many shrines to the Japanese cult of ice. Ginza bartenders take whole courses on ice as part of their training. They carve them into spheres and diamonds, and they inspect every cube before gently introducing it to your booze. Professional ice providers slowly freeze pure water into huge slabs. While freezing over a period of as much as three days, air and minerals are pushed towards the center. The dense block that results is transparent and free of impurities. Sub-slabs, still of considerable size, are cut away, leaving the flawed center as waste to slowly melt down the drain. Once in the bar, sawara-wood buckets are just as good for keeping ice balls cold as they are for keeping dumplings or rice hot.

Order Y&M Kisling's signature Kaikan Fizz (Gordon's gin, lemon juice, whole milk, simple syrup, soda water). This eastern cousin to the Ramos Gin Fizz was invented at the legendary

Kaikan Club Bar by Haruyoshi Honda. The Kaikan Club was a training ground for some of the Y&M Kisling staff, as well as for none other than Kazuo Uyeda. The Kaikan Club Bar may be where the Kaikan stir came from. This is a specific way of stirring a cocktail in which a bar spoon is held low on its shaft, as opposed to at the top. With minimal wrist movement and no shoulder or elbow movement at all, the spoon is gracefully swirled around so as to describe the shape of an hourglass—or better yet, a jigger—in the air and in the glass.

LAST CALL!
More Destinations to Explore in Tokyo

If you still haven't got the message that the Japanese like everything from their tea ceremonies to their social etiquette to be regimented and precise, then you may need to visit a few more bars. **Bar IshinoHana** (Daini Yaki Building, Basement 1, 3-6-2 Shibuya, Shibuya-ku; 81-3/5485.8405; www.ishinohana.com) is in the fun Shibuya area. There, bartender-owner Shinobu Ishigaki will prepare his house specialty, the Claudia (rum, vermouth, pineapple juice, caramel syrup, and a garnish too elaborate to detail). This one was inspired by Italian actress Claudia Cardinale. Further garnish architecture may be unveiled to compliment drinks containing local asterids like dragonfruit and hozuki in a room filled with hip retro furniture.

Bar Orange (AK Building, Basement 1, 1-5-16 Nishi Azabu, Minato-ku; 81-3/5775.2010; www.orange-tokyo. com) was opened in May 2000 by a friendly Stanley Kubrick fan. There is a small painting of Kubrick by Wada Makoto at one end of the bar, and a small framed photo of the four "droogs" from *A Clockwork Orange* (a-ha! Bar

Orange!) at the other. A couple of books on Kubrick co-mingle with a few cocktail and wine guides on a small shelf behind the bar. We had a nice Japanese-sized Negroni (¥1,580, or about $20.50), hard-shaken and deposited in a delicately etched glass with a huge and perfectly square iceberg in it. Bar snacks were dried figs and raisins, with a single sliced cherry tomato and a few tiny pieces of baguette smeared with some relative of peanut butter. As is the case in all Japanese bars, you get one serving of these, and you're done. Eat them slowly. We were pleased that Bar Orange didn't charge us either the "*gaijin* tax" or a seating charge.

Close to Bar Orange is a nice little liquor store called **Shinanoya** (on Roppongi-dori in Nishi-Azabu). We grabbed a bottle of Havana Club 7-year (¥2,310 or about $30). Staff are a friendly mix of Asian and Caucasians, and the selection is solid.

Bar Rage (Aoyama Jin & IT Building, 3rd floor, 7-13-13 Minami-Aoyama, Minato-ku; 81-3/5467.3977; www.mixologist.co.jp) is in trendy and stylish Aoyama. Brand names are what you're shopping for in this part of Tokyo, and the branding continues all night; this bar has a Johnnie Walker Room and a Ron Zacapa Terrace. Tomoyuki Kitazoe's menu is a bit heavy on the "-tinis," but if that's your bag, this is the place for 'em, and they're made with fresh fruit. The Rage group has at least five other bars, too.

Like Bar High Five and Tender Bar, **Doulton Bar** (Soiree de Ginza Building, 4th floor, 6-6-9 Ginza; 81-3/3571-4332) is owned by a man well past what many would consider to be retirement age. Too old to cut the mustard? Nope, Minoru Kokuzawa is just getting started. He stocks a fantastic array of Japan's favorite base spirit, whiskey, but his house specialty is the plain ol' Martini (Beefeater gin, Noilly Prat vermouth, orange bitters, lemon zest). While sipping a Cherry Blossom (cherry brandy, cognac, orange curaçao, grenadine, lemon juice), the insightful Gal Friday Night discovered that the free-pour, which is so frowned upon globally (since it makes it nearly impossible to create cocktails that are accurately repeatable) is actually a point of honor in Ginza. This is why the bartenders train for half a decade before they ever serve a drink; they have to be able to dump liquor from bottle to glass, without pour-spout or jigger, the same way, to the drop, every time. We say, why believe in things that make it tough on you? Use a jigger! The Nippon Bartenders Association holds their flame high in the air and yells, "Free pour!"

Here's a fun one: **Higashiya Tea and Sweets** (Aobadai 1-13-12, Meguro-ku; 81-3/5428.1717) is a tea house and patisserie that does tea infusions, dainty finger sweets, and cocktails using Japanese ingredients like sake and shochu. Shochu is a quick distillate of barley, sweet potatoes, or rice. It is distinctly different from sake, and was considered to be a drink for the lower classes until very recently. The elevation of shochu is a 21st-century phenomenon. Higashiya infuses their shochu with seasonal fruits, and pours a few splendid cocktails. Do you think that the tea, truffles, and cocktails at Higashiya are all served with a penchant for presentation that made even the relentlessly efficient Gal Friday Night squeal girlishly?

Bet on it.

The **Old Imperial Bar** (Imperial Hotel Tokyo, 1-1-1 Uchisaiwai-cho, Chiyoda; 81-3/3504.1111; www.imperialhotel.co.jp) is within the Imperial Hotel, which takes up an entire city block at the edge of Ginza. Designed in 1923 by Frank Lloyd Wright, the bar was rescued when the original Imperial Hotel expanded. Today, the decor retains a hint of Wright's original 1923 design. This being Japan, you'll find a great selection of whiskeys be-

hind the bar. This nation does love its whiskey. The bar is very low, and the stools feel almost child-sized. There is a very well-defined spotlight shining on the bar top in front of each seat. Bar snacks are salted peanuts in a little crystal chalice.

At the door, under a cool vintage drawing of the bar, a sign says: "Anyone with the distinctly exotic experience of having visited the Frank Lloyd Wright Imperial will tell you the very name stirs up delicious art deco images of glamour and intrigue. Relax amidst the ambiance of this remarkable legend over sandwiches and frothy beer, or try a Mt. Fuji, a 1924 Imperial original." We believed the hype, and ordered a lil' tiny Mt. Fuji (gin, orange juice, pineapple juice, egg white; ¥1,365 or almost $18). This was an improvement over most published recipes for this drink, which are typically sake, triple sec, and sweet-and-sour. Verdict: this is the original. Gal Friday Night squeezed her petite frame into an equally miniature Sidecar, which had some stray ice chips in the glass (a particular peeve for my co-pilot and frequent nanny), but this same glass did have a cool checkerboard pattern etched around the rim. We'll take it for a spin.

Kanpai!

SHANGHAI

Just like Marco Polo, but with a ruthlessly efficient personal assistant in tow, the *Destination: Cocktails* caravan rolled into China in the latter half of 2011. We weren't surprised to discover a handful of completely worthy bars in cosmopolitan Shanghai. The only outpost for truly solid cocktails in Beijing is at a spot called Apothecary, which has a sister location in Shanghai, so we won't be discussing Beijing in its own section.

Alchemist Cocktail Kitchen

Sinan Mansions
Block 32 45 Sinan Lu
Shanghai
21.6426.0660
www.alchemistbar.cn

China does not have a drinking culture even remotely akin to the ones in the Western world. Chinese drinking basically consists of three brands of beer, plus various brands of *bai jiu* (essentially sorghum brandy), and they're all terrible. Even the expensive bai jiu is terrible. Even the expensive bai jiu in pretty bottles is terrible. Specialty shops in tourist and expatriate neighborhoods do import Western liquor and beer (mostly Belgian brands), so one could mix drinks at home if so inclined, but a real craft cocktail bar did not exist in China until very recently. But then again, you can say that about Paris, too.

Within Sinan Mansions, a Western-style housing and commercial complex at the edge of Shanghai's embassy district, are not one, but two solid craft cocktail bars, plus a microbrewery and a bar sponsored by Johnnie Walker whisky.

The first one we'll explore is the Alchemist Cocktail Kitchen.

Opened by Kelley Lee of Los Angeles, the titular alchemist might actually be Ryan Noreiks, a friendly native of Brisbane, Australia. He creates four menus a year filled with classic cocktails and house originals.

We spent some time at the Alchemist and ended up sampling a bunch of Noreiks's creations. First among them was the 24½ Century (duck-fat-infused Hennesey VSOP, Talisker 10-year Scotch whisky, Bénédictine, chocolate bitters). This is obviously a reference to the old *Duck Dodgers in the 24½ Century* cartoon, given the duck-fat infusion. The duck, in turn, grounds this drink in China, a nation well-known for its duck-based cuisine. Noreiks commented, "We try to stay in touch with local traditions."

The Jamestown (Mount Gay XO rum, ruby port, unspecified amaro, white curaçao) is a sweet drink with the curaçao forward. Return of Jolly Roger (Damoiseau agricole rum, coffee, falernum, orange juice) comes from the same family as the Mutiny at Fort Lauderdale's Mai-Kai, both in name and in flavor profile. The Straights Sling (Tanqueray gin, Bénédictine, luxardo morlacco) is a solid rendition of the classic. We finished with an improv of Talisker 10-year Scotch whisky, green Chartreuse, and Lillet rouge aperitif wine, a solid twist on the classic Rob Roy, with a big mint sprig floating on top.

The house-made falernum is very mild; the clove taste is subdued, as are citrus notes. "Anything we do here, we do it from scratch," Noreiks comments. That includes introducing 1.6 billion people who have never tried a Manhattan to the concept of the Western cocktail. As a result, Noreiks has trouble training the Chinese bar staff. Since they don't have the experience or palate to know if things are right, consistency is difficult. Creativity is also hard. "Sometimes they want to add some crazy things!" says Noreiks. American bar managers are officially not allowed to whine anymore. About *anything*.

All cocktails are in the vicinity of ¥85, or about $13.50. This is phenomenally expensive for China, but it is about the going rate for the very few Western-style cocktail bars to be found in this country. The thinking here is that Westerners are used to paying prices like this for drinks like this, and the local Chinese aren't usually coming to these places anyway. But, we must also consider that the liquors we have easy access to in North America and Europe come at a dear price to Chinese importers.

Just steps away from the Alchemist, and also just steps away from the Public (see below) is **Boxing Cat Brewery** (21.6426.0360; Sinan Mansions, Unit 26A, 519–521 Fu Xing Road Central; www. boxingcatbrewery.com). We ordered their Black EyePA beer and were really surprised at how un-IPA-ish it was. In fact, it tasted like a pilsner. The Sucker Punch pale ale, surprisingly, tasted exactly like a stout! We realized that the kid behind the bar was pouring pints more or less at random. This is endemic to Chinese drinking culture. The people working at these places have never been exposed to the concept of a stout versus an IPA versus a Belgian-style beer; they've had the same three shitty canned beers their whole lives, and that's it. The idea that beer can be as diverse as it is, and the very conception of why people might care, is completely lost on them. Then, if you open the door to the world of whiskeys or rums or cocktails, you may as well be speaking Chinese to these people. Oh, wait, bad metaphor. Anyway, we observe, we describe, we do not condemn. The beers were certainly the best we had in China. Also in this same complex is the **Johnnie Walker Bar**, which will serve you a glass of whisky. Good to know. Let's move on.

The Public

Sinan Mansions
Building 2, 4th floor, Lane 507
Fuxing Zhong Lu
Shanghai
21.3368.9419

The Shanghai outpost of Apothecary (renamed the Public as of May 2012), opened on April 1, 2011, following the success of the Apothecary in Beijing (Nali Patio, 3rd floor, 81 Sanlitun Lu, Chaoyang District, Beijing; 5208.6040). Both the Shanghai and Beijing businesses were originally owned by Leon Lee and Max E. Levy, both of whom stepped away from the Shanghai location in early 2012. They continue to own and operate the Apothecary in Beijing. To date, the Public has not changed fundamentally since its days as the second Apothecary store. It is a bar first, but they also

offer a full-service menu of American and Creole-inspired food.

Both the food and cocktail halves of these bars espouse an "everything from scratch" philosophy. This is evidenced by glass shelves at the front door containing big jars full of infusions, most with dates on the bottles: kaffir lime bitters, Hess House bitters, grapefruit bitters, coconut rum infusion, xocolat bitters, Sichuan peppercorn, cherry vanilla bitters, aromatic bitters, gentian, cherry bourbon, tequila por mi amante, orange bitters, and cocoa rum. "We try to make as much as we can in-house, from the ice on up," says Lee. "We make 10 kinds of bitters. It's all very utilitarian. We started making them because we couldn't buy them in China." That may change, however. "The Bitter Truth has their entire line here," Lee adds. "Fee Brothers is supposed to be here soon. Angostura will be here soon." As for the ice, it is made from quadruple-filtered water, a necessity in China—particularly for foreign visitors. The water here can be . . . tricky. Or just icky.

We put their claims of being the sole retailer of Rittenhouse rye in China to the test by ordering a rye-based classic, the Preakness (Rittenhouse rye, Dolin sweet vermouth, Bénédictine, house-made aromatic bitters; ¥80, or about $12.75), which we followed up with a Sin Cin (Rittenhouse rye, maraschino liqueur, cinnamon syrup, grapefruit juice, house-made aromatic bitters, Versinthe absinthe blanc; ¥80). Both cocktails were fully up to the standards of any other bar in this book. We were convinced; let's continue. Sold on the Versinthe, we sampled the Bazillionaire (rye, lemon juice, house grenadine, Versinthe absinthe blanc, simple syrup; ¥90, or about $14.25).

We wanted to try the Versinthe straight, but the idea of explaining proper absinthe service to our waiter would have been futile. It was fascinating, really; he was friendly enough and quite professional, but again, he had no background in his product at all. Training an

American to work in a proper cocktail bar can be challenging, but at least things like "gin" and words like "Daiquiri" or "Martini" are almost universally part of the cultural lexicon. The people working these new Chinese bars have never even heard phrases like "on the rocks" or "up, with a twist" in their lives. They have no context at all for what they're doing; it's all completely new to them. *Tabula rasa.* They're like cocktail babies! It will be fascinating to see how China's own cocktail culture evolves as they start to get a grip on the paradigm and develop their own unique context and vocabulary.

We asked Lee about *bai jiu,* the local spirit. The fearless (or reckless) Gal Friday Night wanted to try the local flavors. "Most of it is made from sorghum, and is categorized by fragrance," Lee told us. "They have a rice one, a medicinal one, different categories. They use rice cakes to start the fermentation process. It is aged in clay pots in a cellar." He seemed skeptical about a *bai jiu* cocktail; when we asked about quality, he laughed. "Yeah, there is quality, but we're looking at a different scale. The best *bai jiu* still isn't very good, but it is priced as though it is a rare single malt Scotch."

Opened in 2009, the original Apothecary in Beijing is in a really hard-to-find spot within a shopping plaza called Nali Patio. It is right along Sanlitun Lu, a bustling and festive street full of designer shops, expensive restaurants, and boutique hotels, all being patronized by employees of the nearby embassies (and lots of tourists). We spent ¥170 ($28) for two drinks and a bowl of exquisite hardboiled quail eggs while chatting with Alice, the friendly manager. The bar itself is much smaller, more intimate, and attracts a younger and noisier crowd that does the Public in Shanghai. Naturally, the tinctures, infusions, and macerations are made in-house here by Lee, Levy, and their team.

***

Constellation No. 1

86 Xinle Lu
Shanghai
21.5404.0970

Cosmopolitan Shanghai is the one city in China that may be just as influenced by the West as it is the East. To wit: if Apothecary and Alchemist are doing things New York-style, then Constellation No.

1 is definitely bringing the Japanese Ginza style to Shanghai.

At Constellation No. 1, the long and narrow bar seats 12, with a row of booths against the opposite wall. It is a small and cozy place within the European-influenced French Concession neighborhood. The cocktail list has over 100 recipes present and accounted for. Arranged by base spirit and described in detail, each drink also has a little icon next to the description showing the glassware, and a digit indicating the total amount of alcohol by volume of the final cocktail. The list is mostly classics, with very few house creations. There is, however, a drink simply called the Number Two. Not sure we can order that with a straight face. Is it a mistranslation of the Corpse Reviver #2, or some other similarly numbered beverage? Possibly.

Bartenders in white jackets and black bow ties show a Japanese influence in their dress that also carries over to the drinks—they're small pours (about two ounces total), and the Ginza hard shake is in full effect when appropriate.

Prices are ¥60–¥80, which works out to about $9.50–$12.75. There is a great selection of liquors behind the bar. Everything you need, and a few things you probably don't. The whiskey list is exhaustive and labeled by country (and by region in the case of the Scotch—Highland, Speyside, Lowland, Island of Islay, Island of Arran, Isle of Orkney, Jura, Campbeltown, Isle of Skye). Scotch seems to be the variety of whisky that the Chinese prefer, or at least the one that they have the most access to. Bourbon isn't super common here, and rye is nearly impossible to get.

This was evidenced when we ordered a Hunter, which was described as "rye and cherry brandy." In reality, we were served Canadian Club whisky, Martini and Rossi white vermouth, and the

lovely Guignolet de Dijon cherry liqueur. The drink worked out all right, but one shouldn't advertise rye if they're going to serve Canadian Club; these things are not the same. It was prepared well, carefully stirred in a beaker with plenty of ice. Utilizing another Japanese touch, bartender-owner Lo lined all the bottles up on the bar, labels facing us, as he made the drink.

Bar snacks are things that look like giant rice grains and taste nutty and a little sweet. There is also a small menu of food and cigars, mostly in the ¥80–¥200 range.

In addition to Constellation No. 1, there are two other Constellations in Shanghai, with **Constellation No. 2** (33 Yongjia Lu, 1st/2nd floors; 21.5465.5993) being more of a straight whiskey bar (we were unable to visit Constellation No. 3). Lo is the owner of all three. His wife also inspired a fourth bar in the Lo dynasty, Southern Cross. We stopped into Constellation No. 2 and had a really quick China Cocktail (of course, what else!). Barcardi white rum, generic orange curaçao, really scary cheap-ass grenadine, Luxardo maraschino, and Angostura bitters. It was mixed with detail and care, but when the bartender can't taste the difference in the crappy ingredients, the care is all for show. We sipped it while gazing at their famously huge whiskey collection (seven bays each with three shelves full of bottles per bay), and wondered who was appreciating it. The bar is bigger and brighter than Constellation No. 1, with an English gentleman's club sort of feel—nautical prints on the walls, a big spiral staircase in the exact center of the room, sconces, lots of dark wood, and brass everywhere. Upscale crowd, lots of suits. The other Constellation felt like a Japanese bar; this one feels English. Completely different.

- - - ◀◆▶ - - -

el Cóctel

47 Yongfu lu, unit 202
Shanghai
21.6433.6511
www.el-coctel.com

Chef Willy Trullas Moreno has been making waves in Shanghai for his Spanish-influenced cuisine, and in late 2009, he brought these flavors to el Cóctel. In a very European setting, the bar serves very Japanese cocktails. In China. Unsurprisingly, the bar was

full of European faces when we visited, and just a few Japanese; all of the bartenders have been imported straight from Ginza. Among them is bar manager Munenori Harada.

The simple Agricole Fizz (Clément agricole rum, lime juice, egg white, soda; ¥68) is crisp and a little bitter, possibly due to inferior limes (good limes are scarce in China). We preferred the Sakura Caprioska (Sakura liqueur, dry gin, orange juice, muddled lemon; ¥78 or $12). Harada says that the sakura liqueur actually contains sakura flowers from Japan. Simplifying, we went for the Spring Feeling (Beefeater gin, green Chartreuse, lemon juice; ¥68 or $11), which proved simple and effective.

There is no sign outside, just a shadow box near the door with a picture of a cocktail shaker on it. Up a steep flight of stairs to the second floor, a dividing wall near the entranceway is made up of dozens of metal shakers. There is a whole lot of booze on the wall behind the bar, and a row of Japanese pop culture toys along the same wall. The ceiling is covered in a motif of insects, courtesy of artist Veronica Ballart Lilja of Barcelona. The room and the customers feel like money, more than most Chinese will ever see. There is also a strange little hipster altar in the back room, but overall the atmosphere is cozy, dimly lit, and decorated in earth tones.

Willy Trullas Moreno can't help but bring some food to the table, since that's what he does best. So, el Cóctel is also known for its sandwiches, of all things, which of course are exotic in China. We were intrigued by a combination of warm smoked salmon, walnut, goat cheese, fresh spinach, and apple for the very reasonable price of ¥55 ($9). Another solid concept is much less reasonably priced option of Spanish anchovies and fresh tomato on toasted bread for ¥120 ($19). What's expensive here, the anchovies or the tomatoes? Who can say? This is China, mister.

At street-level in the same building as el Cóctel is **Rhumerie Bounty** (47 Yongfu Lu, 1st floor, Shanghai; 21.2661.9368). They've got a pirate theme and a nice selection of rums available neat (in the ¥70 range), but poor cocktails. Their other location is at 550 Wuding Lu, Shanghai; 21.2661.9368.

We've also heard great things about **Bar Untouchable** (Rm. 103A, Building 6, Lane 555, Gubei Lu, Shanghai; 21.6241.2941), which is owned by Kiyotaka Kobayashi of Yokohama. Lead bartender Tamura-san is often considered to be the best of the Ginza-schooled barmen in Shanghai. Local bartenders track this bar down as their post-shift destination; you may want to also track down Kobayashi's parallel Bar Untouchable location in Yokohama during your Japan trip.

DESTINATION: NIGHTCAP

Your endlessly thirsty author is not a professional bartender. But you can bet your last Kold-Draft cube that he has spent his fair share of time inventing a drink or two, after learning a thing or two watching the fantastic bartenders discussed in this book do their thing. Here are some favorites, presented humbly for your approval and improvement, with a few notes on each.

Cheers.

Vélo

This drink won the monthly St. Germain-sponsored cocktail competition in 2009. The result: a trip to New York to compete against a dozen other bartenders (many of them are mentioned in these pages), all making drinks for a judge of no less distinction than Mr. Dale DeGroff.

> 1.25 oz London dry gin
> 1 oz St. Germain elderflower liqueur
> .5 oz passion fruit syrup
> 4 dashes Peychaud's bitters
> .75 oz lime juice

Shake for a long time with a lot of ice and strain into a wine glass.

To make passion fruit syrup, simmer two parts Goya-brand passion fruit pulp, one part sugar, and one part filtered water until integrated.

Katy's Kiss

This one was inspired by someone mentioning that Pimm's tastes like Chapstick. Why not go for *cherry* Chapstick?

> 1.5 oz bourbon
> .5 oz Pimm's
> .5 oz Peter Heering cherry liqueur
> 1 tablespoon fresh-squeezed lime juice
> 2 shakes Angostura bitters.

Build all ingredients over ice cubes in a Collins glass. Stir and top with seltzer water. Add a cherry garnish.

Feyd

The spice must flow!

   1.5 oz Orinoco rum
   .75 oz Campari
   .5 oz Don's Mix
   .5 oz additional grapefruit
   .5 oz lime juice

Shake and strain ingredients into coupe glass. Don't skimp on the distinctive Orinoco rum!

Swap ratios of Campari and Don's Mix, depending on how bitter you like the drink and how cinnamon-y the Don's Mix turns out.

Don's Mix (small batch): 1 oz simple syrup, ¾ teaspoon fresh ground cinnamon, 2 oz grapefruit juice. Simmer until ingredients are integrated.

Wigwam

"Wigwam" is the new slang for excellent. As in, this drink is *so wigwam!*

   2 oz Elmer T. Lee bourbon
   1.5 oz grapefruit juice
   .5 oz ginger syrup
   1 tablespoon honey
   1 tablespoon fresh lemon juice

Dry shake (without ice) all ingredients, then pour over ice and stir. Adjust ginger syrup to taste.

Note: We're big fans of using honey, agave nectar, or other natural alternatives to refined white sugar as a sweetener. In most cases, you'll need to warm the honey to make it liquid, then dry shake the drink to fully integrate it with the other ingredients. Making a honey syrup works, too (half honey and half water, warmed and then bottled). This can be easier to work with than regular honey. When a recipe calls for honey, use twice as much if using honey syrup (since it is half water).

Gulliver

First quaffed with a sample of the very best of Chicago's famous pizza.

>   2 oz Tinta Tawny Port
>   2 oz Laird's bonded applejack or your favorite calvados.
>   1 teaspoon lemon juice
>   Less than ¼ teaspoon of absinthe

Stir all with a large, solid lump of ice in an Old-Fashioned glass.

Go Man Go

A tiki drink or breakfast? You decide!

>   1.5 oz demerara rum (Lemon Hart is fine, Eldorado 12-year is much better)
>   1.25 oz fresh mango pulp
>   .5 oz Peter Heering cherry liqueur
>   .75 oz Berry Hill pimento liqueur
>   .5 oz lime juice

Liquefy mango pulp in blender. Add to all other ingredients and shake with crushed ice. Pour into double Old-Fashioned glass.

Note: Since Berry Hill is tough to get, you can substitute other brands of allspice dram to taste—but get some of the distinctive Berry Hill if you can!

Mango Mary

The mango/Eldorado combo from the previous drink was working (Hallmark of St. James demerara rum is good, too), but a variant with a bitter note seemed interesting. After trying this one a bunch of ways, the mango/rum balance ended up being the same as in the Go Man Go. If it ain't broke . . .

> 1.5 oz Eldorado 12-year rum
> 1.25 oz fresh mango pulp
> .5 oz Clement Creole Shrubb
> .5 oz lemon juice
> .5 oz Campari

Dry shake to integrate mango. Pour over a big iceberg in double Old-Fashioned glass. Stir.

Rio Gimlet

The problem with making a Gimlet exactly true to the classic recipe is that it calls specifically for Rose's Lime Juice. Back in the day, Rose's was made with real lime juice. Today it is only five percent juice. So, in order to make a "good" Gimlet, one must use fresh lime and sugar, even though a "real" Gimlet uses Rose's. This was the result of playing with Gimlet variations one fine day.

> 1.5 oz gin
> 1 oz John D. Taylor's Velvet Falernum
> .75 oz lime juice (to taste)
> 1 dash orange bitters

Combine ingredients, shake well, and strain into a cocktail glass. Garnish with a lime wheel.

Note: Taylor's Velvet Falernum is pretty sweet, but add a dash of agave nectar if you need it sweeter.

Aku Hall Sour

A needlessly complicated twist on the experience of consuming many Pisco Sours on Easter Island and in Chile. Adding egg white is the custom with a traditional Pisco Sour, but it didn't work in this case.

>   2.5 oz Pisco
>   .75 oz fresh lemon juice
>   .5 oz fresh lime juice
>   .5 oz simple syrup
>   .5 oz Grand Marnier
>   .75 oz falernum (John D. Taylor's)
>   2 dashes orange bitters

Shake all ingredients with crushed ice, pour into tiki mug or Collins glass with a quarter lime rind. Float a tablespoonful of very dark rum on top (try Cruzan Black Strap). Sprinkle with a pinch of brown sugar.

Quarante

Guess who was inventing drinks on his birthday?

>   1.25 oz Clement VO rhum vieux agricole
>   .5 oz Clement Creole Shrubb
>   .75 oz St. Germain elderflower liqueur
>   .5 oz lemon juice

Shake ingredients together with extreme prejudice and strain into a cocktail glass. No brand substitutions are possible for this drink.

Note: Try adding a little bit of absinthe.

Chartreuse Flip

Had to happen.

> 2 oz demerara rum
> 1 oz green Chartreuse
> .75 oz simple syrup
> 1 whole egg
> dash of Angostura bitters

Combine ingredients, then dry shake like you hate it for a long time. Then shake with ice for a short time. Strain into coupe glass.

Bee's Sneeze

A riff on the classic Bee's Knees, with bonus added paramecium!

> 1.75 oz Hendrick's gin
> .5+ oz lemon juice
> .25+ oz yellow Chartreuse
> 1 tablespoon honey
> Float of Deer-brand basil seed drink (aka "paramecium")

Dry shake all except basil seed drink, then shake long and well with ice. Serve up, top with basil seed drink.

Note: We get the Deer-brand basil drink at a market in India town; adjust your search accordingly.

Version 5

An autumn drink.

> 1 oz Laird's apple brandy
> 1 oz Bulleit rye
> .5 oz Commerce Pine-Elixir
> .5 oz Cynar
> .5 oz lemon juice

Work with the Pine-Elixir like you would honey—heat to liquefy. Dry shake all ingredients to integrate Pine-Elixir, then shake with ice. Strain into coupe glass; add a dash of Angostura bitters on top.

Note: Commerce Pine-Elixir is a pine syrup also found at the Indian market. It is similar to maple syrup, but with intense pine flavor.

BAR INDEX

UNITED STATES

INTERNATIONAL

ACKNOWLEDGMENTS

Special thanks to (alphabetically): Naomi Alper, Kirsten Amann, Michelle Baldwin, Meg Bell, Alice Berry, Jeff Berry, Natalie Bovis, Kestrel Burley, Kristen Campbell, Martin Cate, Evgenia Cherkova, April Cheverette, Forest Collins, Dean Curtis, Joe Desmond, Nicole Desmond, Ginger Dzerk, Kari Hendler, Rebecca Hill, Jochen Hirschfeld, Sven Kirsten, Brian Miller, Wendy Miller, Vern Stoltz, Julie Thompson, Allison Vallerga, Jeanne Vedrine, Jimmy Virani, Kim Vollstedt, and Kent Wang, plus Rob Cooper and everyone at St. Germain. Thanks also to everyone who provided photos or agreed to be interviewed for this book.

Very special thanks to Valerie Emerick, who helped with research about various independent distilleries.

A shout-out to Toby Maloney of the Violet Hour, Audrey Saunders of Pegu Club, Adam Seger (formerly) of Nacional 27, and Paulius Nasvytis of Velvet Tango Room. The idea for this book was first hatched while visiting these four bars way back in 2006 and 2007.

Apologies: Charles H. Baker Jr.

PHOTO CREDITS

All photos of bars, restaurants, hotels, and cocktails have been provided courtesy of the businesses or products they depict. The copyright for each photo is owned by the respective business.

The businesses that requested photography credits are: 1886 Bar at the Raymond (acuna-hansen), American Oak (Melissa Rivers), Bar Congress (Jody Horton), the Bar at the Merchant Hotel (Khara Pringle and Glenn Waddell), Barrelhouse Flat (Jesse LiRola), the Bent Brick (David L. Reamer), Candelaria (Danielle Rubi), Columbia Room (Jim Webb), the Cruise Room (Van Buren Photography), Curio Bar (Kari Skaflen), Dry Martini (Jordi Poch), Drink (Justin Ide), Craft and Commerce (Amy K. Fellows), Elixir (Darren Edwards), Equus & Jack's Lounge (Dan Dry of Power Creative), Experimental Cocktail Club (Simona Belotti), Forbidden Island (Gabriel Hurley and Paul McMillan of Zero Coordinate, Inc.), Green Russell (Michael McGill), the Gibson (Sam Vasfi), L'Abattoir (Glasfurd & Walker), L'Experimental Cocktail Club (Simona

Belotti), Longman and Eagle (Clayton Hauck), Maison Premiere (Will Femia), Mark's Bar (Jason Lowe), Michael's Genuine Food & Drink (the Genuine Hospitality Group), the Passenger (Jim Webb), Please Don't Tell (Noah Kalina), Rob Roy (Chad Pryor), Sanctuaria (Jacqui Segura and Egan O'Keefe), Sepia (Tony Soluri), Smuggler's Cove (Jennifer Yin), Sun Liquor (Nathan Hazard), Sun Liquor Distillery (Mark Klebeck), the Tasting Kitchen (Niles Harrison), and West (David Wolowinyk).

Additional photos by James Teitelbaum.

Back cover photos courtesy of the Varnish (left) and Maison Premiere/Will Femia (right).

ABOUT THE AUTHOR

James Teitelbaum is the author of *Tiki Road Trip* (Santa Monica Press, 2007) and *Big Stone Head: Easter Island and Pop Culture* (Tydirium Multimedia, 2009), and has contributed to dozens of magazines and websites, including *American Heritage, Playboy, Alternative Press, Beverage World, Tiki Magazine*, RoadTripAmerica.com, and FilmThreat.com. When not traveling the globe and scribbling about it, James lives in Chicago, where he works in the music business and teaches at a digital media arts college.

ABOUT GAL FRIDAY NIGHT

Born in Iceland, the enigmatic Gal Friday Night (real name withheld) maintains a legal practice in Argentina, where she lives with a paleobotanist and their three albino marmosets. She joins James for travel adventures, lest he make good on his promises not to return. She also makes him eat his spinach, deciphers his handwriting as scrawled on soggy coasters stained with Fernet-Branca, and tells him when "that's a really bad idea in this country."